CANADA WEST

OTTAWA

Also by SHIRLEY E. WOODS, Jr.

Gunning for Upland Birds and Wildfowl
Angling for Atlantic Salmon
The Squirrels of Canada

OTTAWA
The Capital of Canada

Shirley E. Woods, Jr.

DOUBLEDAY CANADA LIMITED
Toronto, Canada
DOUBLEDAY & COMPANY, INC.
Garden City, New York

1980

Library of Congress Catalog Card Number: 79-6101
ISBN: 0-385-14722-8

FIRST EDITION

Printed and bound in Canada by the John Deyell Company
Design by Robert Burgess Garbutt
Typesetting by ART-U Graphics

ILLUSTRATION CREDITS

The front endpaper is a Stent & Laver print of Ottawa
circa 1859 from the collection of Shirley E. Woods, Jr. The
back endpaper is an aerial view of Ottawa circa 1979 ©
Malak, Ottawa. The map of Bytown on pages 74-75 is by
C. C. J. Bond. The public notices reproduced on pages 86
and 115 are courtesy the Historical Society of Ottawa. The
old and new city coats of arms on pages 130 and 131 are
courtesy the Ottawa Municipal Archives.

For my grandmother,
  Amy Gordon Guthrie

and my mother,
  Catherine Guthrie Woods

Foreword

I am doubly delighted to be writing this introduction for Shirley Woods's book *Ottawa:* because the long-needed, flowing narrative history of Ottawa has finally been done; because it has been done so well, by one so knowledgeable.

The history of Ottawa is of special interest to me because I was originally commissioned by Doubleday Canada Limited to write this book for Centennial Year. However, after considerable research, and writing the manuscript up to 1840, I concluded that the increasing responsibilities of my position, and those of bringing up a young family, would prevent me from completing the project within a reasonable time. With great regret I advised the publishers of my decision and returned their advance.

Fortunately, in 1977, following a film showing at Government House, I encountered an acquaintance of years before who mentioned his books to me. It didn't take me long to decide, after reading his first book, that Shirley Woods, from an old and prominent Ottawa family, and a former officer of the Governor General's Foot Guards like myself, possessed both the background and the clarity of style necessary to successfully complete the project, which was still very close to my heart. But would he consider it? After all, much time-consuming research would have to be undertaken and this would be a larger book than either of his others. Then, too, he lacked the formal academic credentials assumed to ensure accuracy and thoroughness. Anyway, I asked him if he would be interested, he agreed, and I warmly recommended him to Doubleday.

The result you see here. The author has fully met my expectations and I am sure you will agree that this is the best book written on the history of Ottawa and the best likely to be written within the foreseeable future. Shirley proves, I think, that the ability and spirit with which one is born is more important than the academic qualifi-cations which one acquires along the way. One can be accurate without being academic. One is more likely to be readable without academic pretensions. I can only hope that this book will have the enormous and continuing success which it deserves. It is the product of a lively, inquiring, perceptive mind devoted to clarity and accuracy.

This is not the book I would have written myself: it is a much better book. I recommend it to you as deserving to be read and deserving a place in every Canadian library. Ottawa is the nation's capital; it represents us all.

ERIK J. SPICER
Parliamentary Librarian
Ottawa, Canada

Preface

One of my reasons for writing this book is to dispel the common belief that Ottawa is a dull civil service town. This misconception has been fostered, in part, by nonresident journalists assigned to the Parliamentary Press Gallery. Their task is to report on Parliament and the government. Quite naturally, their dispatches leave the impression that the only events of interest that happen in the capital are caused by Members of the House or the so-called "Mandarins" (senior government appointees).

It is, however, well to remember that Parliamentarians are for the most part transients who have little or no effect upon the city. A few Prime Ministers, notably Sir John A. Macdonald, Sir Wilfred Laurier, and the Right Honourable Lester B. Pearson, have been permanent residents of stature. And those who run the government departments, the Mandarins, have no more *direct* influence on the people of Ottawa than they do on the citizens of Moose Jaw, Saskatchewan, or Truro, Nova Scotia. I make this point, not to denigrate the country's elected representatives or her public servants—many of whom are talented and dedicated people —but to place their role in the capital in perspective.

Ottawa is a complex and surprisingly cosmopolitan city. It is composed in the main of French and English stock, and many of its residents are fluent in both languages. Because it has three universities, and Canada's largest scientific research establishment, there is a substantial academic community. It also has a great many professional people and a broadly based business community. Ottawa has the largest concentration of senior armed forces personnel in the country, and a diplomatic contingent from one hundred nations. No single group can be said to dominate the life of the capital.

After studying Ottawa's past, I have come to some general conclusions. One is that the riotous pre-Confederation years laid the base for a harmonious relationship between Ottawa's French and English inhabitants. From violence and prejudice there developed a mutual respect that continues to this day. Not only do the French and English people of the capital have a good rapport, but newer ethnic groups have subsequently become full partners in the social and commercial life of the city.

I was also impressed by the courage and fortitude of the early residents during the turbulent square timber era. Fortunes were made and fortunes were lost, with little heed for security. It was in this period that the spirit of the community was forged and a lasting commitment made to private enterprise.

Queen Victoria's choice of Ottawa as the seat of government was a windfall that brought many benefits. Had Ottawa not been selected as capital, the city would be less prosperous and a great deal less beautiful than it is today. In retrospect, the Queen's choice was a good one, for Ottawa has drawn little criticism as a national site, and it has functioned well as the capital.

In writing this history I have had—for reasons of space—to leave out the names of many worthy citizens who contributed to the community. This I regret, for these citizens collectively formed the backbone of the capital. The city has also been fortunate to attract a steady influx of talented men and women from the surrounding Ottawa Valley towns. These fine people have made an immense contribution to Ottawa.

I must mention that this is the second time I have written the history of Ottawa. The first time was many years ago, when I was a schoolboy. That venture took the best part of a day—I spent the morning in the National Archives and then wrote the saga in the afternoon. This attempt has taken considerably longer.

My hope is that you will enjoy this book, and that it will enrich your knowledge of Canada's capital.

S.E.W., Jr.
Ottawa

Contents

OTTAWA

1

The Setting

OTTAWA WAS NOT planned as a capital city; it became one through the stress of war, the demands of commerce, and the shifting wind of politics. Because of these circumstances, the history of Ottawa embodies most of the elements that have shaped Canada's destiny. Friendly and hostile Indians, explorers, missionaries, and soldiers have played important roles in Ottawa's past, as have French, English, Irish, Scottish, and American immigrants, royalty, commercial buccaneers, statesmen, politicians, civil servants and rogues. Their stories make a colourful saga.

Ottawa first attracted international notice when Queen Victoria chose it to be the capital of Canada in 1858. One American newspaper waggishly advised its readers: "Start from the North Pole; strike a bead for Lake Ontario; and the first spot where the glacier ceases and vegetation begins—that's Ottawa!" In fact, the city is located in the province of Ontario, on the south bank of the Ottawa River, a major tributary of the St. Lawrence River. The precise map reference is latitude 45° 25′ north, longitude 74° 42′ west, which places it within twenty miles of the midpoint between the North Pole and the Equator. The Ottawa River runs from west to east and is fed by two smaller rivers, the Gatineau and the Rideau, from the

north and the south. Viewed from the air, these four rivers resemble
a cross, with the city at its centre. Within the city limits a second
waterway—the Rideau Canal—traces its way from the Ottawa
River south to the Rideau River; this canal is of profound historic
importance.

The topography of the Ottawa area is dominated by the sweep of
the Ottawa River, whose average flow is greater than all the rivers
of England and Wales combined. This river is frequently more than
a mile wide, and its drainage basin encompasses 57,000 square miles.
Now partially hidden, the most significant landmark on the waterway is the Chaudière Falls, just upstream from the Parliament
buildings. Originally there were seven distinct cataracts that spanned
the river; today the largest still thunders into a huge pocket in the
stream bed known as the Devil's Hole. The north shore, or Quebec
side, is scalloped with numerous bays including the estuary of the
swift Gatineau River. On the north shore the land is relatively flat,
but gradually becomes more rolling a few miles from the water, and
then rises sharply for a thousand feet when it merges with the
Precambrian Shield—known locally as the Gatineau Hills. The south
shore, or Ontario side—where Ottawa is located—is quite different.
This bank is characterized by steep limestone cliffs, the most famous
being the promontory on which the Parliament buildings stand.
Two miles downstream from Parliament, the shoreline is cleft by
the Rideau River, which cascades over the limestone in a glistening
sheet before dropping into the Ottawa River. The terrain on the
Ontario side is fairly level, with a modest increase in elevation as you
go south.

The Dominion Weather Bureau states that "Ottawa has a marked
continental climate with wide temperature variations throughout
the year." Put more simply, it is hot in summer and cold in winter,
with approximately two thousand hours of sunshine. The winter is
long, as the first frost can be expected around the beginning of
October and the last in the second week of April. The months of
January, February, and March are the core of winter, with a mean
average temperature of -8°C (18°F). Ottawa is colder than Moscow,
and has the dubious honour of being the second coldest capital in the
world (Ulan Bator, the capital of the Mongolian Peoples Republic, is the
most frigid). Fortunately, humidity is low in winter, so it is a dry and
invigorating cold—when the temperature plummets to -25°C the snow
creaks underfoot and the trees crack like pistol shots. The annual
snowfall averages 216 centimetres (85 inches), most of which stays on

the ground due to the constant low temperatures. In 1970 Ottawa had 441 centimetres (144 inches), and by mid-March there was an air of quiet desperation among the city's overworked snow-removal crews. Toward the end of April skeins of migrating Canada geese announce the arrival of spring, which lasts until the middle of May. Summer comes suddenly, with high temperatures intensified by high humidity; in July the city can be as steamy and uncomfortable as New York. The growing season is relatively short, but a balmy mean temperature of 19°C (67°F), for the months of June, July, and August, combined with an annual rainfall of 85 centimetres (35.5 inches), usually ensures good crops.

While Ottawa has a long winter, a short spring, and a hot summer, the autumn is glorious. Most residents agree that October is the golden month, with its frosty nights and sun-filled days. When he was British High Commissioner to Canada during World War Two, the Right Honourable Malcolm MacDonald wrote a charming book, *The Birds of Brewery Creek,* in which he vividly describes the October landscape:

> The whole Ottawa valley then is a field of blazing colours. On a sunlit day it appears as if the Creator had accidentally dropped the contents of His paint-box from heaven and spilled them across the landscape. The earth is like a huge artist's palette. Masses of dark evergreens, pale green, russets, pinks, reds, crimsons, scarlets, yellows, orange and gold are splashed everywhere. Through this splendour flows the sapphire river and overhead is the blue sky.

2

The Struggle for Control

1610 to 1791

THE OTTAWA RIVER, flowing more than 600 miles downstream from Lake Temiskaming to the island of Montreal, was from the beginning the main route to the interior of the continent. By paddling up the Ottawa you could connect with other river systems and reach the Great Lakes, the Mississippi, Hudson Bay, and as far west as the Pacific Ocean. As a tributary of the mighty St. Lawrence, the Ottawa led from the interior to the Atlantic Ocean. Initially the Ottawa was known as the River of the Algonquins, or the Kit-chi-sippi; toward the end of the eighteenth century it was officially designated La Rivière des Outaouais, but both French and English referred to it as the Grande River. In the nineteenth century the name of the waterway was officially changed to the Ottawa River.

Although the first white man arrived at the site of the city of Ottawa in 1610—and was forced by the Chaudière Falls to halt there—no attempt was made to settle the vicinity for nearly two hundred years.

The reason for this paradox was the policy of the successive French governors whose priorities were exploration, the procurement of furs, and the Christian conversion of the Indians. New settlements were not encouraged because they conflicted with the

4

fur trade, which was the backbone of the economy. Population growth was vital to New France, but this requirement could look after itself within the established communities. After Montcalm's defeat on the Plains of Abraham in 1759 the British Government followed a similar policy. For the next twenty years the English concentrated on the exploitation of the fur trade, and the discovery of the West—settlement and the spiritual salvation of the natives were held in abeyance. It was not until Britain lost the American colonies in 1783 that London decided it would be prudent to settle loyal subjects in the undefended wilderness adjacent to the American border.

Thus the limestone cliffs of Ottawa remained uninhabited while an historic procession of explorers, fur traders, and missionaries toiled their way around the Chaudière Falls going to and returning from the interior. During this period the Ottawa River could be compared to a highway, with the Chaudière Falls a major stoplight. The history-makers, to a man, were all travellers bound for distant destinations. Although Ottawa plays a passive role, a brief review of the exploits of some of these adventurers will shed light on subsequent developments in the area.

Étienne Brûlé, who portaged at the Rideau Falls in 1610, was the first white man to view the site of the future capital. Brûlé was a colourful scoundrel who had been sent by Samuel de Champlain to live with the Huron Indians for the winter to learn their language. When he returned to Montreal the following spring (as the first Canadian graduate of a language immersion course), he was a qualified interpreter.

Although Brûlé was only nineteen, his future seemed assured, for Champlain—the Father of New France, who is remembered as a statesman, soldier, explorer, scholar, and saint—had great plans for him. Regrettably, Brûlé turned his back on the colony and chose to live an irresponsible life among the savages. For the next twenty-two years he roamed from band to band, building a reputation as a ne'er-do-well and a lecher. In 1629 he betrayed his country when he guided a British force, led by the Kirke Brothers, down the St. Lawrence to their successful conquest of the garrison at Quebec. The only achievement from his nomadic existence in the wilderness —and it must not be overlooked—was that he covered a great deal of territory, and he is believed to be the first European to reach Georgian Bay, as well as the Great Lakes. Even before Brûlé turned traitor, Champlain said of him: "Brûlé is licentious and otherwise depraved, thus setting a bad example to the savages, for which he should be severely punished." In 1633 Brûlé was severely punished. While living with a band of Hurons in Georgian Bay he was stabbed to death, his body was dismembered, and his remains were consumed by the villagers.

The second white man to go up the Ottawa earned his niche in Canadian history for being a liar. His name was Nicolas de Vignau, and in 1611 he was sent by Champlain to establish an alliance with the Indians who lived above the Chaudière Falls. De Vignau spent the winter on Allumette Island, roughly one hundred miles upstream from the city of Ottawa, opposite the present site of Pembroke. This island, strategically located in the middle of the river, was flanked by impassable rapids from shore to shore. Allumette was occupied by a band of Algonquins, led by a one-eyed chief named Tessouat, who made their living as fur brokers and toll keepers. Everyone descending the river was forced to portage at Allumette Island, and paid a toll for the privilege of crossing Tessouat's property. This arrangement was a powerful incentive for the Indians living upstream to sell their furs to Tessouat, who then marked up the price and resold the pelts to the French.

After spending a pleasant winter with Tessouat's people, de Vignau paddled down to Montreal in the spring of 1612 and caught the first sailing ship for France, where he made his report to Champlain. De Vignau's testimonial to his own good work culminated with the announcement that he had discovered the Northwest Passage. This was stunning news, for the Passage was the water route to the Orient and its riches. De Vignau embellished his tale by adding that he had seen a large British vessel, with a crew of eighty men, which had foundered on the shore of the northern sea. Champlain was elated with the tidings, but as a precaution he had de Vignau sign a formal statement of his discovery before two notaries. Then he made plans to return to Canada to view the route for himself. For some reason, possibly because he was so deeply enmeshed in his lie, de Vignau agreed to accompany Champlain up the Ottawa the following spring.

At the end of May 1613 Champlain and de Vignau left Montreal with four other companions in two canoes. De Vignau shared Champlain's birchbark craft, and one wonders what his thoughts were as they paddled up the river. On June 4 the little party reached the outlet of the Rideau River, where Champlain recorded the sight of the falls in his diary:

At its mouth there is a wonderful waterfall; for, from a height of twenty or twenty-five fathoms, it falls with such impetuosity that it forms an archway nearly four hundred yards in width. The Indians, for the fun of it, pass underneath this without getting wet, except for the spray made by the falling water.

Champlain's description of the water forming an archway is perfect; later French canoeists dubbed it *Le Rideau* (the curtain). However, he misjudged the measurements somewhat—the falls were more like seven fathoms (forty-two feet), and their over-all width was closer to a hundred yards than four hundred.

Less than an hour later the Indian guides brought them to the portage on the opposite side of the river, at the foot of the Chaudière Falls. The falls were an inspiring spectacle, and once again Champlain took careful note:

These falls are a league wide and descend from a height of six or seven fathoms. There are many little islands, which are nothing but cliffs, ragged and unaccessible and covered with poor brushwood. At one place the water falls with such violence upon a rock, that, in the course of time, there has been hollowed out in it a wide and deep basin, so that the water flows round and round there and makes, in the middle, great whirlpools. Hence, the savages call it *Asticou,* which means kettle. This waterfall makes such a noise that it can be heard more than two leagues off.

From Champlain's explanation it is obvious how the Chaudière Falls got their name. Both Indians and Frenchmen agreed that the torrents of water created the effect of a boiling kettle; the Indian name for a kettle was *asticou,* the French equivalent, *chaudière.*

A constant factor in travelling the waterways was the need to portage around obstacles, such as rapids or cataracts, which would swamp or damage the frail canoes. The *coureurs de bois* had this chore down to a science. The canoe was quickly unloaded and the contents distributed without a word, those not carrying packs then put the canoe on their shoulders, and all hands "portaged" (walked) around the obstruction. In the case of the Chaudière Falls, it was a rugged six-hundred-yard tramp for Champlain over slippery stone, on a twisting path that came so close to the maelstrom in places that the travellers were frequently wet with spray.

When they arrived at Allumette Island, a few days later, Champlain was greeted warmly by his "good captain" Tessouat, with whom he had fought the Iroquois in 1603. At the conclusion of the feast that evening, Champlain asked Tessouat for an escort to take his party to the headwaters of the Ottawa. Tessouat declined this request on the basis that it was too dangerous to proceed upstream because of the sorcerers and bloodthirsty Indians who lived around Lake Nipissing. Champlain then explained to Tessouat that those Indians were *not hostile toward white men* because de Vignau had passed through the same country on his way to the great salt sea, two years earlier.

When Tessouat heard this, he became furious and had his braves seize de Vignau, whom he denounced as a liar and a braggart. Under pressure, de Vignau confessed that his story of the Northwest Passage had indeed been a lie. The Indians offered to kill de Vignau, but Champlain would not allow it; instead, he made plans to return to Montreal. This development pleased Tessouat, who no longer had to worry that the French would make contact with the Indians upriver and buy their furs direct. The chief was happy to provide a flotilla of canoes to escort the French downriver—an uneventful journey, except for a ceremony Champlain witnessed at the Chaudière Falls:

> Having carried their canoes to the foot of the fall, they assemble in one place, where one of them takes up a collection with a wooden plate into which each puts a piece of tobacco. After the collection, the plate is set down in the middle of the group and all dance about it, singing after their fashion. Then one of the chiefs makes a speech, pointing out that for years they have been accustomed to making such an offering, and that thereby they receive protection from their enemies; that otherwise misfortune would happen to them, as the devil pursuades them. When he has finished, the orator takes the plate and throws the tobacco into the boiling water, and all together utter a loud whoop. These poor people are so superstitious, that they would not think they could have a safe journey, unless they had performed this ceremony here.

Before leaving the story of the wretched Nicolas de Vignau, it is appropriate to say a few words in his defence. De Vignau definitely did not discover the Northwest Passage, but he may have *spoken* with Indians who had been as far north as Hudson Bay. If this was so, then the tale of a British ship could have had some substance, because Henry Hudson—the legendary arctic explorer who was abandoned by his mutinous crew—had sailed into the northern sea

(Hudson Bay) on his last voyage in 1611. Thus Champlain's judgment of de Vignau as "the most impudent liar that has been seen for a long time" may have been unjust.

The first missionary came up the Ottawa in 1615, on his way to Georgian Bay. His name was Father Joseph Le Caron, and he was one of four Récollet priests who had been brought from France by Champlain earlier that summer. Wearing a coarse black robe and wooden sandals, Father Le Caron was the vanguard of a host of selfless men who dedicated their lives to converting the savages to Christianity; in the next half-century many priests were to die in this endeavour. After surmounting the Chaudière Falls, Father Le Caron continued to the headwaters of the Ottawa, crossed into Lake Nipissing, and paddled down the French River into Georgian Bay. From a letter sent to his superior in France we can get some idea of the hardship of the journey:

> It would be hard to tell you how tired I was with paddling all day, with all my strength, among the Indians; wading the rivers a hundred times or more, through the mud and over sharp rocks that cut my feet; carrying the canoe and luggage through the woods to avoid the rapids and frightful cataracts; and half starved all the while, for we had nothing to eat but a little *sagamite,* a sort of porridge of water and pounded maize, of which they gave us a small allowance morning and night. But I must needs tell you what abundant consolation I found under all my troubles; for when one sees so many infidels needing nothing but a drop of water to make them children of God, one feels an inexpressible ardour to labour for their conversion, and sacrifice it to one's repose and life.

Father Le Caron's "drop of water" was to prove a source of grief to the missionaries on many occasions. This came about because the priests believed it their duty to baptize any dying Indian who had not been converted. When the native subsequently died, the village medicine man would spitefully attribute his death to the ministrations of the "Black Robe."

A few weeks after Le Caron passed beneath the silent cliffs of Parliament Hill, he was followed by Champlain. Unlike the missionary, who went in peace, Champlain planned to fight the Iroquois, and his canoes were loaded with weapons for his Huron allies. At the mouth of the French River he met a band of Indians who wore their hair in a distinctive fashion, tied in a bunch on the top of their heads. Through his interpreter Champlain learned that these were members of the Ottawa or *Outaouais* tribe whose hunting grounds stretched from the west bank of the Ottawa River to Lake Superior.

That September Champlain visited Father Le Caron in Huronia (Georgian Bay), where the Récollet priest had established a small mission with a bark chapel and was busy saving souls. Later in the fall Champlain accompanied a Huron war party that crossed Lake Ontario and laid siege to an Iroquois stockade near Lake Oneida. The campaign failed due to the fierce resistance of the defenders, and a missed rendezvous with Étienne Brulé, who was meant to appear with reinforcements. Champlain received an arrow in the leg which crippled him so badly that he had to be carried in a basket for most of the journey back to Huronia. His wound healed slowly, and it was not until the following spring that he was able to travel down the Ottawa waterway to Montreal.

This was Champlain's last voyage on the Ottawa; for the next few years the European traffic on the river consisted of missionaries and a few *coureurs de bois*. In 1618 Jean Nicolet employed this route to get to the Great Lakes; from there he pushed on to discover Wisconsin. Ten years after Father Le Caron went to Huronia, it became obvious to the mendicant Récollet fathers that they could not cope with the needs of their gigantic parish, so they requested the help of the Jesuit Order (Society of Jesus) in France. The Jesuits were an excellent choice, for they were highly disciplined, well financed, and their founder, Saint Ignatius Loyola, had been a gallant soldier. By 1649 there were eighteen Jesuit priests at Huronia, in addition to more than forty lay staff.

During the 1600s the main source of revenue in New France came from furs, which were trapped in the wilderness by the Indians and sold to the colonists for export. To the south, along the New England seaboard, the Dutch and English settlements also depended heavily on the export of pelts. Theoretically this meant that the Indians had the opportunity to choose the best of three markets to sell their furs. In practice the situation was very different. Age-old animosities between tribes, competition for trapping grounds, and the intervention of the white men—who supported various factions—combined to spark continous violence. So important was the fur trade that even the pious missionaries got involved in it by encouraging their charges to deal with the French. They did so for the good of the colony (rather like the Canadian Trade Commissioners who are sent from Ottawa all over the world), but it complicated their relationships with the natives. As early as 1627

Father Joseph Dallion, a Récollet monk, wrote to his superior in France explaining the problems he was having with the Hurons, who were concerned that he would persuade the neutral tribe to deal directly with the French:

> ... the Hurons, having discovered that I talked of leading them to the trade, spread in all the villages where they passed very bad reports about me: that I was a great magician; that I had tainted the air of their country and poisoned many; that if they did not kill me soon I would set fire to their villages and kill all their children. In fine, I was, as they said, a great Atatanite—that is their word to mean him who performs sacrileges, whom they hold in great horror. ... In a word, the Hurons told them so much evil of us to prevent their going to trade: that the French were unapproachable, rude, sad, melancholy people, who live only on snakes and poison; that we eat thunder, which they imagine to be an unparalleled chimera, relating a thousand strange stories about it; that we all had a tail like animals; that the women only have one nipple in the centre of the breast; that they bear five or six children at a time, adding a thousand other absurdities to make us hated by them and prevent their trading with us.

The most powerful and warlike Indians were the Iroquois, or Five Nations, which was a federation consisting of the Oneidas, Cayugas, Mohawks, Onondagas, and Senecas. The Iroquois controlled the south shore of the St. Lawrence as far downstream as Valleyfield, as well as the Ottawa Valley from the Chaudière Falls to the island of Montreal, and made sorties across Lake Ontario into Huronia. Less militant Hurons and Algonquins occupied the territory to the north and west of the Iroquois. In 1609 Champlain committed a strategic error when he sided with the Algonquins and Montagnais against the Iroquois near Lake Champlain. In that engagement the Iroquois —who had never seen a firearm—were routed, but the roar of Champlain's arquebus was to have a haunting echo. As a result of this skirmish, the Iroquois became allies of the English and the Dutch. In time, the Iroquois were supplied with guns which enabled them to terrorize the French settlers, to vanquish the Hurons and Algonquins, and to wipe out the mission posts. By 1653 the Ottawa River was effectively closed to all traffic, the Indians had been scattered in Huronia, and many of the priests had been tortured to death (eight of the Jesuits who died as martyrs were canonized by Pope Pius XI in 1930).

In 1654 the French and the Iroquois signed a truce at Montreal that reopened the Ottawa River. This truce was so brief that it is historically insignificant except for a coincidence that occurred two hundred years later. In 1853 Joseph-Balsora Turgeon, the mayor of Bytown (as Ottawa was then known), used the anniversary to justify his choice of the name "Ottawa" for the future capital.

By 1660 relations were so bad with the Iroquois that the residents of Montreal expected a mass attack at any moment. Rather than wait for the assault, Adam Dollard des Ormeaux, a young subaltern of the garrison, decided to try and deflect the Iroquois invasion by engaging them upstream from Montreal. With a tiny force of sixteen soldiers, forty Hurons, and six Algonquins, he paddled up the Ottawa. At the Carillon rapids (four miles below the Long Sault rapids) he encountered a war party of two hundred Iroquois descending the river. Taking refuge in an abandoned Algonquin fort, Dollard withstood five days of siege. On the fifth day, five hundred more Iroquois appeared, and his Huron allies defected, except for their chief, Annaotaha. Dollard was now outnumbered fifty to one, but he held his position for three more days, until he ran out of ammunition and the attackers swarmed over the palisade. There were no survivors. Yet Dollard and his companions accomplished their mission; the Iroquois were so impressed with the fighting qualities and valour of this small band that they cancelled their plans to attack Montreal, and withdrew. Had the Iroquois stayed in the vicinity, they would also have killed the legendary fur traders Pierre Esprit Radisson and Médard Chouart-dés-Groseilliers, who, descending the Ottawa six weeks later with a load of furs, were the first to see the charred fort and fly-blown corpses at the Carillon rapids.

The governor did not congratulate Radisson and Groseilliers for running the Iroquois blockade, when they reached Quebec with their precious cargo. Instead, because they had made the expedition without a licence, he confiscated their furs, fined both men, and clapped Groseilliers in jail. Incensed by this treatment the two hot-blooded *voyageurs* went to France but failed to receive satisfaction. Later they made their way to England, where they obtained an audience with King Charles II and offered him their services. The King was so impressed with them that he consented to the formation of the Company of Adventurers Trading into Hudson's Bay, which was financed by British merchants and led by the two entrepreneurs (remembered thereafter by English schoolchildren as "Mr. Radishes and Mr. Gooseberries"). Today this enterprise is still going strong but is known to most people as the Bay, with head office in Winnipeg and assets of more than a billion dollars. It is hard to visualize the turbulent beginnings of this conglomerate when you pass the perfume counter at a Bay store—and even harder to imagine what would have happened if Radisson and Groseilliers had been ambushed at the Chaudière Falls.

For years following the massacre at the Long Sault, travel on the Ottawa River was safe only for large flotillas of canoes or military expeditions. After the British became established in Hudson Bay, the flow of furs to the French settlements began to dwindle, which hurt the economy. In an effort to eliminate this northern competition, the Chevalier de Troyes took a force of one hundred men to James Bay in 1686. The column left Montreal in March, just prior to the spring breakup on the Ottawa River, and for some days the Chevalier had to walk in front of his troops, testing the rotting ice with his sword point. His campaign was a success in that he captured Moose Factory, Rupert House, and Fort Albany. This eased the situation, but it failed to dislodge the British from Hudson Bay. In 1701 a lasting peace treaty was signed in Montreal by a council of 1300 Indians representing thirty tribes. From then on there was a steady stream of French fur traders paddling up the Ottawa on their way to the interior of the continent.

The fur traders, or *coureurs de bois,* were a tough bunch of men who took hardship and danger in their stride and were completely at home in the woods. The missionaries regarded them with a jaundiced eye, because they were freebooters whose main items of barter were guns and rum—a lethal combination for the Indians— and they fathered countless bastards, as well as spread alien diseases such as smallpox and syphilis. Due to the increasing scarcity of game, or competition, these men were often forced to venture far afield; in the process they became important explorers.

The staple of the Canadian fur trade was the beaver, *Castor canadensis.* For more than two hundred years, from 1625 until the advent of the silk "topper" in 1840, the most prestigious and expensive hats for men were made of beaver felt. In the early days it was common practice for smooth-talking traders to cozen Indian braves out of their long beaver cloaks. These garments fetched high prices in Europe because they were usually worn and greasy, with the guard hairs rubbed off, which made them easy to process into felt. After the Indians had sold their cloaks, the trade continued to flourish with freshly trapped skins, although "green" pelts did not command the same premium due to the increased cost of felting.

The first British traveller to portage the Chaudière Falls was Alexander Henry, who ascended the Ottawa River in 1761. Henry was a Yankee carpetbagger who came to Canada from New England right after the fall of Quebec in 1759. Being eager to get into the fur trade, he paddled west until he reached Fort Michilimackinac at the head of Lake Superior and Lake Huron. He arrived on 2 June 1763, just in time to witness the slaughter of the English garrison by Chippewas, who were led by an Ottawa chief named Pontiac. This tragedy was the high point of an Indian campaign (inspired by the French) known as Pontiac's Uprising. Later that summer Chief Pontiac laid an unsuccessful siege against the fort of Detroit, which had been founded in 1701 by another Ottawa explorer, Antoine de La Mothe Cadillac. Ironically, the names of both the founder and the attacker of Detroit have since been made household words by one of that city's automakers.

Pontiac's Uprising was a sign of deep-seated changes taking place in North America. Within the next twenty years two treaties signed in Paris would create two distinct nations on the continent and eventually lead to the birth of the city of Ottawa.

The first Treaty of Paris, in 1763, ceded Canada and all the territories east of the Mississippi to Great Britain. At the time France was in a deplorable position to bargain, for she had just lost the Seven Years War, and her Canadian colonies had capitulated to British forces three years earlier. Nevertheless, the French were given the islands of St. Pierre and Miquelon, as well as fishing rights off Newfoundland. Encouraged by the generous attitude of the British negotiators, the French team then suggested that England might prefer to take the islands of Guadeloupe instead of Canada. The British were surprised at this proposal because Voltaire, France's leading man of letters, had been saying to anyone who cared to listen that Canada was merely "a few acres of snow." Yet it was an intriguing idea, and the question of whether to accept Canada or Guadeloupe was referred to the British Parliament. The pros and cons of the swap were debated at length. On one hand, Guadeloupe was an exotic location that could provide Britain with sugar, rum, and bananas (still the mainstays of her economy, in addition to a Club Med resort). On the other hand, while Canada lacked Guadeloupe's delightful climate, she was 5640 times larger than those tropic islands, and there was reason to suspect that she had natural resources other than furs. Parliament voted to retain Canada.

The second Treaty of Paris, in 1783, gave the thirteen colonies their independence from Britain. When the territorial question came up, Benjamin Franklin, who led the American delegation, suavely suggested that England cede the entire continent to the new republic. This was an audacious proposal, for the colonies were just a necklace of settlements strung along the Atlantic seaboard. Yet it had the advantage of simplicity, and it eliminated the need to haggle over boundaries. The British declined the proposal because they wanted to keep the ports of Halifax and Quebec for their navy, but they agreed to a compromise. The Americans received roughly half the continent, with most of the boundaries to be defined at a later date. Canada lost both the Ohio basin, and a great wedge of territory between Quebec and Halifax. The Treaty of 1783 established a pattern for the future: whenever Britain and the United States sat down to discuss North American boundaries, Canada invariably came out the loser. This was due as much to indifference as to incompetence on the part of the British negotiators.

After the secession of the United States, the Canadian colonies became known as British North America. This name stood until 1867, when the British Parliament passed the British North America Act, which united most of the colonies and changed their name to the Dominion of Canada. Prior to Confederation, each colony had its own constitution and a governor or lieutenant-governor sent from Britain. Each colony was run by an executive council appointed by the lieutenant-governor, and a legislative assembly made up of elected representatives. Legislation was drafted and proposed by the elected members, who then submitted it to the lieutenant-governor (through his council) for approval. In 1784 British North America consisted of six separate colonies: Nova Scotia, New Brunswick, Cape Breton, Prince Edward Island (then called St. John), Quebec, and Newfoundland. The Canadian colonies were headed by a governor-in-chief who wore several hats: he was the senior representative of the sovereign, the senior representative of the British Parliament (through the Colonial Secretary), and the governor of Quebec. The governor-in-chief was responsible for the defence of the country and relations with other nations, and he had final authority over the allocation of Crown lands. For these reasons he was the most important man in British North America. However, while the governor-in-chief and his lieutenant-governors could veto legislation and dissolve the elected assemblies, they had no control over the use of tax revenues. This financial restriction proved to be a recurring source of friction between the governors and the elected officials. The office of governor-in-chief was superseded by the office of governor-general in 1838, and upon Confederation in 1867, the governor-general changed his residence from Quebec City to Ottawa, the capital of the new dominion. Today, his responsibilities are greatly reduced, but he is still the senior representative of the British sovereign.

As a result of the Treaty of 1783 the St. Lawrence River became part of the international boundary, which made the waterway vulnerable to American attack. This prompted the British government to seek an alternate inland route for the movement of troops and supplies between Montreal and Kingston. The same year the treaty was signed, two junior officers of the Royal Engineers were sent from England to explore the feasibility of using the Ottawa River and connecting streams for this purpose. A Lieutenant Jones went up the north shore of the Ottawa to the Chaudière Falls and returned to Montreal via the south shore. His companion, a Lieutenant French, turned off at the Rideau River and followed it through the Rideau Lakes, where he portaged across to the Gananoque River and paddled down to the St. Lawrence. Both officers reported that there was plenty of good land for settlement. More important, Lieutenant French stated that a protected route could be fashioned, using the Rideau system and the Ottawa River, which would link the garrisons of Kingston and Montreal. Lieutenant French's report planted the seed for the Rideau Canal and was also responsible for the recommendation of a British Parliamentary Committee that a community be established at the forks of the Rideau River, in the vicinity of Dow's Lake, roughly two miles south of Parliament Hill.

On Boxing Day, 1791, the British Parliament passed the Constitutional Act dividing the colony of Quebec into two separately administered provinces, to be known as Upper Canada and Lower Canada. The Ottawa River formed a long section of the boundary between these provinces, which were subsequently redesignated the districts of Canada West and Canada East in 1840, and, on Confederation in 1867, took their present names of Ontario and Quebec. Both Upper and Lower Canada offered land grants to induce British subjects, and former subjects, to settle in their territories. Loyal settlers trickled into the Ottawa Valley during the next decade, but the one who is remembered as the "Father of Ottawa" had to swear an oath of allegiance to King George III before he could get a grant of land. The reason for this precaution was that he was a Yankee who had fought against the King's troops at Bunker Hill. His name was Philemon Wright.

3

Philemon Wright

1796 to 1820

PHILEMON WRIGHT WAS a remarkable and complex individual. He is described by his contemporary, John Mactaggart, as "about six feet high, a tight man, with a wonderfully strange, quick reflective wild eye." A natural leader and a practical man, he was also a visionary whose imagination could be fired by the wildest schemes. Underlying these traits was a paternal concern for the common good and a profound belief that the best things in life could only be earned through hard work.

In 1800, when he was thirty-nine—an age when most men are concerned with security—Philemon Wright left his prosperous farm near Boston and took his family to the wilderness of Canada. With him was his wife Abigail and their six children: Philemon, Jr., aged eighteen; Tiberius, thirteen; Polly, ten; Ruggles, eight; Abigail, six; and Christopher, the baby, who was only two. Wright's move was a gamble, but he had shrewdly calculated the odds.

Four years earlier he had gone to Montreal to sample the political and social climate in the British colony. He was favourably impressed, and returned the next year to make a general survey of Crown lands along both banks of the St. Lawrence River, from Quebec City to Montreal. When this was completed, he made a quick trip up the

Ottawa (then known as the Grande River) as far as the Chaudière Falls. The uninhabited Ottawa Valley proved to be exactly what he was looking for: it combined fertile soil with vast stands of timber on a waterway that led to the markets of Montreal and Quebec City. When he went home, he accepted an offer from John Fassett of Bennington, Vermont, to buy a half-interest in a "warrant of survey" covering four newly designated townships in Lower Canada. One of the townships was named Hull and was situated directly opposite the present city of Ottawa. A warrant of survey did not give the holder title to property, but it made him eligible for a substantial land grant from the Crown if he fulfilled certain obligations. These obligations included a survey of the tract, the introduction of a stipulated number of settlers, and the clearing of a given number of acres. Warrants of survey were only issued to men of substance with unquestioned loyalty to the Crown.

Philemon Wright did not know it at the time, but Fassett's warrant had been cancelled because the governor of Lower Canada had learned that Fassett was not only an unrepentant rebel but also a land speculator who had no intention of settling in Canada. Assuming that his warrant was valid, Wright went to Montreal in 1798 and tried to hire two axemen to help him make a detailed survey of Hull Township. He was unable to hire anyone because the North West Company let it be known that they did not want any settlers in their fur territory.

This did not deter Philemon Wright. He simply went home to Massachusetts and engaged two "respectable" men who returned with him the next year. After twenty-seven days of hard paddling, they reached the Chaudière Falls at the end of September, 1779. For the next three weeks they tested the soil, took inventory of the standing timber, and plotted the topographical features. In the course of their investigation they climbed more than one hundred trees to get a panoramic view of the surroundings. One advantage of the dense forest was that it made it easy to climb lookout trees; they simply felled a small tree so that its branches lodged in the boughs of the tall one, and then scrambled up the inclined "ramp." Wright was also pleased to see that, because of the low banks on the Hull shore, the main portage route was on his side of the river. This traffic would be good for trade in the future.

Before leaving Canada Wright stopped in Montreal and advised the governor's land agent of his plans to settle the following year. It was then that he learned that Fassett's warrant was invalid. This was a dreadful blow, but Wright was able to convince the agent of his personal integrity, and received a verbal assurance that the Crown would look favourably upon an application for a warrant on Hull Township in Wright's name. Wright then lodged a formal request for warrant of survey and continued home to Woburn. Aided by the eyewitness reports of his two assistants, Wright had no trouble in recruiting homesteaders and hired hands to accompany him on the long trip north.

Wright's party, consisting of five families and twenty-five men, left Woburn on 2 February 1800. Most of the men walked, while the women and children rode in seven sleighs drawn by fourteen horses and eight oxen. Their provisions were limited to staples such as salt pork and they brought some simple implements. A week later they reached Montreal, where Wright met with the land agent and was given permission to proceed with his plans. His friends used the stop-over to catch up on their sleep before making the final leg of their journey. From Montreal, it took them three days to reach the foot of the Long Sault Rapids, a distance of forty-five miles. This marked the end of the road and the limit of civilization. The next sixteen miles were hard going because they had to reharness the teams in single file and literally hack their way through the bush. To keep from losing their direction they camped beside the river for the next three nights, taking care to choose a site free of dead trees, which could fall on them if a storm arose. They were at the mercy of the elements—the men slept in the snow by an open fire while the women and children bundled in the sleighs—but morale remained high.

At the head of the Long Sault they decided the easiest course was to travel the remaining sixty miles along the river. However, this presented another problem: neither Wright nor his guide knew the ice conditions, and it was impossible to see the weak spots because there was a foot of snow. Wright's solution was to send men with axes in front of the column to laboriously test the surface every few feet. While they were creeping along, they encountered an Indian with his squaw, who was drawing a child on a little birchbark sleigh. The Indian was fascinated by the sight of the horses and oxen. Although neither party could speak the other's language, the Indian quickly grasped the situation, and told his wife to camp on the bank until he returned. Then he went to the head of the company and led them upriver, pausing from time to time to check the ice with his hatchet. Six days later their guide brought them safely to their destination a few miles below the Chaudière Falls. Wright and his party were deeply touched by the kindness of this Indian, for he had been promised nothing for his services. Before their guide left to rejoin his wife and baby, he was given some useful presents and he was "three times huzzaed" by the men.

Wright's settlers completed their five-hundred-mile trek on 7 March and immediately started clearing home sites. Work progressed quickly because most of the felled timber was used on the spot as material for the cabins. Each day was longer than the previous one, the snow quickly melted under the increasing warmth of the sun, and the woods rang from dawn till dusk with the sound of axes. It was not long before the activity in the bush opposite Parliament Hill attracted the notice of passing Indians. Twenty years later Philemon Wright recounted the story of his first visitors in an address to the House of Assembly for Lower Canada:

> ... as soon as we commenced cutting and clearing, the Chiefs of two Tribes of Indians that live at the Lake of Two Mountains came to us and viewed all our tools and materials with astonishment, and would often hoop and laugh as they were quite unacquainted with tools or things of that nature. They also viewed with astonishment the manner in which we harnessed our oxen, horses etc. all being harnessed by pairs. They seemed to view all our things, cattle, etc. with great pleasure. Some of them fetched their children to see the oxen and horses, they having never seen a tame animal before, being brought up on the great Lakes upon the Westward: they would also ask the liberty of using one or two of our axes to see how they could cut down a tree with them, as their axes are very small, weighing only half a pound, our axes weighed from four to five pounds. When they had cut down a tree, they would jump, hoop, and huzza, being quite pleased at having cut down the tree so quick.... They continued very friendly to pass backward and forward for about ten days, often receiving small presents, for which they made me returns in sugar, venison, etc.

Later that first spring Philemon Wright received another delegation of chiefs. These Indians did not come on a social visit but rather to voice their concern at his intention to settle on their land. Through an interpreter named George Brown (who had worked for the North West Company), Wright was asked what authority he had to encroach on native territory. He explained that his authority came from the Great Father, and offered to go to Montreal the next moon to clear the matter with Sir John Johnson, the superintendent-general for Indian Affairs. The chiefs thought this was fair, and agreed to abide by Sir John's ruling. When Wright returned from Montreal another council was held with the chiefs, who were told that Sir John Johnson had confirmed Wright's claim to property in Hull Township. The Indians accepted this news with good grace; in fact, they made Philemon a brother chief in a colourful ceremony that included the symbolic rite of burying the hatchet. From then on the red men and the settlers lived in harmony. Speaking of the Indians in his 1820 address, Wright stated: "I must acknowledge that I never was acquainted with any people that more strictly regarded justice and equity than those people have for these past twenty years."

The early spring in their first year was a blessing because it made the task of clearing easier and gave them time to plant a potato crop. When Wright paddled to Montreal that September to buy provisions for the winter, potatoes were not on his shopping list, for he had just harvested more than a thousand bushels. However, this bonanza was lost because the potatoes were stored beneath the frost line and rotted during the winter.

As soon as the ice went out the following April, Wright returned to Woburn to clear up his affairs and pay off his short-service labourers. Many of these same men accompanied him back to Hull with their families as permanent settlers. Building continued that summer and more than a hundred acres were cleared for cultivation. From July until October Wright headed a crew of ten men who surveyed Hull Township. This was a difficult job due to the hilly terrain, the dense vegetation, and the sinuous meanderings of the Gatineau River. When they were finished, they had placed 377 stakes and surveyed a total of 82,429 acres.

The survey met the final requirement of Wright's application for a grant of land from the Crown. As a result of their work, Wright and his settlers were given a 12,000-acre block in Hull Township by the governor. However, by previous agreement, Wright's associates ceded five-sixths of their land back to him. Today, five-sixths of the grant may seem an exorbitant fee, but in those days it was considered a reasonable payment for the promoter's services in surveying the land and obtaining the grant. Wright kept a leather book in which he recorded the reconveyance of lands to him as well as the purchase and sale of other properties. By 1820 he held personal title to 21,145 acres.

In 1802 he took two important steps in his plan to make the community self-sufficient. He built a sawmill and a grist mill. Both operations were run on water power generated by the Chaudière Falls; thus he became the first man to harness this centuries-old obstacle. That same year he expanded his agricultural program by sowing hemp. Hemp was a versatile plant for pioneers because the stalk fibres could be woven into rope and sturdy cloth, while the oil from the seeds was used to make soap and paint. To maximize his profit Wright built a hemp-processing mill. This proved a wise investment; his first crop accounted for 85 percent of the total hemp sold in Lower Canada. Not only did he have a high yield, but the quality of his plants was outstanding—a fourteen-foot bundle submitted to the Agricultural Committee of the Arts Society in Quebec won him a silver medal for excellence. In this connection, Ottawa is still a fine area to grow hemp, but under present legislation a fourteen-foot bundle of *Cannabis sativa*—colloquially known as grass—would more likely win thirty days in jail.

In 1804 Philemon Wright's work force had grown to seventy-five men, most of whom addressed him as "Squire" Wright, a title he quite enjoyed. That spring he built a tannery, but the main piece of machinery, a special bark-grinding cylinder, did not arrive from New York until the fall. During the summer he also constructed a blacksmith's shop with four water-powered bellows for the forges, as well as a tailor's shop, a shoemaker's, and a gigantic bakery. Road- and bridge-building continued, for it was important to link the spreading community.

By the end of 1805 Squire Wright had spent his original capital of $20,000. If he—and his settlement—were to survive he must find a dependable source of export income (the hemp business was marginal because his hemp peelers were now charging $1.00 a day). Lumber was the obvious commodity to export. Unfortunately, the only way to get the logs to market was down the Ottawa River. No one had ever taken a raft through the Long Sault rapids, and the *habitants*, whose ancestors had lived on the Ottawa for more than one hundred years, were certain that it could not be done. Wright knew the Long Sault rapids, and decided to gamble. To this end he negotiated a contract for 6000 oak staves, to be delivered in Quebec by 31 July of the following year. During the fall and winter his crews worked in the bush, while his sawmill was kept busy cutting boards and preparing five-and-a-half-foot oak staves.

In the spring of 1806 Wright assembled a timber raft at the mouth of the Gatineau River which consisted of 700 logs, 9000 boards, and the 6000 oak staves. On 11 June he set off with his son Tiberius and two crewmen on a history-making voyage to Quebec. Their ungainly raft slid down the Ottawa without incident until they reached the head of the Long Sault. Here, Wright engaged some Iroquois Indians from the Caughnawaga reserve (which was downstream, opposite Lachine) to help him dismantle the raft into "cribs." Each crib contained thirty-five logs, which were overlaid with boards and staves. Guiding the cribs through the rapids proved a dangerous and frustrating task. The powerful current smashed many of the cribs against the rocks; others were forced aground; some were simply swept away. When a jam occurred, the men frequently had to wade waist-deep in the treacherous flow to pry the logs loose with iron-shod pike-poles. Finally, after thirty-six days, they cleared the Long Sault rapids, reassembled the raft, and drifted on downstream. To avoid the Lachine rapids Wright took his raft around the north shore of the island of Montreal, via the Rivière des Prairies, and thence to the St. Lawrence. Due to the abuse his cribs had taken on the journey, his raft came apart several times between Montreal and Quebec. This caused further delays. When they reached Quebec on 12 August Wright was informed that his contract for the staves was void, due to late delivery. He also learned that the timber market was in a decline. There were no buyers for his logs and boards. His sixty-four-day voyage—which marked the beginning of the lumber trade in the Ottawa Valley—appeared to have been in vain.

Wright had no alternative but to wait in Quebec and hope that the market would improve. Three months later, in November, a convoy of British "timber droghers" sailed into port and he sold them his raft. The arrival of these ships so late in the season confirmed a growing rumour that the British Navy was short of stores. Another indication of Britain's interest in the Canadian market was the buying activity of Scott, Idles and Company, who were purchasing agents for the Royal Navy. Wright was unaware that Napoleon planned to seal off the Baltic ports—Britain's traditional source of timber—but he knew that Scott, Idles and Company would be heavy buyers of oak staves and mast timbers the following year. The Navy's specifications for mast timbers of white pine, with a minimum length of 112 feet, and a butt width of 40 inches (after "squaring"), did not worry him in the slightest. The Ottawa Valley was carpeted with giant white pines. As for the Long Sault, he had gained valuable experience on his first passage, and he was confident that his next descent would take a fraction of the time. The prospect of soaring prices fueled his determination to return to Quebec with an even bigger raft.

That winter he sent most of his men to the woods; while their axes bit into the pine, the settlement echoed to the screech of his sawmill. By the time the ice went out, a boom of mast timbers lay at anchor in the river, and the mill was completely surrounded by stacks of lumber. The Squire could hardly wait to sit down with the British Navy purchasing agents. On 8 May his hopes literally went up in smoke. Fire destroyed his mills (including the grist mill and the hemp plant) and all the sawn lumber—there was not a board or a sack of flour left in the settlement. When Philemon Wright surveyed the smoking ruins he was ready to admit defeat. Having no insurance, he was now effectively bankrupt. At this juncture his sons prevailed on him to rebuild with the proceeds from the squared timbers, which were still floating, untouched, in the estuary of the Gatineau. Wright agreed and took the raft safely down to Quebec. While he was absent, his men got on with the job of reconstruction. By the fall Wright's Town (as it was then known) had a new sawmill and a new grist mill. That autumn they had to go to Montreal to buy winter provisions but the community had survived the crisis.

The next five years were spent consolidating the settlement, expanding the lumber business, and improving the standard of agriculture. The Squire was a strong advocate of "scientific farming" as well as selective breeding. In this connection he was the first person in the Ottawa Valley to import prize Devon and Herefordshire cattle. His attention to scientific farming had some tangible rewards: in 1813 he sold three thousand bushels of wheat in Quebec for $3.00 a bushel, an astronomical price provoked by the War of 1812. Another facet of the war is revealed by a cryptic entry in his personal diary. Like many busy men, Wright relied on a diary to keep track of his commitments; many of his entries were scrawled in haste, and he was inclined to spell phonetically. These journals offer an insight into his life; the following was written while he was in Montreal, on 25 July 1814.

> Hired 5 desertors [sic] from the
> American army at 8 dollars
> each month. Pd them 5 dollars
> in advance

Samuel Muntoon
Peter Green
John Williams
JanBatist [*sic*] Chesilow
John Turnir
All for 1 year
time commence 27 July

Philemon Wright's deserters were accepted at their face value, and it is likely that some of them subsequently settled in Hull Township. The situation was quite different during the world wars and the Korean War. Canada and the United States were then co-combatants, so deserters were not only unwelcome but actively prosecuted. One hundred and fifty years would lapse after the Squire hired Messrs Muntoon, Green, Williams, Chesilow, and Turnir, before the Ottawa Valley again tolerated American deserters. This time, they would be fugitives from the war in Vietnam.

Wright's Town, or Wrightville (as Hull was usually called until the name was officially changed to that of the township in 1875), continued to prosper after the War of 1812. This was largely due to a thriving lumber trade, which was bolstered by a system of tariffs favouring the export of timber to Great Britain.

In 1819 the Squire built a major thoroughfare from Wright's Town to a point above the Chaudière Falls. The road followed the old portage trail, close to the river, and was built with simple ingenuity. First, the right-of-way was cleared of trees, then two parallel trenches were dug along the entire route. The earth from these trenches was piled in the space between them, which created a substantial mound. When the mound was graded, the result was a level surface, with a deep drainage ditch on both sides. Initially the highway was called the Britannia Road, but was rechristened the Aylmer Road in 1832, in honour of Lord Aylmer, the Governor of Lower Canada at that time. Still in use today, it is now known as the Lower Aylmer Road.

In the same year Wright decided to augment his cargo boat service on the Lower Ottawa which carried goods and freight to and from Grenville, at the head of the Long Sault Rapids. Because this was the longest navigable stretch between Montreal and Hull, there was a growing demand for a passenger boat service. In response to this demand, Wright built the *Packet* in 1819, and several larger steam vessels in the ensuing years. The *Packet* was powered by sail and oars—mostly oars—and plied her way from the wharf opposite Parliament Hill to the town of Grenville. The Squire kept a close watch on this venture in its maiden year. When sheet ice started forming in the sheltered bays of the Ottawa River, he was quick to take action:

Montreal 22 Nov 1819

To the Master of the Packet boot [*sic*]
from Hull to Granville [*sic*]
Head of Long Sew [*sic*]

Dear Sir,
    I request you as soon as you open this letter to go to our boots [*sic*] which must be near the head of Long Sew [*sic*] with your men, to give them every assistance lyes [*sic*] in your power. Let it require what time it may leaving the mail in the Granville [*sic*] Post Office until you can take it and take what loading you can carry from the boots [*sic*] and get to Hull as soon as possible. For you may depend a foul winter is near on hand. Work as fast to the southward as the wild goose does when hard winter comes in the Eastward.

Your most obedient
humble servant

P. Wright, Senr.

Wright's increasing role in the export of wheat and lumber often made it necessary for him to travel to Montreal and Quebec on business. Despite his commitments in these volatile markets, his thoughts were never far from Hull. When he was away, he wrote regularly to his wife Abigail and his grown sons, Tiberius and Ruggles. These letters give us a picture of Philemon's personality, and clearly reflect his paternal—almost feudal—concern for his little community. Extracts from letters written in 1820 provide two typical examples. Philemon had gone to Quebec City, the capital of Lower Canada, to settle some land questions, one of which concerned the Clergy Reserves. (The Constitutional Act of 1791 provided for one-seventh of Crown land suitable for settlement to be set aside for the support of the Protestant clergy. This provision caused political controversy, and was discontinued in 1854.) Shortly after his arrival in Quebec in November, Wright engaged a scrivener to write his sons on his behalf. The last paragraph in his letter refers to Joseph Wyman, his brother-in-law, who had just come from

Woburn to visit his sisters, Abigail Wright and Lavina Allen (the Allens were one of the five founding families who came to Hull in 1800).

> ... Hope Mrs. Wright and Mrs. Allen feels [*sic*] happy in a brother's visit. There is nothing would give me greater satisfaction that Mr. Wyman's settling among us* providing he could shake off that heavy load of Democracy that he has carried this 20 years about him—and enjoy the fruits of Independency in lieu of returning home under its shadow where Uncle Sam has so many calls and wants which *must* be had from the cash of sons of Liberty. It is an old subject but *yet* new and strong (not threadbare) that I particularily request you will pay strict attention to Agriculture the surest source of gain—my prayers to God for your safety etc.
>
> Yours Affectionately
P. Wright Senr.

A month later the Squire was still waiting in Quebec for the government to deal with his submissions. The atmosphere in the city that December was grim; timber prices were falling; money was scarce. A pair of turkeys could be bought for three shillings, while beef sold for four coppers a pound, and pork fetched only three coppers a pound. Philemon's next letter to his boys contains a hint of loneliness, as well as frustration at the bureaucratic delay, and the usual message of inspiration.

> ... I should take great pleasure if I could inform you when I mean to return but it is out of my power as the government business goes on so slow—there is little done and much yet to be done.
>
> I hope all things goes on well with you particularly the distillery business, I need not say the attention to that department as I am too well acquainted with your perseverance and indefatigable exertion. I have no small spite against an obstruction which presents itself between the Falls and the Columbia Farm called *Woods*—convert it as soon as probable into smoke or pile it up as winter fencing or fencing stuff not forgetting loggs [*sic*].
>
> The Agricultural horizon is a little clearing up and I hope soon to see established a society of this sort in Hull to which I have but little doubt but what you will lend every assistance for I feel that science is the sheet anchor of prosperity and honour and more particularily for a new country where only man may be said to have earned his bread by the sweat of his brow—when you look on the stock of cattle keep

---

*Joseph Wyman subsequently returned to Canada in 1823 and settled in Hull Township.

this in view and preserve the best breeding animals of every kind.

You will give my kind rememberances [*sic*] to all Relations, Friends, brother labourers and good fellows as I am sorry to be compelled to leave them so long but say it is not out of sight out of mind. Committing you all to the care of a good providence, I remain.

P. Wright Senr.

Wright's sons may have chafed under his close supervision, but they heeded his words. When Ruggles came home from a grand tour of Europe, he brought his father a prize bull and a pedigreed goat. The Squire's commitment to Hull was also warmly reciprocated by his people. On his return from an extended trip, the whole community would line the shore to give him a royal welcome, complete with flags, bells, and the crash of cannon.

By 1820 Hull was a well-established village. Philemon Wright lived in a fine house near Leamy Lake, surrounded by eight-hundred acres of tilled land. His residence was called Columbia Farm, and should not be confused with the stone house on St. Joseph Boulevard in Hull (now a restaurant known as La Ferme Columbia) that was built for his son-in-law, Thomas Brigham. The total population at the time was 703 people, all of whom were New Englanders or first-generation Canadians. Among the buildings were five mills, four stores, three schools, two hotels, two distilleries, and a brewery. The livestock count was 123 horses, 418 oxen, 503 cows, 505 pigs, and 558 sheep.

Across the river, Ottawa was still dense bush, occupied by a few widely scattered pioneers. Within the next few years, however, Ottawa would turn into a boom town; within the decade it would eclipse Hull in population and importance.

Philemon Wright contributed significantly to the transformation. Not only was Hull the base of operations for work across the river in the formative years, but his village also provided skilled men and materials. In addition, Wright personally acted as host and advisor to all the key decision-makers. Although he was in his sixties—and Ottawa was in Upper Canada—he pitched into the development of the new community with gusto. During the first crucial stages of the Rideau Canal— and the bridging of the Ottawa River—Wright's intervention frequently saved the day. His presence was a major factor in the healthy birth of the future capital.

Thus Philemon Wright, the dynamic New Englander, is remembered in Canadian history as both the Founder of Hull and the Father of Ottawa.

4

The Formative Years

1800 to 1826

THE FOUNDING AND development of Hull followed the typical pattern of the period. A band of pioneers hacked a community out of the wilderness; the community grew; then small satellite settlements blossomed within a day's ride of the original community. This sequence was reversed in the founding of Ottawa. The satellite settlements of Perth, Richmond, March, and Hull were well established by 1826, when construction of the Rideau Canal created the core community that eventually became Canada's capital.

To understand the development of Ottawa it is helpful not only to record the arrival of the first settlers but to review the situation in Canada prior to the building of the Rideau Canal and to glance at the histories of the satellite communities.

When the Constitutional Act of 1791 divided the old colony of Quebec into Upper and Lower Canada, Lower Canada had approximately 130,000 inhabitants, most of whom were French, while Upper Canada had only 20,000, most of whom were English. General John Graves Simcoe, the first Lieutenant-Governor of Upper Canada, was concerned about the sparse population in his province and took immediate steps to remedy the problem. In 1792 Simcoe issued a formal Proclamation inviting people in the United

Kingdom and the United States to apply for land grants. His message was widely circulated in the state of Vermont, which had just joined the Union after holding out since the American Revolution. In a sense Simcoe's invitation was also a form of amnesty, because anyone—even a rebel— was eligible, provided he was genuinely interested in settling and would take an oath of allegiance to the monarch, George III. United Empire Loyalists were especially welcome, and not only they but their descendants received generous grants. These people, known as UELs, had chosen to leave or were forced to flee the republic following the Declaration of Independence; some were tarred and feathered for their royalist sympathies.

At that time Upper Canada was partitioned into four judicial districts, each of which had its own court and jurisdiction within the boundaries of the district. Ottawa was in the judicial district of Lunenburg, a triangular territory that stretched from the Ottawa River to the Gananoque River. The districts were subdivided into counties for the purpose of electing representatives to the Legislative Assembly. Each county consisted of a number of townships. The township was the unit of settlement; most townships contained from 60,000 to 70,000 acres—those on waterfronts normally measured nine miles long and twelve miles deep, while inland townships were usually ten miles square.

In 1793 John Stegmann (deputy surveyor for Upper Canada) surveyed four townships in the adjoining counties of Carleton and Russell which he designated with the letters A,B,C, and D. In the next decade these letters were replaced with the names of prominent people. Township A was named Osgoode, after William Osgoode, first chief justice of Upper Canada, who ruled in 1803 that the practice of slavery was against English law. Township B was christened Gloucester, in honour of the King's nephew, the second Duke of Gloucester, a pleasant fellow whose limited intellect earned him the nickname "Silly Billy." Township C was called Gower, for a distinguished British admiral, John Levenson-Gower, who served in the waters off Newfoundland. Township D was named Nepean, after the Secretary of State for Ireland, Sir Evan Nepean. All four townships are in the Ottawa area, but the most important in the early days were Nepean and Gloucester. In 1800 the land fronting the Ottawa River immediately west of the Rideau River was Nepean Township, while the land to the east of the Rideau was Gloucester Township. The division is the same today except that successive annexations by the city of Ottawa have eaten into both townships.

Following Simcoe's Proclamation, parcels of land in this region were granted to applicants from the United Kingdom and to United Empire Loyalists. Much of the land in the vicinity of the capital was spoken for, but no one seemed in a hurry to occupy the ground. This was not surprising, as there was plenty of good land near established settlements such as Kingston and York (Toronto), which was the capital of Upper Canada. In addition, many of the original grantees took advantage of Simcoe's offer simply to speculate in real estate. As a result, there were more sellers than buyers, and land prices were depressed in Upper Canada for many years.

From the beginning, Canada had a polyglot monetary system. During the French regime, both French and Spanish silver dollars were used. The first paper money appeared in 1686, and was made of playing cards signed by the Governor and the Intendant. (In New France, the Intendant was an administrative officer responsible for commerce, finance, and police.) Following the British conquest in 1763, the variety of coins in circulation increased, with the most important being the Spanish silver dollar. The British attempted to solve the shortage of small change by allowing large-denomination coins to be cut into pieces. The slang expression "two bits," meaning a quarter of a dollar, is a legacy of this practice. However, the do-it-yourself approach to fractional coins led to wholesale fraud and they were soon prohibited. Not only did rates of exchange for the currencies fluctuate with time, but they also had different geographic values—Prince Edward Island tried to prevent Spanish dollars from leaving the island by punching a hole in the centre of them; these became known as "holey dollars." Among the mediums of exchange were the British pound Sterling, the Halifax pound, the Yankee dollar, Hudson Bay Company tokens (based on a prime beaver pelt), the Spanish dollar, notes issued by private banks (which were reluctantly redeemed at a deep discount), and a Canadian pound, which was lower in value than the British pound. During the War of 1812 the Governor-in-Chief paid for goods and services from the civilian population with "army bills." To further complicate matters, all currencies had to be converted into British or Canadian pounds for accounting purposes. By 1840 Canadian businessmen and politicians unanimously wanted to adopt the American decimal system, but it was not until Confederation in 1867 that Canada finally obtained her wish.

General Simcoe's open-handed land policy in Upper Canada produced some memorable real estate transactions. In 1802 Jacob Carman, the son of a United Empire Loyalist, drew one of the first lots in Nepean Township. Carman paid £10 Halifax currency, for a six-hundred-acre block overlooking the Ottawa River, bounded on the west by Bronson Avenue, the south by Wellington Street, and the east by the Rideau River. The terrain consisted of swamp, beaver meadow, and a limestone escarpment that was only fit for growing rocks. Carman did not settle on his property but was content to sell it, ten years later, to Thomas Fraser of Quebec for £12 Halifax currency. Today this tract is one of the most beautiful, and valuable, pieces of real estate in Canada. Within its boundaries are the National Archives and National Library buildings, the Supreme Court buildings, the Justice building, the Parliament buildings, the Library of Parliament, the Rideau Canal, and the Chateau Laurier Hotel.

The first person to actually settle in Ottawa was Jehiel Collins, a United Empire Loyalist from Vermont. In 1809 Collins built a shanty tavern and store at the canoe landing below the Chaudière Falls, an excellent location to catch the "portage trade" on the south bank of the Ottawa. Originally the shoreline had been christened Nepean Point, but it soon became known as Collins' Landing. A few years later Collins sold out to his clerk Caleb Bellows (a fellow Vermonter who had married Collins' sister) and moved back to the United States. After Collins' departure the name of the area changed again, to Bellows' Landing. The Nepean Point that Ottawans know today is not the same place but a park on a promontory east of the Rideau Canal, approximately two miles downstream from Bellows' Landing.

The first settler in Gloucester Township was Braddish Billings, the son of a Loyalist surgeon who had immigrated to Brockville in 1793. Around 1807 Billings journeyed to Hull and signed on as an employee of Philemon Wright. Later the Squire sent him to cut oak staves on the banks of the Rideau River. Billings was so impressed with the potential of the area that he left Wright's employ in 1810 to go into the lumber business for himself. By 1812 he had cleared several acres on the southeast bank of the Rideau and built a log cabin. This shanty had a large boulder that served as a backstop for the fireplace—the original stones may still be seen in a low monument erected near Billings Bridge. In November of 1813 Braddish Billings married Lamira Dow of Merrickville. Earlier in the year Miss Dow had been hired by Reverend Brown, the Methodist minister in Merrickville, to teach school for three months. Miss Dow's contract stipulated that she would be paid $7.00 a month plus room and board. However, at the end of the school term she learned that she would be paid in wheat receipts rather than cash and that these receipts would be honoured by Mr. Eastman, a storekeeper in Brockville. Miss Dow had no alternative but to walk the twenty miles to Brockville and present the receipts for credit. Mr. Eastman refused to honour her paper, and said he would only provide credit (for goods in his store) when the grain was delivered. Undaunted, the seventeen-year-old girl trudged back to Merrickville, borrowed a team of horses, collected the sacks of wheat, and drove the load to Brockville. Lamira Dow's grit and self-reliance in a male-dominated world earns her a place in the history of the Ottawa Women's Movement.

The first white child born in Gloucester Township was Sabra Billings, the daughter of Braddish Billings and Lamira Dow. In 1814, while Sabra was still an infant, she and her parents were nearly drowned when their canoe was swept over the thirty-foot Hog's Back Falls. Philemon Wright witnessed the accident and was horrified because not even the Indians dared to run this dangerous obstacle. When the canoe bobbed into view at the foot of the falls with the family drenched but safe, he was astounded.

Two of Lamira Dow's relatives, Abraham and Samuel Dow, settled near the Billingses in 1814 and 1816. The Dows' farms bordered the Great Swamp, on the opposite side of the Rideau River. The Great Swamp, which is in Nepean, was flooded during construction of the Rideau Canal. Today we know it as Dow's Lake, a scenic body of water in the heart of the city which hosts a fleet of small sailboats in the summer.

In 1810 Ira Honeywell built a house on the Ottawa River, five miles upstream from the Chaudière Falls. His father, Rice Honeywell of Prescott, obtained a thousand-acre block by purchasing adjacent land grants over a period of years. This parcel—one of the first land assemblies in the Ottawa area—was given to Ira by his father on the condition that he develop the property. Ira not only fulfilled his obligation but was also a leading figure in the early days of the future capital. His son John was the first white child born in Nepean. Direct descendants of Ira Honeywell are still prominent in the community.

In the summer of 1812, the United States declared war against Great Britain and proceeded to attack Canada. The conflict lasted for three years and directly affected most people in the colony. No battles were fought in Ottawa, but the war spurred the building of the Rideau Canal. This, in turn, brought in a wave of settlers, which changed a wilderness depot into a boom town.

The War of 1812 was a spin-off of the Napoleonic War. Part of Britain's strategy was to cordon off the Continent and thereby prevent supplies from reaching her enemy. To enforce the blockade, the British Navy did not hesitate to search and seize American merchant vessels. This practice infuriated the United States, who responded by declaring war against Britain. However, the new republic was in no position to challenge Britain's Navy, which would have been as ludicrous as a mouse attacking an elephant. The only feasible target for American aggression was the lightly populated British colony to the north. Some historians believe that the United States was confident that Canada would capitulate without a struggle. In fact, the American declaration of war had the reverse effect, for it united the French, the English, and the Indians against a common foe. On the other side of the border, many New Englanders were reluctant to fight their friends and relatives in Canada. Rather than strike at the core of the country with a major force, the United States pressed a series of attacks along its border. This strategy was stupid but understandable because the Americans did not have the naval strength to threaten Halifax or Quebec. Indeed, using a naval screen, Sir John Sherbrooke took a force from Halifax and captured a string of settlements on the Maine coast. Among the major towns were Bangor, Eastport, Hampden, Machias, and Castine. All the territory was returned at the end of the war, but customs duties levied at Castine were retained. These funds were used as seed money for the founding of Dalhousie University in Halifax.

The War of 1812 was characterized by bloody skirmishes rather than long campaigns. Among these was the capture of Detroit by Major-General Sir Isaac Brock, with a combined force of Indians under Chief Tecumseh; the massacre of the American garrison at Chicago by Canadian Indians; the Battle of Queenston Heights, where General Brock was killed (his tunic with the bullet hole is on exhibit at the War Museum in Ottawa); the indecisive but gory battle at Lundy's Lane; and the burning of Buffalo by Major General Phineas Riall, which culminated a series of lightning raids by his Indian force.

Although Britain had supremacy on the high seas, the Americans gained control of the Great Lakes when Captain Oliver Perry defeated Captain Robert Barclay at Put-in-Bay (Lake Erie) in 1813. Following this victory the Americans sailed across Lake Ontario and captured York. The invaders put the public buildings to the torch and then left with a considerable amount of booty. Among the items taken was the mace of the city, which was returned to Toronto by President Franklin Delano Roosevelt 121 years later.

One of the most distinguished Canadian units in the War of 1812 was the Glengarry Fencibles, which came from a Scottish settlement fifty miles south of Ottawa. The Glengarry Fencibles Regiment (fencibles is a term for troops on defensive service) was raised by Alexander Macdonell, a Roman Catholic priest. Father Macdonell was a burly Scot whose powerful personality matched his six-foot-four-inch frame. Twenty years earlier, while a missionary in Scotland, Father Macdonell had obtained work in Glasgow for six hundred destitute Highlanders. When this scheme failed, due to a depression brought on by Napoleon's blockade, Father Macdonell persuaded the British War Office to enlist his dependents as soldiers. A special unit was formed, the Glengarry Fencibles, which served in a number of trouble spots. The original Glengarry Fencibles are best remembered for their role in Ireland during the insurrection of 1798. Having been reared in the mountains of northern Scotland, the Highlanders were admirably suited to guerrilla warfare in the Irish hill country, and were so adept at hunting down rebels at night that they became known as The Devil's Bloodhounds.

The Glengarry Fencibles were disbanded in 1803, and once again Father Macdonell was faced with the task of finding employment for his wards. This time he arranged for them to immigrate to Glengarry County in Upper Canada. His people were not the original pioneers, as there was already a Scottish settlement there, founded by another priest with the same surname, Father Scotus Macdonell. From 1804 to 1812 the chaplain (or "Maihster Alastair" as he was affectionately known) worked on behalf of his own flock and the earlier Scottish immigrants. By 1812 he had managed to obtain land grants, or to clear title on provisional grants, in the counties of Stormont and Glengarry totalling 162,000 acres.

When the United States declared war in 1812, Father Macdonell donned his chaplain's uniform and raised another regiment of Glengarry Fencibles. This unit fought in fourteen general engagements and suffered heavy losses. One of their greatest victories was the unauthorized capture of Ogdensburg, New York, on 23 February 1813. Ogdensburg was attacked at first light by a combined force of

Glengarry Fencibles and the Glengarry Militia, who crossed the thin ice of the St. Lawrence led by Colonel "Red George" Macdonell. On the left flank Mr. MacKenzie, the Presbyterian chaplain, marched with a Bible in his hand; on the right flank, Father Macdonell exhorted his parishioners with a cross held high. As they neared the enemy's shore, one of Maihster Alaister's flock drew back. Father Macdonell roared at him to press on, but the young recruit ignored his chaplain's command. Father Macdonell excommunicated him on the spot.

The loss of Ogdensburg cost the Americans many casualties, in addition to four officers and seventy men who were taken prisoner. Before returning to their side of the river, the Canadians destroyed the American barracks, eleven cannon, four armed vessels, and a host of military stores. An incident at the end of the day is mentioned in the *Reminiscences of Alexander Macdonell* which was written by J. A. Macdonell, the chaplain's grand-nephew, in 1890.

A good story of him is told me by my friend, Mr. Kenneth Ross of Lancaster, whose father was wounded in the attack. Ross was carried into the house of an inn-keeper near Prescott, a half-Yankee, like many of his ilk along the border. The Chaplain saw that the wounded man was as much in need of stimulants as of priestly counsel, and went at once in search of some brandy. Excuses of various kinds were made by the woman of the house. Her husband was absent and had the keys, and so on. The Chaplain told her he would take no denial, and that if she did not procure the brandy forthwith he would have it in short order. She still demurred, whereupon he walked to the tap-room door, and with one kick lifted it off its hinges, and not only Mr. Ross, but all others of His Majesty's liege subjects had all the brandy they required after their hard day's fighting. Though Mr. Ross was a Presbyterian and the Chaplain a Catholic priest, I doubt if he could have been better served in his extremity even by a Minister of his own denomination.

In 1826 Alexander Macdonell was consecrated first Roman Catholic bishop of Upper Canada. His appointment coincided with the start of work on the Rideau Canal, which eventually employed several thousand Irish Catholic immigrants. During the next six years Bishop Macdonell frequently vistited his parishioners along the Canal route, and he was also the senior Church authority for the fledgling Roman Catholic ministry in Bytown (as Ottawa was then known).

Bishop Macdonell was an advocate of the ecumenical movement at a time when Protestants and Catholics were poles apart. Shortly after he arrived in Glengarry, Macdonell hosted a fellow man of the cloth, Bishop Jacob Mountain, the founder of the Church of England in the Canadas, and the two formed a lasting friendship. He was also a close friend of Bishop John Strachan, the first Anglican bishop of Upper Canada, with whom he sat on the Legislative Council for many years. This friendship is particularly impressive when one considers that Bishop Strachan was a "hard-line" Anglican. However, the most extraordinary evidence of Macdonell's popularity was the fact that he received a personal tribute from the Orange Lodge of Toronto, a society with radical anti-Catholic views.

Bishop Macdonell's motto was "Peace and goodwill among men of all creeds and our country for ourselves." He loved God, the Crown, and the smell of gunpowder.

His regiment, the Glengarry Fencibles, was subsequently melded with other militia units in the area to become the Stormont, Dundas, and Glengarry Highlanders. This unit, whose rallying cry is "Up the Glens!" has served with exceptional heroism in both world wars. During World War Two the regiment was commanded for eight months in northwest Europe by Lieutenant-Colonel (later Major-General) Roger Rowley of Ottawa. Rowley was twice awarded the Distinguished Service Order for gallantry while leading the "Glens."

The war with the United States ended in 1814, and the peace treaty, which restored the *status quo,* was ratified the following year. On the surface the fighting would appear to have been an exercise in futility since neither side gained any territory and both suffered heavy casualties. However, the intangible results were significant. Canada's French, English, and native people shared a positive experience that helped to unite them, and gave them a pride in their country. The conflict also tended to polarize views on both sides of the border, planting seeds of hostility that bloom from time to time in the form of anti-American sentiment.

In 1815 the Ottawa area was still uncleared acres of bush and swampland. There were a few pioneers in the townships of Gloucester and Nepean, but they lived in isolation because there were no roads and the only way to travel was on the Ottawa and Rideau rivers. These same two rivers were the main links of the proposed Rideau Canal, a project that took on sudden importance in view of the possibility of a second American invasion. The building of the

Rideau Canal was the catalyst for settlement in Ottawa, but it did not begin until 1826. In the meantime most immigrants to Upper Canada went elsewhere. Some of the British troops who had fought in the war agreed to remain in Canada, and they formed the nucleus of two satellite communities near the future capital.

In 1816 the Colonial Office established a military settlement fifty miles southwest of Ottawa. The new community, named Perth, was comprised of disbanded soldiers from the Regiment de Watteville, Scottish immigrants, and some members of the Glengarry Fencibles. The strategy behind this move was that, in the event of war, trained men would be close to the United States border *and* the Rideau Canal. In the next ten years Perth was made the judicial seat for the District of Bathurst, which included Bytown (Ottawa) because it was one of the Rideau Settlements. The appointment of Perth as the judicial seat caused much frustration and hardship for the magistrates of Bytown, especially during the boisterous canal-building days and the rowdy years that followed. At that time Bytown did not have a jail, which meant that prisoners had to be escorted through the bush to Perth. Not only was this a tedious trip, but quite often the accused escaped en route. Perth remained the judicial seat until 1842 when, by Proclamation of the Governor, Sir Charles Bagot, the District of Dalhousie was created with Bytown as its judicial seat.

One of the few settlers who trickled into the Ottawa area between the War of 1812 and the commencement of the Rideau Canal was a man named John Burrows Honey. He was a surveyor from Plymouth, England, who purchased a two-hundred-acre tract south of Parliament Hill, bounded on the north by Wellington and Rideau streets; to the east by Waller Street; to the south by Laurier Avenue; and to the west by Bronson Avenue. When he arrived in 1817 it was an unpromising parcel of swamp and cedar bush. Today it is the core of the downtown business district, with an assessed value in the hundreds of millions. John Burrows Honey cleared a small patch at the corner of Wellington and Lyon streets, where he built his cabin. He made no attempt to develop the property further, but sought employment across the river with Philemon Wright. For this reason he is probably the first Ottawan to commute to work in Hull. Soon after arriving in Canada, Honey shortened his name to John Burrows. A popular explanation for this name change is that he had been a persecuted Methodist in the Old Country and wanted to make a fresh start in the New World. However, a search of the

Plymouth records has failed to support this theory, and it is more probable that he simply disliked his original surname—it may even have embarrassed him.

In 1818, two years after Perth was founded, another military depot was established between the American border and the Ottawa river. Like Perth, the purpose of the settlement—composed of disbanded soldiers from the 99th Regiment of Foot—was to provide a reservoir of troops who could be mobilized to repel an American invasion. The new community, christened Richmond in honour of the Duke of Richmond, the Governor-in-Chief, was located on the Jock River (a tributary of the Rideau), just ten miles south of Ottawa. Because the 99th was disbanded in Quebec, the men and their dependents had to make a three-week journey in Durham boats and barges up the Ottawa. They reached Bellows' Landing—which was renamed Richmond Landing—at the end of August. Here, the women and children lived under canvas while the men set about hacking a trail into their new home. The trail is known today as the Richmond Road, and is the oldest thoroughfare in Ottawa. By November the townsite had been surveyed and rough cabins erected. Most cabins were built of round logs, with a stone chimney and a basswood "scoop" roof. Despite a bitterly cold winter only two members of the community died of exposure. When the snow melted, it revealed a well-planned settlement. One reason for the instant success of Richmond was the adaptability of the troops to strange surroundings. Other reasons were the disciplined co-operation of the men and the fact that each man owned his own land. It being a military depot, land grants were made on a scale according to rank:

Lt. Colonel	1200 acres
Major	1000 acres
Captain	800 acres
Subaltern	400 acres
Sgt. Major	300 acres
Sergeant	200 acres
Private	100 acres

For the first year the settlers were permitted to draw army rations, and were also issued with the following tools and stores:

To the head of each family: 1 axe, 1 broad axe, 1 mattock, 1 pickaxe, 1 spade, 1 shovel, 1 hoe, 1 scythe, 1 draw knife, 1 hammer, 1 handsaw, 2 scythe stones, 2 files, 12 panes of glass and 1 pound of putty, 12 pounds of nails (in three sizes), 1 camp kettle, 1 bedtick, 1 blanket.

For every five settlers: 1 crosscut saw, 1 whipsaw, 1 grindstone.

For the settlement: 2 complete sets of carpenter's tools.

The foregoing lists suggest a marginal living standard, but this was not the case. During the next year Captain George Lyon, now a storekeeper, imported luxury items from Montreal such as bone china, crystal glasses, swan's down silk, fine lawn, and gold jewellery. A further indication of the community's refinement was the demand for books, including the current issues of the illustrated magazine *Life in Paris.*

By coincidence, the same day that the disbanded soldiers of the 99th left Quebec in their Durham boats, a British vessel named the *Iphigenia* sailed into harbour. On board was Charles Lennox, fourth Duke of Richmond, a well-built man with blue eyes, fair hair, and a determined jaw. The Duke was Canada's new Governor-in-Chief, replacing Sir John Sherbrooke, who had suffered a nervous breakdown. Some historians have dealt harshly with Richmond because he was often at odds with the Assembly of Lower Canada over budget matters. In this respect, His Grace was no different from many Crown appointees, and better than most. The Duke was also a notoriously unsuccessful gambler. This weakness—which consumed his personal fortune and most of his wife's dowry—made him an easy target for criticism. Indeed, the Goodwood Cup, a classic British horse race, is run on the track he built at Goodwood, his family seat. Prior to his Canadian appointment Richmond was in reduced circumstances, and it has been suggested that he took the job for the money. This may be true because, in addition to gambling, he was lavish in his generosity and he had *fourteen* children to bring up. Yet the question of the Duke's motivation is really irrelevant. From the day he landed, he was one of Canada's most dedicated Governors-General.

Charles Lennox was both a soldier and a parliamentarian. In 1789, at the age of twenty-five, he commanded a company of the Coldstream Guards. That spring his colonel, the Duke of York, stated in public that "The Lennoxes don't fight!" When the future Duke of Richmond heard this insult to his family he approached his commanding officer at the next parade. The Duke of York dismissed him from the square, but later agreed to a duel. This was a bizarre situation with an unusual twist, for the Duke of York was the son of the reigning monarch, George III, while Charles Lennox's great-grandfather was the illegitimate son of a former monarch, Charles II. The duel proved an anticlimax, but sparked so many rumours that the seconds were compelled to issue an official statement:

> In consequence of a dispute of which much has been said in the public papers, His Royal Highness the Duke of York, attended by Lord Rawdon, and Lieutenant-Colonel Lennox, accompanied by the Earl of Winchelsea, met at Wimbledon Common. The ground was measured at twelve paces, and both parties were to fire on a signal agreed upon. The signal being given, Lieutenant-Colonel Lennox fired, and the ball grazed His Royal Highness' curl. The Duke of York didn't fire. Lord Rawdon then interfered and said he thought enough had been done. Lieutenant-Colonel Lennox observed that His Royal Highness had not fired. Lord Rawdon said it was not the Duke's intention to fire; His Royal Highness had come out upon Lieutenant-Colonel Lennox's desire, to give him satisfaction, and had no animosity against him. Lieutenant-Colonel Lennox pressed that the Duke of York would fire, which was declined upon a repetition of the reason. Lord Winchelsea then went up to the Duke of York and expressed his hope that His Royal Highness would have no objection to say he considered Lieutenant-Colonel Lennox a man of honour and courage. His Royal Highness replied that he should say nothing. He had come out to give Lieutenant-Colonel Lennox satisfaction, and did not mean to fire at him. Lieutenant-Colonel Lennox said he could not possibly fire again at the Duke, as His Royal Highness did not mean to fire at him. On this, both parties left the ground. The seconds think it proper to add that both parties behaved with the most perfect intrepidity.
>
> Rawdon,
> Tuesday evg., May 26th, 1789   Winchelsea.

As a result of this duel Charles Lennox was forced to leave the Brigade of Guards. Between 1790 and his appointment to Canada he was elected to Parliament four times, where he eventually attained the rank of Privy Councillor. From 1807 to 1813 he was Lord Lieutenant of Ireland, a posting that gave him plenty of time for field sports. For the next five years he lived in Belgium, a country with the advantage of being remote from his creditors. The night before the Battle of Waterloo, the Duchess of Richmond gave a splendid ball, which was later immortalized by Lord Byron in his epic poem "Childe Harold's Pilgrimage." The Duke did not see action at Waterloo, but his daughter, Lady Sarah, eloped with one of the heroes of the battle, General Peregrine Maitland. General Maitland was knighted for his role at Waterloo and appointed Lieutenant-Governor of Upper Canada. Sir Peregrine came to Canada on the *Iphigenia* with his father-in-law, and then went up the St. Lawrence to York (Toronto), which was the seat of government for Upper Canada.

During his first year in Quebec the Duke of Richmond worked on a variety of problems which he dutifully reported to the Colonial Secretary, Lord Bathurst. At the end of July 1819 he set off on a tour of Upper Canada. On the way he stopped for a few days at Fort William Henry, his summer residence in Sorel. Here he was bitten on the thumb by a pet fox that belonged to a soldier of the garrison. The incident was forgotten, and His Grace proceeded to York via Montreal and Kingston. He attended a round of functions in York and made an excursion to Drummond island, near Sault Ste. Marie. For relaxation he rode with the officers and played cricket with the enlisted men. On 17 August Richmond and his entourage left York for Kingston. From there the main party continued on to Montreal while the Duke turned inland to visit the military settlements. With the Governor were Baptiste, his Swiss valet, Major Bowles, his military secretary, and Lieutenant-Colonel Cockburn, the deputy quartermaster-general. At their heels frisked Blucher, the Duke's spaniel. His Grace spent three days at Perth, where he made a thorough inspection of the settlement, and dined each night with the officers (who had been retired on half-pay).

On the evening of 23 August the Duke experienced a peculiar difficulty in swallowing some mulled wine. This unusual symptom made him wonder whether the fox that bit him at Sorel had been rabid. The next morning his suspicion was confirmed when the sight of the water in his shaving basin caused him to have a convulsion. He knew this was a classic symptom of hydrophobia, which literally means "an abnormal fear of water." He also knew that rabies virus can take several months to incubate, but once it takes hold, the disease is invariably fatal. Aware that his time was running out, he said nothing to his companions but insisted that they press on to Richmond.

Heat combined with the dense foliage to impede their travel on the narrow bush trail. By alternately riding and walking, they made it as far as Beckwith, where the Duke spent a sleepless night. The next morning it was obvious to Colonel Cockburn and Major Bowles that His Grace was ill. They suggested a return to Perth, but the Duke dismissed the idea. That day they were able to cover only thirteen miles because of the swampy terrain and heavy under-growth. At dusk they stopped at the cabin of a settler named Vaughan, who lived four miles outside of Richmond.

In the morning the Duke was unable to stand the sight of water and Baptiste, his valet, had to pass him a wet towel so that he could shave. His Grace, looking ghastly, entered the settlement of Richmond at ten o'clock, and before lunch made a tour of the town, which included a stroll by the Jock River. Not wishing to offend his hosts, he followed the route, but kept his eyes averted from the stream. That afternoon he heard petitions from several villagers; in the evening he was entertained by the officers of the depot at the Masonic Arms Hotel (renamed the Richmond Arms after the Duke's visit). During the toasts he was only able to drink by raising his glass sideways, and each attempt triggered a spasm. Colonel Cockburn asked the Duke about his indisposition, and was told wryly, "It is fortunate I am not a dog, or I should have been shot some time ago."

That night the Duke wrote a long letter to his eldest daughter Mary. When Major Bowles checked on his master at five o'clock the next morning he was handed the letter with instructions to give it to Lady Mary should anything happen to the Duke. Although he was too sick to eat any breakfast, His Grace was determined to maintain his schedule, which called for him to be at Richmond Landing on the Ottawa River that evening. It was arranged that he and Major Bowles would take a canoe down the Jock River to Chapman's Farm, where they would transfer to horses. Colonel Cockburn recorded the departure in his journal:

> ... accordingly about 7 or ½ past, we left the Tavern and accompanied His Grace to the Canoe, on his embarking there was something particularily striking in the manner in which he took his little Dog Blucher into his arms and kissed him—he made no objection to entering the Canoe but on getting in he asked for assistance lest he should fall down ....

Shortly after they embarked, the Duke was overcome by the effect of the water and had to be put ashore. As soon as the canoe reached the bank he jumped out and ran wildly into the woods. Eventually Major Bowles caught up with his master, and with the help of Colonel Cockburn, the two men helped the Governor to Chapman's farm. It was a harrowing journey for the three because there were many rivulets, each of which caused the Duke to react violently. One incident (from Cockburn's journal) shows the mettle—and the sense of humour—of the dying man:

> Just before our arrival we passed the Cottage of a poor Man who was standing at his door, the Duke on perceiving him asked him how his clearance went on, the Man expressed his thanks to the Duke for asking the question—when His Grace turning to us observed "he ought to be obliged to me if he knew the pain it gave me to ask him the question."

When they reached Chapman's farm, the Duke declined to go into the cabin because it overlooked a stretch of the Jock River; instead, he went behind the shanty to the dim barn and lay down on some corn shucks. During the next hours he was wracked by paroxysms of pain and bouts of delirium. In his lucid moments he calmly dictated his farewells and last wishes to Major Bowles. Late in the day Surgeon Collis bled the Duke and gave him a laudanum pill; the opium provided temporary relief but his condition continued to deteriorate. At dusk he was carried into the cabin; by midnight he was in a coma. The Duke died in the arms of his valet at eight o'clock the next morning. One of his last wishes concerned his beloved spaniel: "Give Blucher to Mary, it will make her cry at first, but turn him in when she is alone, and shut the door."

The Governor's body was taken to Richmond Landing in a wagon provided by Philemon Wright. He was given a state funeral in Quebec City, and is buried in a vault in the chancel of the Anglican Cathedral of the Holy Trinity. A few miles outside of Ottawa, on the Richmond Road, a stone cairn marks the site where he died.

The township of March, which fronts on the Ottawa River immediately west of Nepean Township, was named after the Duke of Richmond's eldest son, the Earl of March. The first settler in March Township was Captain John Monk. In 1819 Captain Monk erected a house on the shore of the Ottawa at a place he christened Mosquito Bay—a most appropriate name—but the region is now called Constance Bay. Captain Monk, late of the 97th Regiment, preceded a score of officers and gentlemen who moved into the township during the next few years. By 1822 the waterfront of March was occupied by Ottawa's original aristocracy. Among the earliest gentry were Hamnett Pinhey, Major-General Arthur Lloyd, Captain Benjamin Street (RN), Captain Andrew Lett, and Lieutenant Thomas

Read (Royal Marines). Hamnett Pinhey, one of the few civilians, eventually emerged as leader of the March Township elite. Pinhey's thousand-acre grant had been given to him by a grateful British Government for his services as a courier on the Continent during the Napoleonic War. It took him five years of hard work and self-denial to develop his estate to the standard he wished. His Georgian stone house, "Horaceville," sheltered many distinguished guests, including the Governor-in-Chief, Lord Dalhousie, and the Anglican bishop for Upper Canada, Bishop Strachan.

The gentlefolk of March emulated London society in their customs and protocol; Pinhey not only had a full staff with footmen and a butler, but his wife was carried to the family church in a sedan chair. Despite their preoccupation with the Old Country, the leaders of March Township played an important role in the early affairs of Ottawa. Many of the families are still active in the community today. In the 1940s Don Pinhey, a direct descendant of Hamnett Pinhey, thrilled fans at Lansdowne Park when he played halfback for the Ottawa Rough Riders. One of his specialties was the hazardous job of returning punts.

From 1818 to 1822 more settlers—particularily Scots—came to the Rideau Settlement as a result of the British Government's stepped-up immigration policy. During the same period the Ottawa River turned into a busy thoroughfare for vessels, including those of Philemon Wright which carried passengers and freight between the Chaudière Falls and Grenville on their way to and from Montreal. Traffic became so brisk at Richmond Landing that a second tavern opened its doors to the public in 1819. The new inn, located upstream from Caleb Bellows establishment, was owned by a jolly fat man named Isaac Firth. In addition to dispensing grog, Firth's wife (who had been a milliner in Edinburgh) made highly prized otter caps for the men who worked on the boats. By all accounts Firth's tavern was a popular watering hole. John Mactaggart, clerk of works for the Rideau Canal, wrote fondly of Firth's tavern in his two-volume memoir, *Three Years in Canada,* saying "we hold our big nights there with much hilarity." Mactaggart spoke with authority, as the poor fellow was dismissed from the Canal job in 1828 for drunkenness.

George Ramsay, ninth Earl of Dalhousie, succeeded the Duke of Richmond as Governor-in-Chief of the Canadas in 1820. Prior to this appointment he was Lieutenant-Governor of Nova Scotia where, among other things, he founded Dalhousie University. Having been a commanding general at Waterloo, Dalhousie was inclined to attack problems with force rather than finesse. Like his predecessors, he believed the wishes of the Crown should be obeyed without question; as a result, he quarrelled with the Assemblies of Nova Scotia and Lower Canada. Although he was unbending, he was fair. This was borne out by the citizens of Bordeaux, France, who presented him with a gold mounted sword in appreciation for the gentlemanly conduct of his troops, who occupied that city during the Napoleonic Wars.

One of Dalhousie's first priorities was a tour of Upper Canada. In those days a tour meant hardship; in addition to travelling by canoe and horseback, one had to slog through the bush on foot. When Dalhousie reached the Ottawa area in the summer of 1820, he took careful note of the terrain and rivers with the future Canal in mind. At Richmond he was the guest of honour at a dinner given by the half-pay officers. Much of the conversation that evening concerned the urgent need for government storage facilities at Richmond Landing. At that time all shipments to and from Montreal were left in the open, with no protection against the elements or thieves. Dalhousie agreed that the Crown should buy the property—known as Lot 40—and openly instructed his secretary to locate the owner, Robert Randall, and effect the purchase.

The story behind Lot 40 is an interesting one. This property, which included a portion of the Ottawa River, was bounded on the west by Bayswater Avenue, to the south by Carling Avenue, and the east by Bronson Avenue. Randall had bought the parcel in 1809, when the region was an uninhabited wilderness, with the aim of harnessing the flow of the Chaudière and establishing a milling complex. Randall, who had come from Maryland in 1798, was not an idle speculator but a well-financed industrialist. The Bridgewater Works, one of his two companies at Niagara Falls, was the first plant in Canada to manufacture wrought iron, while the other, Bridgewater Mills, was the first mill to grind wheat flour in Upper Canada for export.

The same year that he purchased Lot 40, Randall's agents in Lower Canada and Britain went bankrupt. This caused Randall's commercial empire to collapse, and he was sent to debtor's prison in Montreal for seven years. While he was in prison, the War of 1812 broke out, and his mills at Niagara Falls were burnt by the invaders. Randall could have survived these calamities had he been permitted to liquidate his real estate in an orderly manner. Tragically, he was completely ruined by the concerted efforts of the Family Compact— a small but powerful group of men who dominated the government of Upper Canada for many years—and his own lawyer, Henry F. Boulton, who subsequently became Solicitor General for Upper Canada. A contemporary described Boulton as "simply unendurable" and went on to say:

> His capacity was barely such as to enable him to discharge his official functions and what he lacked in ability he made up in bluster. He had an abominable temper, a haughty over-bearing manner. He was always committing blunders, which he refused to acknowledge, and he roared and bullied his way through one complication after another in a fashion which disgusted even those with whom he acted.

One of Boulton's most malevolent acts against Robert Randall was to force the sale of Lot 40. Few people knew of the pending sale, but one of those who did was Captain John Le Breton. This man had served with conspicuous bravery in the War of 1812, and lived at Britannia, on the Ottawa River some five miles upstream from the Chaudière Falls. He was also one of the officers who attended the dinner for Lord Dalhousie at the Richmond Arms Hotel. Captain Le Breton scuttled around to a number of wealthy people in an effort to get financing so that he could purchase the property. The night before the sale, Livius P. Sherwood, a highly respected Brockville lawyer, agreed to finance the venture on a partnership basis. The next morning, 10 December 1820, Le Breton bought Lot 40 for £499. The title was then changed so that he owned the west half and Sherwood owned the east half.

A short time later Le Breton went to Quebec and offered Lot 40 to the Governor for £3000. Lord Dalhousie was furious, and told Le Breton that under no circumstances would the Crown buy the property.

Dalhousie's rejection of Lot 40 caused a significant change in plans for the Rideau Canal. Had the Crown been able to place the entrance locks at the foot of the Chaudière Falls, it would have meant a shorter and cheaper route to Dow's Great Swamp. More important, another set of locks could have skirted the falls and given access to the whole Upper Ottawa River. Le Breton's speculation literally influenced the course of Canadian history. To prevent further profiteering, Dalhousie quietly purchased the Fraser parcel in 1823 for £750. As previously noted, this six-hundred-acre block included Parliament Hill, and was bounded to the west by Bronson Avenue, to the south by Wellington Street, and to the east by the Rideau River. The same year the government of Upper Canada commissioned a detailed survey and cost estimate of the Rideau Canal. The following year, 1824, Lord Bathurst, the British Colonial Secretary, offered Upper Canada a loan of £70,000 to begin construction. Upper Canada considered this offer and decided, because the waterway would benefit both provinces, she would only undertake the Canal if Lower Canada shared the cost. Lower Canada declined to participate, so Upper Canada withdrew from the project and turned her attention to improving navigation on the St. Lawrence River.

This was the first of many wrangles between Ontario and Quebec over the sharing of joint responsibilities. In some of these disputes Ottawa has found herself "the ham in the sandwich." A current example is the problem of pollution control in the Ottawa River. The boundary between Ontario and Quebec runs down the middle of the river, which means that both provinces must work in concert. Ontario has taken steps to process raw sewage on her side, but Quebec refuses to take similar action. As a result, the Ottawa continues to be heavily polluted.

When Lord Bathurst's attempt to shift the cost of the Rideau Canal to the colony failed, the project went into limbo. A few months later the British Government agreed to finance and build the canal.

In 1827 Captain Le Breton (who was still *persona non grata* in official circles) wrote a long letter to the Governor protesting his innocence in the Lot 40 affair. Part of Le Breton's defence was that had he wished to corner the waterfront, he could also have bought Fraser's land for a pittance. Lord Dalhousie—who was convinced the sale had been illegal, and personally financed Isaac Firth's claim to squatter's rights—replied to Le Breton:

Military Secretary's Office
Quebec, 9th May, 1827

Sir,—

I am directed to acquaint you that the Commander of the Forces has received your letter, to which His Lordship would not have thought it worthwhile to return any answer, but for the purpose of having a true statement of the subject committed to record. With this view I have received His Lordship's commands to transcribe and convey to you the following statement, drawn up by Himself on a perfect and clear recollection of the whole of the transaction to which it relates.

"In 1820 I made it my first duty on my arrival in the Province to visit it as extensively as the period of the season permitted. I passed up the Ottawa and crossed the Country from Hull through the Military Settlement then just begun. At Richmond Major Burke with a party of the Half Pay Officers there (as many as the house could hold) dined with me; the chief subject of conversation was the means of promoting the public prosperity in that newly settled tract. It was evident to all, that a Government Depot for stores and supplies was highly important at the Richmond Landing, so called on the Ottawa, to establish an accessible point of communication and a certainty of supplies for the large population likely to assemble in that new Country.

"The land belonged to a Mr. Randall, an absentee, and who could not then be found. No improvement had been made on it, and it was probable that the purchase might be made for a trifling sum; I gave an instruction to Major Burke, as Superintendent and in the presence and hearing of all at table, to take steps to effect the purchase, or to watch any advertisement of the sale of it, but to report to me before he concluded.

"Captain Le Breton was then present, heard my sentiments, heard my instructions and in my idea, as a member of that settlement, as an officer and a gentleman was, in honour bound, to give assistance. He did not do so, he availed himself of the information and set about a speculative purchase to make a profitable bargain and then offer it to Government.

"I heard nothing more on the subject until when Lieut. Col. Cockburn informed me that the Richmond Landing had been sold, and that Capt. Le Breton was in Quebec to offer it to Government. It was stated to me that he had bought it for £400, and offered it at £3000, but in all probability might yield at £2000. I desired to see Captain Le Breton personally, and he came with Col. Cockburn up to my writing room. I asked him if he seriously proposed such a demand. He said he did, and justified himself, I forget in what terms. I, at once, and very angrily, told him, I would not permit so scandalous an imposition on H. M. Government, and I have all my reasons for so thinking:

"1st, A breach of confidence in availing himself of the information which passed at my table.

"2ndly. It was not becoming a British officer to catch at such a speculation.

"3rdly. The difference from £400 to £3000, or even £2000 before he himself had paid his price, was indecent and shameful imposition.

"From that one interview I formed an unfavourable opinion of Captain Le Breton and I have seen no cause to alter it since. I know nothing of his character. I thought then and think still that due notice of the Sheriff's sale was not given, and although the Solicitor General did report to Sir P. Maitland that it was done in due form, the later Memorials of Mr. Randall himself incline me to think the sale was not legal, and therefore Mr. Le Breton's title altogether bad, and the purchase of the lot an illegal transaction. I do not believe one word of Mr. Le Breton's assertion that he could have obtained from Mr. Fraser at £15 the lot for which that gentleman obtained £750 from Government.

"With regard to the family of Firth, I did say I would support that family if ill treated by those illegal proprietors, and I will do so still at my own private cost.

"I know nothing of Dr. Thom, Mr. Sherwood or any of those people named.

"No further answer will be made on this subject if continued."

(Signed) DALHOUSIE,
I have, etc.
H.C. Darling,

7th May 1827

Lord Dalhousie was theoretically correct in assuming that the sale of Lot 40 was illegal. However, while the proceedings *prior* to the land going on the block were a travesty, the sale itself was legal, and the new proprietors did in fact have clear title. Henry Boulton (who was also Sherwood's brother-in-law) was the Solicitor-General who advised Sir Peregrine Maitland that proper notice of sale had been given.

In the ensuing years Le Breton and Sherwood sold their portions of Lot 40 for a handsome profit. Today their former holdings are still known as the Le Breton Flats and Sherwood Heights. Livius Sherwood's family have been prominent in Ottawa since that time; one of the city's oldest real estate firms is owned by direct descendants, while Livius A. Sherwood, a great-great-grandson, is a judge of the Ontario Court in the capital.

Henry Boulton was promoted to Attorney General in 1828 and dismissed from that position in 1833. Following his recall to England, he was then appointed Chief Justice for Newfoundland where he was again dismissed for incompetence in 1838. Boulton finished his career in Toronto, where he served two terms in the Assembly. His client, Robert Randall, ended his days in ruin. Randall is buried in the military cemetery at Lundy's Lane; his tombstone reads:

HE DIED OF COLONIAL MISRULE

One other notable real estate sale took place in this period. In 1821 John Burrows Honey was compelled to return to England on a family matter. To raise funds for his passage he tried to sell his two-hundred-acre parcel (fronting on Wellington) to Philemon Wright. The Squire, who had more than 20,000 acres on the Quebec side—and may have been short of cash—declined to buy. However, one of Wright's hired hands, Nicholas Sparks, was very interested, and after some trouble managed to borrow £95 to close the transaction. It is said that when Sparks toured the property after the sale, he was appalled at the worthless scrub and swamp he had bought. In less than a decade this unpromising terrain would transform Nicholas Sparks into a real estate baron. By 1836 he would sell lots of one seventh of an acre for £400.

The reason for his good fortune was the Rideau Canal, which not only created a boom town but passed through the eastern edge of his property.

5

The Rideau Canal

1826 to 1832

THE RIDEAU CANAL was a gigantic undertaking, even by today's standards. Had the British Government been aware of the scope of the task and known of its eventual cost to the British taxpayers, it is doubtful the Canal would ever have been built.

The purpose of the Canal was to provide a navigable waterway for steam vessels between the Ottawa River and Lake Ontario. Although the project was feasible (due to the Rideau River and other connecting streams), the Precambrian Shield complicated its realization. The Shield is an ancient rock formation covering much of northern Canada as well as part of Upper New York, which rises in a massive hump between the Ottawa River and Lake Ontario. This topographic feature has its high point on the Rideau system at the Upper Rideau Lake, which is 277 feet (84.4 metres) above the Ottawa River and 162 feet (49.4 metres) above Lake Ontario. The Upper Rideau Lake, being the height of land, divides the watershed: at one end of the lake the water flows downstream to Kingston; at the other end the water flows in the opposite direction down to Ottawa. The only way a vessel could mount and descend the spine of the Precambrian ridge was by means of a series of locks.

Canal locks operate on a simple principle. To ascend, a boat enters the first or lowest lock at river level. The gates of the lock are shut behind the vessel, sealing it into a watertight "box." Water is then released through sluice gates from the lock above, causing the water in the "box" to rise to the same level as the lock above it. When this happens, the downstream gates of the upper lock are opened and the vessel moves into the second box. The operation is repeated with successive locks until the summit is reached. To descend, the procedure is reversed. The boat enters the top lock and the gates are shut behind it. The water is then *lowered* in the top lock until it corresponds to the level of water in the one below it. A lock system consumes a substantial amount of water; for this reason, provision must be made for a reservoir upstream from the highest lock.

In addition to channel dredging, the excavation of "deep cuts," the shoring of banks, and the construction of dams (which flood out rapids and form reservoirs of water to operate locks), the main channel of the Rideau Canal was to have forty-seven locks. On the 123-mile (198-kilometre) journey between Ottawa and Kingston, a vessel would be locked up and down a total of 439 feet (133.8 metres). This figure gains perspective when one considers that the average height of Niagara Falls is 162 feet (49.4 metres).

The logistics of the project were also formidable, as the Canal was to be built in the wilderness and most of the work would have to be done by unskilled labour, by hand. The British authorities based their final calculations for the Rideau Canal on a report submitted to the government of Upper Canada by a respected engineer, Samuel Clowes, in 1824. Clowes's detailed survey and cost estimates were checked by a British commission of Royal Engineers who went over the proposed route in 1825. The military surveyors agreed with Clowes's recommendation that the Cataraqui River be used from Kingston to the Rideau Lakes, rather than the Irish Creek or the Gananoque River. They also accepted his cost estimates but added £20,000 to them so that the locks could be increased to 108 feet in length, 20 feet in width, and 5 feet in depth. The addition of £20,000 brought the total estimated cost of the Rideau Canal to £164,000.

Responsibility for constructing the Canal was given to the Corps of Royal Engineers, who appointed one of their senior staff officers, Lieutenant-Colonel John By, as superintending engineer of the project. Colonel By had served in Canada earlier in his career, from 1802 to 1811. During his nine-year stay in Canada he had worked on the fortifications in and around Quebec City and had been a supervisor for the construction of the Cedres Canal on the St. Lawrence River. In the spring of 1811 he was sent to Spain, where he served with distinction in the Peninsular War against Napoleon. Later the same year he was recalled to England, where he was placed in command of the Royal Gunpowder Mills at Faversham, Purfleet, and Waltham Abbey. He performed his duties faultlessly, but in 1821 he was retired on half-pay as a result of a sharp reduction in the strength of the British Army, which was part of a national cost-cutting program. While in temporary retirement he was promoted from the rank of major to lieutenant-colonel.

Colonel By was of average height, with a strong face, florid features, and dark hair. Although he was inclined to stoutness, his erect carriage and military bearing gave him an unmistakable air of authority. He was an excellent choice as superintending engineer for the Rideau Canal. In addition to being a disciplined soldier, he was also an able administrator whose courtesy and good nature permitted him to get along with people in all walks of life. As an engineer, he worked by the manuals, but when a problem exceeded their scope he was not afraid to innovate his own solution. On his appointment in 1826 he was forty-seven years old, in robust health, with unlimited energy. During the next six years the job would call upon all his talents and resources.

Colonel By arrived at Quebec City with his wife Esther and his two daughters on 30 May 1826. Here he paid his respects to the Governor-in-Chief, Lord Dalhousie, and to Colonel Durnford, the commandant of the Royal Engineers in British North America, and then set to work reviewing the reports on the Canal. After studying Samuel Clowes's survey and cost estimates, he immediately wrote his superiors in London and told them the Rideau Canal would cost at least £400,000.

Colonel By's revision of the estimate was conservative, for the project eventually cost twice that much. It also foreshadowed an ongoing problem between the superintending engineer and the British Treasury, which was aggravated by change-orders, bad communication, political considerations, and the malicious intervention of several people. Within the year officials were muttering in London that Samuel Clowes had gulled the British government into the project. A report of the Ordnance Department in 1827 refers to Clowes's survey, "made out from the reprehensible motive of endeavouring to benefit the Colony by embarking His Majesty's Government in this undertaking upon the faith of an estimate which the author of it, himself, admits he considered to be fallacious and inadequate."

Unaware of the financial clouds on the horizon, Colonel By went to Montreal in the summer of 1826 and set up a temporary office. A few weeks later he journeyed up the Ottawa to inspect the Canal site. At that time there were only a dozen scattered families in the adjoining townships of Nepean and Gloucester. For this reason Hull, with nearly a thousand inhabitants, had been chosen as the base of operations for preliminary work on the Canal, even though the village was on the opposite side of the Ottawa River. Colonel By was accompanied by Thomas MacKay, a masonary contractor who had recently done the stonework on the Lachine Canal. The two men reached Hull on 21 September, and were hospitably received by Philemon Wright.

The next day Colonel By and Thomas MacKay were rowed across the Ottawa to Governor's Bay (an indentation in the shoreline just east of the Prime Minister's residence), which was the proposed site for the headlocks. After walking the ground By and MacKay concluded that the high limestone formation in the area made this spot unsuitable. In search of a better location, they scrambled through the bush along the river's edge as far upstream as the Chaudière Falls, a distance of approximately two miles. Colonel By's first choice for the locks was in the vicinity of the Richmond Landing, but the property was owned by Captain Le Breton and this site was out of the question. His second choice was Sleigh Bay, some three quarters of a mile below the Richmond Landing (between the Parliamentary Library and Nepean Point).

Sleigh Bay got its name from an incident that occurred there in the winter of 1819. Tiberius Wright, Philemon's son, had arranged to be married in Hull by a Justice of the Peace from Perth. However, the Justice of the Peace was not authorized to marry people in Lower Canada, so the wedding party crossed the frozen Ottawa River to a sheltered cove on the south shore, where the ceremony was performed in the centre of a ring of sleighs.

A few days after Colonel By and MacKay reconnoitred the Ottawa shoreline, they were joined by Lord Dalhousie who made a special trip from Quebec City to approve the final plans for the Canal. Dalhousie was intensely interested in the project. He was convinced the entrance locks would be more than the northern terminus of the waterway; they would be the focal point of a significant new community. Dalhousie reviewed the situation carefully and then acted with dispatch. On 26 September the Governor-in-Chief gave Colonel By written authority to proceed with the Canal, and the Countess of Dalhousie symbolically turned the first sod for the Entrance Locks at Sleigh Bay. In his memorandum Dalhousie made specific reference to the six-hundred-acres he had purchased from the Fraser estate three years earlier:

> I take this opportunity of meeting you here to place in your hands a sketch of several lots which I thought it advantageous to purchase for the use of Government, where the canal was spoken of as likely to be carried into effect. These not only contain the site for the headlocks but they offer a valuable locality for a considerable village or town for the lodging of Artificers and others necessary in so great a work. . . .
>   I propose that these [lots] should be clearly surveyed and laid out in lots of two to four acres, to be granted according to the means of settlers and to pay a ground rent of 2/6d per annum to the Crown annually. The location to contain the positive condition of building a house on the line streets according to plan to be made of it. Allow me to caution you against the immediate rush of applicants for these lots that will be made. Make particular inquiries as to individuals and others before you consent to their petitions. It will be highly desireable to encourage half-pay officers and respectable people should they offer to build on these lots.

Just before returning to Quebec Lord Dalhousie authorized the construction of a 640-foot bridge across the Ottawa River. This bridge (subsequently christened the Union Bridge because it united Upper and Lower Canada) was essential to speed the flow of men and materials between Hull and the Canal site. In this age of bureaucratic red tape it is refreshing to read how quickly work was begun. Dalhousie gave the go-ahead for the Union Bridge, which was not a single structure but eight separate spans linked by the rock islands below the Chaudière Falls, on the morning of 27 September. Work commenced immediately, and the Governor laid the first stone *the same day*.

In accordance with Dalhousie's wishes, Colonel By laid out a ground plan for two communities, one on either side of the Canal, separated by what is now Parliament Hill. The settlement to the east, which was mostly beaver meadow and cedar bush, was called Lower Town. The settlement to the west, also cheerless terrain but on higher ground, was named Upper Town. Upper and Lower Town each had a ninety-nine-foot-wide main thoroughfare, which is noteworthy because the maximum width for a street was normally sixty-six feet, or one English chain. To obtain the necessary width in Upper Town, Colonel By purchased a thirty-three-foot strip of frontage from Nicholas Sparks. The thoroughfare in Lower Town was called Rideau Street, while the one in Upper Town was called Wellington, after the Duke of Wellington under whom Colonel By had served. These streets are still important traffic arteries in the city today. As soon as the ground plans were completed, lots were surveyed in the two settlements and offered to the public. The lots were snapped up quickly, but many reverted back to the Crown when the holders failed to build a structure (minimum size thirty feet square) on their property within twelve months.

Colonel By awarded his first contracts during the autumn of 1826. Thomas MacKay received one to build the stone arches of the Union Bridge, and another one to construct a two-story commissariat building in the valley above Sleigh Bay. The commissariat building still stands on the west bank of the Canal entrance locks, but is now the Bytown Museum, a showplace of Ottawa's past, run by the Historical Society of Ottawa. A second stone building, to house a workshop and administrative offices, was commissioned on the opposite side of the locks. This structure was demolished at the turn of the century. Colonel By also arranged for a modest two-story dwelling to be erected on the headland east of Sleigh Bay as his personal residence. By's house stood in Major's Hill Park (behind the Chateau Laurier Hotel) and had a magnificent view of the Ottawa River. Originally the area was known as Colonel's Hill, but the name was changed when Major Daniel Bolton, By's successor, moved into the house in 1832.

Work progressed steadily on the Union Bridge during the autumn of 1826 and throughout the winter, despite subzero temperatures and the hazards of freezing spray from the falls. The Lower Canada terminus of the bridge was near Philemon Wright's mills; the Upper Canada end, a short stagger from Firth's tavern. The spans leapfrogged from island to island and were constructed simultaneously from both shores.

Due to the relocation of the headlocks, a detailed survey had to be made of the territory between Sleigh Bay and the southern loop of the Rideau River. John Mactaggart, clerk of works (who was already supervising work on the Union Bridge), undertook this task in November 1826, but found the dense swamps impenetrable. His second attempt, in December, was more successful for he managed to reach Dow's Great Swamp, which emptied into the Rideau River. However, it took him *five days* of hard slogging, although the swamp was only two linear miles from Sleigh Bay. One reason for his slow progress was the frequent need to take levels of the surrounding countryside—the proper way to determine the lowest ground for the Canal route. On this expedition Mactaggart and his companions traced a circuitous path through a necklace of swamps and beaver ponds, and eventually got as far as the Hog's Back Falls on the Rideau. The following excerpt from his memoir, *Three Years in Canada,* graphically describes the conditions they encountered:

Placed in thick and dark snow-covered woods, where, unless the axe-men cut holes, a prospect of five yards could not be obtained; doubtful what kind of land lay on either side, or directly before; calculating at the same time, the nature of canal-making in such places, the depths to dig, or the banks to raise, so that the level might be kept from one sheet of water to another, the former eighty feet above the latter; while the weather was extremely cold, and the screws of the theodolite would scarcely move; these things all considered, were teasing enough to overcome, and required a little patience.

When night drew on, two of the axe-men were sent off to rig the wigwam shanty by the side of the swamp. This was done for two reasons or say three: first because water could be had in the swamps to drink and cook with, if the ice were broken to get at it: secondly, the boughs of the hemlock grow more bushy in such places, and are so far more easily obtained to cover the shanty: and thirdly, there are generally dry cedar-trees found there, which make excellent firewood, and the bark of a dry cedar is the best thing in the world for lighting a fire with.

When the party got to the place, there was a very comfortable house set out, a blazing fire with a maple back log, ranging along for a length of twenty or thirty feet. There on the bush hemlock would we lie down, roast pork before the fire on wooden prongs, each man roasting for himself; while plenty of tea was thrown into a large kettle of boiling water, the tin mug was turned out, the only tea cup, which being filled, went round until all had drunk; then it was filled again, and so on; while each with his bush-knife cut toasted pork on a shive of bread, ever using the thumb-piece to protect the thumb from being burned; a tot or two round of weak grog finished the feast, when some would fall asleep,—others to sleep and snore; and after having lain an hour or so on one side some would cry Spoon!— the order to turn to the other—which was often an agreeable order, if a spike of tree-root or such substance stuck up between the ribs.

Reclining thus, like a parcel of spoons, our feet to the fire, we have found the hair of our heads often frozen to the place where we lay. For many days together did we lie in these wild places, before we could satisfy ourselves with a solution of the problem already posed represented. In Dow's great swamp, one of the most dismal places in the wilderness, did five Irishmen, two Englishmen, two Americans, one French Canadian, and one Scotchman, hold their merry Christmas of 1826,—or rather forgot to hold it at all.

Colonel By spent the winter of 1826 in Montreal attending to administrative matters, much of his time devoted to negotiations with potential contractors. In this connection a tender system was used for the three main categories of work—masonry, fabrication, and excavation. Colonel By tried to brief the contractors as fully as possible, and urged them to consider their capacity and resources before submitting a bid. The masonry and fabricating contractors were for the most part experienced and competent operators, but many of those who applied for excavating contracts did so on a highly speculative basis. For this reason it is not surprising that most of the stonework and carpentry was executed in a satisfactory manner, while a substantial number of excavators went bankrupt or were unable to fulfill the terms of their contract. When a contractor defaulted he had to be replaced. This created delays and additional expense in the construction of the Canal.

Early in the new year the Legislative Assembly of Upper Canada passed a special Act to expedite the Canal project. This Act, dated 17 February 1827, invested Colonel By with the same powers as the government of Upper Canada for the construction of the Rideau Canal, including the right to expropriate property. Colonel By scrupulously observed the limitations of the Act, but problems still occurred. From the outset venal landowners claimed exorbitant damages and insisted on outrageous prices for their property. These landowners were aided in their suits by members of the legal fraternity in Brockville, Prescott, and Cornwall who were only too happy to cadge fees for obstructionist tactics on behalf of their clients.

The fall and winter of 1826 had been devoted to the preliminary phases of the project. In 1827 work began on the Canal itself.

Thomas MacKay was awarded the contract for the headlocks at Sleigh Bay, which was renamed Entrance Bay. This was a major undertaking because the total "lift" from the Ottawa River to the summit was eighty-one feet. MacKay's task was to build eight connecting locks that would climb Entrance Valley from the Ottawa River like giant steps on a stairway.

Colonel By arrived at the site in March 1827. He was early, for snow still carpeted Entrance Valley and ice pans dotted the Ottawa River, but the absence of leaves allowed him to make a detailed survey of the surrounding terrain. One of his first decisions was to drain a twelve-acre swamp that lay directly on the Canal route, some two hundred yards south of the summit of Entrance Valley. By means of strategic cuts and the installation of a dam, he reduced the swamp to one third its former size. It was a clever bit of work that created a docking basin, or "lay by," as well as a controlled reservoir to feed the headlocks. A wooden sluice gate in the dam released excess water in the Lay By down a stream that ran through Lower Town and emptied into the Rideau River. Because the stream removed the overflow in the Lay By, it was called the By Wash. The By Wash poured from the eastern rim of the Lay By, across Rideau Street, north along Musgrove to George Street, then diagonally across to York Street, where it turned east and continued to King Edward Avenue. At King Edward the stream veered north again for approximately five hundred yards until it swept down a gully near St. Andrew Street into the Rideau. In the early days the volume of water in this drain was sufficient to run a small mill on York Street. Today the only evidence of the By Wash is the extraordinary width of King Edward Avenue, which was part of its stream bed. The Lay By, which has also gone, was opposite the National Arts Centre.

Colonel By travelled the entire length of the Canal route in May 1827. It was a good time to make the trip because the blackflies had not emerged, and he was able to view the countryside through the pastel filagree of new leaves. When he reached Kingston he checked with the contractors who had just begun work at the southern terminus of the canal. For this tour "the little emperor," Sir George Simpson, Governor-in-Chief of the Hudson's Bay Company, provided Colonel By with a company canoe and five crack *voyageurs*.

On his return to Ottawa By found the settlement a hive of activity. Excavation had started in Entrance Valley and the Deep Cut. People seeking work were pouring into the site daily; many lived under canvas, or in rude shanties, although a few of the lucky ones were able to get a bed in the newly constructed civilian barracks on George Street. Most of the labourers, or "navvies," were recent immigrants from Ireland who had arrived in Canada with nothing but the clothes on their back. Because of their desperate poverty they could not pay rent, so Colonel By allowed them to squat in hovels along the muddy bank of the Deep Cut, which was Crown land. This collection of shanties was called Corkstown because so many of its inhabitants came from County Cork in the south of Ireland. Corkstown—Ottawa's first slum—disappeared soon after the completion of the Canal.

Entrance Valley, the site of the headlocks, was a challenge to excavate because of boulders, and the sensitive Leda clay, which flows like soup when disturbed. The Deep Cut, a 1,400-yard channel, ran southeast from the summit of the entrance locks to a point near the Mann Avenue overpass. This section was excavated entirely by hand by a crew of navvies whose only tools were picks and shovels. It was also a tricky place to work because of the unstable nature of the clay, which often precipitated landslides. Today this same stretch of Canal hosts pleasure craft in the summer and ice skaters in the winter; it is difficult to visualize a horde of barefoot men toiling in the slippery blue muck. At the end of the Deep Cut the route swung south along a fold in the ground for approximately 3,100 yards until it was blocked by a ridge of high ground. The lowest point in the ridge was just behind the Exhibition Grounds, near the Bank Street bridge, and was known as the Notch. When the Notch was opened to the proper width, the rest was easy going because a stream bed led directly to Dow's Great Swamp, some 1,100 yards to the west. Two dams converted the swamp from an impenetrable morass into Dow's Lake. Philemon Wright built the main dam on the south shore, while a man named Jean St. Louis built the smaller dam on the north shore.

The Canal then followed a feeder stream from the south end of Dow's Lake for approximately 800 yards. Here a double set of locks, built by Thomas MacKay, provided a lift of twenty-two feet. These are known as Hartwell's Locks and are situated just west of Carleton University. Some 1,800 yards above the Hartwell Locks the Canal connects with the Rideau River, at the Hog's Back Falls. This was a problem area for Colonel By. The locks were relatively simple: a separate channel running parallel to the river skirted the falls, and two locks constructed by MacKay overcame the thirty-foot rise. However, the Rideau River had to be dammed at this spot to create a seven-mile stretch of navigable water upstream. Both the force of the current and the precipitous banks on each side of the Hog's Back made the construction of a dam an immense challenge. Colonel By's original plans called for a structure three hundred feet wide and forty-five feet high. These dimensions were startling, because the largest dam in North America at that time was only twenty-eight feet high. The first attempt to build the Hog's Back dam was made by a contractor named Fenelon, who began construction in the summer of 1827.

The distance by water between the Entrance Locks and the Hog's Back Falls is approximately four and a half miles (7.2 kilometres). All of this section of the Canal lies within the city limits of Ottawa. Today one can trace the route by car from Sussex Street, near the Entrance Locks, thence along Colonel By Drive to the Hog's Back Falls.

On 1 June 1827 the 15th Company of Royal Sappers and Miners arrived at the Canal site from England. They were joined by another eighty-one-man contingent, the 7th Company, on 17 September. The task of these units was to provide expert assistance on the Canal, to build thoroughfares in Upper and Lower Town, and to construct a bridge over the Deep Cut that would connect the two communities. Both companies were billeted in tents at Richmond Landing while three stone barracks and a twenty-bed hospital were being erected for them on Parliament Hill, which at that time was called Barracks Hill. In addition to housing the military establishment, the British Government intended to fortify Barracks Hill so that it could guard the Entrance Locks. To protect the southern approach to the Hill, a shallow crescent-shaped moat was to be dug from the Lay By to Bank Street. Because the Crown did not own sufficient land for the moat, Colonel By expropriated a 104-acre block of swamp and cedar bush from Nicholas Sparks. Plans for the fortification and the moat were subsequently cancelled and the property was returned to Nicholas Sparks in 1847.

The first stone of the Entrance Locks was laid by a famous arctic explorer, Captain (later Sir) John Franklin, at 4:00 P.M. on 16 August 1827. Franklin had stopped to spend the night as a guest of Colonel By on his way down the Ottawa from a three-year expedition to the Coppermine River. Thus, the laying of the first stone was a fortuitous event due to the appearance of an unexpected visitor. However, the laying of the cornerstone by the Governor-in-Chief, on 29 September, was a carefully staged celebration.

When Lord Dalhousie arrived, a few days before the ceremony, the Union Bridge was in use by pedestrians. The 212-foot span over the Great Kettle—still far from completion—was being built with the aid of a suspension bridge as a work platform. To get a cable from one bank to the other, a projectile with a rope attached had been shot from a brass cannon. The first two attempts to get the rope across had failed when the half-inch hemp had parted with the explosion. The third attempt, with a one-inch rope, was successful and the line was secured on the opposite bank. Heavy chains were then hauled across the gap to make the suspension bridge. This catwalk sagged dangerously close to the torrent and swayed alarmingly when anyone stepped on it.

From his diary it is clear that Lord Dalhousie was fascinated by the engineering concepts of the Union Bridge:

September 1827
    On the 26th we left Grenville about 1 o'clock P.M.; next day reached Hull about noon; it was a fine day and induced us to proceed immediately to the chain of bridges now completed so as to walk across the whole extent. I have ordered a General Plan of the whole to be done for me, at present I'll only state the dimensions of each in the chain. It commences from the North side near to Philemon Wright's mills
    No. 1 and 2 Bridges are stone arches drybuilt but coped with lime and large stones on edge each arch is 57 feet.
    No. 3 a long straight Bridge of wood, rough beams, two supports fixed on the flat rocky bed—180 feet.
    No. 4 is to be a wooden Bridge 212 feet span with an easy spring of Arch 20 feet. There is however now only a temporary suspension bridge to facilitate the preparations, and give a walking passage to people employed—of this I must refer to the drawing, only saying that it is a support on three cables, with planks as pathway and a handrope to hold by. I have ordered a model of this which I intend to send to Dalhousie Castle.
    No. 5 a straight Bridge 104 feet in length, with three supports.
    No. 6 a wooden Arch 117 feet long, spring 9 feet, this and No.
4 are done on a mechanical principle common in America—the uprights tie together in triangular divisions, and give great strength to the beam, or Arch on which the path rests—it is not pleasing to the eye, but that will not be considered, if it answers in more material points.
    I may mention en passant a singular coincidence which Drummond the Carpenter told me the following day—that on 27th Sept. last year I laid the first stone of No. 1 Bridge, and that Col. By then said, if I would revisit their work on that day 12 month, he promised I should

walk the whole extent—the circumstance was never thought of by us, but it did so happen that Lady Dalhousie did walk across the whole line on that day twelvemonth—even that trembling and nervous part of it, the Suspension Bridge—which in fact Col. By himself had not ventured to do, until Lady D. called me back to accompany her over—and then he kept his own secret—I admit it was a bold thing for a Lady, but I was satisfied before of the safety of it.

On arriving we dispersed to our quarters, old Philemon Wright with his usual kindness put up Col. Ramsay with us. All the rest went to the Inn, now a very good one—and I would have gone there too, but that Philemon would have been offended.

On 28 September the Governor-in-Chief toured the Canal on horseback from the Entrance Locks to Black Rapids, some five miles upstream from the Hog's Back Falls. The next morning he discussed land claims with the surveyor-general, laid out two new townships to be settled by immigrants working on the Canal, and "satisfied a great many very anxious petitioners." His diary for that day contains a vivid account of the festivities that followed the laying of the cornerstone.

At 3 P.M. we met at Col By's house and proceeded to lay the foundation stone of the 1st Lock on the Canal, where he had assembled a great number of his Irish labourers—Lady D then accompanied him and Mrs. By in his carriage all around the new road and Villages, Barracks, etc. etc. Meanwhile he had ordered a Puncheon of Rum at the Lock to be opened, and a fair allowance to each family had been previously detailed on certified tickets—All was well regulated, all was joy— Dances and jigs were soon set agoing, and we looked down from the bank above, on the ranting lads below—quarrels and blows soon followed the jigs, but again good humour resumed, and they danced a new.

We went to dinner at Col By's, and at dark were agreeably surprised in seeing prodigious bonfires lighted on all the prominent points and headlands up to the Chaudiere Falls—When we took leave we were marched thru a double line of the people each holding a Cedar torch with bark of birch giving a blazing light, and as we passed all followed on—We heard by some, muttered loud enough to be heard "Long life to your Honour, and good luck wid you" another had a bad fiddle and played the "God Save the King" as if he were going to sleep on it—and another had a fife on which he made also a very lame attempt; but when we put off in our Batteaux, all gave three Glorious cheers, and made a general fire of the torches— there was no drunken man there, all admirably contrived and well behaved. The scene was quite magnificent, and as we passed up the river it became still more spirited, by the shouting hurrahs on every point and fires, returned to them by the loud mixture of the Canadian Boat Song from Finlay and my 14 rowers—the whole river was illuminated so as to have easily read a book and a bright full moon in all her splendour stood high in Heaven over the Grand Cataract without any exaggeration so finely, that it might have been imagined. Col By had chosen the moment a month before—an hour sooner or an hour later it must have been a somewhat less Glorious scene.

On his tour of the Canal Lord Dalhousie was pleased to note the good work being done by the Royal Sappers and Miners. A few weeks before his arrival the 15th Company had begun construction of a stone bridge over the Deep Cut. This span, subsequently called Sappers Bridge, was to link Rideau Street in Lower Town with the footpath (now Sparks Street) that led around the base of Barracks Hill to Upper Town. The bridge, finished in December 1827, was a fine example of the stonemason's craft. When it was demolished in 1912 to make way for the Union Station, dynamite did not even shake the structure; a two-ton stone had to be dropped from a height of fifty feet for three hours before the arch finally collapsed.

In December Colonel By sent a trusted aide, Lieutenant Henry Pooley, to England to present a detailed progress report on the Canal. This report contained a strong recommendation that the locks be increased in size to accommodate naval vessels patrolling the Great Lakes. The report also contained the unpleasant news that the estimated cost had risen from £400,000 to at least £474,000. By's superiors delegated a commission to go to Canada to appraise the situation. After touring the Canal the commission concluded in June 1828 that the extra expense was justified, and agreed to an increase in the lock size to 134 feet in length, 33 feet in width, and 5½ feet in depth.

By the end of 1827 there were roughly 150 houses in the Nepean settlements; virtually all were made of wood and most were situated in Lower Town. During that year the communities flanking the headlocks became known as Bytown. This name was proposed in jest, but Bytown was so appropriate that it quickly came into common usage. When the township of Nepean got its first post office in 1829, the name became official. All the mail was postmarked Bytown.

The year 1828 was a difficult one. In February one of the huge scows propping the 212-foot span of the Union Bridge was torn loose by floodwaters. This caused one of the three chains supporting the nearly finished structure to snap, and eight men working on the bridge were pitched into the icy river, one of whom drowned. The next day a second chain parted and the bridge collapsed. Thomas Burrowes witnessed the drama and wrote: ". . . the whole structure fell with an astounding noise, and was shattered to splinters. Nothing could be more complete than its demolition; the wreck floating down the River, grounding upon a shoal, and presenting to us a most melancholy appearance." After analyzing the cause of failure Colonel By ordered that the bridge be rebuilt using specially forged chains from the naval dockyard at Kingston.

In the same month floodwaters broached the dam being built by Mr. Fenelon at the Hog's Back Falls. Fenelon was relieved of his contract, and a crew of Sappers and Miners was called into repair the damage. In April a flood caused by snow-melt washed out the dam completely. Colonel By then arranged for Philemon Wright to build a flood barrier upstream from the dam, employing timber cribs filled with rocks. Sixty Sappers and one hundred civilians were detailed to rebuild the dam.

During that summer "swamp fever" broke out along the Canal route and in the settlement of Bytown. Swamp fever was a severe form of malaria, transmitted by the bite of a mosquito. Although malaria is now restricted to tropical and subtropical countries, it was prevalent in eastern Ontario at that time. Up until 1925 the only cure for malaria was sulphate of quinine, which was obtained from the bark of the Peruvian *cinchona* tree. In Canada in 1828 this remedy was almost unobtainable and few could afford to buy it. In consequence, the death toll was frightful, and a half-acre of land had to be set aside for a cemetery in Bytown. This plot (between Queen and Sparks streets, flanked by Elgin and Metcalfe streets) was divided into three sections for Anglicans, Presbyterians, and Roman Catholics. Swamp fever stopped work on the Canal in several places, and was a contributing factor in the desertion of sixteen Royal Sappers and Miners. To check further desertions, Colonel By arranged for each soldier to receive a free grant of one hundred acres upon completion of his term of service.

Much of the construction took place under appalling conditions. In addition to extremes of temperature, swamps, and pestilence, the actual work involved considerable risk. John Mactaggart described some of the hazards encountered by the unskilled labourers:

Even in their spade and pickaxe business, the [men] receive dreadful accidents; as excavating in the *wilderness* is quite a different thing from doing that kind of labour in a cleared country. Thus they have to *pool in,* as the tactics of the art go—that is, dig beneath the roots of trees, which not infrequently fall down and smother them... Some of them... would take jobs of quarrying from contractors, because they thought there were *good wages* for this work, never thinking that they did not understand the business. Of course, many of them were blasted to pieces by their own *shots,* others killed by stones falling on them. I have seen heads, arms, and legs, blown in all directions; and it is vain for overseers to warn them of their danger, for they will pay no attention. I once saw a poor man blow a red stick, and hold it deliberately to the *priming* of a large shot he had just charged. I cried out, but it was of no use. He seemed to turn round his face, as if to avoid the smoke; off went the blast... he was killed in a moment.

With the advent of cooler weather that September the mosquitoes disappeared and the malaria epidemic subsided. In October 1827 the 212-foot span over the Great Kettle was completed; the Union Bridge was now finished and vehicles could pass freely between Hull and Bytown. Despite the reverses during the year Colonel By was pleased to report to his superiors in London that 60 percent of the work on the Rideau Canal was completed. Unfortunately, he also had to advise that the estimated cost had risen to £576,755. This latter information caused some consternation, and was subsequently reduced by the Board of Ordnance to £558,000.

In March 1829 spring floods caused leaks to appear in the Hog's Back Dam, which was within a few feet of completion. Colonel By was called to the scene and did his best to stop the erosion. However, on 3 April the ground started to shift beneath his feet as he stood on the dam directing a crew of forty men. Everyone ran for his life. The dam gave way at the base and then washed out completely. Surveying the ruin of so much work, Colonel By is alleged to have said that he would continue rebuilding the dam until it stood, even if he had to build it with half-crown pieces! He investigated the failure and discovered that frozen clay had been packed into the base during the winter; in the spring, the clay had thawed, which caused the foundation to settle. He then went back to the drawing board and produced a fresh plan, which was executed under the close supervision of Captain James Victor, Royal Engineers.

Early that year the 7th Company of Royal Sappers and Miners was transferred to the hamlet of Newboro, which was at the height of land near Little Rideau Lake, some forty miles from Kingston. This region was one of the worst areas for swamp fever. During the following summer, 787 of the 1,316 men employed between Newboro and Kingston were stricken with the fever.

The Canal route from the Entrance Locks to Dow's Lake was completed in 1830. To celebrate the occasion Colonel By issued rum to all hands, and a whole ox was roasted on a spit. In October the Hog's Back Dam was finished with a macadamized top, which also served as a bridge across the Rideau River. One hundred and fifty years later, this dam still ranks as a major engineering achievement.

Colonel By had hoped to finish the entire project by the end of 1831, but a series of unforeseen delays postponed completion until the spring of the following year. In his report to England at the end of 1831 he advised that the total cost, including blockhouses for defence of the locks, would be £776,023, plus another £30,000 for sundry expenses. The documentation supporting these figures mysteriously went astray, so a duplicate set had to be sent later in the winter.

By was unaware that forces were massing in England to destroy his reputation. One factor was public sentiment against the cost of the Canal which was agitated by a number of virulent newspaper articles. In this connection, H. Howard Burgess, a former 1st clerk to the Royal Engineers in Bytown, fed the newspapers scurrilous information, which stated that Colonel By had misused government funds. Burgess had been dismissed from the Rideau Canal project in 1830 for drunkenness. His credibility may be judged by a report from Dr. M. H. Tuthill, the military surgeon at Bytown, dated November 23, 1830, which reads in part: "I attended Mr. H. H. Burgess in the months of January, February, and March last, during which time, he was subject to fits of insanity which I understand were produced by intemperance." Another more subtle factor was the stance of the British Ordnance Board, which had wanted to see the Canal completed and had not kept the British Parliament fully informed of the mounting costs. To shift the blame from themselves they blandly gave Colonel By's report to the British Treasury without explaining that they had authorized By to proceed at his own discretion. The Lords of the Treasury took a cursory glance at the Ordnance submission on the Rideau Canal and immediately referred the question to the British House of Commons. A Parliamentary Committee was then appointed to investigate the unauthorized expenditure by Colonel By of £82,576 in the construction of the

Canal. The Colonel was summoned to appear before the Committee in the summer of 1832. Secure in the knowledge that he had done the work meticulously, By thought his appearance before the Committee would be a formality prior to being knighted for his achievement. Disillusionment awaited him.

The Rideau Canal was officially opened on 24 May 1832. Colonel By, with his family and friends, made a triumphal journey in the steam vessel *Rideau* from Kingston to Bytown. It was a leisurely, joyous trip that took five days to negotiate the 123 miles and 47 locks between Lake Ontario and the Ottawa River.

Later in England, Colonel By was exonerated of wrongdoing by the Parliamentary Committee. However, his reputation had been tarnished and his chance for recognition lost. He retired from the army and spent the next four years in failing health at his home in Frant, Sussex. He died on 1 February, 1836 at the age of fifty-three.

When word reached Canada of the shameful treatment given to Colonel By, citizens from Kingston to Bytown were outraged. Yet, within a generation, most people had forgotten the once-familiar figure on his black charger who founded the future capital.

His colleague, Lord Dalhousie, whose term as Governor-in-Chief expired in 1828, was also forgotten. Dalhousie's foresight and personal intervention—when Ottawa was still wilderness—deserves to be remembered. Yet no monument has been erected. A city electoral district, and a nondescript business thoroughfare in Lower Town are the only things that bear his name.

In 1915 two stones from Sappers Bridge were placed in Major's Hill Park to mark the site of Colonel By's house. Seventeen years later the Historical Society of Ottawa erected a stone monument to Colonel By beside the Canal. This cube was to be the base for a bust of the superintending engineer, but lack of funds prevented completion of the project. In 1954, at the instigation of Mayor Charlotte Whitton, the Queen Mother rechristened the old Hog's Back road Colonel By Drive. The following year the engineers of Ottawa erected a memorial fountain to Colonel By on the west bank of the Canal, near Laurier Bridge. This ornamental fountain originally stood in Trafalgar Square, London, and still bears shrapnel marks from the German Blitz during World War Two. While the National Arts Centre was being built, the fountain was placed in storage and then relocated on parkland near the corner of Laurier Avenue and Elgin Street. In 1971 Governor-General Roland Michener unveiled a full-length bronze statue of Colonel By that stands on the east shoulder of Entrance Valley overlooking the locks.

Notwithstanding these belated tributes, the finest monument to John By is the Canal itself.

6

Early Bytown

1826 to 1842

BOTH LORD DALHOUSIE, who chose the land with foresight, and Colonel By, who laid out the settlements with care, envisioned Bytown as a model community. During the prosperous Canal-building era the conduct of the inhabitants, if not exemplary, was unspectacular by frontier standards. When the Rideau Canal was completed, and Colonel By had returned to England, the economy slumped and there was a general exodus from Bytown. Those who remained were forced to depend on the brawling lumber trade for their survival. Within a few years Bytown became known as the most lawless community in British North America. Travellers were warned to avoid the place if they valued their lives.

Although much thought went into the formation of Bytown, the nature of its population and the political climate of the day guaranteed a stormy beginning. One barnyard historian likened the genesis of the future capital to that of a cow giving birth to a roll of barbed wire.

From its inception in 1826 until Confederation in 1867 Bytown had a substantial transient element. The first were the Irish skivvies on the Canal, they were followed by French, Irish, and Scottish lumber workers, most of whom were the roughest of roughnecks.

The resident population of Bytown was a yeasty mixture of English, French, Irish, and Scots. Each of these ethnic groups—which fairly represent Canada's founding peoples—brought to the wilderness their own values, prejudices, and memories. Seventy years earlier, the French had surrendered the country to the English, a fact the French had not forgotten. The Scots, who had also been conquered by the English, entered this new environment with a spirit of fierce clannish independence. The Irish came to Canada in desperation and despair, having suffered repression and privation in their native land at the hands of the British. The English, for their part, held few animosities, for they were secure in the belief that God had ordained them to be leaders.

These racial differences, fuelled by the availability of cheap whisky, made street brawls an everyday occurrence. John Mactaggart observed that

> ... *raw grain* whisky may be produced at a couple of shillings per gallon, the flavour of which is qualified by frosty potatoes and yellow pumpkins. Such *aqua* is extremely delicious; and those who know what *Glenlivet* is, may, perhaps, touch it with a long stick, confining their nostrils at the same time.

He also noted that potato whisky

> ... is the absolute poison of Upper Canada,—the laudanum that sends thousands of settlers to their eternal rest every season. There is a particular charm about the name whisky, which Irishmen and Scotsmen feel more strongly than the natives of any other country: which is one of the causes why this infernal liquid gets hold of and overcomes so many of them as it does.... No hell broth that the witches concocted of yore can equal it.

In addition to racial bias, there was also a sharp division along religious lines between Roman Catholics and Protestants in Bytown. The French and most of the Irish were Roman Catholic, while most of the English and Scots were Protestant. In Bytown the French and Irish were united by the Mother Church (although there were stresses within the union), but the Protestants were fragmented until an Orange Lodge was established in Brockville in 1830.

The Orange Order was a secret society founded in 1686 to unseat James II, the Roman Catholic King of England, and replace him with his Protestant daughter Mary, who was married to William of

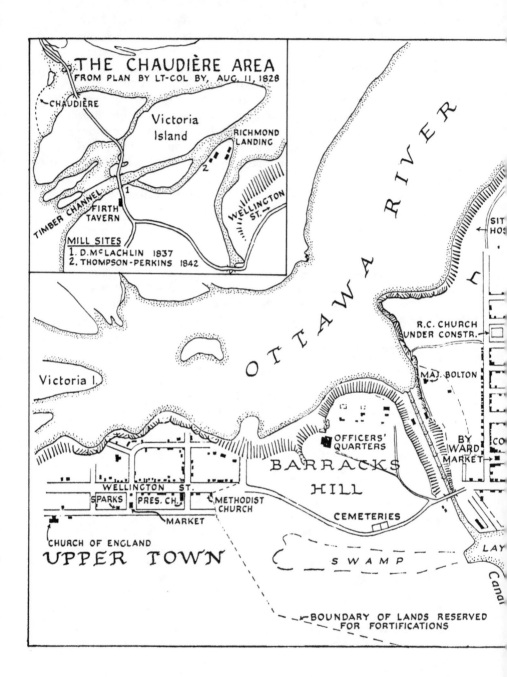

THE CHAUDIÈRE AREA
FROM PLAN BY LT-COL BY, AUG. 11, 1828

CHAUDIÈRE

Victoria
Island

RICHMOND
LANDING

TIMBER CHANNEL

FIRTH
TAVERN

WELLINGTON
ST.

MILL SITES
1. D. McLACHLIN 1837
2. THOMPSON-PERKINS 1842

OTTAWA RIVER

SIT
HOS

R.C. CHURCH
UNDER CONSTR.

MAJ. BOLTON

Victoria I.

OFFICERS'
QUARTERS

BY
WARD
MARKET

CO

BARRACKS
HILL

WELLINGTON ST.
SPARKS
PRES. CH.
METHODIST
CHURCH

MARKET

CEMETERIES

CHURCH OF ENGLAND
UPPER TOWN

SWAMP

LAY

Canal

BOUNDARY OF LANDS RESERVED
FOR FORTIFICATIONS

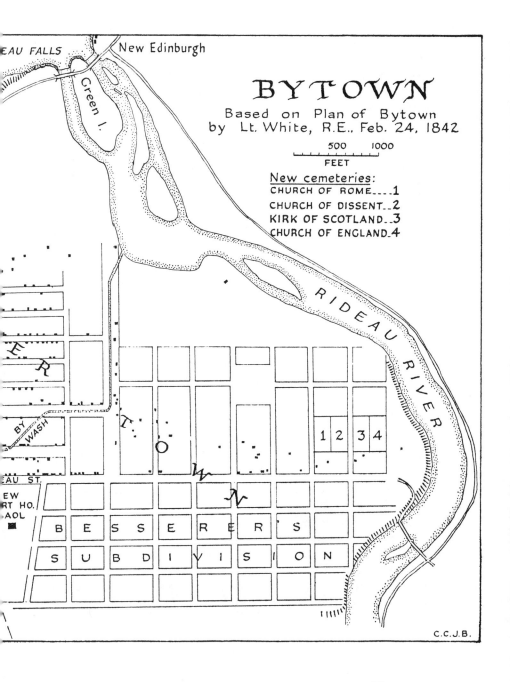

EAU FALLS   New Edinburgh

Green I.

BYTOWN
Based on Plan of Bytown
by Lt. White, R.E.. Feb. 24, 1842

500   1000

FEET

New cemeteries:
CHURCH OF ROME....1
CHURCH OF DISSENT..2
KIRK OF SCOTLAND..3
CHURCH OF ENGLAND.4

RIDEAU RIVER

1 2 3 4

BY WASH

EAU ST.
EW
RT HO.
AOL

B E S S E R E R S

S U B D I V I S I O N

C.C.J.B.

Orange. The annual celebration of the society takes place on 12 July, which is the anniversary of the Battle of the Boyne, when William of Orange (later William III) defeated James II and subdued Ireland. The annual parade is a colourful affair with a fife and drum band, "King William" on a white horse, and symbolic banners, including the Union Jack signifying loyalty to the British sovereign. The Orange Order in Canada in the nineteenth century was a significant anti-Catholic political force that stood for Protestant Christianity and the Empire. Membership in the Orange Order has declined over the years; today there are only two lodges left in the city of Ottawa. However, the order still flourishes in the outlying settlements, such as Richmond, where more than two thousand people from the Ottawa Valley attended the 1979 celebrations. The society's views have also modified with time—it is now primarily a fraternal organization—although the toast commemorating the Battle of the Boyne remains unchanged: "To the glorious, pious, and immortal memory of the great and good King William, who saved us from popery, slavery, knavery, brass money and wooden shoes—and a fig for the Bishop of Cork!"

Bytown was further stratified by economics, politics, and geography. In 1827, the year that construction actually started on the Canal, nearly a thousand people poured into Upper and Lower Town. Except for those who lived in the Irish ghetto along the Deep Cut known as Corkstown (who occupied the property on sufferance) all the occupants of Upper and Lower Town were tenants of the Crown.

Most of the newcomers were Irish and French labourers who settled in Lower Town because of its proximity to the work site. Before this area was fit for habitation, a large swamp had to be drained by a series of cuts that emptied into the By Wash. The first resident of Lower Town was an enterprising man named Jean-Baptiste St. Louis who built a house on Cumberland Street and then erected a grist mill around the corner on York Street which harnessed the flow of the By Wash. St. Louis was the contractor who built the dam on the north shore of Dow's Great Swamp, and he later erected a sawmill at the Rideau Falls. During 1827 many shanties and small businesses appeared on Sussex and Rideau streets (the main arteries of Lower Town), as well as the side streets of York, George, Clarence, and Cumberland. From the start it was a bustling, rough-and-tumble, predominantly Roman Catholic community.

Upper Town, consisting of part of Wellington and Kent streets, had far fewer residents. It was settled by the more affluent and better-educated citizens, including senior artificers on the Canal and some of the gentry from March Township. Most of these people were of English or Scottish descent, and most were Protestant.

Until the 1840s Bytown was effectively controlled by a small number of men, many of whom lived in, or adjacent to, Upper Town. Among the most influential early Bytowners were G. W. Baker, J. Bareille, G. T. Burke, J. Chitty, A. J. Christie, D. Fisher, S. Fraser, J. Lewis, G. Lyon, E. Malloch, T. MacKay, J. B. Monk, D. O'Connor, G. Patterson, H. Pinhey, N. Sparks, and W. Stewart. They came from a variety of trades and professions, but all were staunch Tories who believed in the perservation of the British Empire and the *status quo*. Most of these men felt it was their civic duty to manage Bytown's affairs, and they did a creditable job of it under trying circumstances.

Colonel By, in addition to his military and engineering duties, governed Bytown as magistrate during the first months of its existence. At that time the Lieutenant-Governor would not permit Bytown to have its own town council, thus the magistrate had sole authority over municipal affairs and also dispensed justice for minor offences such as drunkenness and disturbance of the peace. In the spring of 1827 Captain Andrew Wilson (RN) petitioned the Lieutenant-Governor of Upper Canada to appoint permanent magistrates from the civilian population. Captain Wilson, an old sea dog, had a large house on the banks of the Rideau River near Mooney's Bay. He had settled there before the Canal was started and his home, called Ossian Hall, had provided hospitality to many of the early surveyors and travellers on the Canal route. He was an exceptionally well-read man—Ossian Hall had one of the finest libraries in Upper Canada—and a boon companion of Dr. Alexander Christie, who was also a man of letters.

While awaiting the outcome of the petition, Colonel By made Captain Wilson an acting magistrate. This delighted the peppery sailor, who revelled in his new-found authority. The petition was a controversial document that underwent numerous changes and was the subject of a town meeting before it finally reached the Lieutenant-Governor, Sir Peregrine Maitland. After it was dispatched, one of the candidates, Dr. Thomas F. McQueen, sent a letter of his own to the Lieutenant-Governor's secretary:

By Town 18th October 1828

Sir,

Having placed my name to a petition some time ago addressed to His Excellency Sir P. Maitland for the appointment of Magistrates for this place. Since the above I have been informed that the names of several persons have been appended to the said petition "after it having been fitted up" by Mr. Heron [sic] Roman Catholic Priest of this place in a clandestine manner as being the most fit and proper persons for the appointments and as its having been done by the voice of the people, if I have been informed right, the persons recommended, to my knowledge with the exception of one, are most ignorant, and have not even the rank of gentlemen. They are Mr. T. McKay who came to this country a few years ago a common stone mason and is now a contractor on the canal, it is with difficulty he can write his own name, Mr. Penefather [sic] one of the lower class of Irish, Mr. Burgess a clerk in the Government office, and Doctor Christie a man very unfit for any public office, he is continually at the bottle, he does not want for talent, if these are the persons recommended I beg you will withdraw my name. I am also authorized to state that Capt. Alex. McQueen also R.D. Fraser Esq., would wish their names erased.

I am Sir

G. Hillier Esq.,   Your Obed't Serv't
Secretary   Thos F. McQueen
York U.C.   Surgeon

Dr. McQueen's scathing remarks reflected the haughty stance of the Bytown gentry. In the same year, Hamnett Pinhey writing to Jonas Jones described the Wrights as "old squatters"—a preposterous statement that ignored the fact that Philemon Wright held legal title to more than 20,000 acres and was on warm terms with the Governor. Education and breeding were the important criteria for admission to Upper Canada's aristocracy; wealth could be a handicap.

It is interesting to check Dr. McQueen's uncharitable observations (which contain an element of truth) with the information we have today on the persons mentioned in his letter.

The Roman Catholic priest "Mr. Heron" was the Reverend Father Patrick Horan, who had been stationed in Richmond and was transferred to Bytown by Bishop Macdonell in 1828. It is possible Father Horan "fitted up" the petition to give the Roman Catholics fairer representation. One could not fault him if he did so since the French and Irish—who far outnumbered the English and Scots—were sparsely represented in municipal affairs until the 1840s. Father

Horan had some personal shortcomings, including a penchant for alcohol and a distressing inclination to sell Church land for his own profit. At the request of the church wardens, he was removed from the parish of Bytown in 1829 by Bishop Macdonell. One of the church wardens was the "Mr. Penefather" in Dr. McQueen's letter, whose name was actually John Pennyfather, a leading member of the Irish community. Whether Pennyfather was "lower class" is a matter of opinion. However, we do know he was the contractor for the excavation of the Entrance Locks, which was one of the most difficult jobs on the entire Canal.

Thomas MacKay began his career as an apprentice mason in Scotland. He was a man without pretensions and probably would not have minded in the least being called a "common stone mason." By 1828 MacKay was well established financially and had developed many skills—including the ability to play the bagpipes. He was a perfectionist who never cut corners in the interest of profit, yet everything he touched seemed to turn to gold. An example of his good luck was his experience with the Entrance Locks. After signing the contract MacKay found that all the stone he needed to build the locks was available at the site, in the form of waste from the excavation. On the opposite shore of the Ottawa River he discovered a quarry that had stone for making mortar that was superior to the cement he had been importing from England. His search for perfection won him a gold medal at the London Exposition in 1850 for blankets woven in his mill at the Rideau Falls. In addition to his stonework on the canal and the Union Bridge, MacKay built the Scotch Kirk, a grist mill, a carding mill, the County Court House, and the Nicholas Street Gaol. At his death in 1855 he owned approximately 1,100 acres of land that encompassed the district of New Edinburgh, all of Government House grounds, and the present village of Rockcliffe Park. Not only was he the founder of New Edinburgh, but his house, known as MacKay's Castle, was purchased from his estate by the Canadian Government as the residence of the Governor General. MacKay, who represented Russell County in the Upper Canada Legislature and the Legislative Council of United Canada, made a tremendous contribution to the future capital. At this writing, his accomplishments are almost forgotten.

Dr. McQueen's objection to the candidacy of Burgess, "a clerk in the Government office," was probably based on snobbishness. This was H. Howard Burgess, who was dismissed from the Canal two years later for drinking himself into a state of insanity. As mentioned in the preceding chapter, when Burgess got home to England he conducted a smear campaign and published falsehoods concerning Colonel By's conduct.

The castigation of Dr. Christie by Dr. McQueen is historically significant because it is the only publicly recorded instance of a member of Ottawa's medical fraternity being critical of a fellow member. Christie was also mentioned in another letter of protest to the Lieutenant-Governor; George A. Rankin wrote that Christie was "a person with whom no gentleman can associate without dishonour."

Alexander Christie was not only a physician but a journalist and political manipulator *par excellence*. Born in Scotland in 1787, he came to Canada in 1817, following service in the Napoleonic Wars. Christie practised medicine for a few months and then became editor of the Montreal *Herald* newspaper. This venture soured when he was jailed as a result of a partnership dispute. In 1821 he applied for a lot in March Township and got himself appointed as a medical officer to the Richmond Settlement. His professional credentials are hazy, and there is reason to doubt whether he ever received a degree in medicine. A glance at his financial journal (which may be seen in the Bytown Museum) suggests that he was not too particular about how he turned a shilling. One of his first patients was Captain John B. Monk; in July 1821 Christie extracted teeth for two of the children; in September he sold the captain eight pounds of shingle nails; the following March he sold Monk a pair of moccasins, in May he vaccinated Monk's youngest child.

After being flooded out for several springs, Dr. Christie returned to Montreal in 1824 and took over as editor of the *Gazette*. The following year he returned to March and when work began on the Canal he secured a position from Colonel By as an assistant medical officer. McQueen's assertion that Christie was "continually at the bottle" had some foundation, for Christie was undoubtedly fond of the grape. On one occasion Christie and Andrew Wilson became disoriented after they lurched out of Firth's tavern and nearly perished in the Ottawa River. Alexander Christie was one of the first residents of Upper Town; his name keeps popping up in the affairs of the community from 1827 until his death in 1843.

Before leaving the story of Bytown's first municipal officers, it may be worth mentioning that Dr. McQueen did not linger in Bytown but moved to Brockville, where he practised medicine until his death in 1866.

Having considered the petition—and supplementary letters—the Lieutenant-Governor appointed the following gentlemen to life terms as magistrates: Daniel Fisher, Daniel McKinnon, George Rankin, Charles Shirreff, and Captain Andrew Wilson.

Upon their appointment, these men assumed responsibility for maintaining law and order in Bytown. The first major test of their effectiveness occurred in 1829 when Bytown had its inaugural fair. Tents had been pitched in two rows in the vacant lot beside St. Andrew's Church, and grog flowed freely. In the afternoon, horse races were run along Wellington Street, using the intersection of Bank Street as the starting point. Inevitably a dispute arose over the outcome of a race. Tempers flared and a mass brawl ensued. Because most of the able-bodied citizens were involved in the fray, the magistrates were unable to deputize any constables. The donnybrook lasted for three hours and finally guttered out at the end of the day. Many years elapsed before Bytown had another fair.

Soon after Upper and Lower Town were surveyed, additional property became available for settlement to the east and west of the Canal. However, due to the Ordnance lands between Upper and Lower Town, a substantial vacant area continued to exist in the core of Bytown.

Thomas MacKay started amassing land to the east of the Rideau River shortly after he arrived in Bytown. His 1,100-acre tract (which would eventually become the district of New Edinburgh and Rockcliffe Park) remained unoccupied until the mid-1830s because of its remoteness from the Canal and the inconvenience of having to cross the river.

In 1828 Louis-Theodore Besserer, a notary from Quebec City who had served in the War of 1812, was granted a large parcel of unproductive land south of Rideau Street. His block, known as Sandy Hill, was bounded on the west by Waller Street (adjacent to Nicholas Sparks's property), to the south by Laurier Avenue, to the east by the Rideau River, and to the north by Rideau Street. Besserer was an absentee landlord, thus the area was neglected, save for a handful of squatters, until William Stewart became his agent in 1838. Stewart, who subsequently attained political prominence, laid out a street plan for Sandy Hill and began to sell lots in a businesslike manner. One of the streets in this old residential district still bears his name. Besserer eventually moved to Bytown in the 1840s and built a substantial stone house—with a kitchen in the basement, serviced by a dumb-waiter—at the corner of King Edward and Daly avenues.

The major landowner west of the Canal was Nicholas Sparks. Until 1848, when the Ordnance Board returned the property they had expropriated for a moat, the only portion of his land available for settlement was the portion west of Bank Street.

To the south of Barracks Hill and the "moat property" was a six-hundred-acre parcel that had been granted to Grace McQueen in 1801. This block was bounded by Laurier Avenue to the north, Bronson Avenue to the west, Gladstone and Mann avenues to the south, and the Rideau River to the east. Colonel By bought the property in 1832, just before returning to England, for £1200. He died four years later, and the land remained uninhabited until the 1850s due to legal complications in connection with his estate.

While Upper and Lower Town showed marked growth in the first twenty years, and property was developed on the outskirts of these settlements, no one lived in the centre of Bytown. Part of Barracks Hill and some land below Wellington Street was pasture; as one went south, the terrain changed to bush.

The first school in Bytown was opened in the summer of 1827 by an Irishman named James Maloney. It was called the English Mercantile and Mathematical Academy and was located on Rideau Street, near the By Wash. A few years later the academy moved to a log structure at the corner of Mosgrove and Besserer streets; in 1838 it moved to larger quarters at 112 Clarence Street. James Maloney, the founder and principal, taught in Ottawa for fifty-two years, until his death in 1879. He was totally dedicated to his profession and deserves an important place in the history of the city.

The first church in Bytown was a wooden building erected at the corner of Rideau and Chapel streets by the Methodists. The guiding force behind this project was John Burrows, the former owner of Nicholas Sparks's property. Soon after the church was completed, it burnt to the ground, and a new edifice of stone was built in Upper Town, near the corner of Elgin and Sparks streets, on land donated by Nicholas Sparks. The Methodists generously allowed their church to be used by the Anglicans until that denomination built their own place of worship in 1832.

St. Andrew's, at the corner of Wellington and Kent streets, was the first Presbyterian Church in Bytown. It was built in 1828 on a lot purchased from Nicholas Sparks for £200. Thomas MacKay, one of the elders of the congregation, donated the stone for the kirk and

Samuel de Champlain, "The Father of New France," is depicted in this water-colour painting on one of his exploration trips. *(Public Archives Canada #C 13320)*

Philemon Wright circa 1825. Wright founded Wright's Town—now the city of Hull—in 1800. *(PAC #C 11056)*

TOP LEFT: Sir Richard Scott, mayor of Bytown in 1852 and influential advocate of Ottawa as Canada's capital. *(OMA #CA 0903)*

TOP RIGHT: John Bower Lewis, mayor of Bytown in 1848 and first mayor of Ottawa in 1855. *(OMA #CA 0905)*

RIGHT: Henry Friel, an important and colourful figure in the 1850s and 1860s. Served terms as mayor of both Bytown and Ottawa. *(OMA #CA 0916)*

LEFT: Monseigneur J. E. Bruno Guigues, OMI (1805-74), first bishop of Ottawa and founder of Ottawa University. *(PAC #C 2150)*
RIGHT: Mère Elisabeth Bruyère who established a community of Sisters of Charity in Bytown, and founded the Ottawa General Hospital. *(PAC #C 4023)*

TOP: Watercolour painting circa 1828 of trussed wooden span to Bytown of the first Union Bridge. *(PAC #C 35954)*
BOTTOM: Main wooden span over the Great Kettle of the first Union Bridge. *(PAC #C 16331)*

ABOVE: Painting of Rideau Canal and locks circa 1835. Hog's Back Falls in background. *(PAC #C 92906)*
BELOW: View of Entrance Locks from East Block, Parliament Hill, circa 1888. *(Ottawa Municipal Archives #CA 0170)*

ABOVE LEFT: Bust of Colonel John By, Royal Engineers, the man responsible for the entire construction of the Rideau Canal. *(Historical Society of Ottawa)* BELOW LEFT: The Honourable Thomas MacKay circa 1850. MacKay was the contractor for the Entrance Locks and an immensely influential figure in early Bytown. *(Keefer family collection)*

LEFT: George Ramsay, ninth Earl of Dalhousie, Governor-in-Chief of British North America 1820-28. Dalhousie laid out the settlement of Bytown in 1826. *(PAC #C 5958)*
BELOW: Charles Lennox, fourth Duke of Richmond, who died of rabies at the settlement of Richmond in 1818. The dog in the portrait is a fox terrier. *(PAC #C 23610)*

arranged for his masons to build the church during a lull in the Canal work. The original kirk, a plain structure measuring forty-five feet by fifty-five feet, was enlarged in 1854 and completely rebuilt in 1873. Today the congregation of St. Andrew's plan to build a seven-story office complex where the old stone church hall now stands. The decision was not unanimous, and it is regretted by many outside the congregation.

St. Andrew's was the only church in Bytown to obtain a land grant under the terms of the Clergy Reserves Act. On 19 May 1836 it was given a parcel of 178 acres bounded on the north by Carling Avenue, to the west by Bronson Avenue, to the south by Fifth Avenue, and to the east by Main Street. This tract became known as the Glebe, which is an old French word for parsonage land. St. Andrew's Church disposed of the property during the next century, the last lots being sold in 1948. It is not known why the Anglican and Methodist denominations did not take advantage of the Clergy Reserves Act before it was rescinded in 1854. Possibly they were not as canny as the Scots.

The first Roman Catholic Mass was celebrated in a house on Bank Street by the Reverend Father Patrick Horan in 1827. For the next five years services were held in temporary premises in Upper and Lower Town. In 1832 a small wooden chapel was built on St. Patrick Street near Sussex Street. In 1839 plans were made for a substantial stone church on Sussex Street, between Guigues and St. Patrick streets. The cornerstone was laid in 1841, but due to the scope of the work and unforeseen delays, the structure was not completed until 1853, at which time it was designated Notre Dame Cathedral. In 1879 Notre Dame Cathedral was elevated to the rank of Basilica. The slender spires of this church are one of the finest examples of twin Gothic architecture in North America.

In 1832 Nicholas Sparks donated a piece of land for an Anglican church at the west end of Wellington Street. Initially his fellow parishioners refused to support the project because they considered the site too remote. As a result Sparks was forced to pay most of the cost of the stone building (which seated three hundred) out of his own pocket. The first service was held in Christ Church on 21 July 1833. Despite the importance of the occasion, the collection plate yielded a paltry seven shillings, sixpence. The church's first minister, the Reverend Amos H. Burwell, was an eccentric who became a member of a radical Protestant sect known as the Irvingites. Reverend Burwell stayed in Bytown only four years. Before leaving, he wrote a treatise expounding the evil influence of democracy on spiritual values. Published in 1837, this is believed to be the first book printed in Bytown. Burwell was succeeded by the Reverend Samuel S. Strong, who served the church for twenty years.

In 1841, Nicholas Sparks donated additional land so that Christ Church could be enlarged. Although the congregation was growing, the weekly collection failed to cover Reverend Strong's stipend. By 1843 Strong was owed £107.42 and his bishop, the Right Reverend John Strachan, wrote to him saying, "I should not hesitate a moment in withdrawing you from Bytown after the extraordinary conduct of your congregation, were it in my power to render your situation more comfortable." The Bishop's letter had the desired effect, and the congregation have met their financial obligations from that day to the present. In 1873 Christ Church was completely rebuilt; in 1896 it was elevated to the status of Cathedral for the Bishop of Ottawa. Christ Church is set on a promontory overlooking the Ottawa River; within this stately cathedral are many reminders of the past, including the frayed colours of some fine Ottawa regiments.

In 1832, the year the Rideau Canal was finished, Bytown suffered its first epidemic of Asiatic cholera. This disease, borne in fecal matter, is characterized by violent diarrhoea and vomiting which lead to severe dehydration. Death occurs in more than 50 percent of untreated cases. To cope with the epidemic, a Board of Health was established under the chairmanship of Dr. Alexander Christie. Because the disease was brought to the settlement by immigrants, Christie tried to prevent boats from stopping at Bytown, but was unsuccessful. Those who succumbed were treated in a hastily erected wooden shed near the Royal Canadian Mint. Below this primitive hospital a temporary wharf (known as Cholera Wharf) was built to intercept boats before they entered the Canal. Many people died of the cholera, particularily in Lower Town where the waste weir of the By Wash trapped much of the community's sewage. After the epidemic ran its course the following winter, the Board of Health was disbanded.

In 1834 Bytown was again swept by cholera, and the Board of Health was reactivated. This time Charles Shirreff was the chairman, and three other medical practitioners, Drs. Gellie, Scanlon, and Van Cortlandt, were on the board. Dr. Christie was the secretary. In the course of their meetings a bitter dispute took place between Dr. Christie and the other three doctors which precipitated Christie's resignation.

In February 1836 a weekly newspaper, the *Bytown Independent and Farmer's Advocate,* was published by James Johnston, a self-styled independent reformer. This brave venture, which was owned, published, and edited by Johnston, folded after a few issues.

Three months later Dr. Alexander Christie, an experienced journalist and rabid Tory, published the *Bytown Gazette and Ottawa and Rideau Advertizer.* It was a success from the first issue, and one can not help but draw the conclusion that Christie had finally found his *métier*—one that allowed him to practise journalism and to exercise political influence. At that time there was agitation for the union of Upper and Lower Canada, which had first been proposed to the British government in 1822. From the outset Christie's paper promoted the feasibility of Bytown as the capital of the united provinces.

In 1840 the British Parliament passed the Act of Union, which came into effect on 10 February 1841. The Act created the Province of Canada by uniting Upper and Lower Canada, which were now designated Canada West and Canada East. The Province of Canada was to have a single appointed Legislative Council, and an elected House of Assembly, with an equal number of members from Canada West and Canada East. The Act provided for the Governor-General, Lord Sydenham, to choose the new capital of the Province of Canada. Sydenham chose Kingston.

Following the passage of the Act, an election was called to choose representatives for the House of Assembly. Bytown was permitted to elect one member for Canada West. Four men tossed their hats in the ring: Alexander Christie, Conservative; Robert Shirreff, Reformist Conservative; James Johnston, Independent; and William Stewart, Independent. In September 1840, seven months before the election, Lord Sydenham made a special visit to Bytown. After holding a levee for the townspeople at Major Bolton's residence (formerly Colonel By's house) the Governor-General held a private conference with all the candidates except William Stewart, who was away on business. As a result of this meeting Christie, Shirreff, and Johnston agreed to withdraw their names from the ballot in favour of Stewart Derbyshire, the Governor's candidate. Derbyshire was a barrister by profession who had come to Canada with Lord Durham in 1838; in 1840 he was publishing a Tory newspaper, *The Courier,* in Montreal. When William Stewart returned to Bytown and learned that he was expected to step down for Derbyshire he flatly rejected the idea and vowed to defeat the Governor's candidate. In the ensuing months Derbyshire attracted a great deal of critical comment, especially as he rarely visited Bytown. In this absence, Alexander Christie's *Bytown Gazette and Ottawa and Rideau Advertizer* campaigned on his behalf. There was also a fair amount of mudslinging, as the following poster attests:

ELECTORS OF BYTOWN.

Gentlemen,---

A report is current and disseminated among my fellow Townsmen, that I said, "Every Irishman in Bytown could be bought by a glass of Grog."

The contradiction to this is carried on the very face of it. Every person who know me, are well aware that I am not capable of uttering such an *untruth*. I therefore challenge any person to come forward and prove it.

1 remain, Gentlemen,
Your friend and servant,
WM. STEWART.
Bytown, 1st March, 1841.

Only eighty-five of Bytown's 3,122 inhabitants were eligible to vote on Election Day, 8 March 1841. The reason for this unusual situation was that in order to cast a ballot a man had to own mortgage-free property. The election took place under the surveillance of George Baker, Bytown's postmaster. (Baker succeeded Matthew Connell, who had opened a post office near the By Wash in 1829 and died of cholera in 1834.) The vote was done by a show of hands, and Derbyshire won a clear majority. However, William Stewart refused to accept the verdict and insisted on a written ballot. This took place the following day, with the result being fifty-two votes for Derbyshire, twenty-nine for Stewart. Stewart then protested the outcome on the basis of irregularities (there were many), but it did him no good. In this connection, the returning officer could hardly be described as impartial. Having announced Derbyshire the winner, George Baker stood on the platform and sang "Rule Britannia" at the top of his lungs—then he jumped into his sleigh and led the victory parade!

Derbyshire served his constituents well, even though he was a stranger who had been thrust upon the voters of Bytown by the Governor. Soon after taking his seat in the House of Assembly he earned the approval of most of his critics. Within a few months he and his arch-rival William Stewart were on cordial terms. Derbyshire was one of the first and strongest proponents of Bytown as a capital. As early as December 1840 he wrote Alexander Christie stating his belief that Bytown had the potential to be the capital not only of the Province of Canada, but of all British North America.

In 1842 William Stewart obtained a seat in the House of Assembly as a result of a by-election in the adjacent county of Russell. This vacancy occurred when the sitting member, Thomas MacKay, was appointed to the Legislative Council. In the next election, 1844, Stewart ran again in Bytown and won by a comfortable majority.

Bytown was named the judicial seat of a new district called Dalhousie, by an Act passed in March 1838. This was welcome news because until that time Bytown had been part of the District of Bathurst, which had its judicial seat in Perth. The Act stipulated, however, that Bytown would not become the judicial seat until a satisfactory Courthouse and jail were erected. In 1840 Nicholas Sparks donated an acre of land for these buildings, east of the Canal, on what is now Nicholas Street. Thomas MacKay was the chief contractor for both structures.

In 1840 Lord Sydenham signed a Municipal Act creating district councils. Each district was to have *one* elected warden, *two* elected councillors from *each* township, and an appointed clerk. This act transferred control of municipal affairs from the appointed magistrates to elected representatives. On 9 August 1842 the first council meeting for the District of Dalhousie was held in Bytown. Thomas MacKay was the warden for the district, the councillors from

Nepean being George Baker and John Johnson. The district clerk was Dr. Alexander Christie.

On 6 March 1842 a proclamation confirmed the existence of the District of Dalhousie. Bytown now had its own stone Courthouse and jail. Both buildings would see plenty of use in the years to come.

7

The Square Timber Trade

1806 to 1855

THE INDEPENDENT ACTIONS of two men, Philemon Wright and Napoleon Bonaparte, started the square timber trade in the Ottawa Valley. Within a generation this region became the foremost producer of lumber in British North America.

In 1806 Wright proved that it was possible to raft timber down the Ottawa River to the port of Quebec. The following year Napoleon issued his Berlin Decree, which closed the Baltic timber ports to Britain. In the ensuing months Russia and the United States (excepting Vermont) also closed their markets to Britain. Napoleon's Decree threatened England's naval supremacy, and forced her to turn to British North America for masts, spars, and wooden building materials. For the Canadian colonies it was a windfall.

Up until that time Britain had relied upon the Baltic for her naval stores because the Baltic ports were close to England, their wood was of high quality, and the cost was reasonable. Prior to the American Revolution New England had also supplied a portion of Britain's needs, but this became an unreliable source following the Declaration of Independence. High shipping and labour costs placed the colonies in a poor position to compete with the Baltic. At the turn of the century Canadian timber, cut in the Quebec City region and the valley of the St. John in New Brunswick, accounted for less than 2 percent of Britain's imports.

To promote the growth of a forest industry in British North America—and to create an alternate source of naval stores—the British Government instituted a tariff on the importation of foreign timber in 1795. This tariff, known as the Colonial Preference, was intially levied at the rate of 10 shillings per load (a load being fifty cubic feet), which was insufficient to overcome the price spread. In 1805, when the war began to create shortages in British shipyards, the tariff was raised to 25 shillings. That year Britain imported 15,000 loads of square timber from Canada. In 1807, the year of Napoleon's Decree, she imported 30,000 loads from the colonies. For the next four years British North America supplied nearly 90 percent of Britain's naval stores. In 1814, following the collapse of Napoleon's blockade, the Preferential Tariff was increased to 65 shillings. This rate more than compensated for the competitive advantages of the Baltic countries, which were once again in the market. By 1820 Britain was importing nearly 300,000 loads of timber from the colonies on an annual basis. In 1821 the Preferential Tariff was reduced to 55 shillings, and remained at this level until it was abolished in 1842.

The staple woods of the timber trade were white pine, red pine, and oak. The most sought after was white pine, which can grow to a height of more than two hundred feet, with a diameter at its base of six feet. Because of its exceptional length, its strength-to-weight ratio, and its weather resistance, white pine was a favourite wood for main masts. Red pine does not grow as tall as white pine and is a denser, heavier wood, but it was well suited for spars and structural work. Oak, particularly white oak, was used for barrel staves and the decking of vessels.

Square timbers, deals, and staves were the units of export. A square timber was made from an entire tree, which was squared by lopping off the cylindrical sides with a broad-axe. Only the tallest trees were cut for square timber. Deals were rough-cut planks three inches thick, eleven inches wide, and twelve feet long. The extra thickness of the deals was specified by the British buyers so that they could dress them into boards in their own mills. Staves were normally made of white oak and were one and one-half inches thick, five inches wide, and five and one-half feet long.

The timber trade had a profound effect upon the Ottawa Valley. From the outset it was the main source of income for Wright's settlement. Upon completion of the Rideau Canal, Bytown became the hub of the industry as a supply depot and enlistment centre for men going into the bush. Both the social life and the economy of Bytown reflected the community's dependence on the forest. Lumbermen and shantymen were a devil-may-care breed who imbued the town with a raw frontier spirit, while timber, a notoriously unstable commodity, caused periods of affluence and depression.

Almost everybody in the Ottawa Valley was directly or indirectly engaged in the lumber trade. When settlers cleared their land, they sold or bartered the trees. Farmers grew hay and produce to supply the shanties, and also cut wood on their "back forty." Some farmers spent the winter in the bush as shantymen or teamsters. Merchants relied upon the lumber operators for the bulk of their business; hotel and tavern-keepers wooed the shantymen. Businessmen invested in lumbering ventures and occasionally took a raft of their own down to Quebec. Sawmills not only provided employment but also consumed the harvest of the forest. Scores of men—with varying success—became lumbering entrepreneurs. It is impossible to list all the participants, but a glance at the operations of two of the first timber families, the Wrights and the Hamiltons, may indicate the scope of the trade.

When Philemon Wright entered the square timber trade in 1806 he was sole proprietor of his business. As such, he was involved in all phases of the venture, from the felling of the trees to the navigation of his raft. A few years later he formed a company, P. Wright & Sons, in which his sons Tiberius and Ruggles Wright played a significant role. Eventually P. Wright & Sons employed more than two hundred men in shanties on the Ottawa, Blanche, Gatineau, and Rideau rivers. In an average year this firm sent twenty rafts of timber to Quebec. Although Philemon Wright cut deals and staves in his own sawmills, and his son Ruggles built a revenue producing timber slide, the main emphasis of the family firm was the harvesting of pine for square timber.

In 1807 Thomas Mears established a sawmill in Hawkesbury, at the head of the Long Sault rapids. Mears subsequently defaulted on a contract with Messrs. George and William Hamilton, Quebec City lumber merchants. Because Mears was unable to repay the advance he had received from the Hamiltons on the contract, he was obliged to surrender his mill to them. It turned out to be a questionable asset for the Hamiltons because it burned to the ground in the spring of 1812, a few months after they had acquired title to the property.

The mill was rebuilt and began operating under the management of William Hamilton, who was also responsible for the firm's timber limits along the Rideau River.

Several years later William sold his interest to his three brothers, George, John, and Robert. This change in ownership provided the mill with a competitive edge through "vertical integration." Brother George looked after the mill and timber limits, John was a lumber merchant and broker in Quebec (with his own rafting cove), and brother Robert was a wholesale lumber dealer in Liverpool. This meant that the Hamiltons were able to avoid the expense of middlemen, and were also in control of their product—except for the ocean voyage—from the time it grew in the forest until it was sold in England. Another advantage of the Hawkesbury mill was its location. Many small operators would take their rafts as far as Hawkesbury and then sell their timber to the Hamiltons rather than go through the trouble of running the Long Sault rapids. The Hamilton firm exported square timber, but the main thrust of their business was the sawing of logs. By midcentury, Hamilton Bros. was one of the largest producers of deals in British North America.

It was relatively easy to become an entrepreneur in the square timber business. The first requirement was to obtain a licence to cut on Crown land. Licences were granted to most applicants, and the fee ranged between $1.00 and $1.25 per *square mile.* The next step was to negotiate a contract with a merchant in Quebec City, or his agent in Bytown, to purchase the timber you intended to cut on your newly acquired limits. If your credentials were sound, the contract might contain a provision for the advancement of funds to offset your expenses during the winter. If not, you borrowed money (which was known as "raising the wind") from a bank, merchant, or individual on the strength of your contract. Both a firm contract and financing were critical to the success of the endeavour, but they could also be the source of ruin if you failed to meet your obligations. A contract was necessary because of the volatile nature of the timber market: to cut without one was a form of Russian roulette. Outside financing paid for the winter expenses and allowed you to increase the scale of your operations—with other people's money.

The timber was cut by a shanty "team" of from 30 to 120 men. The shanty was managed by a foreman whose word was law. There was also a clerk who kept the books, a "culler" who graded the wood, and a cook. The term "shanty" was also applied to the building in which the men lived. A shanty was a low structure built of logs with a small door and a large hole in the roof for ventilation. Most shanties accommodated forty men and each had a central fireplace, framed with sand, where the food was cooked. Double bunks lined three walls of the shanty. The men slept in pairs, fully clothed, under two grey wool blankets on a mattress of balsam boughs. Each shanty had a chore boy whose task was to keep the fire fed with logs. Because the only source of ventilation was the hole in the roof, smoke permeated the shantymen's clothes and clung to them for weeks after they returned to civilization.

In September the men and provisions for the shanty were hauled into the woods by teams of horses and oxen. Oxen were favoured over horses for work in the bush because of their strength and their ability to subsist on much coarser forage. The staple foods were salt pork, flour, peas, molasses, and tea. Shantymen were great tea drinkers, and they liked their tea brewed as strong as battery acid. When the men reached the area they were going to lumber, their first task was to build a shanty. The shanty had to be located in the centre of the pinery and within four miles of a waterway so the logs could be floated out in the spring.

The men worked hard during the winter. Shortly after dawn cutting crews of three axemen and a teamster fanned out from the shanty. Throughout the day the axemen felled and squared trees, while the teamster "skidded" the trunks to the waterway. The crews returned to the shanty at dusk. Sunday was a day of rest when the men could sleep in, attend to personal chores, and relax. Occasionally a circuit riding minister or priest would visit the shanty on the Sabbath and conduct a service.

Cutting ended with the first thaws in March. At this time some of the shantymen were paid off and returned home. Those who remained in camp waited impatiently for the "drive" to start. The drive, which took place as soon as the ice went out, was the most dangerous and exciting phase of the year. When the spring breakup came, the logs on the banks were rolled into the snow-swollen streams and sent on their way to the Ottawa River. Often, the loose sticks piled up or jammed at a bend or narrows in the tributary. This was called a log jam and if not dealt with quickly the blockage could become so severe that the year's work would be lost. Joshua Fraser, author of *Shanty, Forest and River Life* (published 1896), describes the actions of the men on the drive when they encountered a jam:

> A wild and exciting scene of bustle and activity now takes place. Every man is on the alert, and throwing his whole strength into the work. The only man who is cool and collected is the foreman, and he needs to be; if ever experienced and calculating judgment, as well as nerve and ability, is required, now is the time. As soon as he finds out the salient points of the jam, and above all the *pièce de resistance,* he attacks it with all his force and skill. With wild whoop and yell the men respond to his summons, and go at it with a will.
>   ... the climax of interest in this scene is when the jam is giving way and bursting; with the crash and noise of thunder it sweeps away everything before it, and in a furious, whirling, seething jumble of logs, up-rooted trees, and foaming torrent, rushes down the gorge with lightning speed. Every man has now to look out for himself, and make for the shore the best way he can. As they leap from stick to stick, in the tumbling, whirling mass, it is almost miraculous how they escape. And as they go bounding along, every man is whooping at the pitch of his voice "There she goes, There she goes, Hoorah! Hoorah!"

When the sticks of timber reached the Ottawa River they were trapped by a "boom" stretched across the mouth of the tributary. (A boom is a necklace of floating logs connected by chains; today one can still see tear-shaped booms of pulp logs being towed down the Ottawa.) On the main river the logs were made into "cribs" containing from twenty to thirty-five sticks. Each crib had a frame of four timbers on which the sticks were laid, and two timbers (called "floats") to hold the load in place. Both the framework and the floats were secured by oak pins. A raft was made by joining from thirty to one hundred cribs together. This was done with the aid of withes, chains, and wooden cap pieces that linked the oak pins of adjoining cribs. When the raft was finally assembled, it looked like a gigantic patchwork quilt.

A square timber raft was a self-contained community. On board were sleeping and cooking facilities for the crew, which on large rafts could number more than fifty men. The focal point of the raft was the cookhouse, or "camboose." The camboose had a sand-filled hearth, similar to those in the shanties, and a lean-to roof for protection against the elements. The company flag flew from a pole attached to this structure. Scattered around the raft were portable sleeping shelters, which were semicylindrical in shape, made of bark, and accommodated one man. Up until 1825 rafts on the Ottawa were powered by a combination of sails and twenty-four-foot oars, called "sweeps." In later years some of the rafts were towed to Quebec by steam vessels.

In 1826 Colonel By constructed a channel on the south shore of the Chaudière Falls for the passage of individual sticks of timber. This channel reduced the amount of damage to the timber, but it still meant that rafts had to be completely dismantled to negotiate the falls. Hardwood, which lacks buoyancy, had to be transported around the falls by wagon. In 1829 Ruggles Wright built a timber slide on the Hull side which was twenty-six feet wide, permitting the passage of an entire crib. Wright learned the technology for his slide on a visit to Scandanavia. This slide was available to anyone—on payment of a toll—and did much to encourage lumbering on the Upper Ottawa. Within six years shanties were cutting as far upriver as Lake Temiskaming. In 1836 George Buchanan built a slide for cribs on the Bytown side of the river, between Victoria Island and Chaudière Island. Buchanan's slide, which started three hundred yards above the falls and ran for nearly three-quarters of a mile, was Bytown's first (and only) tourist attraction. In *Shanty, Forest and River Life* Joshua Fraser counselled his readers:

> Shooting the slides on cribs is capital sport; in its excitement and velocity it reminds you of tabogganing. Two men manage the crib, one at the stern, the other at the bow, who, with their immense oars, steer it fair for the mouth of the slide, and, catching the current, it glides down the steep incline with immense rapidity; so great indeed is its velocity that it often completely submerges itself in the calm water below. When you shoot the slides you should have your top boots on, if you wish to keep your feet and legs dry.
>
> Shooting the Chaudière slides at Ottawa is a favourite amusement of adventurous visitors, but it is not unattended with danger, especially to nervous ladies. I would advise no one to undertake it except in company with some lumbering friend; and on a carefully selected crib, and one strongly bound together. If you can manage to get on the "cookery crib," which carries all the provisions and cooking utensils, then you may consider yourself quite safe, as it is constructed with all the skill and care that the most experienced raftsmen can bestow.

Joshua Fraser's words of caution were well justified, for there were many rafting accidents at the Chaudière Falls. When a crib missed the slide and was sucked over the falls by the current, the results were usually fatal. One incident bears retelling because it suggests that bilingualism in Bytown in the past century was a matter of courtesy, rather than a means of job classification for civil servants, as it is in Ottawa today. On 3 June 1848 the *Packet* of Bytown reported:

> Yesterday, about ten o'clock, A.M., an accident of a serious nature occurred. Two men were upon a crib of oak timber, endeavouring to make the head of the Chaudière Government slides, but the current, proving too strong, carried them out of the channel. They observed their danger too late, and were carried with the crib over the lost channel. One of the men, named Baptiste Beaudran, jumped off the crib, and was carried over the chute. The other, named Paul Filardeau, kept his hold of the crib until it struck against the table rock. His situation was even here critical, for a dreadful rapid lay between him and the main shore, distant about one hundred and fifty yards. A crowd of the inhabitants, about 500 in number, were soon on the spot, and measures immediately taken to remove the poor fellow from his unpleasant situation. Messrs. McLachlin, Farley, Sullivan, Keefer, and Larmouth, were most active in the attempt. A small cord was first thrown over, to which was attached a stronger one, and finally a cable or hawser, to which cords were attached, and one end thrown over to the rock. Filardeau then tied the cords around his body, and slung himself to the rings. Great excitement occurred when he let himself off. He was immediately pulled in along the main rope, not, however, without touching the water several times. When the poor fellow reached the shore, he with the greatest coolness turned to his deliverers, and thanked them in both languages for their kindness.

When all the cribs of a raft had cleared the Chaudière, they were reassembled in the quiet stretch between the base of the falls and Parliament Hill. Depending upon the water conditions, a raft would take four to six weeks to travel from Bytown to Quebec City. On arrival at Quebec the raft would be taken to one of the coves, owned by the timber dealers, which lined the waterfront for a distance of ten miles.

Lying offshore would be several hundred droghers waiting for cargoes. Droghers were ancient vessels that had special ports cut in their bows to facilitate the loading of timber. These ships had all seen better days and their reputation for seaworthiness was so bad that they were nicknamed "floating coffins." This was an accurate description when one considers that in 1872 no less than fifty-seven droghers foundered or sank in the Gulf of St. Lawrence. It should also be mentioned that most of the immigrants who came to Canada in the nineteenth century crossed the Atlantic in droghers.

After the raft was moored, the cove owner would send out a culler to evaluate the timber. Negotiations between the raft owner (or his agent) and the timber dealer would follow. As soon as the sale was concluded, the raftsmen would be paid off. Not all the raftsmen went directly home because there were many temptations in the port of Quebec. Joshua Fraser wrote in despair of the fate that awaited many of the men:

> Like Jack Tar when he gets into port, the poor shantyman has now to run the gauntlet of the very worst and vilest temptations that can assail a man . . . As he leaps with a light heart and a heavy pocket from the raft on to the shore he is at once beset with a host of hell-runners in the shape of calash drivers, boarding-house agents, brothel sirens, and crimps and sharpers of the blackest stamp. "Come and have a drink, my jolly buck," is generally the first salutation that greets his ears, and in the joyous hilarity of his soul, the poor fellow thinks it is only "good manners" to comply. . . . The liquor with which he is plentifully plied is poison of the blackest and rankest kind, and on account of his long abstinence from all intoxicants produces a more immediate and potent effect than it otherwise would. As the fiery spirit mounts to his brain, and his pulses, already exhilarated, become doubly so under its influence, he soon loses all caution and self-command. His love of ostentatious spending and open-handed treating give themselves full fling—he treats right and left, and delights in being the hero of a thirsty crowd of spongers and thieving vagabonds, and flourishes his bank notes and tosses them on the counter with the air and tone of a millionaire. Of course the upshot of the whole business can be readily surmised. Between bad whisky and worse men and women he is plucked as clean as a Christmas goose, and in an incredibly short time too.

Carousing shantymen were accepted in Bytown as part of the price the community had to pay for its dependence on the timber trade. However, in the early 1830s a violent faction emerged that not only terrorized the citizens but also threatened the future of the forest industry. The members of this unruly element were known as "Shiners."

Shiners were Irish labourers who were stranded in Bytown without jobs following the completion of the Rideau Canal. These men had come to Canada to escape the poverty and hopeless circumstances of their homeland. Canada proved little better than Ireland. In Bytown they were treated as second-class citizens, they lived in mud huts or shacks along the Canal, they did the most menial work (for the lowest pay), and many died in the cholera epidemic of 1832. When the Canal was finished, their only source of employment was the timber trade. But, being recent immigrants, the Shiners could not compete with the French as woodsmen. In consequence, they remained unemployed. To vent their frustration at "the system" the Shiners turned to alcohol and violence. French raftsmen and shanty-men bore the brunt of Shiner hostility, which was motivated by envy rather than ethnic prejudice.

There are several theories concerning the origin of the term "Shiner." One of the most plausible is that these Irishmen—like the Irish "Bowery Boys" of New York—soaped the long hair at their temples to make it shiny; both groups were called "Shiners."

An article in the Toronto *Daily Globe* of 25 December 1856, from their Ottawa correspondent, who signed himself "Chaudiere," said of the Shiners:

> At first these ruffians acted independently of one another, and without concert—jeering and insulting the defenceless and unprotected, and occasionally "pounding an enemy." Anon, they moved about in couples or small gangs, like wild beasts, seeking whom they might destroy. As one party commenced a murderous attack on a passer-by, other gangs, as if by common instinct, immediately rushed to the scene of the slaughter, to witness "the sport," perhaps to cheer their fellows on, and perchance to prevent succour reaching the unfortunate.
>
> ...these fiends in human form have been known to fill unfortunate females, or the innocent companion of the wandering Indian, with liquor, till they become insensible, and after indulging their beastly lusts to satiety, proceed to strip their victims naked, and lay them out in a public place, and arrange a number of lighted candles around, so as fully to expose the naked body of their victim, and otherwise indulge themselves in acts of brutality and blasphemy sufficient to horrify any but the most depraved and abandoned villain.

The Shiners became a cohesive force in the autumn of 1834, when they came under the leadership of a timber baron named Peter Aylen. Their new "king" was a self-made man who had come to Canada as a cabin boy and jumped ship when the vessel docked at Quebec. Aylen later made his way up the Ottawa, and entered the employ of Philemon Wright. In 1816 he went into the timber business for himself. By 1834 Peter Aylen had extensive lumbering operations on the Gatineau, Bonnechère, and Madawaska rivers, as well as real estate holdings in Upper and Lower Canada, including a mansion in Bytown and a substantial home in Aylmer.

Aylen had obvious appeal to the Shiners, for in addition to his leadership qualities he provided them with jobs and lavish hospitality. Why Aylen, a successful businessman and member of the "establishment," chose to lead the Shiners is more obscure, but the evidence suggests that he used them as an instrument to wield personal power.

Peter Aylen's right-hand man was Andrew Leamy, a prosperous mill owner, after whom Leamy Lake in Hull is named. His bodyguard was a hulking brute named Martin Hennessey. Among others he relied upon were the seven Slavin brothers, "Jimmy the Wren," a dead shot with a stone at any distance, and Thomas Burke, whose forte was murder. As for the Shiner king, "armed to the teeth, he would parade himself on the highways and in the 'groggeries' with the air of a despot—a bold wild reckless outlaw, for whom nothing was too hot or too heavy, who lived without the pale of society, and who neither feared God nor honoured the King."

In the spring of 1835 the Shiners escalated their campaign of terror and intimidation against the French raftsmen. Rafts were seized at the Chaudière Falls and the crews severely beaten. The Shiners took control of the Union Bridge, which they used as a site for ambush, tossing their victims into the Great Kettle. The purpose of these actions was to force the French off the river so that the Shiners could take over their jobs. Initially the French reacted passively to these outrages, but in July they retaliated by destroying a raft manned by Shiners as it passed behind the island of Montreal. However, this was one of their few victories. The French were not properly organized to resist their tormentors, although they had one formidable champion in the person of Joe Montferrand.

Joseph Montferrand, the son of a North West Company fur trader, was born in Montreal in 1802. While still in his teens he gained fame as a boxer, and for prodigious feats of strength. He was a handsome man of six feet, two inches, with brown hair and blue eyes. Montferrand was not a brawler and he never fought for money, but he could certainly use his fists. On one occasion he defeated the heavyweight champion of the Royal Navy in a seventeen-round bout held at the Queen's Wharf in Quebec. In 1829 Joe Montferrand became a rafting foreman for Gilmour &

Company on the Ottawa River. This brought him in frequent contact with the Shiners. There are many tales concerning Mont-ferrand's role in these engagements, and it is difficult to separate fact from fancy. Yet one thing is certain, Joe was more than a match for any Shiner. He was also a genuine Canadian folk hero. Mont-ferrand died peacefully in Montreal on 4 October 1864.

The gentry of Upper Town ignored Aylen and his gang until the Shiner king assaulted and seriously injured Daniel McMartin, a respected lawyer from Perth. Aylen was arrested, placed in the garrison jail, and then escorted under heavy guard to Perth, where he served a short sentence. In the meantime the Shiners, knowing that McMartin was convalescing in Chitty's Hotel (near the corner of Wellington and Kent streets), tried to burn down the establish-ment. Only the reading of the Riot Act, and the calling out of the garrison guard prevented a conflagration.

By midsummer of 1835 the situation in Bytown was completely out of control. The Shiners did as they pleased and no one stopped them. This state of affairs was due to a lack of law enforcement. The garrison troops, except in special circumstances, restricted their activities to the protection of government property. The handful of magistrates and their battered deputies were hopelessly outnum-bered. In addition, the magistrates were divided because Daniel O'Connor, one of their most effective members and the only Irish-man on the slate, sympathized with the Shiners. O'Connor—after whom a street leading to Parliament Hill is named—was a well-educated man who to this point had been a pillar of the ruling class. He first showed his bias for his countrymen in the Galipaut affair.

Two years earlier Martin Hennessey had paid a call on Joseph Galipaut, the owner of a Lower Town tavern much frequented by French raftsmen. Due to the fact that Hennessy was mounted on his horse when he entered the tavern, Galipaut interpreted his visit as a hostile act and shot Hennessey in the eye. After that Galipaut's days were numbered. In June of 1835 another Shiner, Matthew Power, broke into Galipaut's tavern to take revenge. Power was also felled by a ball from Galipaut's pistol. Magistrate O'Connor was called in, and proceeded to imprison Galipaut for assault. While Galipaut languished in a garrison cell, the Shiners burned his tavern to the ground. As soon as he was released, Galipaut fled from Bytown with his family.

By late summer it was clear that the Shiner tactics of intimidation and harassment were taking effect. George Hamilton of Hawkesbury complained to officials about the "bravoes & ruffians" being imported by some lumbermen, while Ruggles Wright lamented to Hamilton that ". . . we shant [sic] be able to engage Canadiens to go into the interior of the Country at any price."

In October of 1835 a meeting of concerned citizens was convened in Upper Town to form a vigilante group known as the Bytown Association for the Preservation of the Peace. More than two hundred volunteers enlisted in the Association, and a system of nightly patrols was instituted. This helped matters somewhat, but the Association was hampered by a lack of co-operation from the Lieutenant-Governor, Sir John Colborne, who would not issue them arms or permit them to lodge offenders in the garrison jail.

The year 1836 was marked by continued Shiner violence. Assault and battery, rape, murder, and arson were practised with vicious efficiency. Explosives were also used, but were not always as successful. "Chaudiere" in his *Daily Globe* article of 25 December 1856, recounted an attempt by Shiners to blow up the house of John Little, who lived at the Hog's Back:

> They employed a keg of powder, and the villain who applied the match was blown up with it. His remains lay there all blackened and seared as they were, for some time, and no one of his confederates would acknowledge him, until a little shoemaker came along, who recognized the shoes he had on, which he had made for him. The deceased was known as "hairy Barney," a very troublesome man in life, and an unfortunate man in death.

The Shiner tide crested in 1837. On 2 January Peter Aylen led a gang of his men to the township meeting, which was being held in Stanley's Tavern, Kent Street. His plan was to take control of Bytown by having a slate of Shiners elected. When Aylen stood up and demanded that everyone in attendance be allowed to vote, he was reminded by the chairman, James Johnston, that only men owning unmortgaged property in Nepean had this privilege. The Shiner king's response was predictable. He started a riot. In the ensuing bedlam James Johnston was singled out for a special beating.

On 14 February, St. Valentine's Day, the wife and daughters of a prominent Orangeman named Hobbs were attacked in their sleigh by a gang of Shiners. The girls were savagely pummelled, and Mrs. Hobbs, who was pregnant, was also beaten. In trying to escape Mrs. Hobbs caught her coat in the woodwork of the sleigh and was dragged by the frightened horses. As she skidded along the frozen ground, the Shiners ran alongside and belaboured her with sticks. The Hobbses were eventually released, but the Shiners kept the sleigh and team. The next morning Mr. Hobbs found his horses wandering aimlessly in the snow. Both animals had their ears and tails cut off; one had a gaping hole in its side.

A week later, on 21 February, a contingent of heavily armed country people arrived in Bytown and told the magistrates that they had come to help arrest a man named Gleeson who was responsible for the outrage. The Shiner leaders, and Magistrate O'Connor, then spread a rumour that the Orangemen were coming to attack the Roman Catholics. This ploy (which was used on other occasions) brought the law-abiding Catholics in Bytown to the aid of the Shiners. The stage was set for a pitched battle. Fortunately the magistrates were able to pursuade the country people to go home, and bloodshed was averted. In the confusion Gleeson was quietly arrested.

That evening it was rumoured that Hobbs was spending the night at the home of James Johnston. Johnston, a popular merchant and publisher of the short-lived *Bytown Independent and Farmer's Advocate,* was an outspoken critic of the Shiners. Peter Aylen, who hated Johnston (as well as Hobbs), marshalled his gang and marched on Johnston's residence. The Shiners were unable to force their way into the house, nor could they put it to the torch, because it was made of stone. After milling around for some time they fired shots through the windows and then dispersed.

The 17th of March, St. Patrick's Day, was fraught with danger but passed without incident. This was due to the good influence of Father Cannon, the Roman Catholic priest, and the swearing-in of extra constables by the magistrates.

On 24 March three Shiners attempted to waylay James Johnston, but were forced to withdraw when Johnston drew a pair of pistols. The would-be assassins, Thomas Burke, Patrick O'Brien, and James McDonald, had been commissioned by Peter Aylen to kill Johnston. (Aylen may have felt diffident about undertaking the task himself because at that time he was awaiting trial for inciting three riots and assaulting an old man on the Richmond Road). The next night, the three Shiners cornered Johnston on the Sappers Bridge, which spanned the Canal between the present-day Chateau Laurier Hotel and the War Memorial. In an effort to elude them Johnston jumped over the parapet to the ground twelve feet below. When he landed, he sank into soft snow up to his armpits and was helpless. While McDonald and O'Brien fired pistols at their quarry from the bridge, Burke clambered down the bank to finish Johnston off with the weighted butt of his whip. Burke nearly succeeded—Johnston's skull was fractured in two places—before some townspeople came to the rescue of the beleagured man.

Bytown was incensed at this outrage and the three Shiners were arrested. Aylen boasted they would never stand trial. This pledge nearly came true; the Shiners stormed the Perth jail and freed their comrades, who then fled to the United States. The three men were recaptured in Upper New York State on 3 May and subsequently served prison terms for attempted murder.

The attack on Johnston marked the beginning of the end for the Shiners. In Bytown the sense of apathy and helplessness on the part of the citizens was changing. The forces of law and order were on the increase. This was especially evident at the close of the year, when the Mackenzie and Papineau rebellions broke out in Upper and Lower Canada. There were no skirmishes in Bytown, but the insurrections had the effect of uniting the townspeople. On 11 December 1837 William Stewart said in a letter to one of his Montreal suppliers: "This week has been one of excitement here, we had a public meeting, there are about four hundred men who took the oath of allegiance, the most of whom turn out voluntary to drill every day, and we mount Guard every night over the Gov't property."

Not only in Bytown but also in the surrounding communities people rallied to the colours. William Stewart's brother Neil, a political leader of the Scots in Glengarry, wrote to his brother on 16 December 1837:

>...I have been pretty much engaged on duty for the last week to receive *arms* and ammunition from Kingston for the St. Andrew Militia... A great political meeting was held at my house 10 days ago from 7 to 800 attended which showed our opponents in this quarter their own insignificance.... You must send me your *Bonnet* and feather and pipes also, they would be of the utmost service to our highlanders—those pipes must not be kept locked if they would be the means of doing good and stirring people up to their duty in these critical times.

With patriotism running high, and most of the able-bodied men in Bytown enlisted in the militia, no one was prepared to tolerate the

Shiners. Peter Aylen, a shrewd man, realized that his "reign" was over. He sold his house in Bytown and slipped across the river to Aylmer. This move put him out of reach of the law because Aylmer, being in Lower Canada, was a different jurisdiction.

James Johnston recovered from his bludgeoning and later entered politics. After stepping down in favour of Stewart Derbyshire in the Bytown election of 1841, he ran for the County of Carleton seat in 1844 and won easily. His tenure in the Parliament of the United Canadas was a brief one. Shortly after being elected, he got into a drinking bout with a fellow member, Dr. "Tiger" Dunlop, who dared Johnston to resign his seat. Johnston marched into the house and did so. The next day when he tried to enter the Assembly he was banished by the Speaker. Johnston contested the ensuing by-election but was badly defeated.

Andrew Leamy, Aylen's chief lieutenant, turned his full attention to his sawmills in Hull and died a rich man.

Martin Hennessey, Aylen's bodyguard, died from a poker blow on the head which he received while attempting to roast an opponent in the hearth of a Lower Town tavern.

In time Peter Aylen underwent an astounding change of character and became a model figure in the town of Aylmer. He died a wealthy and respected man in 1868, and was fondly remembered by the children of that day for his gentle nature. Aylen had six sons, all of whom became professional men. The Aylen name in Ottawa legal circles has been synonymous with integrity for more than a century. At this writing, Peter Aylen's great grandson, John A. Aylen, Q.C., is the oldest practising lawyer in the city of Ottawa. John A. Aylen's grandson David Aylen, is the fifth generation of Aylens to practise law in the Ottawa area.

Most of the rank-and-file Shiners subsequently became law-abiding citizens. Many of their descendants have distinguished themselves in battle—on behalf of their country—as well as in sports, business, and the professions.

The square timber trade offered a glittering opportunity for profit, but it was also a high-risk business. A fundamental problem within the industry was the compulsion to pyramid profits. If an operator had a good year, he automatically increased his cutting—and his borrowing—the following year. This practice was similar to a gambler playing "double or nothing" until he lost. Because of the unstable nature of the timber market, and the lemming-like penchant for everyone to overproduce on the heels of a good year, timber prices frequently collapsed. One bad year, or two at most, was all that was needed to wipe a lumberman out.

The square timber trade contained numerous perils, some of which were beyond the control of the operator. The spring breakup was an annual risk. If the winter was mild, or if the snow melted gradually, the flow of water in the tributaries could be insufficient to carry the logs to the mainstream. Storms on the Ottawa or St. Lawrence River could easily wreck a raft: in 1856 more than one million feet of square timber and deals washed up on the beaches of Anticosti island. Rafts sent to Quebec to fulfill a firm contract could be severely reduced in value because of damage incurred on the journey, or unfair valuation by cullers in the employ of the buyer. When a lumberman sent a raft to Quebec on speculation, he was faced with the dilemma of whether to anchor in the St. Lawrence or a privately owned cove. If he chose the former, his raft could be shifted by the tide, and was also a hazard to shipping. In the latter case no other merchant would bid for his timber, which left him at the mercy of the cove owner. Cove owners were rarely noted for their philanthropy.

Both the lumbermen and the environment would have benefited if there had been a central body to monitor production and to control cutting. The government could have played a significant role in this connection, but restricted its efforts to the issuance of licences and the collection of tolls. (Toll money from the passage of sticks down the Ottawa was meant to be applied to improving the river and its tributaries, but the funds were not always used for this purpose.) The lumbermen in the Ottawa region did get together, in 1836, and formed the Ottawa Valley Lumber Association, but this group was mainly concerned with cost-sharing of timber slides. In a sense the lumberman was his own worst enemy. Being fiercely independent, he would not tolerate government interference, and he preferred to live by the law of the jungle than to work in concert with his competitors.

Most of the lumbermen eventually came to financial grief. Philemon Wright's firm teetered along the edge of bankruptcy from its inception until is closed its doors in 1842. The Hamilton brothers' operation went into receivership in 1822, managed to survive the crisis, and then suffered financial woes in the ensuing years. Even Peter Aylen, who retained most of his winnings from the trade, was jailed in L'Orignal (a village on the Ottawa River fifty miles east of the capital) by his creditors, and had to remain there until he sold enough assets to pay his debts.

By midcentury many of the old names in the trade had disappeared. At that time the largest operators on the Ottawa were John Egan, Allan Gilmour, and Joseph Aumond.

In 1830 Egan was a storekeeper in Aylmer selling supplies for the shanties. In 1838 he entered the trade as a lumberman when he founded the firm of John Egan & Co. His business flourished with the aid of contracts and financing from the Quebec firm of LeMesurier, Tilson & Co. Within a decade Egan had approximately one hundred shanties on the upper Ottawa and its tributaries. In a good year he would employ up to four thousand men and send more than fifty rafts to Quebec. Despite the scope of his operations and his close connection with Quebec buyers, he was vulnerable to a drop in the price of timber. Several bad years for the trade in the late 1840s and early 1850s, crippled him financially. In 1854 he went bankrupt.

Joseph Aumond started his career as a shopkeeper in Bytown in 1828. He turned to lumbering about the same time as John Egan and also enjoyed a meteoric rise. In the early 1840s Aumond's company employed up to one thousand men and sent as many as forty rafts to Quebec in a season. The depression years of 1848-49 resulted in heavy losses for Aumond, affectionately known as "Grand Joe," and he never recovered.

Gilmour & Co., founded by Allan Gilmour from Glasgow, was the second largest concern in the Ottawa Valley. Gilmour & Co. not only controlled extensive timber limits but also owned its own cove in Quebec. In the 1840s this firm shrewdly shifted the thrust of its operations from square timber to sawn lumber. As a result the company remained on the Ottawa scene for nearly a century. In 1891 the Hughson family bought into Gilmour & Co. and the name was changed to Gilmour & Hughson.

The decline of the square timber trade started in 1842, when Britain removed the Preferential Tariff and turned once again to the Baltic countries. It was accelerated as steel came into common use for ship hulls and steam replaced sail as a means of locomotion.

Before this form of lumbering came to an end, it consumed approximately one million trees in the Ottawa region and denuded miles of forest. Many of the operators were commercial buccaneers who indulged in wasteful cutting practices with no thought for the morrow. Yet these men were willing to accept risk, and they exploited the resource at a time when there was no other viable export commodity. Square timber sustained Bytown during its formative years and laid the base for the lucrative sawn lumber industry. This violent and tempestuous era is an important part of Ottawa's heritage.

On 5 June 1854 a Reciprocity Treaty was signed with the United States which allowed British North America to export sawn lumber to the republic free of duty. This agreement gave the lumber industry in the Ottawa Valley a much-needed stimulus and opened a new economic era. Attracted by the hydraulic lots on both sides of the Chaudière Falls, a group of American entrepreneurs came to Bytown between 1849 and 1853 to establish sawmills. These men were A. A. Baldwin, A. F. Bronson, J. M. Currier, M. K. Dickinson, E. B. Eddy, Captain J. J. Harris, C. B. Pattee, W. G. Perley, and L. Young. Bytowners referred to them as the "American Colony." In 1855, the year after the American market for sawn lumber was opened, the mills in Ottawa produced more than 39 million board feet.

Rafts of square timber were still seen on the Ottawa until the end of the century, but they were an increasingly rare sight. The last raft was sent down the river by J. R. Booth in June 1904. John Rudolphus Booth had come to Wright's settlement from the Eastern Townships in 1852. When he arrived, he had $9.00 in his pocket, and he started work as a carpenter on Andrew Leamy's new sawmill. In the intervening years he acquired his own mills, more than four thousand square miles of timber limits, and his own private railway. As one of the greatest lumber magnates in the world—and a connecting link between the old era and the new—it was fitting that Booth should dispatch the last raft of square timber.

8

Bytown Comes of Age

1843 to 1854

THE OUTSTANDING SOCIAL event in Bytown in 1843 was the Arch Riot. This occurred on Sunday, 20 August, the day after a visit to Bytown by the Governor-General, Sir Charles Metcalfe. As was the custom, ornamental arches had been erected on the main thoroughfares. One of these arches, heavily bedecked with tiger lilies, was sponsored by the Orange Order. Because the arch was stretegically located on the Rideau Street bridge over the By Wash, the Orangemen chose to leave their arch in place so that the Roman Catholics would be forced to pass beneath it on their way to Mass the next morning. To ensure that the plan would be successful, the arch was guarded by loyal Orangemen throughout the night. On Sunday an agitated crowd gathered at the bridge, and the magistrates were called to the scene. The magistrates then ordered the Orangemen to remove the offending structure, but the Orangemen refused to comply. When the magistrates enlisted the aid of bystanders to dismantle the arch, a riot ensued. Many of the participants in the resulting mêlée were battered and bruised, but fortunately no one was killed.

In May 1843 construction started on a wire suspension bridge at the Chaudière Falls to replace Colonel By's wooden truss bridge, which had rotted and collapsed in 1836. In the intervening years the two Canadas were linked by a one-horse ferry. This service was operated by a man named John Perkins, whose paddle-wheel craft was powered by a horse in the boat walking on a treadle. The new bridge was designed by one of Canada's foremost engineers, Samuel Keefer, and the masonary contractor was Alexander Christie, the son of Dr. A. J. Christie. The bridge was fashioned by anchoring steel cables to towers on each bank, from which members were slung to support the roadway. In its day the Second Union Bridge, with a clear span of 243 feet, was one of the finest structures on the continent. It was opened on 17 September 1844 "amidst the discharge of cannon, the waving of flags, and the cheers of the multitude."

In the autumn of 1843 William Harris, a leading liberal and a prominent member of the Reform Party, founded a newspaper called the *Packet*. Six years later the *Packet* was sold to a staunch Conservative named Robert Bell. On 22 February 1851 (four years before Bytown changed its name) the *Packet* was rechristened the *Ottawa Citizen*. In 1896 William Southam of Hamilton bought the paper and sent two of his sons, Wilson and Harry, to Ottawa to run it. Hugh Clark, the first editor for the Southams, wrote: "The change in management will have no effect whatsoever upon the *Citizen's* editorial policy. Conservative it was born and Conservative it would die, if such a thing as death were possible for the *Citizen*. Managements may come and managements may go; but the *Ottawa Citizen* goes on forever."

Editor Clark's confident words were partially correct. Today the *Citizen* is the oldest and largest newspaper in Ottawa, and its circulation continues to grow. The *Citizen* is popular not only in Ottawa but widely quoted throughout Canada. Since 1897 the political views of the paper have run the gamut from Conservative to Social Credit, and are now somewhere left of centre. Both Harry and Wilson Southam were noted philanthropists who made significant gifts to the capital.

On 9 December 1843 the Ordnance Vesting Act was passed by the government of the Province of Canada. This Act released the Ordnance lands in Upper and Lower Town for sale. The effect of this legislation was to promote growth and investment in Bytown. It also radically altered the balance of political power because it created a whole new class of property owners, primarily French and

Irish, who supported the Reform Party. Up until 1843 the Conservative gentry had dominated the polls.

In 1844 Bytown's population of approximately five thousand souls was evenly divided between Roman Catholics and Protestants. Of the Roman Catholics, 60 percent were Irish, the balance French. At that time Bytown was part of the Roman Catholic Diocese of Kingston, and the spiritual needs of the community had been served by a succession of secular priests.

In 1844 the Oblate Order of Mary Immaculate established a mission in Bytown with two French priests, Father Pierre-Adrien Telmon and Father Damase Dandurand. These were excellent men, but because they were French, they aroused the hostility of the Irish parishioners, who felt they were being neglected. Shortly after Fathers Telmon and Dandurand arrived in Bytown, an Irish delegation petitioned Bishop Phelan of Kingston to send them an Irish priest. Bishop Phelan passed on their request to the Oblate Order, but was advised that the Oblates did not have a qualified man in Canada. The months dragged by and the situation became so critical that the future of the Oblate mission was in jeopardy. During this difficult period a bilingual Oblate of great tact and diplomacy, Father Joseph Bruno Guigues was temporarily posted to Bytown, and Bishop Phelan made a number of visits to pacify the Irish majority.

On 16 September 1845, a hastily ordained thirty-nine-year-old priest, Father Michael Molloy, arrived in Bytown from Ireland. On the way Molloy was nearly killed when he failed to heed a warning to duck when the barge he was riding passed under a low bridge; the impact pitched him head first into the hold and damaged his hearing. At the outset Father Telmon was less than impressed with his new assistant and reported that Molloy was no more familiar with the Breviary than the Koran. Despite Father Molloy's modest credentials, he soon earned the affection and respect of the entire community. During his forty-four-year tenure he founded the House of Mercy, a refuge for fallen women (who were known as "Father Molloy's girls"), a boardinghouse for single women, a home for the aged, and the Irish Catholic Temperance Society.

Of equal importance, Father Molloy's presence reconciled the Irish with the Oblates, which permitted the fathers to get on with their good works. Since 1845 the Oblate Order has maintained congregations of English and French priests in the capital. Through the years the Oblate fathers have made an immense contribution to the education and spiritual welfare of the city.

At the request of Bishop Phelan, the Grey Nuns of the Cross in Montreal sent six of their nuns to Bytown in 1845. Their arrival on 20 February was a cause for rejoicing; more than eighty sleighs and cutters sped down the frozen Ottawa to greet the sisters when their sleighs were sighted near Gatineau Point. These nuns—three English and three French—were the nucleus of a new religious community that subsequently became known as the Sisters of Charity of Ottawa. Their leader, and foundress, was a remarkable twenty-six-year-old woman named Sister Elisabeth Bruyère, who had formerly been a schoolteacher.

The first residence of the nuns was a one-story wooden house (measuring eighteen by twenty-four feet) on St. Patrick Street, which was built for them by Father Telmon. As soon as they were unpacked, Sister Bruyère set about fulfilling her obligations to tend the poor and to establish a hospital and a school. In a matter of days schoolrooms were arranged in a shed adjoining Notre Dame Cathedral (on St. Patrick Street), which was still in the course of construction. This school—the first bilingual learning institution in Ottawa—opened on 3 March 1845.

At the beginning of May, Father Telmon purchased another house for the sisters, which was identical to, and just fifty feet from, their convent. This dwelling was speedily converted into a seven-bed hospital. (Up until that time the twenty-bed garrison hospital was only available to the citizens of Bytown on an emergency basis.) The nuns' hospital opened its doors on 10 May 1845. One of the first patients was a twenty-year-old Negro from Bermuda with a gangrenous foot that had been frozen while he was working in a lumber camp. This young man was a favourite of the nuns, who called him "Boule-de-Neige" ("Snowball"). Dr. Edward Van Cortlandt, the surgeon of the garrison hospital, and Bytown's best-qualified medical practitioner, donated his services to the nuns' hospital for the first year.

By the middle of 1846 it was apparent that both the school and the hospital were too small for the needs of the community. Sister Bruyère petitioned the Marquis of Anglesey (Commissioner of Ordnance Lands) for property on which to build larger facilities and a mother house for the order. In December the Sisters of Charity were granted six lots of Ordnance land on the north side of Water Street (renamed Bruyère Street).

In 1847 Bytown was swept by a typhus epidemic. Typhus is a contagious disease that is transmitted by body lice, and is characterized by high fever, a rash, and delirium. This disease, also known as prison fever, or ship fever, was brought to Canada by emigrants from the British Isles, most of whom were Irish people fleeing the Potato Famine. These unfortunates crossed the Atlantic in the fetid holds of timber ships, which became floating charnel-houses.

Bytown was given a month's warning of the impending scourge, and set up rude sheds on the west bank of the Canal, near the headlocks, where emigrants could be examined. The Sisters of Charity offered their newly acquired lots to the emigration agent, George Burke, as a site for a typhus hospital. This hospital was built with the aid of Father Telmon and his two curates. All the emigrants came by barge from Montreal down the St. Lawrence to Kingston, and thence to Bytown via the Rideau Canal. Upon arrival they were given a medical inspection by Dr. Van Cortlandt at the Canal sheds, and seriously ill people were transferred to the typhus hospital.

The first typhus case sent to the nuns was a child named Mary Cunningham. She was admitted on 5 June, in a semiconscious state, and was so filthy that her clothes had to be cut off from the back. Three days later she died. The number of typhus victims soon swelled to a flood, and a wing was added to the hospital. Even with the additional beds, twenty-three patients were forced to sleep out in the rain one night. A letter from Sister St. Joseph describes the initial treatment:

> When they arrived, we cut their hair, we shaved the men, we washed them and changed their clothes. When their bath was over and they saw themselves in a clean bed, many of them would say they were not sick any more, because they found themselves so comfortable. It is true that they must have felt some relief when we had removed from their body a plateful of lice, each as large as a grain of wheat and as red as fire.

More than three thousand emigrants landed in Bytown during June and July of that sweltering summer. As the disease took its toll, the lay population withdrew (excepting the doctors), which left the Protestant and Catholic clergy to care for the sick. This situation became so acute that at night the nuns had to drive the dead in carts to the cemetery for burial by Father Telmon and Brother Sweeney. Many of the stricken were never admitted to hospital. Father Dandurand recounted:

One summer evening, around 9 o'clock, I was called to assist a family who were lying on the lawn of what is now Parliament Hill. The father, after his confession, gave me a key with the following instructions: "I have six children who may all be dead. If by chance, one survives, give him this key to open the trunk which is by my side and which contains family documents." I then assisted the mother, who died shortly after. Around her were five dead children. I looked for the sixth child, when at some distance, under the moonlight, I discovered a 15 month baby who smiled at me with open arms. . . .

To stop the flow of emigrants the Rideau Canal was closed to all traffic on 2 August. During the next five months the scourge gradually ran its course. In that year the sisters treated 532 typhus cases; 172 of these died. Because of their constant exposure to the disease, seventeen of the twenty-one nuns came down with typhus, as did Fathers Telmon, Molloy, and Dandurand, but all recovered. (Father Dandurand, the first Canadian Oblate, live to be 102.) Several of the hard-working Protestant ministers were also felled in the epidemic; the Reverend William Durie, the minister of St. Andrew's Church, died of typhus on 12 September 1847.

At the conclusion of the typhus epidemic, the lazaretto on Bruyère Street was disinfected and converted into what is now the Ottawa General Hospital. Over the years the original structure has grown into a massive stone complex with more than five hundred beds. Until 1959 the Sisters of Charity had sole responsibility for the Ottawa General, but since that time it has become a provincially assisted institution under the aegis of the Ontario Hospital Commission. The Sisters of Charity have retained title to the land and buildings but now run the hospital with the help of a lay board of trustees.

Mother Bruyère's two-room school in the shed beside Notre Dame Cathedral not only started bilingual education in Bytown but also laid the foundation for Ottawa's separate school system. The order she founded—which many people still call the Grey Nuns— has provided inestimable service to the community in the areas of health, welfare, and education. The Sisters of Charity are the largest single religious congregation in Ottawa.

In 1847 the legislature of the Province of Canada passed an Act that incorporated Bytown as a town. This Act gave Bytown self-government by permitting the citizens to elect their own mayor and seven councillors. Lower Town was divided into two wards, each of which elected two councillors, while Upper Town was designated a single ward with three councillors. In the 1847 election Lower Town returned John Scott, Thomas Corcoran, Henry Friel, and John Bedard; Upper Town elected Nicholas Sparks, John Lewis, and Nathaniel Blaisdell. At the first council meeting John Scott was chosen as mayor. All town business was enacted on the basis of a majority decision of the mayor and his council.

Two years later, in 1849, Bytowners were stunned to learn that Queen Victoria had vetoed the Act of Incorporation. This meant that the actions of the mayor and council in the preceding years were invalid. It is believed that Queen Victoria vetoed the Act on the advice of the military, who did not wish civilian interference in a garrison town. By the time word filtered through to Bytown of this development, Nicholas Sparks's 104-acre parcel (which was expropriated for a moat) had been returned and the Act was being resubmitted for the Queen's approval. On New Year's Day, 1850, Bytown was incorporated as a town for the second and final time.

Bytown became the seat of a new Roman Catholic diocese in 1847. The first bishop of the diocese was Joseph Bruno Guigues, OMI, who was consecrated in the unfinished Notre Dame Cathedral on 30 July 1848.

Shortly after taking his post, Bishop Guigues founded St. Joseph's College of Bytown, a bilingual school staffed by his fellow Oblates. In 1849 the name of this institution was shortened to the College of Bytown, and changed again in 1861 to the College of Ottawa. In 1866 the school was granted university status. Today the University of Ottawa occupies eighty-three acres in Sandy Hill. Its campus reflects both a vigorous building program and the legacy of the past. Interspersed among grey painted houses awaiting demolition are modern structures as well as solid stone buildings from an earlier era.

The University of Ottawa tries to maintain an equal division between French and English courses for its 10,000 students. It has the only law faculty outside the Province of Quebec that grants both a Licentiate in Quebec Law (Droit Civil) and a Bachelor of Laws degree. The medical faculty offers postgraduate degrees and is active in medical research; the Ottawa Civic and the Ottawa General are major teaching hospitals affiliated with the university. Its Child Study Centre, which specializes in treating children with learning disabilities is recognized throughout the world.

Sir John A. Macdonald, the Father of Confederation and first Prime Minister of the Dominion of Canada. *(PAC #C 2831)*

Thomas D'Arcy McGee, the Canadian statesman of Irish descent who was assassinated on Sparks Street by a Fenian sympathizer in 1868. *(PAC #C 51976)*

RIGHT: Second Union Bridge across the Chaudière Falls, designed by Samuel Keefer and completed in 1844. *(PAC #C 20644)*
FAR RIGHT: View of the Chaudière District from Parliament Hill, circa 1870. The huge piles of lumber on both banks were a constant fire hazard. *(PAC #C 6589)*

FAR LEFT: J. R. Booth—circa 1925—standing beside a trainload of timber from his vast limits. *(Historical Society of Ottawa)*

TOP LEFT: One of Booth's square timber rafts in a cove near Sillery on the St. Lawrence in 1891. Timber "droghers" in background. *(PAC #6073)*

LEFT: Log jam on the Gatineau River circa 1900. Long rowboat was an especially designed craft known as a "pointer." *(PAC #PA 8919)*

Feu-de-Joie being delivered by troops in front of the unfinished Houses of Parliament, May 1868. The centre tower was later capped with a dome. *(PAC #C 2837)*

The architectural staff of the Parliament Buildings on site circa 1860. Thomas Fuller is seated far right; behind him (wearing a pill-box hat) is King Arnoldi. *(OMA #CA 0161)*

The Rideau Falls circa 1880, showing the "curtain" effect of the water. *(PAC #C 21796)*

Dufferin Bridge under construction in 1874. The Lay By or turning bay for canal traffic may be seen in the background. *(PAC #C 493)*

The Honourable Thomas Ahearn, Ottawa's electrical genius and industrial magnate. *(PAC #PA 12222)*

Samuel Bingham, one of the city's most charitable and best-loved mayors. *(OMA #CA 0936)*

Ice palace on Nepean Point, February 1895. *(OMA #CA 0060)*

Rideau Street in 1898, looking west toward the Parliament Buildings. *(PAC #C 1585)*

Lady Aberdeen's May Court fête at Rideau Hall in 1898. This gathering was the genesis of the May Court Clubs of Canada. *(PAC #PA 28022)*

Lord Dufferin, standing at left with broom raised, in the Rideau Hall curling rink circa 1875. *(PAC—Topley Collection)*

In 1965 the University of Ottawa was reorganized and became a provincially assisted institution. At this writing, the university is guided by the Reverend Dr. Roger Guindon, OMI, and a thirty-two-person board of governors. The University of Ottawa owes much to its founder, Bishop Guigues, and the Oblate fathers who served this institution for more than a century.

Although Bytown became more civilized after the arrival of the Sisters of Charity and the Oblate fathers, it was still a frontier town. An altercation between two of Bytown's leading citizens on 18 August 1848, resulted in the following notice being prominently displayed in Upper and Lower Town:

TO THE PUBLIC.

HAVING been grossly and wantonly insulted yesterday, in the Streets of Bytown, by Edward V. Cortlandt, and having promptly demanded from that individual (through a friend) the usual satisfaction, which that cowardly miscreant, without assigning any reason, refused to grant.

I have no other course left to me, but to proclaim to the world, and I now do so, that *Edward Van Cortlandt, Surgeon,* of this place, is a mean and contemptible liar, slanderer, and ruffian; a miserable, drivelling, cowardly scoundrel, a pitiful poltroon, and utterly unworthy of the notice of any one having pretensions to the character of a gentleman.

R. HERVEY, Jr.

Bytown, Saturday Morning,
19th August, 1848.

Dr. Van Cortlandt came to Bytown in 1832 as surgeon to the garrison and continued in practice until the 1870s. He was a brilliant man with many interests, including history, geology, and literature. One of his contemporaries described him as being "odd and eccentric in manner and dress, brusque and sharp, and often rough in speech; but beneath his rough exterior there was always a kind and sympathetic nature."

Diligent research has failed to reveal the cause of the dispute between Hervey and Dr. Van Cortlandt, but neither party suffered any lasting harm. Robert Hervey was elected mayor of Bytown the following year, and when Dr. Van Cortlandt died (in 1875), he was given a final salute by the Ottawa Field Battery.

In 1849 feelings ran high in Bytown between supporters of the Reform Party and the Conservatives, or Tories, over the Rebellion Losses Bill. That year, Lord Elgin, the Governor-General, had approved a bill proposed by the Reform Party that indemnified everyone (except those convicted of treason) for losses sustained in the Papineau-Mackenzie uprisings of 1837. Montreal Tories were so incensed at the passage of the bill that they burned the Parliament buildings, and stoned Lord Elgin's carriage. This prompted the British Government to look for another site for the capital of the Province of Canada.

When word reached Bytown that Lord Elgin planned to visit the town that autumn, there was great excitement. The Reformers wanted to extend a royal welcome, but the Tories felt the Queen's representative should be ignored. Moderates in both camps saw the wisdom of a nonpartisan reception, which could favourably influence the Governor-General into choosing Bytown as the new capital. A committee of moderates approached the mayor, Robert Hervey, Jr., and asked him to call a public meeting to draft a greeting for Lord Elgin. Hervey, a rabid Tory, refused to comply, so two Reform councillors, Charles Sparrow and Joseph Turgeon, exercised their prerogative and called a meeting in the By Ward market for Monday, 17 September. Mayor Hervey retaliated by calling a rival meeting, to be held at the Upper Town market on Wednesday, 19 September.

Both factions turned out for the meeting in Lower Town on Monday. The meeting opened with a proposal that former Mayor John Scott take the chair. This was countered by a proposal from the floor that Mayor Hervey be chairman. A shouting match ensued, and Joseph Turgeon stood on a chair to restore order. Before he could do so, the chair was pulled out from under him. John Scott and several others mounted the platform to aid Turgeon and the platform collapsed. Pandemonium erupted, punches were thrown, and the mob spilled into the street. In a short time both sides had taken up positions in the buildings surrounding the market, and were sniping at each other with small arms and stones. Many people were injured; one man, David Borthwick, was killed by a ball in the chest. The fracas was eventually stopped by a company of garrison soldiers commanded by Brevet-Major F. W. Clements. While the troops were quelling the violence, the Tories reopened the meeting under the chairmanship of Dr. Hamnett Hill and passed a motion censuring the conduct of the Governor-General. This day is remembered in Ottawa's history as Stony Monday.

On Tuesday both factions rallied their forces for Mayor Hervey's meeting. On Wednesday morning more than a thousand Reformers gathered in Lower Town. Some of these men came from the Gatineau and from Wright's Town; on the way they had picked up several hundred small arms and three cannons from Wright's armoury. An even larger and better-armed force of Tories assembled in Upper Town. Many of these people were Orangemen who had come in from the adjacent townships. The only thing that separated the combatants was the Sappers Bridge. At midmorning, the Tories started for the bridge, led by a fife and drum band with the Orange Banner in the van. A mass of Reformers waited on the other side, near the corner of Sussex and Rideau streets, with two of their cannon—loaded to the muzzles with ox chain—trained on the bridge. At this ominous juncture Major Clements and his Royal Canadian Rifles stormed onto the bridge and faced both parties with fixed bayonets. It was a daring move because the troops could have been annihilated, but it worked. After milling around for some time the antagonists slowly dispersed.

The next day Major Clements took a mounted troop to impound any weapons left in Wright's armoury. On the way he caught Henry J. Friel, who was racing in a caleche to warn the Wrights. After arresting Friel, Clements went ahead with two subalterns, and was just in time to see three men—Andrew Leamy, Ruggles Wright, Jr., and Joshua Wright— wheeling a cannon out of the armoury. The men tried to turn the gun on Clements, but were subdued in a brief scuffle. Clements took his prisoners to Bytown, where Henry Friel was released. (Friel, for whom Friel Street is named, was subsequently elected mayor of Bytown in 1854 and was twice mayor of Ottawa.) The other three men were transferred to Wright's Town for justice. When they were brought before the magistrate, they defended their actions by saying they thought Clements and his officers were rioters *disguised* as soldiers.

The violence of Stony Monday and the near-bloodbath on Wednesday were more than a clash of political views; there was also an element of religious friction, and serious unrest in Bytown because of unemployment in the timber trade. As a result of the discord Lord Elgin postponed his visit for another three years.

On 1 January 1850 Bytown was officially confirmed a town. The mayor for that historic year was John Scott, who had the curious distinction of being the first mayor of Bytown twice (in 1847 and 1850). In March, Bytown was linked to Montreal by telegraph. This proved a blessing, but the connection with the outside world was a tenuous one. Within two weeks a reward was posted for the person or persons who had cut down several telegraph poles in Cumberland Township.

The year 1853 was one of peaceful developments in Bytown. The British Government agreed to let vessels from the United States use the facilities of the Rideau Canal, which boosted trade in Bytown, particularily the export of lumber. Lord Elgin visited Bytown in July, and was warmly received by the inhabitants. Late in the year the British Government gave the Canal to Canada West, and the garrison was withdrawn from Parliament Hill.

In 1850 a group of Bytowners and men from Prescott were granted a charter to build the Bytown & Prescott Railway. This line would run from Bytown to Prescott, where it would connect with the main railway between Montreal and Toronto, thus providing Bytown with rail access to most of the continent. Construction started at Prescott in 1851, but progress was extremely slow; it was not until December 1854 that the tracks were laid within sight of the Rideau River. At this point the company ran out of rails and money. With a stroke of genius—prompted by desperation—the chief promoter of the venture, Robert Bell, substituted wood scantlings made of three-inch maple capped with steel strapping, for iron rails. This temporary measure allowed him to complete the line along the east bank of the Rideau River, to the village of New Edinburgh. New Edinburgh, on the far side of the Rideau from Bytown, would seem an odd choice for a terminus, except for the fact that Thomas MacKay was a major shareholder, and the president of the line, John MacKinnon, was his son-in-law. On Christmas Day the *Oxford* steamed into New Edinburgh amidst cheers from the residents. The following summer a bridge was built across the Rideau, and the tracks were extended to the main terminus, which was at the corner of Sussex and McTaggart streets. (The bridge has gone, but the stone abutments may still be seen.)

From the outset, even though it was funded in part by Ottawa, Kemptville, and Prescott, the Bytown & Prescott Railway was a financial disaster. It also suffered from gross mismanagement. At one stage R. W. (later Sir Richard) Scott, the railway's solicitor, had to personally buy one of the company's locomotives at a sheriff's auction and lease it back to the line. In addition, the main terminus was badly located to serve the sawmills at the Chaudière Falls.

Aside from these shortcomings, the Bytown & Prescott Railway linked Bytown with the rest of North America, and it was a vital asset in the choice of a capital city. Without a railway Ottawa would not have stood a chance.

On New Year's Day, 1855, the town of Bytown was incorporated as the city of Ottawa. This change in name and status had been earnestly petitioned by Mayor Joseph Turgeon in 1853, and by Mayor Henry Friel in 1854. There were valid reasons for an elevation in status: in addition to its increasing importance, Bytown had a population of nearly ten thousand and paid more than 40 percent of the taxes for the twelve municipalities. There was also sound logic behind a change in name; Bytown was angling to be chosen capital of the Province of Canada, and it was believed that a different name—any name—would help people forget the community's appalling reputation.

9

The Struggle to Be Capital
1856 to 1867

IN SEPTEMBER, 1827 Lord Dalhousie stood on Barracks Hill and said to Colonel By: "I may not live so long, but whoever lives to see the Canadas united, will from this eminence, see the seat of the United Legislature." This proved a hollow prophecy: when the Act of Union took place in 1841, Kingston was designated capital of the Province of Canada.

However, the legislators soon became disenchanted with Kingston (later described by Sir Edmund Head as a "dead place") and voted to move the capital to Montreal. Montreal, in addition to being the commercial hub of British North America, was a much livelier location. It was so lively that in 1849 a mob of dissident Tories burned the houses of Parliament to the ground. Left in the street, the legislators hit upon another solution: the seat of government would be shared by Quebec City and Toronto, on alternating four-year terms. This nomadic system had one advantage in that it helped to enlighten regional bigots, but it was most unsettling to the public servants, it was expensive, and there was always the risk of government documents being lost. In 1856 the Legislative Assembly decided to put an end to the perambulations of Parliament and voted to make Quebec City the permanent capital. This plan was aborted by the Legislative Council, which refused to approve funds to start construction of Parliament buildings in Quebec. For the next eight months there was bitter debate (fuelled by parochial interests) on a suitable location for the seat of government. Finally, on 24 March 1857 Parliament turned the decision over to Queen Victoria:

To the Queen's Most Excellent Majesty
    May it please your Majesty,
      We, Your Majesty's dutiful and loyal Subjects, the Commons of *Canada*, in Parliament assembled, humbly approach Your Majesty for the purpose of representing:—
    That the interests of *Canada* require that the Seat of the Provincial Government should be fixed at some certain place.
    That we have resolved to appropriate the sums requisite for providing the necessary Buildings and accommodation for the Government and the Legislature at such place as Your Majesty may see fit to select.
    And we therefore humbly pray Your Majesty to be graciously pleased to exercise the Royal Prerogative by the selection of some one place as the permanent Seat of Government in *Canada*.

Upon being advised of Parliament's request, the Governor-General, Sir Edmund Head, immediately solicited memorials from the mayors of Montreal, Quebec, Kingston, Toronto, and Ottawa. These memorials, extolling the virtues of each city as capital, were then forwarded to Henry Labouchère, the Colonial Secretary. Ottawa's eloquent brief, signed by Mayor John Lewis and City Clerk William Lett, was written by the city's member of Parliament, Richard W. Scott.

When the Governor-General dispatched the city memorials to the Colonial Secretary, he also sent along a confidential memorandum stating his personal views on the subject. Head's lucid ten-point appreciation of the Canadian problem included the following observations:

Ottawa is the only place which will be accepted by the majority of Upper and Lower Canada as a fair compromise . . . Ottawa is, in fact, neither in Upper nor Lower Canada. Literally it is in the former; but a bridge alone divides it from the latter.
    The main objection to Ottawa is its wild position, and relative inferiority to the other cities named. But this wild position is a fault which every day continues to diminish. The present population may

be called 8,000 or 10,000, not of the best description.

A secondary consideration, but one of some importance as affecting the popularity of the choice, is the fact that the Rideau Canal, now handed over to the Provincial Government, would probably increase its traffic, and become more productive by the transfer of the seat of Government to Ottawa. At present this great work is a dead loss so far as money is concerned.

On the whole, therefore, I believe that the least objectionable place is the city of Ottawa. Every city is jealous of every other city except Ottawa. The second vote of every place (save, perhaps, Toronto) would be given for Ottawa.

Canadian folklore suggests that Queen Victoria chose Ottawa on a whim. One legend says that the Queen played "pin the tail on the donkey" with a map of Canada—and her finger landed on Ottawa. Another story says the Queen made her decision on the strength of a water-colour sketch of Parliament Hill by Lady Head. In fact, the Colonial Office selected Ottawa after a careful review of all the documents, including an unsolicited memorial from the city of Hamilton. The Colonial Office then presented their recommendation to the British Cabinet, with copies of the memorials and Sir Edmund Head's confidential memorandum. After the Cabinet agreed upon the site, the Colonial Office approached Queen Victoria for her approval. The Queen and her beloved consort Prince Albert took a keen interest in the question and also sought outside opinions. When Prince Albert sent the dossier with the Queen's signature to the Colonial Secretary (in December 1856) his covering note read: "I return the enclosed papers with very best thanks. Ottawa must indeed be a beautiful situation and all the detached descriptions must tend to confirm the impressions that the choice is the right one. We must now trust that the Province will look upon it in the same light, when it becomes known."

Because the Province of Canada was in the throes of an election, the Queen's decision was withheld until the end of the year. Formal notice was conveyed to Sir Edmund Head by Henry Labouchère in a letter dated 31 December 1857. The final paragraph of the letter stated: "I am commanded by the Queen to inform you that, in the judgement of Her Majesty, the City of Ottawa combines greater advantages than any other place in Canada for the permanent Seat of the future Government of the Province, and is selected by Her Majesty accordingly."

The Queen's choice was announced on 17 January 1858. Ottawans were jubilant, but their euphoria was soon tempered by critical comment from the other cities. In England an Oxford don named Goldwin Smith waspishly observed that Ottawa was "a sub-arctic lumber-village converted by royal mandate into a political cock-pit" (Smith's assessment contained just enough truth to make it sting). While an uncharitable reaction was expected from some quarters, it was assumed that because Parliament had asked the Queen to choose the capital, Parliament would also abide by her decision. However, this was not the case. Soon after Parliament was convened at Toronto under the new ministry of John A. Macdonald and George Etienne Cartier, the issue was put to a vote. On 28 July a motion that "the City of Ottawa ought not to be the permanent seat of Government of the Province" was carried by a majority of sixty-four to fifty. Macdonald and Cartier chose to interpret this vote as a want of confidence in their ministry, and resigned.

The Governor-General then called upon the leader of the Reform Party, George Brown (Macdonald's arch-enemy), to form a new government. Brown was unaware that Macdonald and Sir Edmund Head were working in concert, and promptly stepped into a trap. Expecting the Governor-General to dissolve Parliament for a new election, and in compliance with the rules governing a new ministry, Brown and his shadow cabinet resigned their seats. However, the Governor-General did not dissolve Parliament, and two days later the leaderless Reform Party was defeated by a want of confidence vote. The Governor-General then recalled Macdonald who, to avoid the same fate as Brown and his ministers, engaged in what has since become known as the "Double Shuffle." Taking advantage of a statute that exempted ministers who held a portfolio for less than thirty days from having to seek re-election, Macdonald appointed his old Cabinet to different ministries in the afternoon of 5 August 1858. A few minutes after midnight the second part of the shuffle took place; all the ministers shifted back to their *original* portfolios. While Brown and his colleagues fought by-elections, the Opposition was left in disarray.

The question of whether Ottawa should be the capital was not put to another vote for many months. In the interim an intense lobby for the city was mounted by Richard Scott, who was ably assisted by William F. Powell (the Conservative member for Carleton County) and George Etienne Cartier. Finally, on 10 December 1859, when Parliament was sitting in Quebec, the motion that had toppled the administration on 28 July 1858 was once again tested on the floor. An account in the Montreal *Pilot* captures the drama of the division:

> Two minutes must elapse after the ringing of the peal before the vote can be taken—they seem to all an age. The seats begin to change their look—well-known forms rush in to occupy them. From the gallery, we see the crowd of heads more closely packed than we ever noticed them before. Ah, Scott, of Ottawa, well may you nervously twitch your fingers, and look in fifty places for that division-list you put there not a moment since. Calm and unruffled though you try to look, you cannot deceive a close observer! Powell, of Carleton, thin and pale as death, wrapped in furs, walks in upright; but we see how great an effort it is for the sick man as he sinks down into his chair. . . . Silent as the ice-covered Bay outside, are all the members. With one impulse, yet without noise, the Opposition rise as Mr. Speaker invites the ayes to the amendment to declare themselves. . . . The numbers increase; fifty-seven, *fifty-eight,* FIFTY-NINE! . . . How will the tide of battle turn? For whom will be the victory? The Honourable Attorneys General Cartier and Macdonald lead the van. There are a few "hear, hears," when Dubord votes, a few when Holmes is found all right. But the anxiety becomes too great to cheer as we count sixty, sixty-one, sixty-two. Now we are safe. . . . Yeas 59; Nays 64— says the clerk. The Ottawa men shout hurrah! Scott goes into extacies of joy for once. A burst of cheering follows. . . .

Richard Scott's contribution to this victory cannot be overstressed. In addition to his role in the selection of the city as capital, he served as Mayor of Bytown in 1852, he held senior Cabinet positions in various administrations, and he was Government Leader in the Senate. In 1909, four years before his death, he was knighted for his service to the country. Sir Richard's grandson, Colonel Cuthbert Scott, Q.C., and his great grandson, David Scott, Q.C., are partners with Peter Aylen's descendants in the Ottawa law firm of Scott & Aylen.

In the spring of 1860 a public competition was held for the design of the Parliament building and the two flanking structures, which were originally designed as departmental buildings. More than fifteen designs, reflecting a variety of architectural periods, were submitted. The selection committee (headed by Samuel Keefer, who had built the second Suspension Bridge at the Chaudière, and was responsible for the government buildings being placed in an open quadrangle) chose the firm of Thomas Fuller and Chilion Jones for the Centre Block. The firm of Frederick Stent and Augustus

Laver won the design for the departmental buildings. Both sets of drawings specified stone buildings in a modern Gothic style.

One of the architects, Thomas Fuller, deserves special mention. Fuller, a recent emigrant from England, was considered to be the foremost Gothic architect in North America, and later designed the former state capital building in Albany, as well as several major buildings on the campus of Cornell University. In 1881 Thomas Fuller was appointed Chief Architect for the Dominion of Canada, a post that was also occupied by his son, Thomas W. Fuller, in the 1920s. His grandson, Thomas G. Fuller, who appears in a later chapter, is a prominent Ottawa building contractor.

In September 1859 tenders were called for the construction of the buildings, and the contracts were awarded just two months later. In December—barely a year after the decision against Ottawa had been reversed—the first sod was turned.

On 1 September 1860 the Prince of Wales (later Edward VII), laid the cornerstone of the Centre Block. It was the first time a prince of the realm had visited Ottawa, and the citizens made it a gala occasion. The cornerstone, a block of white marble quarried from the Upper Ottawa, was suspended from a gigantic Gothic arch. The inscription on the stone read:

> *This corner-stone of the building*
> *intended to receive the Legislature of Canada was laid by*
> *Albert Edward, Prince of Wales*
> *on the first day of September MDCCCLX*

Some journalists made carping remarks about the remote location of the capital, the ankle-deep mud in every direction, and the hesitant use of the word "intended" on the cornerstone. Notwithstanding these criticisms, both the Prince and the townspeople enjoyed the celebrations immensely.

The Prince, who was only nineteen at the time, was under the guardianship of the elderly Duke of Newcastle. Unbeknownst to the Duke, but with the approval of Cartier and Macdonald, on the night of the cornerstone-laying the Prince made an incognito tour of Lower Town. This clandestine adventure was arranged by Father Damase Dandurand, who not only accompanied the Prince, but also provided clothes for his disguise. Father Dandurand recounted that the Prince was fascinated by the antics of the populace, and kept repeating, "Charming! Charming!"

A year after the Prince's visit construction on the buildings came to an abrupt halt. By this time the £225,000 allocated for the total job had been spent, and it was estimated that the cost to completion would run to nearly three times that amount. The haste with which the project had been launched resulted in numerous problems: because proper soil tests had not been done, it was necessary to dig much deeper foundations; no provision had been made to heat or fireproof the buildings, and the logistics of transporting materials and water to the site were, for practical purposes, ignored.

For the next eighteen months the half-finished piles on Barracks Hill stood silent while a Royal Commission investigated the over-all situation. During this period 1700 workers were unemployed and many of the skilled artisans left the city. Ottawa suffered a severe depression. Once again there were grave doubts as to whether Ottawa would ever be the capital.

In January 1863 the Royal Commission tabled a report that attributed the cost overrun to administrative bungling and recommended that contracts be renegotiated with the original firms so that construction could resume. The report also included a recommendation that Thomas Fuller be appointed chief architect for all three buildings. The government accepted these recommendations, and work commenced within a matter of weeks.

By 1864 the government buildings were attracting favourable comment. George Brown wrote to his wife in August and said, "They are really magnificent. Fit for the British, French and Russian Empires, were they all confederated!" Dr. Stephen Sewell, who was both a prominent medical man and a literary figure in Ottawa, wrote in Mitchell's *City Directory* (1864-65): "These buildings are characterized by purity of art, manliness of conception, beauty of outline, and truthful nobility of detail. There is no modern gothic purer of its kind, or less sullied with fictitious ornamentation." Dr. Sewell was not simply being polite; he also described the public buildings in the *city* as being "remarkable for the laborious ugliness and want of taste which characterizes them all."

By the autumn of 1865 the buildings were sufficiently completed to allow the transfer of approximately 350 civil servants from Quebec City. The first session of the Legislature was convened on 8 June 1866. During this session Confederation, which had been proposed the year before at the Charlottetown and Quebec conferences, was the main topic of discussion. One of the points agreed upon by the legislators was that Ottawa would be the capital of the new federation—a decision influenced to no small degree by the fact that $2,600,000 had been poured into the Parliament buildings.

In December 1866 delegates from New Brunswick, Nova Scotia, Ontario, and Quebec met in London to work out final details for the union of the provinces into the Dominion of Canada. The result of their labours—the British North America Act—was sanctioned by the British Parliament on 29 March 1867, to take effect on 1 July 1867. Ottawans were greatly comforted by the clause in the Act that stated: "Until the Queen otherwise directs, the seat of Government shall be Ottawa."

The 1st of July 1867 was a momentous day for Ottawa. Five minutes past midnight a 101-gun salute boomed a farewell to the Province of Canada and welcomed in the new Dominion. As the echoes died away, the sky was lit by bonfires and fireworks.

Shortly after sun-up, people started to stream into the bunting-clad city, and everyone headed for Parliament Hill. By ten o'clock, when the Governor-General, Viscount Monck arrived, the hill was jammed with spectators and troops; more than eight hundred soldiers of the 43rd Carleton Battalion (popularly known as the Carleton Blazers), the Ottawa Provisional Brigade of Artillery, and the Civil Service Rifles were formed up in front of the Parliament buildings. The first ceremony was the swearing-in of Viscount Monck as Governor-General of the Dominion of Canada. After the oath was administered by the Chief Justice, the Governor-General, acting on behalf of the Queen, bestowed honours upon some of the fathers of Confederation. Prime Minister John A. Macdonald was made a Knight Commander of the Bath, while the Honourable Messrs. Cartier, Galt, Howland, McDougall, Tilley, and Tupper were created Companions of the Bath. The official party then went outside to watch a march-past of the troops. His Excellency—who took the salute—provided a striking contrast in the sea of bright colours, for he was the only one dressed in sombre clothing, and wore no badge of office or decorations of any kind.

The formal part of the ceremonies ended at noon with a cannon salute from Major's Hill and a *feu de joie* from the troops assembled on Parliament Hill. The rest of the day was devoted to athletic contests in various parts of the city, and to general merrymaking. When the shadows lengthened, everybody returned again to Parliament Hill where giant bonfires were lit and a splendid fireworks display took place.

Since that night, celebrating Dominion Day—now known as Canada Day—on Parliament Hill has become an annual tradition for many Ottawans.

10

The Transformation Begins
1855 to 1874

OTTAWA BECAME A civilized community during the last half of the nineteenth century. This evolution began on New Year's Day, 1850, when Bytown ceased to be a village and was incorporated as a town. William Pittman Lett, who served as city clerk from 1855 to 1891, noted in his *Short Panoramic View of Ottawa's History* (Citizen Press, 1877) that following the Stony Monday Riot in 1849 "... there has not since been a single fight worth looking at." Another giant step took place on 1 January 1855, when Bytown was incorporated as a city and changed its name to Ottawa. These milestones—plus the tantalizing prospect of being capital—awakened a sense of civic responsibility amongst the populace.

At that time City Hall was located on the upper floor of a wooden building on Elgin Street where the National Arts Centre now stands. This structure, erected on land donated by Nicholas Sparks, was originally intended to house the West Ward market. (A scheme that would have provided convenient shopping for residents of the neighbourhood, as well as enhancing the value of Sparks's adjacent real estate.) However, the By Ward market was so well established that few people patronized the new facility in Upper Town. After some difficulty Sparks persuaded the city to use the empty building.

The mayor and his ten-man council took the upper floor, while a unit of the fire brigade occupied the ground floor.

John B. Lewis—Ottawa's first mayor to be elected by the public rather than by his fellow councillors—did not pass any startling legislation in 1855, but he lent great dignity to the proceedings by wearing his newly acquired robe and chain of office. Downstairs, the fire company conducted itself with efficiency and decorum, except for an incident recorded in the *Bytown Gazette* of 22 June:

IMPROPER.—One of the city fire companies (the Ottawa No. 2) turned out on Monday evening last in full uniform, with their engine for practice. They dragged it down to the neighbourhood of the Sappers' bridge, near the canal wharf, where they could have a supply of water convenient. Having obtained this they exercised the engine for some time. Whoever directed the hose-pipe held it in such a position that it threw the water over the Sappers' bridge to the great annoyance of the passers-by. Two ladies, who happened to be going along the bridge at the time were completely drenched by it. The exertions of the firemen to render themselves efficient are certainly laudable, but they would be none the less valuable if not accompanied with such improper and unmanly conduct. When they turn out next time, we trust that whoever has charge of the engine will take care that none of the citizens, particularily delicate females, are subjected to such treatment.

The most significant accomplishment of the first city council was the adoption of a new coat of arms to replace the simple picture of an oak tree that had served as a civic crest and postal mark in the Bytown years. The new coat of arms, designed by George Hay, manager of the Bank of Ottawa, was a Victorian tour de force:

The shield was flanked by a blacksmith at his anvil (representing the dignity of labour) and a blindfolded lady with sword and scales (Justice). Above the shield was a sheaf of wheat (indicating plenty), a hand holding a broad-axe (for the square-timber trade), a beehive (industry), and a plow (agriculture). The shield itself was quartered: the first quarter depicted a locomotive and tender (rail transportation); the second quarter, a lake with a tree and two stags in the foreground, a range of hills and the setting sun in the background (indicating a country blessed with sunshine, timber, and game); the third quarter showed the locks of the Rideau Canal (water transportation); the fourth quarter, the Chaudière Falls and Union Suspension Bridge (water power). Beneath the shield were a rose, a thistle, and a shamrock (representing the English, Scottish, and Irish backgrounds of the citizenry). The fleur-de-lis was conspicuous by its absence. "Advance" was the motto.

This spurious coat of arms was used by the city of Ottawa for exactly one hundred years. In 1955, at the instigation of Mayor Charlotte Whitton, Ottawa adopted its present coat of arms, which was designed by the late Alan Beddoe, Canada's leading heraldry expert, and patented by the Kings of Arms. Included in the new armorial bearings (pictured opposite) is a bezant displaying an oak tree—the original seal of old Bytown.

Ottawa's main thoroughfares were lit by gas lamps for the first time on New Year's Eve, 1855. Gas lamps provided brighter and more reliable illumination than whale oil lamps, but a lamplighter still had to make his rounds each night with a ladder to light them. The gas, made from coal processed in a plant on King Edward Avenue, was much more expensive than whale oil. Because of the cost, City Council stipulated in its first contract with the Bytown Consumers Gas Company that their lamps would only be lit during the dark phases of the moon, regardless of the weather. This new form of lighting was first used on Sussex and Rideau streets; by 1876 gas lamps had replaced oil lamps throughout the city.

The gas company expanded its operations over the years and changed hands several times before it was purchased by the city of

Ottawa in 1949. In 1956 the city sold the assets of the gas company to Consumers Gas, a publicly held company. Two years later, when natural gas was piped into Ottawa from Alberta, the new owners found that this inexpensive "clean" fuel created a serious problem. The reason for this was that the original pipe joints had been caulked with oakum, a fibrous material that kept its seal so long as "wet" gas was used. When "dry" natural gas was run through the pipes, the caulking shrank and dangerous leaks developed. As a result, there were a number of well-publicized explosions, including a $2,000,000 catastrophe on Bank street on 25 October 1958. Since the defective seals were replaced, Ottawa Gas (a subsidiary of Consumers Gas) has had an excellent safety record.

The city's oldest and most influential business association, the Ottawa Board of Trade, was founded in 1857. Eight years after its inception Mitchell's *City Directory* stated: "There is here a Board of Trade, but as hitherto the members have signalized themselves by doing nothing, there is nothing to be said for or against them."

In 1857 a three story-stone house—later named Earnscliffe—was completed on a promontory overlooking the Ottawa River, north of Sussex Drive. This Gothic Revival mansion was built for John MacKinnon, Thomas MacKay's n'er-do-well business partner and son-in-law. MacKinnon died intestate in 1866, leaving his widow Annie penniless and the house heavily mortgaged. Thomas Coltrin Keefer, another MacKay son-in-law and executor of the patriarch's estate, came to Annie's rescue by purchasing the house when it was auctioned on 7 November 1866. Keefer, who paid $48 for the mansion (and assumed the existing $6,000 mortgage) let Annie live there until she could comfortably move her familiy to Rockcliff Manor, where her mother lived. Rockcliff Manor also overlooks the Ottawa and is now the residence of the Apostolic Pro-Nuncio.

In 1868 Keefer sold Earnscliffe to an Englishman named Thomas Reynolds, who had recently purchased the bankrupt Bytown & Prescott Railway for ten cents on the dollar. Reynolds loved the house and spent a substantial amount on improvements, but was soon forced by ill health to return to England. In 1871 Sir John A. Macdonald became a tenant; twelve years later he bought the house, and christened it Earnscliffe.

Following Sir John's death in 1891 the house was rented to several distinguished tenants and then, in 1900, sold to Mrs. Ella Harriss, whose first husband had been a Pennsylvania "iron king." Her second husband, Dr. Charles Harriss, was an English musician who organized the first Canadian Festival of Music. In 1928 Earnscliffe was bought by the British Government as the official residence of the British High Commissioner.

The Earnscliffe story also has a happy twist to it. In 1873, three years after his wife Elizabeth died, Thomas Keefer married Annie, John MacKinnon's widow. Thomas and Annie moved into Rockcliff Manor and enjoyed more than thirty years together; she died in 1906, he died in 1915.

John Rudolphus Booth—familiarly known as J.R.—started in the lumber business by cutting shingles after work in the back yard of his lodgings on Queen Street. At the beginning of 1859 Booth had managed to acquire a few hundred acres of timber along Constance Creek, upstream from the Chaudière Falls, but he was still operating on a hand-to-mouth basis. During 1859 Booth took two gambles that laid the foundation for a gigantic industrial empire. In November he recklessly undercut his competitors for the contract to supply lumber for the Parliament buildings. Then, having obtained a line of credit from the Bank of British North America, he outbid the timber barons for John Egan's vast limits on the Upper Ottawa. Lumbermen shook their heads at the folly of paying $45,000 for Egan's limits, and prophesied that Booth would soon follow Egan into bankruptcy. Through hard work and shrewd management Booth cleared a $15,000 profit on the Parliament buildings, and used this money to finance a substantial sawmill at the Chaudière Falls. By 1865 his annual output of 8 million board feet made him the third largest producer at the Chaudière (the largest firm was Harris, Bronson & Co. with 15 million, followed by Perley & Pattee with 10 million). Twenty-five years later Booth's milling complex at the Chaudière had the highest daily output in the world.

Booth did not look like a magnate. He was short, he had a slight stoop, and he wore unfashionable clothes that were often discoloured with age. However, a glance at his face, with its square-set jaw and steel-blue eyes, showed that J.R. was a man to be reckoned with.

Booth possessed an iron will; without this trait he would have failed, for he suffered numerous setbacks, including several disastrous fires. Work was his passion; the few times he went fishing (on a lake within his limits) he soon tired of the sport and would wander the shoreline looking for stray logs. Some of the facets of his personality were contradictory. He was frugal and cautious, yet when he seized upon a scheme he would spend money with abandon. Normally he shunned publicity, but when he dispatched the last raft of square timber he made a grand spectacle of the affair. He understood his men and often shared their food and quarters; however, when a strike for higher wages occurred, his reaction was as autocratic as an emperor's. Some said that he was "tighter than the bark on his trees"—it would be fairer to say that he considered thrift a major virtue. Although he was serious by nature, he sometimes revealed a flash of Irish wit. On one occasion he was chided for giving much smaller tips than his son, C. Jackson Booth. J.R. parried this criticism by observing, "That boy has a rich father, but I am an orphan."

After being confirmed as capital, Ottawa enjoyed a period of phenomenal growth. By 1863 Ottawa's population exceeded 14,000, and the city boasted several hundred stone buildings, in addition to many substantial structures of wood. Lower Town was the most heavily developed area in the city, although Sandy Hill, to the south of it, had relatively few houses. The entire length of Wellington Street, from Elgin to the Chaudière, was lined with shops and homes. Bank Street was the same, and there were quite a few dwellings on Sparks and Metcalfe streets. To the west, the Chaudière waterfront was jammed with sawmills and foundries. Behind these plants, on the Le Breton Flats, Mount Sherwood, and Nanny Goat Hill were the closely packed homes of the workers as well as palatial residences belonging to some of the industrialists. To the east, a small milling complex at the Rideau Falls provided employment for residents of New Edinburgh and Lower Town.

Medical facilities were much improved in 1863. In addition to the General Hospital, which had expanded to approximately 120 beds, there was the Protestant General Hospital with forty beds, which had been built by private subscription in 1852. The Protestant General was a two story-stone building at the corner of Rideau and Wurtemburg; in 1871 this institution occupied Wallis House at the corner of Rideau and Charlotte streets. Since then the Protestant General (formally known as the County of Carleton General Protestant Hospital) has become part of the Ottawa Civic Hospital, and Wallis House is now a militia depot.

In 1863 law enforcement in Ottawa was placed on a professional basis—and removed from political influence—with the establishment of a police commission. Prior to this time Ottawa's police force consisted of volunteers chosen by City Council. Headquarters for the first police chief, Thomas Langrill, and his ten constables was the ground floor of City Hall (the old Upper Town market building) which they shared with the Number 2 Fire Company. Two years later the chief and his men were placed on salary rather than being paid a percentage of the fines resulting from the arrests they made. The following year, 1866, the city fathers agreed to supply the force with uniforms.

The Rideau Club, Ottawa's oldest and most prestigious men's

club, was incorporated by an Act of Parliament on 18 September 1865. The petition requesting incorporation was signed by sixty-three prominent Canadians, headed by the Honourable John A. Macdonald.

Later that year the club rented a room in Doran's Hotel at 200 Wellington Street. From 1870 to 1876 the club premises were located in the Queen's Restaurant on Wellington Street at the east corner of Metcalfe Street. In 1876 the club moved to 84 Wellington Street, directly opposite the centre gate to the Parliament buildings, and erected its own clubhouse. Adjoining land was purchased in 1887, and the building was expanded to accommodate the growing membership. In 1910 the facilities were again increased and the premises were completely refurbished.

Until fire destroyed the building in 1979, the focal point of the club was its main lounge, located on the second floor, at the head of a divided staircase. The east wall of this room was dominated by a three-quarter-length portrait of the club's first president, Sir John A. Macdonald. The lounge, with its comfortable leather chairs, high ceilings, Corinthian columns, and fine woodwork, had an old-fashioned charm.

The club has many long-standing traditions. One is that briefcases must be checked with the hall porter, and no business papers may be displayed in the public rooms. Another custom, dating back to January 1879, is "That a Servant in livery be stationed just inside the entrance door of the Club, whose duties shall be to keep a record of all callers, answer all inquiries, take up all messages to those Members who may be in the Club, and prevent all Strangers from ascending the Club stairs."

In recent years the Rideau Club has been lampooned by the press as a stuffy bastion of the Establishment. In defence of the club, it should be pointed out that since its inception, the atmosphere has been as informal as one's home. Sir John A. Macdonald and his boon companion, the Honourable Thomas D'Arcy McGee had many song-filled evenings in the club's room at Doran's Hotel. One of their favourite ditties ended with the refrain:

A drunken man is a terrible curse
But a drunken woman is twice as worse.

The foregoing illustrates the convivial nature of some club gatherings, rather than an opinion of the fairer sex. Indeed, as early as

1922, a resolution was tabled at the annual meeting for the establish-ment of a ladies' dining room. This proposal was *not* rejected, but it was placed in abeyance. Less than forty-two years later, in May 1963, a Ladies Lounge and Dining Room was opened in the northeast corner of the ground floor.

In 1865, the same year the Rideau Club was founded, the Cana-dian government leased Rideau Hall from Thomas MacKay's estate as a residence for the Governor-General. Originally, the government had intended to build a vice-regal residence on Nepean Point, but this plan had been shelved because of the skyrocketing costs of the Parliament buildings. As a compromise, the government rented MacKay's eleven-room Regency villa (with an option to purchase the property), for $4,000 per annum. During 1865 and 1866 a two-story wing containing 10,000 square feet was added to the villa, and a brick house, Rideau Cottage, was built for the Secretary to the Governor-General.

Viscount Monck, who played a valuable role in Confederation, did not favour Ottawa as capital, but he immediately liked Rideau Hall. In a letter to his son, written while construction was still in progress, Monck said, "We are all agreeably surprised by this house." George Brown was considerably less charitable; in a letter to John A. Macdonald he grumbled, "The Governor-General's residence is a miserable little house, and the grounds those of an ambitious country squire." Everybody agreed that the road from Rideau Hall to the Parliament buildings was dreadful. Viscount Monck's solution to the dust and potholes of Sussex Drive was to have a six-oar cutter, with a Royal Navy crew, transport him between Governor's Bay and the Parliament buildings.

In 1867 His Excellency gave a benefit concert for the building fund of St. Bartholomew's Anglican Church. The following year an attractive Gothic chapel was erected at the corner of Victoria and MacKay streets in New Edinburgh, on land donated by Thomas MacKay. From the outset St. Bartholomew's was the parish church of Government House, and it has since been designated as the chapel of the Governor-General's Foot Guards. The interior of St. Bartholomew's contains many reminders of these connections, including memorials and heraldic shields of past Governors-General and the regimental colours of the Governor-General's Foot Guards. The first two pews in the church have traditionally been reserved for the Governor-General and members of his household.

In 1868 the Canadian Government purchased Rideau Hall and

eighty-eight surrounding acres from the MacKay estate for $88,000. Following this transaction, further additions were made, including an octagonal guardhouse and ornamental iron gates at the main entrance.

Viscount Monck was succeeded by Sir John Young (later Baron Lisgar) in November 1868. During Lisgar's three-year tenure there were few physical changes at Rideau Hall. Lisgar was replaced by another Irish peer, Lord Dufferin, in June 1872. Dufferin was not a staid public servant but a romantic with great enthusiasm for Canada. His vivacious wife Hariot shared his outlook and was a tireless hostess. Together, they expanded the vice-regal role and put new life into Rideau Hall.

Dufferin's first impressions of Ottawa were mixed. In an early letter he described the city as ". . . a very desolate place, consisting of a jumble of brand new houses and shops, built or building, and a wilderness of wooden shanties spread along either side of long, broad strips of mud." However, he had kinder words for the inhabitants: ". . . dignified, unpretending, and polite, very gay and ready to be amused, simple in their ways of life and quite free from vulgarity or swagger."

To meet as many Canadians as possible, Dufferin travelled extensively and also entertained frequently at Government House. Their Excellencies embraced the Canadian winter with gusto. Curling, skating, and tobogganing parties—complete with music and brightly coloured lanterns—were held throughout the coldest months. Lord Dufferin footed many expenses out of his own pocket, including the cost of an enclosed curling rink. This rink has since been demolished, but open-air curling is still practiced on the original site. In 1873 a ballroom was added to Rideau Hall. The most famous party held there, attended by more than a thousand guests from across Canada, was the masquerade ball given by Lady Dufferin on 13 February 1876. In addition to various entertainments, diplomatic ceremonies and formal investitures have traditionally taken place in the ballroom.

The Dufferins' vigorous approach to their task resulted in numerous improvements at Government House and forged a warm rapport with many Ottawans. When the couple left Canada in 1878, the city bid them farewell with genuine regret.

The official residence of the Prime Minister of Canada is situated on a bluff overlooking Governor's Bay, directly opposite the main gates to Rideau Hall. This grey stone mansion, originally christened

Gorphwysfa (which is Welsh for "place of peace"), was built in 1868 by a prominent businessman, Joseph Merrill Currier. The house soon became known for its hospitality because, in addition to his association with the Maclarens of Buckingham (who controlled the mills at the Rideau Falls), Currier was also the Member of Parliament for Ottawa. In 1870 Currier added a ballroom so that he could royally entertain Prince Arthur of Connaught, Queen Victoria's third son. After Joseph Currier died in 1884, his widow, Hannah, a granddaughter of Philemon Wright, continued to reside at Gorphwysfa until her death in 1901.

In 1902 the house was sold to another lumber baron, William Cameron Edwards, who had purchased the mills on both sides of the Rideau Falls and at Green Island in 1894. Edwards, a noted art collector as well as an astute businessman, was later appointed to the Dominion Senate. After Senator Edwards' death in 1921, Gorphwysfa remained in the Edwards family for another quarter-century. In 1946 the government of Canada expropriated the property as a residence for the Prime Minister.

Since then, a succession of contractors and interior decorators have effected many changes. An indoor swimming pool has been added, and the property has been heavily fenced. The house is no longer known by its lyrical Welsh name but simply by the street address: 24 Sussex Drive.

The Fenian Brotherhood—a violent republican movement—was spawned in Dublin in 1858 and carried to the United States by Irish immigrants the following year. At the end of the American Civil War some demobilized troops of the victorious Union Army joined the Fenians in a bizarre attempt to conquer Canada. The logic behind this strategy is obscure, but it was meant to advance the Fenian cause in Ireland. Despite the magnitude of the undertaking, the "Song of the Fenian Brotherhood" treats the invasion of Canada rather casually:

> *We are a Fenian Brotherhood, skilled in the arts of war,*
> *and we are going to fight for Ireland, the land that we adore.*
> *Many battles we have won, along with the boys in blue,*
> *and we'll go and capture Canada, for we've nothing else to do.*

In the spring and summer of 1866 the Fenians staged raids along the Canadian border at Campobello Island, New Brunswick; Fort

Erie, Ontario; and the Eastern Townships in Quebec. Another assault by Fenians who had gathered at Ogdensburg, on the United States side of the St. Lawrence River, was aborted by a show of strength from Canadian and American authorities. Although these attacks were inconsequential (and actually helped New Brunswick decide to join Confederation), the Fenian movement was perceived as a threat to Canada for the balance of the decade.

The most effective critic of the Fenians was the Honourable Thomas D'Arcy McGee, who, in addition to being a Father of Confederation, was also a poet, a journalist, and an eloquent speaker. McGee possessed special insight into the movement because he had once been an Irish revolutionary himself, and had been forced to flee to the United States in 1848 disguised as a priest. Between the time he landed in New York and his move to Montreal in 1857 McGee became convinced that there was no place for Irish prejudice and hatred in North America. He entered politics shortly after coming to Canada and was elected to the House of Assembly as an Independent in 1858. Six years later he was invited by John A. Macdonald to join his Cabinet as Minister of Agriculture. When the Fenian problem arose, McGee made a number of hard-hitting speeches stressing the need for Irish immigrants of both religions to stand together for the good of Canada.

On St. Patrick's Day, 1868, McGee was the chief speaker at a huge banquet in Ottawa sponsored by a joint committee of Roman Catholic and Protestant Irish citizens. Among those in attendance were Sir John A. Macdonald and many of his Cabinet. The following excerpt summarizes McGee's message that evening, which drew applause from the guests but enraged the Fenians:

> As for us who dwell in Canada, I may say finally that there is no other way we can better serve Ireland than by burying out of sight our old feuds and old factions, in mitigating our ancient hereditary enmities, in proving ourselves good subjects of a good government, and wise trustees of the equal rights we enjoy here, civil and religious
>
> Let us put that weapon into the hands of our friends in Ireland at home, and it will be worth all the revolvers that ever were stolen from a Cork gunshop and all the Republican chemicals that ever were smuggled out of New York.

Three weeks later, on 7 April, McGee was assassinated. The murderer waited in the shadows outside Mrs. Trotter's boardinghouse on Sparks Street (between Metcalfe and O'Connor) and crept up behind his victim while McGee was inserting his key in the door.

His death was a shock to the country, and was observed by a day of national mourning. Within eight hours of the tragedy Mayor Henry Friel posted a $2,000 reward for the arrest of the assassin on behalf of the city and added a further $2,000 from his own purse. Patrick Whelan, a recently arrived immigrant from Ireland, and a Fenian sympathizer, was subsequently arrested and tried for the murder of McGee. Although summary justice was demanded by the people, it would appear that Whelan received a fair trial. He was defended by a distinguished lawyer, the Honourable John Cameron (an Orangeman), and prosecuted by an equally famous member of the Bar, James Reilly (an Irish Roman Catholic). Whelan was found guilty on the basis of both circumstantial evidence and the eyewitness testimony of the shooting by a Mr. Langevin. On 11 February 1869 Whelan was publicly hanged at the Nicholas Street Gaol. His last words were: "God have mercy on my soul!"

The Ottawa City Passenger Railway, the capital's first streetcar service, commenced operation in July of 1870. The O.C.P.R. owned a single track between New Edinburgh and the Suspension Bridge at the Chaudière Falls—a distance of four miles—which ran via Sussex, Sparks, Wellington, and Duke streets.

In summer, when the horse-drawn trams could use the rails, it was possible to go from one terminal to the other in fifteen minutes. For the rest of the year it took considerably longer. In winter, because of the heavy snow, sleighs were necessary; despite six inches of straw on the floor, these conveyances were cold as a tomb, and the passengers were often pitched against each other en route. Horse-drawn buses were employed in the spring and late autumn, when mud and potholes made the roadbed a nightmare. It was said that a bus ride between the Chaudière and New Edinburgh, with the vehicle swaying forty-five degrees from one side to the other, offered a greater opportunity for seasickness than a voyage across the Atlantic.

The Ottawa City Passenger Railway, incorporated in New Edinburgh in 1866, was largely financed by the estate of Thomas MacKay. Two years later Thomas Reynolds, the new owner of the Bytown & Prescott Railway (which had gone through receivership and was now called the St. Lawrence and Ottawa Railway) bought control of the O.C.P.R. Reynolds made this investment because he planned to have the streetcars transport lumber at night from the Chaudière mills to the McTaggart Street terminal of the St. Lawrence and Ottawa Railway. It was a good idea, but in practice he found that the sharp curves in the tracks would not tolerate heavy loads. In 1871 Reynolds built a branch line to the Chaudière from a point near Billings Bridge to a terminal on Broad Street. That same year he sold Thomas Keefer his controlling interest in the streetcar company. For the next two decades this company, and its plodding horses, provided the main means of public transportation in Ottawa.

Two new militia regiments were organized in the capital shortly after the Governor General's residence was moved to Ottawa. The Ottawa Troop of Cavalry was formed in 23 May 1872, and the Governor-General's Foot Guards on 7 June of the same year. The original role of these units was to provide escorts, or guards of honour, for the Governor-General on ceremonial occasions. Both regiments subsequently saw a great deal of active service, and distinguished themselves in World Wars One and Two.

In 1879 the Ottawa Cavalry Troop changed its name to the Princess Louise Dragoon Guards, in honour of Princess Louise, the wife of the Marquis of Lorne, Canada's Governor-General at the time. A number of Dragoons were in the Canadian contingent that served in South Africa in the Boer War. During World War One the PLDG (familiarily known as the Plugs) provided reinforcements for several battalions overseas. The last mounted full-dress parade of the regiment was in May 1939, when King George VI and Queen Elizabeth visited the capital. The Dragoons, with their dark blue uniforms, chain mail, and plumed silver helmets made a sparkling sight as they jingled past on their black horses. At the outbreak of World War Two the regiment was mechanized and converted into a reconnaissance squadron attached to the 1st Canadian Division. The PLDG suffered heavy casualties in Western Europe and Italy and were awarded battle honours in both campaigns. When the federal government reduced Canada's militia forces in 1964, the Princess Louise Dragoon Guards were disbanded.

The Governor-General's Foot Guards can be traced back to the Civil Service Rifles, which were formed in Quebec City in 1861, when that city was the seat of government. The Civil Service Rifles were transferred to the new capital in 1865, and their members formed the nucleus of the GGFG. When Queen Victoria approved the formation of the Governor-General's Foot Guards, she stipulated that they would have a similar uniform to the Foot Guards in

England: scarlet tunic, navy blue trousers, and a tall fur headdress (which is properly called a bearskin). The Queen further stated that the new unit was to have "the same precedence and status in the Active Militia as is held by Her Majesty's Foot Guards in the Imperial Army." (The GGFG became affiliated with the Coldstream Guards in 1929.)

The first time the Governor-General's Foot Guards saw active service was during the British campaign against the Sudanese (nicknamed "Fuzzy-Wuzzies") in 1884. One officer and four noncommissioned officers led a special detachment of 154 Ottawa valley *voyageurs* whose task was to ferry troops up the Nile. These men played an indirect but important part in the attempt to relieve General Charles George Gordon at Khartoum. (He was killed two days before relief forces arrived.)

In 1885 the regiment contributed three officers and a company of fifty sharpshooters to help quell the Northwest Rebellion. There were so many volunteers for this mission that lots had to be drawn. On 2 May 1885 the unit suffered its first casualties—and won its first battle honour—at the Battle of Cut Knife Hill, against Riel's ally, Chief Poundmaker. A statue of a guardsman, with arms reversed, stands in Confederation Park in memory of the two men killed at Cut Knife Hill.

At the turn of the century the GGFG provided four officers and sixty other ranks for the Canadian Contingent that went to South Africa. The regiment was subsequently awarded a battle honour for their efforts against the Boers. A bronze statue in Confederation Park, of a soldier with his pith helmet raised above his head, commemorates the Ottawa men killed in the South African War. This statue was paid for by 30,000 Ottawa schoolchildren, each of whom donated a penny.

During World War One the Guards maintained a training depot that provided reinforcements for the 2nd Battalion of the Canadian Expeditionary Force. This unit, known as "The Iron Second," suffered 1,353 fatal casualties in France and Flanders, and was one of the first Allied units to be gassed by the Germans. In 1915 the Guards depot provided the nucleus of the 77th Battalion. Three members of the 77th went on to win the Victoria Cross; two of these were awarded posthumously. At the end of the war the 77th was redesignated the 2nd Battalion, Governor-General's Foot Guards.

In World War Two the GGFG were mobilized for active duty at

the end of May 1940. The regiment was converted from infantry to armour and went overseas in 1942 as the 21st Canadian Armoured Regiment. The unit served in France, Holland, Belgium, and Germany.

After the war the GGFG reverted to infantry and once again became a reserve battalion. In addition to normal militia training, the unit has performed many ceremonial duties, such as guards of honour for visiting dignitaries and the Opening of Parliament. From 1970 to 1978 members of the regiment participated in the Changing of the Guard ceremony on Parliament Hill.

The Governor-General's Foot Guards hold a special place in the hearts of many Ottawans. One reason is the number of families in the city who have friends, relatives, or loved ones who have served in the regiment. There are also historical reasons: the Guards have been at the Drill Hall on Cartier Square since it was built in 1879, and the regimental band has been giving public concerts for even longer than that. But the main reason is even more simple: when the Guards are on parade, you can count on a good show.

In 1873, the year after the Ottawa Cavalry Troop and the Governor-General's Foot Guards were formed, traffic had become so heavy between Upper and Lower Town that a second bridge was built over the Rideau Canal, parallel to the Sappers Bridge. The new span, made of stone and iron, connected Rideau with Wellington Street (the Sappers Bridge forked to the south from Rideau onto Sparks Street).

City Council decided to call the new structure Dufferin Bridge in honour of Lord Dufferin who, although he had been in Ottawa less than a year, was already a very popular Governor General. When Dufferin heard of this, he sent a note to Council recommending that the bridge be named after Her Royal Highness, Princess (later Queen) Alexandra, wife of Albert Edward, Prince of Wales. Even though a suggestion from the Governor-General carried considerable authority, City Council voted to proceed with their plan, and Mayor Eugene Martineau politely advised Lord Dufferin to this effect. Dufferin acceded to Council's wish and graciously accepted the honour.

In 1874 Lord Dufferin laid the cornerstone of a large Gothic building that was to be the permanent home for Ottawa's first public high school, Lisgar Collegiate Institute. This institution had functioned as a grammar school, under several names, and in five different locations from 1843. When the first principal, a young divinity student from Kingston named Thomas Wardrope, arrived in Bytown in 1843, he found that the Dalhousie District Grammar School had neither pupils nor premises. With the help of the chairman of the school board, the Reverend Samuel Strong, a one-room house was rented on Waller Street and classes began that autumn. Wardrope resigned two years later to devote his full time to the ministry. His successor, another man of the cloth, managed to run the enrolment down from sixty to thirteen pupils before the school board relieved him of his position in 1850. The headmasters who followed this gentleman recouped his loss and steadily increased the number of students.

In 1871 the grammar school was elevated to the status of a collegiate institute (high school) and took the name of the Governor-General, Baron Lisgar. The limestone schoolhouse on Lisgar Street (formerly Biddy Street) was gutted by fire in 1893 and rebuilt the following year. An east wing was added in 1902, and a west wing in 1908. These additions brought the capacity of the school to approximately one thousand students. Other than repairs to the east wing as a result of fires in 1915 and 1942, little was done to the school for the next half-century.

Lisgar Collegiate Institute is historically significant because it predates Confederation, and it was one of the first six public schools established by the government of Upper Canada. However, Lisgar is even better known for its exceptional academic standards and the success of its graduates in every field of endeavour (among those who have gone into television are Lorne Greene, Peter Jennings, Adrienne Clarkson, Betty Kennedy, and Rich Little). Since the inception of Rhodes Scholarship Awards, approximately one out of every ten Rhodes Scholars from Ontario has been a graduate of Lisgar.

Because of the school's consistently high results, and because it still offers courses in Latin and stringed instruments, Lisgar has been branded by some people as an elitist institution. Nothing could be further from the truth. The students at Lisgar have always represented a cross-section, both socially and economically, of the city's population. In addition, many of the pupils have had to overcome language problems; in an average year, the enrolment encompasses sixty different national and ethnic groups. Until recently the facilities at Lisgar were the most antiquated in the Ottawa school system. Lisgar's tradition of excellence is due to a combination of factors: the dedication of the teaching staff, a desire on the part of the students to learn, and old-fashioned school spirit.

In the early 1970s the Ottawa School Board gave serious consideration to closing Lisgar Collegiate. This action was contemplated because of the prohibitive cost to renovate the building, plus the shift in population from the core of the city to the suburbs. The Board's proposal brought a massive wave of protest from Lisgar parents, students, and graduates. On 2 April 1974, a night of freezing rain, more than 1,300 people squeezed into the Lisgar auditorium to organize support for the school (the attendance was impressive because of three competing attractions: an Ottawa 67s play-off game, the annual Sportsmen's Dinner, and the Academy Awards). In the ensuing months the Committee for the Future of Lisgar managed to persuade the Board of Education to allow the school to continue. As a result of the committee's efforts and the generous support of the National Capital Commission, Heritage Ontario, the city of Ottawa, and the general public, funds were collected to renovate the old structure. The restoration modernized the interior of the school but carefully preserved the exterior character of the building. The total job, estimated to cost approximately $5 million, was completed at a saving of nearly $1 million. This feat, alone, justifies a place for Lisgar Collegiate in the history of the capital.

In 1874, the same year that Lord Dufferin laid the cornerstone for Lisgar Collegiate, the city of Ottawa assumed full responsibility for the fire department. Initially, firefighting was done by volunteers, with equipment paid for by private subscription. The first fire engines in Bytown were hand pumps built by and named for Montreal insurance companies, the *Alliance* and the *Mutual*. Up until 1848 the only participation by the city was to pay for the water used in dousing fires. Later, fire protection was in the hands of independent units, and the municipality paid the total cost. In 1853 the city purchased three modern hand pumps, the *Rideau*, the *Ottawa*, and the *Chaudière*, and erected sheds to house them.

In 1860 the corporation equipped Upper and Lower Town with identical hook-and-ladder carts. These 2,340-pound rigs were meant to be drawn by horses, but as the municipal budget did not provide for horses (although they could be commandeered in an emergency), the carts were normally pulled by twenty men. When a dispute arose in 1864 as to which hook-and-ladder team was entitled to be called Number 1 Company, a race was held on Rideau Street to settle the issue. Practically all of Ottawa turned out to watch the race, which was run between Sussex and Wurtemburg streets. Lower Town won the contest—which was a squeaker—as well as the $300 purse donated by the city. Upper Town demanded a rematch, but this was cancelled when Existe Berichon, the lead "horse" for Lower Town, broke his leg while jumping chairs in the fire station during a practice session.

Prior to its reorganization in 1874, the performance of the fire-fighting units had been erratic. On several occasions the toll of the fire bell at city hall was completely ignored. To encourage a better response the corporation offered a cash incentive to the firefighting companies; the first unit to play a stream of water on the blaze was given a prize of 20 shillings. Because the fire engines usually had to depend on water from horse-drawn puncheons, a bonus of $5.00 was also paid to the first professional water carrier to arrive on the scene—even if most of the water had sloshed out of his cask en route.

The reorganization of the fire department in 1874 brought sweeping changes. For the first time the firefighters became salaried employees of the city. William Young, who had been chief since 1872, headed the eighteen-man force. To say that they worked full time is an understatement; they were on duty twenty-four hours a day, with no time off. (In 1919 the department adopted the platoon system so that the men could work shifts; two years later, Ontario law specified that the firemen must have one day off a week.)

In addition to the change in employment status for the firemen, their equipment was increased and modernized. In 1874 there were five fire stations, linked by telegraph, and each station was issued with a five-hundred-foot roll of hose on a horse-drawn drum. The city acquired the *Conqueror,* a steam-driven engine made in England, which had the capacity to pump 1,400 gallons a minute. (Four years earlier the mill owners at the Chaudière had bought a smaller steam engine, the *Union,* for their private use.) The next major equipment purchase by the municipality was a Silsby rotary engine, which was named after a volunteer fireman and long-serving By Ward alderman, John Heney.

As a digression, it might be mentioned that while the Irish were involved in much of the turbulence in early Bytown, they also made an incalculable contribution to the community in later years. John Heney, known to all as "Honest John," illustrates this point. Heney arrived in Bytown from County Cavan in 1844 with nothing but the clothes on his back. During the next five years he established himself as a shoemaker and became Father Molloy's lay leader in the Irish Catholic Temperance Society. In 1868 he expanded his business to general contracting and then founded a wood and coal company, John Heney and Son, which grew to be the largest fuel dealer in the city. (John Heney and Son was bought by Texaco Canada Limited in 1959.) Honest John served on numerous civic committees and charitable boards. For his work on behalf of the temperance cause, Pope Leo XIII conferred upon him the title of Chevalier of the Sepulchre and awarded him a gold medal.

The Ottawa Fire Department underwent few changes until Chief Young retired in 1897, following a series of disastrous fires. His successor, Peter Provost, formerly of the Montreal Fire Department, instituted an expansion program coupled with numerous changes in personnel. Under Chief Provost a great deal of modern equipment was purchased, and the department soon became a disciplined, highly efficient unit.

During Peter Provost's tenure, which ended with his death in 1909, the foundation was laid for the Ottawa Fire Department's international reputation for excellence.

11

Hull: The City
Across the River
1875 to 1900

IN 1875 WRIGHT'S Town was incorporated as a city, and changed its
name to Hull. For a quarter of a century the Chaudière Falls had
been the industrial core of both Ottawa and Hull. The following
description, looking upstream from Parliament Hill, in *Picturesque
Canada*, published in 1882, indicates the extent to which the mills
dominated the landscape:

Upon every point of rock near the Chaudiere Falls, and upon acres of
massive, wooden, stone-filled embankments connecting them, to
which the upper waters could be led, there have been reared the huge
mill structures of the lumber kings...
   On the right... are mills and still more mills, and an immense
factory for the production of matches and pails—one of the "sights"
of the locality. On the left, perched high on a labyrinth of monster
piles, by which the giant force of the river has been dammed up and
curbed, runs a long line of saw-mills, and entering these, the unearthly
din, made up of whirr, buzz and shriek, becomes absolutely deafening.
   The scene at night—for work continues both by night and day—is
extremely novel and picturesque. Some of the lumbering firms now
use the electric light, and the effect in that pure, clear glare, is of the

most Rembrandt-like character. The contrast between the darkness outside, and the weird unearthly figures of the busy crowd of workers; the dark, rough backs of the dripping logs, as they are hauled up from the water, catching the reflection, and the sharp flash of the steel as it dances up and down—all contribute to make a picture of the horrible which would captivate the pencil of Doré and give Dante a new idea for a modern *Inferno*.

In 1875 Hull depended upon the mills for its existence, and much of the city had become an industrial slum. Philemon Wright's model community had changed greatly since his arrival in 1800. Until the middle of the century 90 percent of the population was English; in 1875 it was equally divided between English and French; by 1900 the population was 90 percent French. Unlike Ottawa, which had the Civil Service and a substantial middle class, Hull was predominantly a working-class community. When Hull was incorporated, the Wright family still owned most of the property. This land was occupied by low-income tenants, who had neither the means nor the incentive to improve their dwellings. Fires were common and difficult to control because of the closely packed wooden houses. One of the worst fires occurred in 1875. This conflagration destroyed many homes and ravaged the mills of the city's main employer, Ezra Butler Eddy.

Eddy was an American who had come to Hull from Bristol, Vermont, in 1851, at the age of twenty-four. He brought with him a fierce determination to succeed, a fine wife, and very little money. By 1875 he was a millionaire and well on his way to being the largest match manufacturer in the British Empire. His first factory (where he made matches from pine stubs discarded by the mills, and then sold his product door to door) was located on the upper floor of a building rented from Ruggles Wright. As his business grew, he extended his sales territory as far as Toronto. Still later he bought machinery to automate most of the manufacturing process. (In the beginning, girls dipped the match heads by hand. Because mixing the volatile composition was a high-risk job, a male employee accomplished the task by placing the components in a pail and then jumping up and down on a springboard with the pail between his legs.)

In 1857 Eddy expanded his product line to include wooden pails, clothes pegs, and corrugated washboards. Ten years later he built a large sawmill on land purchased from the Wrights, and bought timber limits on the Upper Ottawa to feed the mill. In 1870 he erected a huge match factory on an island at the Chaudière, which had also belonged to the Wrights. When fire swept his mills in 1875, he was producing nearly a million matches a day, and approximately fifty million board feet of lumber annually.

Eddy bought the rights to a process for making indurated fibre ware in 1886. To raise funds for his entry into the pulp and paper field, he changed his operation from a sole proprietorship to a limited company the same year. In 1888 he built a pulp mill a half-mile downstream from the Chaudière, which employed huge grinders to crush the logs. However, within a short time Eddy converted this mill to the Mitschelich chemical process for making pulp. The quality of his sulphite pulp was such that most of the fifty tons produced each week was sold to customers in the United States. In 1890 he branched out into fine paper, which was also a success. By 1900 all of Eddy's enterprises had paid for themselves and his company was free of debt. In 1899 he decided—because of the high insurance premiums—to cancel his insurance policies and self-insure his plants. The following year the Great Fire destroyed most of his life's work. (The loss amounted to $3 million, offset by a reserve fund of $50,000 and an unexpired insurance policy worth $100,000.) Eddy had faced ruin from fire before, and was undaunted. Before the ashes were cool he gave orders to rebuild. The new plants were built with borrowed money; when E. B. Eddy died six years later, most of the loans had been repaid and his company was once again on a sound footing.

In 1927 the Eddy match factories—whose production capacity was 120 million matches a day—were sold to a British corporation. In 1943 Willard Garfield Weston, a Canadian tycoon residing in England, bought control of the E. B. Eddy Company from a Canadian expatriate, Viscount Bennett of Mickleham, Calgary, and Hopewell. (R. B. Bennett was Conservative Prime Minister of Canada from August 1930 to October 1935). Following World War Two, J. R. Booth's heirs sold his fine paper mill on the Ottawa side of the Chaudière Falls to the E. B. Eddy Company. In 1959 Weston acquired the balance of shares in the E. B. Eddy Company, and made it a wholly owned subsidiary of George Weston Limited. In 1972 the National Capital Commission purchased Eddy's sulphite mill and forty-four acres of adjacent property for the Portage Bridge and public parkland. Today the company owns approximately thirty acres on the Hull side of the river and approximately ten acres on the Ottawa side. The company manufactures a variety of paper products ranging from fine paper to White Swan toilet tissue.

For the first century after Hull was incorporated as a city, the E. B. Eddy Company was the largest industry and the largest employer in the community. Ezra Butler Eddy's contribution was more than that of a capitalist; Eddy was an alderman in Hull for ten years and served six terms as mayor. The relationship of his company to the city was neatly summarized by the late Ottawa historian, A. H. D. Ross in *Ottawa Past and Present* (Musson Book Company, 1927): "Hull without the E. B. Eddy Company would be like Shakespeare's play of *Hamlet* with Hamlet left out."

12

Public and Private Enterprise
1874 to 1888

OTTAWA LAGGED BEHIND other Canadian cities in the construction of a municipal system of waterworks. This was surprising because the capital was well served by rivers, and one of the residents, Thomas Coltrin Keefer, was the foremost hydraulic engineer in Canada.

Thomas Keefer was a half-brother of the renowned structural engineer, Samuel Keefer. The Keefer brothers were two of the founders of the Canadian Society of Civil Engineers, and Thomas was one of only two Canadians in the past hundred years to be elected president of the American Society of Civil Engineers.

Until 1874 Ottawa's water services were primitive. Two wells— one dug in Lower Town in 1840, the other sunk in Upper Town in 1843—were the sole municipal facilities. Both the residents and the fire department were forced to depend upon professional water carriers, who drew their water from the river and sold it in puncheons for 15 cents a gallon in summer and 25 cents a gallon in winter.

In 1859 City Council requested Thomas Keefer to design a waterworks and sewage system. Keefer, who had just completed the waterworks system for Hamilton, submitted an imaginative plan utilizing Parliament Hill for the reservoir, a site chosen because the elevation would create sufficient pressure to gravity-feed the pipes. Council were enthusiastic until they learned the estimated cost—$1,675,000—and then they dropped the idea.

Five years later, when the Parliament buildings were nearing completion, the demand for a waterworks surfaced again. City Council declined to consider such an expensive frivolity, but said they would encourage any private group who wished to undertake the task. The following year, 1865, the federal government installed a water system operated by a small steam pump in the Parliament buildings.

In 1868 the city engineer recommended that a pump-driven plant be built, at a cost of $100,000, to draw water for the fire engines from Nepean Bay. The meeting, convened to discuss the question, was turned into a shambles by protesting water carriers, and the proposal was shelved. A year later a civic committee recommended to Council that Thomas Keefer be appointed to build a waterworks for a cost not to exceed $300,000. Showing remarkable thrift, the city fathers ignored their committee's recommendation.

Two major conflagrations finally woke Council to the city's desperate need for a system of waterworks. In the summer of 1870 forest fires ravaged both sides of the Ottawa Valley. By 19 August a wall of flames threatened to engulf the entire west end of the capital. That day the garrison was called out, bells and bugles sounded the alarm, and people prepared to evacuate the city. Overhead, the sun was blotted out by a heavy pall of smoke. Ottawa was saved by the quick thinking of some men who cut the St. Louis dam on the north bank of Dow's Lake. Water poured down Preston Street to the Ottawa River, forming a moat that blocked the advancing flames. The fire consumed thousands of acres and left 2,000 residents of Carleton County homeless. In October of the following year a spectacular fire in Chicago destroyed 18,000 buildings and claimed more than 100 lives. This disaster had such an impact on the citizens of Ottawa that the city donated $2,500 to Chicago for fire relief.

In 1872 City Council approved construction of a $1 million waterworks system designed by Thomas Keefer. This system drew water from the Ottawa River above the Chaudière Falls through wooden pipes to a pump house on Fleet Street. Turbines in the pumphouse were fed by an aqueduct, cut through the rock, which tapped the flow upstream from the Chaudière and discharged the flow below the falls. The original capacity of this plant was ten million gallons of untreated water every twenty-four hours.

While the waterworks were being built, the city's first main trunk sewer system was also being installed. The main trunk ran at a depth of twenty feet from Slater Street (near the Ottawa Technical High School) in an easterly direction; after passing under the Canal, it turned north at Musgrove Street and zigzagged across to King Edward Avenue, which it followed due north to Sussex Street; after crossing Sussex, the sewer emptied into the Ottawa River behind the National Research Council building.

When the first stage was completed in 1873, a city inspection party, led by Alderman John Heney, made its way through the sewer from Elgin Street to the outlet. Before descending the manhole to the sewer everyone took a big swig of brandy, except Honest John—the pillar of the temperance movement—who swallowed some disinfectant. Holding lanterns, they crept along the brick-lined, egg-shaped tunnel (which was only three feet nine inches high) toward Musgrove Street. En route, the city medical officer advised the men to light their pipes as a fumigant. When they reached Musgrove, the sewer increased in size to a height of six feet six inches, which permitted them to walk upright. However, at King Edward, the party was forced to make an unscheduled exit through a manhole because of noxious fumes and greasy deposits from the Ottawa Gas plant. They clambered out of the Stygian darkness, blinking like moles in the sunlight, and walked the rest of the way above ground. At the outlet, the contractor, James Murphy, had thoughtfully provided a copious supply of champagne, which helped the inspectors forget the rigours of their journey.

Water flowed to Ottawa taps and hydrants for the first time on 28 October 1874, fourteen years after Thomas Keefer presented his initial plan for a municipal system. The untreated water had a marshy taste and was highly coloured but it was no worse than the slop sold by the water carriers, and a great deal more convenient. In an address to the Ottawa Field-Naturalists' Club on 13 January 1882, the Reverend A. F. Kemp described the results of filtering his tap water with a piece of cotton cloth. Reverend Kemp informed his fellow members that he had identified 140 animal and vegetable forms, in addition to "some fantastic things" that he could not name. His largest catch was a leech *(Hirudo medicinalis)* one and one-half inches long.

Among the bacteria present in the Ottawa water system was the typhoid bacillus, *Salmonella typhosa*, which accounted for an average of twenty deaths each year. (Typhoid fever is characterized by a high fever, a rash, bronchitis, intestinal haemorrhaging, and diarrhoea.)

In 1890 the thirty-inch wooden intake pipe from the river was replaced by a forty-inch steel pipe. Two turbines were added to the pumphouse in 1907, and a second steel pipe, with a section of reinforced concrete leading from the river to Lett Street, was installed. This concrete section subsequently developed cracks that allowed raw sewage from an adjacent sewer to enter the water system, and as a consequence the city suffered severe typhoid epidemics in the winter of 1911 and the summer of 1912. Approximately three hundred died in these epidemics.

To combat this pollution the water was then treated with ammonia and chlorine. In 1915 a pumping station, which drew its water from the centre of the Ottawa River, was built at Lemieux Island. Thirteen years later an experimental filtration plant was erected on the same site. This pilot operation was a preliminary step to the erection of a major treatment facility at Lemieux Island, which was opened in 1932, with a daily capacity of thirty-five million gallons. Purification of the water was achieved by means of a sophisticated sand process that incorporated screening, coagulation, sedimentation, filtration, and the injection of chlorine gas. This treatment—which is basically the same in use today—produced a clear, tasteless water of exceptional purity. Ottawa water has been fluoridated since 1965; lime is also added to make it slightly alkaline, which helps to prevent rust and corrosion in pipes and storage tanks.

The city waterworks have been greatly expanded in the past half-century. Now the Lemieux Island plant has a daily capacity of sixty-three million gallons, while a second facility—built at Britannia in 1961—has a capacity of fifty-five million gallons. Six free-standing reservoirs in the Ottawa area provide a total storage capacity of approximately forty-seven million gallons.

The old stone pumphouse on Fleet Street, erected in 1874, is interesting historically because one can stand by the open aqueduct that curves in from the Ottawa River and trace the course of the waterway through the building. A few feet downstream, the water passes under Pooley's Bridge, which is now just a stone arch in the roadbed. The original structure was built of peeled cedar logs in 1827 by Lieutenant Henry Pooley, R.E., and was so distinctive that

Colonel By named it for him. This bridge spanned the gulley leading to Richmond Landing, and was an essential link in the first road from Bytown to the Chaudière Falls.

The plant is more than just an historic site. It is an integral part of the municipal waterworks system and pumps half the output from Lemieux Island through the city. Although the building has been enlarged three times and the original equipment has been replaced, the turbines are *still* turned by the force of the Chaudière channelled in the aqueduct. In these days of soaring energy costs the taxpayers of Ottawa can be thankful for the genius and foresight of Thomas Coltrin Keefer.

In 1877, three years after the waterworks started operating, a new City Hall was opened. It was desperately needed because the old wooden market building, which had served since 1855, was totally inadequate and overrun with vermin. The old and new City Halls shared the same property on Elgin Street which was originally donated to the city by Nicholas Sparks. When the new building—an ornate limestone structure in the Italian style, with a tall tower—was completed, the old market hall was demolished. The new City Hall was renovated in 1910, and again in 1925. Six years after the second renovation, on 31 March 1931, fire gutted the stone structure beyond repair. Ottawa was in the throes of the Depression at that time and could not afford to rebuild.

As a temporary measure the city rented space in the Transportation Building, at the corner of Rideau and Little Sussex, which had been built by C. Jackson Booth. City Hall remained there for the next twenty-seven years. Part of the delay in relocation was due to the Depression and World War Two, but more than ten years were wasted after the war because the elected representatives could not agree on a site for the new City Hall. Finally, in the late 1950s, Mayor Charlotte Whitton coerced Council into voting for Green Island.

It was a sound decision. Green Island, just upstream from the Rideau Falls, provides a splendid setting for City Hall. Being an island, it is slightly apart from the rest of the city, yet easily accessible from Sussex Drive and the Minto bridges. This ten-acre property is also a heritage site, for it was here that the first grinding mill was located, and the island was owned by two of Ottawa's most influential citizens, Thomas MacKay and Senator W. C. Edwards.

The new City Hall—a functional eight-story building with an exterior of limestone, glass, and aluminium—was opened by Princess Margaret on 2 August 1958. It was the first fully air-conditioned building in Ottawa. Above the main entrance is an aluminium and bronze manganese casting of the city's coat-of-arms. This attractive work, which combines the modern and the classic, was executed by Art Price, a local artist.

The most noteworthy feature of City Hall is its three-story entrance section. The ground floor of this part contains a spacious marble-walled foyer with a spiral staircase that leads to the second floor. The second floor is occupied by the mayor's spacious office and the oak-panelled Council Chamber. Most of the third floor is taken by the Public Gallery.

The top floor of the main building has an observation deck from which one can see the Ottawa River and miles of surrounding country. The view is spectacular at any season of the year, but especially so in the autumn, when the Gatineau Hills are aflame with colour.

In 1877, the year that Ottawa got its first proper City Hall, the residents were given a glimpse of an invention that would change their lives—the telephone. On 13 September 1877 a prototype of Alexander Graham Bell's telephone was demonstrated at the Ottawa Exhibition. A panel of judges, which included two medical doctors, the sheriff for Carleton County, and Joseph Currier, the federal Member of Parliament, solemnly pronounced that "this method of conveying sounds to distant points must eventually result in universal adoption."

Their prediction was accurate, but there were technical problems to be overcome. The first commercial installation took place on 21 September 1877, when a line was strung between Prime Minister Alexander Mackenzie's office at the Department of Public Works (a portfolio he held in the hope of preventing graft) and the Governor General's residence at Rideau Hall. Soon after the sets were hooked up, Mackenzie complained that the line was unreliable and ordered the service removed. This would have been done had Lord Dufferin not overruled the Prime Minister and insisted that the telephones remain in place. Dufferin took this stand because his wife enjoyed having Captain François de B. Gourdeau of the Marine Department sing to her guests over the telephone in Mackenzie's office. During these long-distance concerts Lady Dufferin liked to accompany Gourdeau on her piano.

Another milestone in the development of the telephone occurred in 1879, when Thomas Ahearn established a successful connection between Ottawa and Pembroke, a distance of 110 miles. This feat was achieved with two handmade sets, which Ahearn had fashioned from cigar boxes, and were in fact an infringement on Bell's patent because Ahearn had copied Bell's invention from an article published in the *Scientific American* Magazine. However, Ahearn was an innocent transgressor of the patent laws. When he built the sets and tapped the existing telegraph line, he had merely wanted to be able to chat with a fellow telegraph operator in Pembroke. A few months later he sold his cigar boxes for $16 to settle an hotel bill.

Tom Ahearn was born in the crowded Le Breton Flats in 1855 of Irish parents. At the age of fourteen, he started work as a "runner" for the Montreal Telegraph Company at their Chaudière office, located on J. R. Booth's premises. He was a bright, hard-working lad with an engaging sense of humour, and he got along well with his fellow employees. Within the year he had learned to operate a telegraph key, and was promoted to the company's Sparks Street office. When he was nineteen, he left Ottawa to seek his fortune in New York and was hired by Western Union. Two years later, in 1876, he returned to Ottawa as chief operator for the Montreal Telegraph Company. When Bell Telephone was incorporated in 1880, Ahearn was engaged to manage Bell's Ottawa operation (a move by the company that may have been influenced by the premise that a skilled poacher makes a fine game warden).

Tom Ahearn did an excellent job promoting the telephone in Ottawa, and in 1882 was responsible for the installation of a Bell switchboard in the Parliament buildings. This was important because in the next five years two rival companies appeared on the scene: the Ottawa Telephone Company and the Wallace Company. Competition, in this instance, did not result in better service, for each company had its own circuit, and Ottawa subscribers could only speak with people on the same circuit. This situation was eventually resolved in 1899, when Bell bought out the other two concerns.

In 1882 Tom Ahearn went into partnership with an American, Warren Y. Soper, former manager of the Dominion Telegraph Company in Ottawa. The two men formed an electrical engineering and contracting business, Ahearn & Soper, which undertook a variety of tasks, including the erection of long-distance lines to Pembroke, Montreal, and Quebec for the Bell Telephone Company. Tom Ahearn subsequently resigned as manager of Bell in Ottawa but remained with them for many years in a consulting capacity. In 1915 Ahearn was made a director of this giant utility.

Ahearn & Soper were interested not only in the development of the telephone but in many applications of electricity. Their dynamic partnership figures prominently again at later stages in the city's history.

The Langevin Block was one of the first government office buildings in the capital. This massive structure, which stands on Wellington Street directly opposite the Parliament buildings, took six years to build; from 1883 to 1889. On a winter's night when frost clings to its sandstone exterior, it has a somewhat sinister appearance. One is reminded of a secret police headquarters in an Iron Curtain country. This impression is particularily vivid when you look at the edifice from Confederation Square; the east end has a covered laneway that disappears into the gloom, and it is obvious that the walls could defy cannon.

Thomas Fuller designed the Langevin Block as a functional structure that would also harmonize with the Parliament buildings. It is four stories high, with a copper mansard roof; the architectural style being a combination of Second Empire and High Victorian Gothic. The interior had broad hallways and numerous large rooms (where rows of clerks worked under the watchful eye of an overseer perched on a high stool). Initially the entire building was heated by fireplaces, but central heating was later installed. The plumbing arrangement is odd because the original plans called for a separate building to house the washrooms. During construction the plans were changed to permit access to the washrooms from the half-landings in the stairwells. When the contract for the Block was let in 1873, the estimated cost was $250,000 but by the time it was finished, it cost nearly $720,000.

The Langevin Block was named in honour of Sir Hector Langevin, Minister of Public Works from 1869 to 1873 and again from 1879 to 1891. Sir Hector was the leader of the Quebec wing of the Conservative Party and a close friend of Prime Minister Macdonald. Unfortunately, soon after the Block was completed, a scandal erupted that subsequently led to Langevin's downfall. In the preceding years, two brothers, Thomas McGreevy (Member of Parliament for Quebec West) and Robert McGreevy (an influence peddler from Montreal) had channelled Public Works contracts to the firm of Larkin, Connolly and Co. A portion of the proceeds found its way into the pockets of the McGreevy brothers, and some went to Langevin's political war chest. This happy arrangement was halted in 1890 when Thomas McGreevy—the Member of Parliament—took the incredible step of suing his brother because he was not getting his fair share of the swag. The press leapt on the scandal, and embarrassing questions were raised in the Commons. One of Langevin's rivals for the Quebec leadership, Sir Joseph Chapleau, Minister of the Printing Bureau, gleefully approached the Prime Minister with a proposal that an inquiry be held into the operations of Public Works. The matter was dropped when Sir John suggested that it might also be in the public interest to investigate the operations of the Printing Bureau.

When the House convened following the election of 1891, a newly elected member, Joseph Tarte, formally charged that funds had been misappropriated in certain Quebec Harbour contracts (an area of government spending with a notable history of irregularities). A standing committee was appointed to investigate this charge, and a few weeks later Sir John A. Macdonald died. Had Langevin not been tainted by graft, he might easily have succeeded Sir John. As it was, the evidence presented at the inquiry left Langevin no alternative but to resign in exchange for a majority opinion from the committee exonerating him of wrong-doing. McGreevy was treated more harshly: he was expelled from the House. Langevin's old enemy, Sir Joseph Chapleau—who was not implicated in the scandal—succeeded Langevin as leader of the Quebec wing, and in 1892 was appointed Lieutenant-Governor of Quebec.

A variety of government departments occupied the Langevin Block between 1889 and 1973. In 1974 the building underwent extensive renovations including the installation of air-conditioning, wall partitions, and false ceilings (the original ceilings were from seventeen to nineteen feet high). One of the few areas left unchanged was the impressive entrance hall, with its graceful staircase flanked by columns of polished granite.

Today the Langevin Block could be described as the headquarters building of the Canadian Government. It contains an office for the Prime Minister and a spacious Cabinet Room (normally used when the House is in recess) in addition to quarters for the Privy Council staff and the staff of the Prime Minister's Office. The Privy Council Office functions on behalf of the government departments, and is staffed by public servants. The Prime Minister's Office is the executive arm of the government in power, and is run by political appointees. Since 1940 the Clerk of the Privy Council (who heads the PCO) and the Secretary to the Cabinet (who is in charge of the

PMO) have been one and the same man. The person with this dual responsibility is the most powerful man in the public service.

Many of the offices are equipped with paper-shredding machines that destroy sensitive material at the end of each day. When a government changes—as it did in 1979—the paper shredders whirr for hours on end. Because of its occupants, and the nature of their business, the Langevin Block is protected by a detachment of Royal Canadian Mounted Police as well as sophisticated electronic devices, such as closed-circuit television. It is a fascinating old building, with a great many secrets.

The *Ottawa Evening Journal*, which began as a four-page newspaper in 1885, was founded by A. J. Woodburn. Its first editor was John Wesley Dafoe, who had been a cub reporter in the Parliamentary Press Gallery. However, because Dafoe's political views clashed with the Tory leanings of his publisher, he left the *Journal* the following year. Dafoe then went to the *Winnipeg Free Press* and subsequently became the most respected Canadian journalist of his time. (He received many honours, including an offer of knighthood, and served as chancellor of the University of Manitoba from 1934 until his death in 1944.) In 1899 the *Ottawa Evening Journal* was purchased by Philip D. Ross of Montreal. Ross was an imposing figure who urged his staff to read poetry and to use short words to improve their prose.

In 1917 the *Journal* started publishing a series of morning papers in addition to their regular evening paper. Each night successive editions would be dispatched by trains up the Valley and as far north as Sudbury. In 1919 Ross bought the *Ottawa Free Press* and acquired the services of its editor, E. Norman Smith. Smith was an all-round newspaperman who made an immense contribution to the *Journal* until his death in 1957. From 1930 Smith's editorial partner was Gratton O'Leary, whose superb essays achieved national prominence for the paper. O'Leary was barely five feet tall, but he had a presence, and he could captivate a political audience with eloquence and blarney. He also possessed the puckish sense of humour of a leprechaun. Appointed to the Senate by John Diefenbaker in 1962, O'Leary died in 1976.

Traditionally the *Journal* has depended upon rural people for much of its support while its longtime rival, the *Citizen*, has been more committed to urban readers. The population shift in recent decades—from the country to the city—has been a factor in widening the circulation gap between the two papers. In 1959 the *Journal* was sold to F. P. Publications Limited. Nine years later the paper moved into an office tower press building at the corner of Kent and Laurier. Despite these modern premises, *Journal* readership continued to lag. By September of 1979, after a long and bitter strike, the circulation of the *Journal* was approximately 75,000 compared to 120,000 for the *Citizen*. In the same month the *Journal* returned to publishing morning editions and made significant changes in the layout and content of the paper. This strategy was prompted by the negative impact of television news in the afternoon, and an obvious gap in the market: Ottawa had no local morning paper.

One thing that has not changed is the Tory stance of the *Journal*, even though the editor-in-chief, John W. Grace, is a boyhood friend and confidant of John Turner, former Liberal Cabinet Minister, and potential leadership candidate. Today the *Journal* styles itself as Independent-Conservative, but more than one observer has noted that it is only Independent *between* elections.

Ottawa reaped the benefits of electricity in the last two decades of the nineteenth century. Many people were involved in the early development of electrical services, but the dominant force was the firm of Ahearn & Soper.

In 1881 E. B. Eddy installed arc lighting in his main mill on the Hull side of the Chaudière Falls. (Arc lamps radiate light from a current that jumps between two electrodes, and are only suitable for specialized purposes.) The following year Levi Young installed two arc lamps in his mill on the Ottawa side of the Chaudière. Young's lamps were run by a small dynamo designed by Hiram Maxim, the American inventor of the Maxim machine gun. These lamps were such a novelty that literally hundreds of people gathered each night to see them.

The forerunner of the modern light bulb—the incandescent lamp, which radiates light when an electrical charge heats a filament suspended between two electrodes—was demonstrated at the University of Ottawa in 1883. A few months later the House of Commons and the Senate were lit by incandescent lamps. The first public lighting was a cluster of arc lights suspended from a sixty-foot tower on Christ Church Hill, which overlooks the Le Breton Flats. Before this experiment was tried, there were a number of serious letters in the papers protesting that the residents of the city would be unable to sleep because "night would be turned into day." In fact, no one lost any sleep except the proponents of the scheme. The power generator, located at the Fleet Street pumphouse, proved to be totally inadequate for its task.

In 1885 Council awarded the newly formed Ottawa Electric Light Company a contract to install 165 arc lamps on the city's streets, at an annual cost of $78 per lamp. This transaction reflected little credit on the city because the Royal Electric Company of Montreal had proposed the scheme and been promised the business. At the last moment Tom Ahearn and his associates had stepped in with a lower price, which Royal Electric was asked to match. When the Montreal firm did so, Council revealed its parochial bias by giving the contract to the local group.

On the strength of this contract, the Ottawa Electric Light Company built a power station that contained three small dynamos driven by a water wheel. The method of operating the station—which had an initial capacity of only sixteen horsepower—was exceedingly simple. Because there were no switches or meters, John Murphy, the general factotum, would judge the output by the speed of the water wheel, and when he had to stop a dynamo he would casually pull the wires loose with his bare hands. During the next few years the equipment was improved, and the capacity of the station was increased tenfold.

By this time many business establishments were using incandescent lamps in addition to the old arc lamps. The first residential installations were in groups of five to ten bulbs on a common circuit, like an old-fashioned string of Christmas tree lights. When one light was turned on or off, the entire set went on or off. Problems arose when two houses shared the same circuit; one lady nearly caused a brawl with her neighbour because she kept demonstrating the miracle of electricity to her guests by flicking the lights. Around 1890 separate circuits were introduced, which permitted each bulb to be operated independently.

In 1887 Ahearn formed the Chaudière Electric Company in Hull, which supplied power to businesses in that community and later extended its operations to Ottawa. In 1895 Ahearn merged the Chaudière Company with the Ottawa Electric Light Company, and at the same time bought out his main competitor, the Standard Electric Company. The new corporation, simply called the Ottawa Electric Company, had, for practical purposes, a monopoly on electric services in the capital.

During 1890 W. H. Howland, a former mayor of Toronto, offered to provide the city of Ottawa with an electrically powered streetcar service. Following lengthy negotiations Council agreed to grant Howland a charter, but at the last moment Howland declined to post a $5,000 performance deposit. Thomas Ahearn, who had been following the proceedings with interest, then formed a corporation, the Ottawa Electric Railway Company, and submitted a modified version of Howland's proposal—with the required deposit. The Ottawa Electric Railway was speedily granted a twenty-year charter. Most people welcomed the prospect of electric transportation, although some misgivings were voiced that Ottawa snow conditions would block the streetcars. The Sparks Street merchants, long noted for their devotion to trade, objected because they feared electric trams would upset horse traffic and keep customers away from their area.

On 25 June 1891, the first horseless streetcars rumbled through Ottawa in a five-tram cavalcade. Thomas Ahearn was the motorman in the lead coach while his partner Warren Soper drove the second car. Aboard the shiny wooden trams were Mayor Thomas Birkett, civic dignitaries, and many bowler-hatted spectators who had turned out to watch the procession. When winter came, Ahearn equipped some of his fleet with plows and rotating brushes to keep the single track clear. In 1893 three of his cars were furnished with 500-volt heaters, which made them the first electrically heated streetcars in the world.

The same year that Ahearn and Soper formed the Ottawa Electric Railway they also purchased the existing horse line, the Ottawa City Passenger Railway. In 1893 the two companies were merged. This move increased the Ottawa Electric's trackage, and allowed Ahearn to use the perpetual charter of the horse railway as a lever to extend the charter of the Ottawa Electric Railway from twenty to thirty years. Council inserted a clause in the new charter which gave the city the right to purchase the Ottawa Electric Railway when the term expired in 1923. No action was taken on this clause, and the charter was renewed until 1950, when the city bought the Ottawa Electric Railway for $6,300,000. At that time the fleet consisted of both buses and electric streetcars; buses were first tried in 1924 but did not come into permanent service until 1939. The last electric cars swayed to the barns on 1 May 1959.

Today the city has a fleet of approximately 750 vehicles, which carry an average of 6 million passengers every month on more than one hundred lines. Ahearn and Soper's old company, now officially

called the Ottawa-Carleton Regional Transportation Commission—
OCTranspo for short—is considered to be one of the most efficient
surface transportation systems in North America.

A more modest achievement by Ahearn, in 1891, was the installation of an electric motor to run the frieght elevator in the Russell
House. This sumptuous hotel stood on Confederation Square and
was, from the 1860s until the Chateau Laurier was opened in 1912,
the "political headquarters of the Dominion" as well as the gathering
place of Ottawa society. Having several entrances, it was well suited
for intrigue and romantic dalliances because one could easily come
and go without being observed. The choice of the freight elevator
rather than a passenger elevator was dictated by prudence, in view
of the erratic performance of the early generating stations.

In 1913 Tom Ahearn left his mark on the Windsor Hotel (a
favourite haunt of prominent Valley families, which occupied the
northeast corner of Metcalfe and Queen streets) when he allowed
them to use one of his inventions, the electric stove. An entire menu
was prepared, according to the *Ottawa Journal* of 29 September,
" . . . by the agency of chained lightning." The paper went on to say
" . . . the interesting and peculiar fact about the edibles was that from
the roast turkey down to the berry pie, everything had been cooked
by electricity, the first instance on record . . . The tea and coffee were
boiled on one of Mr. Ahearn's new heaters and everything was
cooked to perfection." Ahearn did not make any money from this
invention because he sold the patent to the American Heating
Corporation, in exchange for stock, and the company later went
bankrupt. He did, however, receive a gold medal from the judges at
the Central Canada Fair of 1892.

Ahearn was also a pace setter in the area of personal transportation. The *Ottawa Citizen* of 12 September 1899 noted:

> The first Automobile or horseless carriage was seen on the streets of
> Ottawa yesterday morning. Mr. Thomas Ahearn who has the dis-
> tinction of being the first in Ottawa to use the carriage, was in charge
> and manipulated it with apparent ease. The speed of the carriage can
> be varied from two to fifteen miles per hour and the motor is
> furnished by electricity. The motion is silent but swift. It is expected
> that a number of these carriages will be on exhibition at the next Fair.

The electric car enjoyed a brief popularity with ladies of fashion in
the city because of its sedate handling characteristics, but was

superceded by gasoline-powered vehicles, which had much greater range and speed. This segment of the past is rather droll in view of the September 1979 announcement by General Motors that the corporation planned to market a revolutionary automobile, powered by electricity, in the next decade.

In the 1890s City Council became seriously alarmed at the Ottawa Electric Company's monopoly on power in the capital. During the preceding years Council had issued charters to a number of rival firms with the hope that they would create competition and force down rates. However, this strategy failed because Ahearn systematically bought the new companies. When the city granted a charter to Consumers Electric in 1899, it stipulated that the company could not be sold to any other private concern. Thomas Ahearn reacted by lobbying in Parliament to have this clever restriction removed. The matter dragged on until 1905, when Philip Ross (publisher of the *Journal*) suggested to Mayor James Ellis that the city quietly buy the Consumers Electric. This was accomplished the same year—for $200,000 the taxpayers got a small substation, a distribution network, and approximately 1,300 customers. What they did not get was a generating plant—all their electricity had to be purchased from the Ottawa and Hull Power and Manufacturing Company (later the Gatineau Power Company, expropriated by the Quebec Government in 1963). This prevented the city acquisition, renamed the Municipal Electric Department, from expanding because Ahearn managed to block any increase in its allotment. The city got around this obstacle in 1907 by arranging with the Hydro Electric Commission of Ontario to buy power on behalf of the Municipal Electric Department. The following year Ahearn and Soper tightened their grip on the city's utilities when they bought the Ottawa Gas Company, which they then merged with Ottawa Electric to form the Ottawa Light, Heat and Power Company.

The turning point in the struggle between the private and municipal utilities came in 1915. That year the city joined forces with the Ontario Hydro Electric Commission, and the Municipal Electric Department became the Ottawa Hydro Electric Commission. Being part of the provincial network, Ottawa Hydro was able to call the tune and rates fell dramatically—the Ottawa Light, Heat and Power Company had no choice but to lower their rates as well. Both enterprises continued to grow during the next three decades, while the residents of Ottawa enjoyed relatively cheap energy. This situation came to an end in 1950, when the city bought the Ottawa Light,

Heat and Power Company for $7,600,000. At the time of the take-over, Ottawa Hydro had fewer than 20,000 customers, while the private firm had more than 35,000 subscribers. Among the assets purchased were two generating stations on the Ottawa River and a large office building at 56 Sparks Street (which has since been sold).

Ottawa Hydro now serves more than 100,000 customers in the capital region. Because its power is sold at a fraction above cost, its rates are among the lowest in Canada.

From Confederation—when the Department of Agriculture was established with a staff of twenty-seven—until World War One, farming was Canada's main industry. In 1886 Parliament authorized the Department of Agriculture to build five research stations across the country. The purpose of these stations was to determine the best livestock breeds, plant varieties, and farming methods for the different regions in Canada. The headquarters station, which would also be responsible for the provinces of Ontario and Quebec, was to be located in Ottawa. In October 1886 William Saunders, who had just completed a survey of research facilities in the United States and other countries, was appointed the first director. A month later 466 acres were purchased on the western edge of the city for the Central Experimental Farm.

Saunders was not only a highly competent and frugal administrator but an intellectual prodigy. By the time he came to Ottawa he was a renowned botanist, he had been professor of Materia Medica at the University of Western Ontario, and he had founded the Ontario School of Pharmacy. These credentials were remarkable for a man who was forced to leave school at the age of thirteen and who was almost entirely self-educated.

The experimental stations soon became involved in all phases of research, from buffalo-breeding to bee-keeping. From the outset Saunders stressed the need for practical rather than theoretical results. Despite his administrative load, he found time to engage in research. Among his personal research contributions were hybrid grapes, currants, and gooseberries that could withstand harsh winter conditions. By crossing giant Siberian crab-apple trees with hardy Canadian apple trees, he produced varieties that could survive as far north as Fort Vermilion, Alberta, where the temperature can drop to -50 C. Working with his son Charles (who was later knighted), he developed a number of frost-resistant grains, the most famous being Marquis wheat. By 1917 Marquis wheat accounted for 90 percent of the Canadian crop. The importance to Canada of cereal crops that can produce high yields in a short growing season, continues to this day. In 1979 Canada's exports of wheat alone were worth approximately $2 billion. When William Saunders retired after a quarter of a century as director, he had won a string of degrees and honours, and the Dominion Experimental Farm System was known throughout the world. Today, there are forty-eight stations across the country, staffed by nearly four thousand employees.

The Central Experimental Farm in Ottawa now covers nearly 1,200 acres. This area encompasses a number of office buildings, including the Sir John Carling Building—headquarters of the Department of Agriculture—as well as ornate wooden barns, various outbuildings, and greenhouses. A 2,800-acre satellite farm was established in the Green Belt, west of Woodroffe Avenue, in 1970. The satellite farm is devoted to animal research and the control of diseases; for this reason the property is restricted to visitors. The main farm is the site of soil-testing experiments, research into forage and cereal crops, botanical gardening, and laboratory research. The Central Experimental Farm sends tens of thousands of seed samples to farms across the country, and bulletins on a host of topics. An advisory service handles an enormous correspondence dealing with agricultural inquiries. By simply picking up the telephone, residents of Ottawa can get free advice on such diverse questions as the control of aphids or the best time to plant petunias.

A visit to the Central Experimental Farm is a rewarding experience. Set apart from the office buildings there is an arboretum with an incredible variety of trees, a charming rock garden, greenhouses, and ornamental gardens, manicured parkland, and vast fields under cultivation. During the summer one can stroll along shaded paths or enjoy a conducted tour on an open wagon drawn by a pair of Clydesdales. Since 1912 the Farm has held an annual Chrysanthemum Show, which is now the largest on the North American continent: more than 4,000 plants with approximately 12,000 blooms are displayed. These flowers represent every conceivable variety, ranging in height from eight inches to ten feet. It is not unusual for five thousand visitors to tour the greenhouses in a single day.

The Central Experimental Farm is the largest farm entirely surrounded by city in the world. For Ottawans it is an oasis that enhances the beauty and tranquility of the capital.

In the bleak month of November 1887 a lanky young Scot named Charles Ogilvy opened a dry-goods store at 92 Rideau Street. He sold quality goods at a reasonable mark-up and refused to stock high fashion or frivolous items. During the next forty years Ottawans patronized his establishment in growing numbers, and his premises expanded from 600 square feet of floor space to encompass most of the block.

Charles Ogilvy was a religious man who curtained his show windows on Sundays because he considered this form of advertising a violation of the Sabbath. He was both a strict disciplinarian and a generous philanthropist. Having no children, he looked upon his employees as part of his family. In the 1930s he instituted a pension plan for his staff (which was unusual at the time) and before his death actually gave the store to the employees—an unusual action at any time. Although he amassed a large fortune, he lived an abstemious existence until his death in 1950. His only obvious indulgence was to have three identical houses built in various parts of the city. This permiited him to travel—within the confines of the capital—safe in the knowledge that wherever he was staying the furniture and the light switches would always be in the same place.

In 1929 a sixteen-year-old boy named D. Roy Hyndman was hired to work in the sporting goods department. His first assignment was selling roller skates, which were priced at 42 cents a pair (a tie-in with the store's forty-second anniversary). During the Depression years Hyndman not only kept his job but was promoted to the business office. When war was declared in 1939 Hyndman left to join the Royal Canadian Air Force. After he made this decision he was asked by Mr. Ogilvy to stop by his house to say good-bye. Ogilvy, who was living at the corner of Chapel and Wilbrod streets at the time, thanked Hyndman for his past services and gave him one hundred shares of company stock. These were the first shares to be given to an employee. D. Roy Hyndman retired from the Air Force as a wing commander in 1945 and returned to the store the same year.

The president of Charles Ogilvy Limited from 1950 to 1962 was Lewis A. Burpee, who had guided the store throughout the difficult postwar era. Burpee died in 1962, the same year that Ogilvy's opened a large branch in the Billings Bridge Shopping Plaza. Ten years later a second major branch was opened in the Lincoln Fields Shopping Centre. D. Roy Hyndman succeeded Lewis Burpee as president in 1962—in 1979 Hyndman marked his fiftieth year with the firm.

Charles Ogilvy Limited is the oldest and largest independent store in Ottawa. It is also the only major merchandiser owned by its employees. Despite competition from the large chains, which can buy in quantity and offer deep discounts, Ogilvy's continues to prosper. Charles Ogilvy's belief that residents of the capital would pay a fair price for sensible, long-wearing goods would appear to be as valid today as it was in 1887.

In 1888 a small group of ladies founded the Ottawa Humane Society. Initially the Society was concerned with the care of children and the aged as well as animal welfare. These multiple tasks proved too much for the Society; by the end of the century, care of the aged was the sole responsibility of specialized institutions. In 1905 child welfare was assumed by a newly formed organization, which is now called the Children's Aid Society of Ottawa-Carleton.

The Ottawa Humane Society seeks to prevent cruelty to animals and to relieve their suffering by means of a four-pronged approach.

It maintains a shelter and an ambulance service (instituted in 1905) for the care of animals. It intervenes in cases of cruelty, and if necessary prosecutes these offences in court. It petitions government to improve animal legislation. It works to educate the public—particularly children—through lectures and shows. Since 1905 the Society has sponsored an annual essay competition in Ottawa elementary schools.

In 1933, with the aid of public donations, the Society built a shelter on municipal property at 49 Mann Avenue. When the city sold this land in 1949, the Society lost both the site and its building. Largely through the efforts of its president, the late Stanley Lewis (a former Ottawa mayor), the Society was given another lot on Bayview Avenue by Council for the token price of one dollar. A modern shelter was erected on this site in 1950, which was expropriated in 1966 for $187,000. The proceeds from this sale were used to build the present shelter on Champagne Street, which includes a veterinary hospital. The hospital is not operated by the Society but leased to private interests with the understanding that animals in the shelter can be treated there at any time.

In an average year the shelter receives approximately 10,000 dogs and 9,700 cats, as well as several hundred other animals, which range from gerbils to beavers. Between five and six hundred birds are brought to the shelter. Many of these are fledglings that cannot fly or migrating birds (including ducks and geese)that have been injured. Whenever possible, wild species are released as soon as they are well, and foster homes are found for domestic pets. During the past decade radio station CKBY and the *Ottawa Journal* have helped this program by advertising animals available for adoption. Each year some 2,500 unwanted dogs are placed in homes, in addition to approximately two thousand lost dogs being returned to their owners; these figures are somewhat lower for unwanted and lost cats. An equal number of dogs and cats are never claimed. These unfortunate creatures must be euthanized because the Society has neither the space nor the funds to keep them.

For many years the Society has employed a full-time inspector who is authorized by the city to enforce laws relating to animal cruelty. Among the numerous calls each day (recently a woman phoned to ask if mice were really baby rats) there are often reports of animal abuse. Investigating these complaints can be a depressing and frustrating task because of the difficulty in prosecuting offenders.

In April 1948 the inspector paid a call on the Argentine Ambassador in response to complaints that the Ambassador was maltreating his dogs. His Excellency was innocent, but was so incensed at the accusation that he charged the inspector with violating diplomatic immunity. Some days later the Consul-General of the Dominion Republic inquired after the health of the Argentine Ambassador's dogs—which had died of distemper—and the Argentine took umbrage at the question. This incident escalated into a fiasco when the Consul-General challenged the Ambassador to a duel. Neither party gained satisfaction.

The Ottawa Humane Society received another unusual call on 7 January 1972. This time a female deer had crossed the frozen Ottawa River, ascended Entrance Valley, made her way along the Canal, and ended up in the National Arts Centre. When the inspector arrived, the deer had been chased into a washroom, and it was a toss-up as to which was the more agitated, the doe or the staff of the Centre. The inspector quickly tranquillized the frightened animal and took it back to the shelter in the ambulance. A few days later the doe was released in the Gatineau Hills, none the worse for her experience.

The Ottawa Humane Society is run by a dedicated staff, whose

Managing Director since 1946 has been Mr. G. K. Switzer. Originally, the Executive Committee was restricted to women, but in 1900 the constitution was amended to allow up to 50 percent males, and this restriction was later dropped entirely. The Ladies Auxiliary works hard throughout the year in various fund-raising activities. Donations and membership support comes from a broad cross-section of the population of Ottawa.

Now that Ottawa is subject to regional government, the Society has greatly increased its scope of operations. This change is reflected in its new name, The Humane Society of Ottawa-Carleton.

13

Recreation in the Capital
1879 to 1891

THE OTTAWA FIELD-NATURALISTS' CLUB was founded in 1879 by James Fletcher, the first Dominion botanist and entomologist. In his opening address to the members, Fletcher said: " . . . everything in nature is interesting and beautiful; and I defy anyone to bring me a single object, picked up by a country roadside, which is not beautiful, and even exquisitely so—a stick, a piece of straw, a leaf, or a stone, it matters not what, if properly examined and understood, they are all lovely."

These words sum up the wide-ranging curiosity, the appreciation of nature, and the search for knowledge that characterize the club to this day. Monthly soirées held during its first year covered such diverse topics as the "Contractibility of the Spores of *Palmella hyalina,* (a form of algae), and "Graphite Deposits in the Ottawa Valley." The most fascinating soirée was a "Practical Demonstration of the Brain" by Dr. J. A. Grant, who dissected a human brain in the gas-lit meeting room.

The origin of the Ottawa Field-Naturalists' Club can be traced back to the Bytown Mechanics Institute (a body dedicated to intellectual pursuits, not the use of tools), which was established in 1847. Six years later the Bytown Mechanics Institute added "Athenaeum" to its name to highlight its literary endeavours. A rival organization, the Natural History Society of Ottawa, was founded in 1863. The Mechanics Institute and the Natural History Society merged in 1869 to form the Ottawa Literary and Scientific Society, which boasted a small library. The Ottawa Literary and Scientific Society faded in the next decade, and most of the surviving members then joined James Fletcher's Ottawa Field-Naturalists' Club.

The club has always kept a careful record of significant findings from field trips and personal research. For the first seven years important papers and demonstrations were noted in the *Transactions*; in 1877 the *Transactions* were melded into a new magazine, *The Ottawa Naturalist*. To properly reflect the scope of its contents, *The Ottawa Naturalist* changed its name in 1919 to *The Canadian Field-Naturalist*. This scientific quarterly has an international list of more than two thousand subscribers, many being institutions. In 1966 the club started a second magazine, *Trail and Landscape*, to cover local topics of a "popular" nature, which had previously been dealt with in periodic newsletters. *Trail and Landscape* is published five times each year.

Today the Ottawa Field-Naturalists' Club has more than 1,200 members, many of whom reside outside of Canada. The club has an excellent field trip program and is a vital force on conservation issues. The published findings of club members over the past century represent a wealth of important data on the natural history of Canada.

In 1879, when the Ottawa Field-Naturalists' Club was founded, the population of the capital was approximately 25,000. Because of the size of the city and the affluence of its inhabitants, the time was ripe for the formation of other recreational clubs. Between 1882 and 1891 three sporting institutions were established that are still flourishing (under slightly different names) today: the Ottawa Tennis Club, the Britannia Aquatic Club, and the Ottawa Golf Club.

Organized cricket, curling, and lacrosse started in the middle of the century. The Bytown Cricket Club (renamed the Ottawa Cricket Club) founded by Magistrate George Baker in 1849, played its matches on the green at Barrack Hill. The game was so popular that John MacKinnon, president of the Bytown & Prescott Railway, was continually badgering his business manager to leave the office and play cricket. When construction of the Parliament buildings forced the cricketers off Barrack Hill, they were welcomed at Rideau Hall by Canada's first Governor General, Lord Monck. Since 1866 the grounds of Government House have been used by Ottawa devotees of this British game. Today Rideau Hall still provides a pavilion and two well-rolled pitches for local cricketers. On summer weekends one can watch the players, dressed in traditional white, engaged in league matches.

The Ottawa Rowing Club, located at the water's edge below Lady Grey Drive, was founded in 1867. This club chose a near neighbour, Sir John A. Macdonald, as its first president. Because rowing is a strenuous and specialized sport, the membership has always been relatively small, but the members have frequently been among the Canadian oarsmen at the Olympics. This club is unique in many respects; during World War One every member enlisted, in World War Two, all but one man joined the armed forces. In the late 1940s the club went into a decline, and by 1967 it had only three members. Fortunately the club has been on the upswing ever since that crisis. In addition to a surge of new members, the Ottawa Rowing Club sponsors more than one hundred novices from the University of Ottawa, Carleton College, Ashbury College, and Woodroffe High School. It is now the oldest rowing club in Canada, and has the dubious distinction of owning the oldest wooden rowing clubhouse in North America. Most of the oarsmen practise after work—on a still summer evening it is a pretty sight to see their slender shells gliding along the Ottawa.

The Bytown Curling Club was founded in 1851 by one of Ottawa's pioneer lumbermen, Colonel Allan Gilmour. The club changed its name to the Ottawa Curling Club when Bytown was incorporated as a city in 1855. Colonel Gilmour and a succession of his nephews—the Manuels—not only sponsored the club financially but also served as presidents from 1851 to 1922. One of the club's early notables was George Hutchinson who, despite the handicap of a wooden leg, threw a cunning "rock" (Hutchinson also played goalie for a local lacrosse team). The first permanent rink of the Ottawa Curling Club was a brick structure, built in 1862, on Cartier Square. When the Drill Hall was erected a few years later, the club was forced to move. After playing in several uptown locations, the club eventually settled at its present site on O'Connor Street. The Ottawa Curling Club has not only hosted many important bonspiels, but has also produced some of Canada's top curlers. The Rideau Curling Club, founded in 1888, is another venerable institution dedicated to this sport in the capital.

The first game of lacrosse—Canada's national game—was played in Ottawa in 1859. On Dominion Day, 1867, a lacrosse match was one of the main events. Two Ottawa teams, the Stars and the Capitals, were famous throughout Canada in the latter part of the century; in 1877 the Capitals won the "world" championship. Until the end of the 1960s Ottawa had a city league that was supported in the main by players from Lower Town. As a result of a major urban renewal program in Lower Town during the next decade, many of these players moved away. Today the adjoining municipalities of Gloucester and Nepean have junior lacrosse leagues, but the capital no longer has a league of its own.

The Ottawa Tennis Club, founded in 1881, was an offshoot of the Ottawa Cricket Club. However, the first racquet game played in the capital was court tennis, not lawn tennis. Court tennis differs from lawn tennis because the walls and ceiling as well as the floor of the enclosure are used to keep the ball in play. Lord Dufferin built a wooden addition for court tennis at Rideau Hall in 1873. The interior of this structure could also be disguised with hangings to make it suitable for informal entertaining. For more than a century the court has been draped in candy-striped cotton, and it is now called the Tent Room.

The game of lawn tennis—invented in 1876—was introduced to Ottawa by British officers on the vice-regal staff. Dufferin had a grass court built for them in the grounds of Rideau Hall around 1878. The cricketers tried their hand at the new game and liked it so much that in the autumn of 1881 a group of them got together to form the Ottawa Tennis Club. The club's first courts were conveniently located between Lisgar and Cooper streets on land donated by C. T. Bate, a prominent businessman and former Mayor. The club had a gala opening in June 1882, and when winter came, the enthusiastic members played their matches in the Drill Hall on Cartier Square. (Eighty years later, the erection of an indoor tennis court was hailed as an Ottawa milestone.) In 1888 the club moved to a site just behind the Drill Hall, but was forced to relocate again in 1902. This move, to Patterson Avenue, coincided with the expansion of the Ottawa Golf Club, which attracted many Ottawa Tennis Club members. To bolster its sagging fortunes, the tennis club added lawn bowling to its facilities and changed its name to the Ottawa Tennis and Lawn Bowling Club. This was a wise decision because the lawn bowlers became the mainstay of the club in the ensuing years. The club purchased another site, on Third Avenue, in 1907 and remained there until 1922. During this period differences in opinion arose between the lawn bowlers and the tennis players.

In 1912 a group of the tennis players resigned from the club, and established the Rideau Lawn Tennis Club.

The Rideau Lawn Tennis Club acquired a large property on the east bank of the Rideau River, which soon attracted the best players in the city. Since then the club has hosted the Canadian Junior Championships for many years as well as a number of Davis Cup matches. The Rideau—now called the Rideau Tennis and Squash Club—has recently become a year-round racquet facility with the installation of squash courts, and a fabric bubble over four of its nineteen tennis courts. The standard of play continues to be above average, although the club now has nearly two thousand members.

In 1922 the Ottawa Tennis and Lawn Bowling Club moved to Cameron Avenue, on the north bank of the Rideau River. The next forty years were difficult ones for the tennis division, but good management plus the tennis boom have reversed this situation. Today the club has regained much of its former prestige, and its eighteen courts are in excellent condition. The bowling division, which "carried the pail" during the lean years, has two well-manicured rinks, each with eight lanes. The combined membership of the club is approximately 1,400.

The Britannia Aquatic Club came into existence, in an informal way, around 1887. The first clubhouse was an abandoned mill, situated on a point that juts into the Ottawa River at the foot of Lake Deschenes. In 1891 the club changed its name to the Britannia Nautical Club; then four years later, to indicate its role as a community centre, the name was changed to the Britannia Boat House Club. In 1896 a new clubhouse was built, but the membership was growing so fast that this building proved inadequate from the day it was opened. In 1902 the executive persuaded a fellow boating enthusiast, Thomas Ahearn (who controlled the Ottawa Electric Railway, which ran an excursion line to the Britannia Pier), to build them a clubhouse at the end of his pier. Ahearn did so with a flourish. When the building was completed in 1905, it immediately became the headquarters of the club, and their other clubhouse was used for storage purposes. Ahearn's premises were a great success—membership soared to two thousand—until they were destroyed by fire in 1918. The club lost a great deal of equipment, records, and trophies, and did not recover from this blow until after World War Two. In 1928, when it became obvious that the pier clubhouse would never be rebuilt, the club changed its name to the Britannia Boat Club and settled permanently in its original site.

In the early days paddling and rowing were major activities. A Britannia team won the Canadian War Canoe Championship in 1902, and a Britannia man, Frank Amyot, won a gold medal for the 1000-metre singles paddling event at the Berlin Olympics in 1936. Paddling and rowing gradually died out, and the emphasis shifted to sailing. In this connection, several Britannia sailors have distinguished themselves in world competition. In 1950 the club changed its name, for the fifth time, and became officially known as the Britannia Yacht Club, Inc. Today its membership is approximately 1,200, and its greatly improved harbour has mooring facilities for some six hundred small craft.

The Ottawa Golf Club was founded by a newly arrived Scot, Hugh Renwick, in 1891. Initially the members had a nine-hole course on fifty acres of land in Sandy Hill, which is now Strathcona Park. The popularity of the game prompted a move five years later to a 108-acre tract, sufficient for a twelve-hole course, on the Chelsea Road in Hull. This property included a substantial stone clubhouse, the former residence of Thomas Brigham, Philemon Wright's son-in-law. In 1902 the Ottawa Golf Club sold its course to the International Portland Cement Company for a handsome profit. (The course covered the huge limestone deposit used by Thomas MacKay when he built the Canal locks in 1827 and is still being worked by the Canada Cement Company to this day.) With the proceeds of the sale, the golf club bought 125 acres on the Aylmer Road opposite the Champlain Bridge. A clubhouse was built, and play commenced at the new location in 1903. Since then the clubhouse has been demolished by fire on two occasions, in 1909 and 1930, and the club has increased its holdings to more than 300 acres. In 1912 the Ottawa Golf Club enhanced its status when King Edward VII granted permission for its name to be changed to the Royal Ottawa Golf Club. Today the Royal Ottawa boasts a fine clubhouse, a ladies' nine-hole course, and a championship eighteen-hole course. The club has approximately 1,200 members, and there is usually a waiting list. Belonging to the capital's oldest golf club carries a certain *cachet* that is not related to one's skill on the links.

Skiing was introduced to Canada in 1887 by a visitor to Government House, Lord Frederick Hamilton. Lord Frederick (who was staying with his sister, Lady Lansdowne, wife of the Governor General) demonstrated a pair of skis at Rideau Hall which he had picked up in Russia. His first stately glide down the gentle slope brought jeers and catcalls, which marred the historic occasion. This churlish reaction may seem surprising in view of the ski mania that pervades Ottawa each winter, but at that time tobogganing was a far more exciting pastime. Lord Frederick told in his memoirs of the antics of his nephews, The Honourable Henry Petty-Fitzmaurice aged fifteen, and the Honourable Charles Petty-Fitzmaurice aged thirteen:

> The Lansdowne boys were very expert on toboggans, and could go down the Ottawa slides standing erect, a thing no adult could possibly manage. They had fitted their machines with gong-bells and red and green lanterns, and the "Ottawa River Express" would come whizzing down at night with bells clanging and lights gleaming.

Even snowshoeing was considered more fun than skiing. Lord Frederick inferred that snowshoeing—which he noted brought unaccustomed muscles into play, causing *mal de raquettes*—held a subtle social appeal: "In my time, snow-shoe tramps at night, across-country into the woods, were one of the standard winter amusements of Ottawa, and the girls showed great dexterity in vaulting fences with their snow-shoes on."

Snowshoeing and toboganning are still popular recreations, but the vast majority prefer to ski. Within a few minutes' drive of the capital are superb facilities for this sport, including Camp Fortune, the largest ski club in the world. Today, skiing provides untold enjoyment for thousands of Ottawans—and a reliable source of income for the city's orthopaedic surgeons.

Lord Lansdowne was succeeded as Governor General by Lord Stanley in 1888, the year after Lord Frederick Hamilton's skiing visit. Stanley's name is also associated with winter sports, for he donated the Stanley Cup, which is emblematic of hockey supremacy in North America.

One of Lord Stanley's duties that year was to officiate at the opening of the first Central Canada Exhibition. Prior to 1888 there had been a number of large fairs in Ottawa, but they had been sporadic rather than annual events. The purpose of the Central Canada Exhibition, which had been organized by some of Ottawa's leading citizens, was to exhibit local agricultural products and live-stock. However, from the outset it was recognized that popular entertainment was also essential to make the fair a success. Paradoxically, the popular entertainment part of the exhibition has always had the most problems.

The inaugural year was no exception; a horrifying accident occurred in connection with a parachute descent from "Professor" C. H. Grimley's balloon. It took most of an afternoon to fill the bag of the balloon, and once it was fully inflated, twenty men were required to hold it in place on the ground. When the signal to let go was given, one man, Thomas Wensley, did not do so and was carried aloft. The *Ottawa Journal* graphically described the tragedy:

> At about 1000 feet the man released his grasp and began a descent to earth, while hundreds of those who stood nearby, unable to endure the spectacle, hid their faces. Grown men blanched; women wept hysterically; others fainted outright. For perhaps 20 feet the man, whose identity was still unknown, fell in a perpendicular position, and then slowly it was altered to the horizontal with legs and arms outstretched. The thud when he struck the earth behind Mr. Holt's dwelling on Bank Street was distinctly audible throughout the western part of the grounds. He met instant death.

The home of the Central Canada Exhibition, which is now the oldest and largest agricultural show in Canada, has always been Lansdowne Park, a sixty-acre site between Bank Street and the Rideau Canal. During recent decades the focus of the Exhibition has shifted from the farmer to the merchant. Each year the media become more strident in urging people to attend the "Ex," implying that it is one's civic duty. At the same time citizens who live in the vicinity of Lansdowne Park have become increasingly vocal in their protests that the Exhibition creates unacceptable noise and traffic jams.

Fortunately the conflict between the ambitions of the Exhibition Committee and the wishes of the surrounding neighbourhood may soon be resolved. As long ago as 1953 the National Capital Commission offered the Central Canada Exhibition Association a 250-acre site in the township of Gloucester. This is now being seriously considered by the Exhibition Committee, and a move may take place in the future. Should the fair relocate to this rural setting, it will be an ideal place for agricultural displays as well as commercial and carnival attractions.

14

The Jews:
An Influential Minority
1882 to 1979

T HE FIRST JEWISH resident of Ottawa was a great strapping
rough-tongued man named Moses Bilsky. He arrived in the
capital in 1857 from nearby Kemptville, where his father had owned
a small store. Born in Lithuania twenty-seven years earlier, Bilsky
has been described as Ottawa's original wandering Jew. In 1861 he
made a long and unsuccessful trip to the Cariboo country of British
Columbia in search of gold. Upon his return, he went south to fight
for the Union forces in the American Civil War. At the close of the
Civil War he inadvertently became a gun-runner to the opposing
factions in the Mexican Civil War. This employment was lucrative
but not without hazard, so he returned to Ottawa and set up a
trinket shop on Rideau Street. In 1874 Bilsky travelled to New York
and married Pauline Reich, the daughter of a wealthy Brooklyn
businessman. Had Bilsky's father-in-law known how poor he was,
the marriage would never have taken place. Moses and his sixteen-
year-old bride lived briefly in Ottawa, and then moved on to Montreal and Mattawa. In the mid-1880s Bilsky settled permanently in
the capital where he bought a house on Daly Avenue, and established
a jewellery store-*cum*-pawnshop on Confederation Square.
It was not until 1888 that there were enough Jewish families in

Ottawa to form a minyan (ten males over the age of thirteen), which is the minimum number for group religious services. For the next four years religious services were held in the homes of Moses Bilsky and John Dover, another early resident. In 1892 the Adath Jeshurum congregation built a synagogue on Murray Street and sent Bilsky to New York to recruit a rabbi. The man Bilsky chose was a Russian-born rabbinical student named Jacob Mirsky. His synagogue—Ottawa's first—proved to be badly located because it was adjacent to a food processor whose staple product was pork and beans. During Sabbath services the air in the synagogue was laden with the odour of cooking pork, a sacrilege in Judaism because the pig is considered an unclean animal. To solve this problem the congregation moved from Murray Street to King Edward Avenue.

In 1899 a bright young Lithuanian born Jew named Archibald Jacob Freiman came to Ottawa and opened a department store in partnership with a middle-aged resident, Moses Cramer. The partnership could have been a happy one if Mrs. Cramer had not insisted on treating Freiman—who was only nineteen at the time— as an inexperienced boy. In 1903 Archie Freiman married Lillian Bilsky, one of Moses Bilsky's daughters. The same year he went into partnership with his father and opened a rival emporium at 73 Rideau Street, the Archibald J. Freiman Department Store. This partnership lasted fourteen stormy years until Archie Freiman could no longer stand his father's continual criticism and bought him out. Operating as sole proprietor, Freiman then obtained a hefty bank loan, which he used to build Ottawa's largest department store, which occupied almost an entire block on Rideau Street, between Sussex and Mosgrove. The store flourished, and remained in the family until 1971, when it was sold to the Hudson's Bay Company. Three years after the sale City Council changed the name of Mosgrove Street to Freiman Street.

Archie Freiman was a remarkable man who, more than thirty years after his death, is still considered by many members of Ottawa's Jewish community to be the outstanding figure in their history. When he came to Canada from Lithuania he could not speak a word of English, and he had only four years of schooling in this country. Despite these handicaps he was a millionaire by the time he was thirty-three. In 1913 Freiman bought a mansion on Somerset Street (originally built for the lumber baron C. B. Pattee) which is now the Army Headquarters Officers Mess. A few years later he built a sumptuous summer residence on 525 acres in the Gatineau Hills.

This granite house had all the amenities, and was perched on a hill with a superb view of Meach Lake. Although he had no background of wealth, by the time he was forty, Archie Freiman was on comfortable terms with the Prime Minister and many internationally prominent people.

Archibald Freiman was the undisputed leader of the Ottawa Jewish community, and as a past president of the Federation of Zionist Societies, a major contributor to world Zionism. Both he and his wife Lillian devoted much of their time to helping less fortunate people, regardless of race or religion. Lillian Freiman was awarded a Vimy Medal for her work on behalf of ex-soldiers following World War One, and in 1934 she was made an officer of the Order of the British Empire. Their only son, Lawrence, born in 1909, served three terms as president of the Zionist Organizations of Canada, and was made an officer of the Order of Canada in 1967.

Archibald Freiman's death was linked to that of his old friend, Rabbi Jacob Mirsky, the spiritual advisor of the Jewish community. On 4 June 1944 Freiman gave a moving eulogy to Rabbi Mirsky at the unveiling of a memorial tablet in the synagogue, and then, moments later, quietly died in his seat.

The Jews came to Ottawa in small waves, starting in the 1880s, which coincided with the *pogroms* in Europe. Most arrived as destitute immigrants, but they were not a drain on the civic purse because the Jewish community looked after its own. Today the Jewish population in the capital is approximately ten thousand and there are five synagogues. This minority group has its own social structure whose focus is the Jewish Community Centre. Ottawa's Jews are noted both for their business acumen and their support of the arts. Lawrence Freiman is an obvious example of a man who has played this dual role. During his tenure as president of A. J. Freiman Limited, he was also an important promoter of the Ottawa Philharmonic Orchestra, a fund raiser for the Stratford Festival, and the first chairman of the board of trustees of the National Arts Centre.

All of the early Jewish business concerns started on the proverbial shoestring. The story of the Pure Spring Company—founded in 1912 by Rabbi Mirsky's eldest son, David—is a typical one. David Mirsky had little education, and was forced to go to work at the age of fourteen. He started as a "newsie" peddling fruit, pop, and magazines for the Canadian Pacific Railway Company on their Gatineau train. Five years later he was promoted to the job of freight agent.

Working in the station, he noticed the tremendous volume of soft drinks being imported into the city. This gave him the idea of manufacturing soft drinks locally. Through the kindness of the manager of Bradings Brewery, Colonel Plunkett Taylor (father of Canadian industrialist, E. P. Taylor) young Mirsky was allowed to build a shack beside the brewery and to tap the spring that flowed down the granite escarpment at the foot of Bronson Avenue. Mirsky called his product Pure Spring after this special water supply. His ginger ale was a popular seller from the outset and his business grew quickly. During the next two decades Mirsky made some errors—such as turning down the Coca-Cola franchise because he did not believe it would sell—but he was right more often than he was wrong, and he was able to expand his investments into other areas. David Mirsky lost everything in the Depression except for his original bottling plant beside the brewery. He managed to keep his business solvent through World War Two but sugar rationing prevented any increase in sales.

David Mirsky's sons, Norman and Mervin, were responsible for the company's phenomenal growth in the postwar years (Mervin had served overseas with the Canadian Army, attaining the rank of lieutenant-colonel). In 1963 the Mirsky family sold their business to Crush International Limited for several million dollars. Pure Spring ginger ale—marketed mainly in the Ottawa area—has the highest per capita sales of any ginger ale in North America.

Another success story concerns Moses Loeb, who left Russia in 1910 and settled in Ottawa two years later. Loeb saved up $200 and bought a confectionary store on the corner of Wellington and Broad streets, (opposite the Canadian Pacific Railway station, where David Mirsky had been employed). This location had the drawback of only being busy twice a day—when the trains came in—so Loeb let his wife manage the store while he supplemented their income by peddling candy with a horse and cart. The peddling business proved more profitable than the candy store and was subsequently incorporated as M. Loeb Limited, wholesale distributors of tobacco and confectionary products.

Moses Loeb had six children, all boys, two of whom became physicians. Four of his sons, including Bertram, served in the Canadian Army during World War Two. To help out his father Bertram went into the business at the end of the war. When Moses Loeb died in 1951, Bertram was elected president of M. Loeb Limited by his brothers. They made a sound choice; to describe Bertram Loeb as "dynamic" is an understatement.

In 1952 M. Loeb Limited acquired the IGA supermarket franchise for eastern Ontario and western Quebec. This franchise enjoyed phenomenal growth, and M. Loeb Limited added further impetus to its earnings by buying several other major concerns. During the 1960s and early 1970s Bertram Loeb's brothers sold most of their shares in M. Loeb Limited, and effective control passed from family hands. In 1977 Bertram Loeb sold his personal holding for approximately $6 million and retired from the business. At that time M. Loeb's annual sales were in excess of $1 billion. Bert Loeb—who majored in philosophy at university—now devotes his time to charitable work, and is presently chairing the fund-raising drive for the Ottawa Civic Hospital. During the past twenty years the Loeb family have given more than $1 million to worthwhile local causes.

Ottawa has been free of virulent anti-Semitism. Since the arrival of Moses Bilsky, Jews and Gentiles in the capital have respected each other, even though the two groups did not mix socially until recent years (the Rideau Club admitted its first Jewish members in 1964). When John Dover canvassed for donations to build the first synagogue in 1892, the largest gifts came from two Christians, J. R. Booth, and Senator W. C. Edwards. Their generosity has been repaid handsomely. In 1969 J. Harold Shenkman, a real estate magnate and art patron (whose father came from Russia in 1905), donated $500,000 for the new Young Men's Christian Association building on O'Connor Street.

While very few of Ottawa's Jews are millionaire philanthropists, most are civic-minded, law-abiding citizens. These virtues were installed by Moses Bilsky, who set high standards of conduct for his fellow immigrants. On one occasion Bilsky was dismayed to learn that a Jew was being held in the Nicholas Street Gaol at the onset of some High Holy Days. Bilsky marched in to see his old friend, Alonzo Dawson, the Governor, and demanded that the prisoner be released into his custody until the religious period was over. Dawson acceded to this unusual request. When Bilsky returned his charge a few days later, he told the Governor: "You can have the son-of-a-bitch. No Jew should be in jail in the first place, and certainly not during High Holy Days!"

15

Steps in the Right Direction

1897 to 1899

IN 1897 THERE were celebrations throughout the British Empire to mark Queen Victoria's sixtieth year on the throne. At Rideau Hall, the Countess of Aberdeen founded the Victorian Order of Nurses for Canada as a memorial to the Queen's Jubilee.

Lady Aberdeen, a buxom, warm-hearted woman with immense energy and little tact, was a zealous advocate of social reform. During her husband's tenure as Governor General (from 1893 to 1898) Lady Aberdeen helped to found several clubs for underprivileged people, the Ottawa Maternity Hospital, the Ottawa branch of the Young Womens' Christian Association, the May Court Club, and the National Council of Women for Canada. She was the founding president of the latter organization and also served as president of the International Council of Women for many years.

In May 1896 a resolution from the Local Council of Women of Vancouver stressed the critical need for nurses to serve in the outlying districts of Canada. A few weeks later the Local Council of Women of Halifax wrote their president at Rideau Hall suggesting that a district nursing order be established to honour Queen Victoria's Jubilee. A committee consisting of Lady Aberdeen and five other executive officers (including Lady Ritchie and Mrs. H. F.

Bronson of Ottawa) considered these submissions and agreed upon the formation of such a nursing order.

At a meeting with Lady Aberdeen on 31 January 1897 Prime Minister Laurier gave his support to the concept and agreed to ask Parliament for a grant of $1 million. During February public meetings were held in Ottawa, Montreal, Toronto, Vancouver, and Halifax to promote the Victorian Order. With the Parliamentary grant in mind, Lady Aberdeen also gave a personal briefing to representatives from the Senate and the House of Commons.

Just as the Order appeared to be safely launched, a storm of protest arose from the Canadian medical fraternity. The reason for this sudden outburst was their fear that the nurses would be inadequately trained and would compete with local doctors. These allegations were unfounded, but the harm had been done. In newspaper advertisements the Ontario Medical Association trumpeted that the Victorian Order was "a scheme deleterious to the health of the country." The press gave considerable space to these protests, and Sir Charles Tupper (who was angry with Lord Aberdeen for refusing to sanction political appointments after Tupper's election defeat as Prime Minister in 1896) also threw his weight against the Order. Support for Lady Aberdeen's project vanished.

At this critical juncture Lady Aberdeen was introduced to Dr. Alfred Worcester, director of the District Nurses' Training Institute of Waltham, Massachusetts. Dr. Worcester was so impressed with the concept of the VON that he came to Canada and successfully defended the Order before hostile audiences in Toronto, Montreal, and Ottawa. He also permitted Lady Aberdeen to engage Miss Charlotte MacLeod, the superintendent of his school, as chief superintendent of the Victorian Order of Nurses for Canada. Miss MacLeod, who was born in New Brunswick, had been especially trained for her duties in England by Florence Nightingale. Miss MacLeod's first task when she arrived in Canada was to set up training establishments in five major cities. In November 1897 the first twelve nurses were admitted to the Victorian Order at a ceremony at Rideau Hall. On 18 May 1898 the Order received its Royal Charter from Queen Victoria.

In the early summer of 1898 the Dominion Government sent a two-hundred-man military detachment—the Yukon Field Force—to Dawson City to maintain order during the Klondike Gold Rush. Four VON nurses accompanied the Force, marching shoulder to shoulder with the men over 150 miles of appalling terrain. The outstanding work of these nurses proved to skeptics that Lady Aberdeen's scheme would be of immense benefit to the nation.

Since its inception the Victorian Order has concentrated on providing skilled nursing service in the home. In addition, nurses of the VON have served in two World Wars, numerous epidemics, and several national disasters, including the Halifax Explosion of 1917. In the first quarter of this century the VON established and staffed forty-four "cottage hospitals" in remote parts of the country. The last of these hospitals was turned over to local authorities in 1924. During the past eighty years the demand for home care has increased steadily; 333 VON nurses paid 51,577 visits to the sick in 1918. 736 nurses made 1,503,121 visits in 1978. The costs of these visits is based on the patient's financial status; in cases of genuine need no charge is made for the VON service.

The VON has seventy-one active branches in nine provinces. It is financed by private subscriptions, fees from patients, fees from provincial health plans, and government grants. Many VON services, such as "Meals on Wheels," are provided by volunteers. Ottawa is both the birthplace and the national headquarters of the Victorian Order of Nurses for Canada. The close connection of the Order with Rideau Hall is maintained to this day, for the Governor General is by tradition its Patron.

Samuel Bingham occupies a special place in the history of the capital because of his progressive views and personal generosity. First elected mayor in 1897—the year Ottawa celebrated Queen Victoria's Diamond Jubilee—he served a second term in 1898 by acclamation.

Samuel Bingham, known to everyone as "Sam," was born in Lower Town of Irish Catholic parents in 1845. Most of his adult life was spent on the Gatineau River as a "driver." In 1879 he went into partnership with the Gilmour and Edwards lumber firms to form the Gatineau Boom Company. The functions of the Gatineau Boom Company were to facilitate the annual log drive and to collect all the timber at the mouth of the river in booms, where it was sorted for the respective owners. (This company is now a wholly owned subsidiary of the Canadian International Paper Company and the booms may still be seen from the Gatineau Bridge.)

Because of the seasonal nature of his business, Sam had ample time for civic affairs. From 1880 until 1893 he served consecutive terms as alderman for Ottawa Ward in Lower Town. In the mayoralty race of 1897 Sam defeated two other candidates who were heavily favoured by the press. A few days after the election, the *Ottawa Daily Citizen*, which had supported one of his rivals, had this to say of the new mayor: "He is thoroughly honest, is a man of means and considerable independence of character; and is moreover, a genial, whole-souled, warm hearted Irishman."

Sam Bingham was all of these things and more. His "independence of character" was reflected in numerous ways, including the conviction that English-speaking Ottawans should learn French. He told the *Daily Citizen*: "There are two languages in this country and you cannot get away from the fact. The French learn English because they need to. But the English should learn French because their education is not complete if they do not know it."

During his tenure as mayor, he gave all his salary to charity. Although he was an Irish Roman Catholic, these gifts went to French and Protestant causes as well as Roman Catholic institutions. Not only his good works, but his eccentricities made him a campaign manager's dream. Everyone knew Sam Bingham, for he loved horseback riding and he would tour a part of the city each day. His house on Sussex Drive (where the National Research Council now stands) was also well known because it was the only dwelling in the capital with a red, white, and blue picket fence. He enjoyed snowshoeing, and on one occasion visited the Governor-General, Lord Aberdeen, on snowshoes, wearing a blanket coat and toque (by way of contrast, his previous call at Rideau Hall had been in a coach and four, wearing full dress, including a wig).

One of his greatest concerns was the welfare of young people. In an interview with the *Ottawa Journal* he told the reporter: "The school hours are too long in Ottawa. There should be more time for play. I believe ninety-eight percent of the criminals and incorrigibles can be kept out of penitentiaries, jails and reformatories by giving the boys a chance to play, and get into proper competition with other boys."

This was not idle talk. While he was in office, Bingham donated a piece of property on Cathcart Street (formerly used as a cattle market) to the city for a playground. Having given the land, he also equipped it at his own expense.

On 16 June 1905 Sam Bingham spent a strenuous day supervising the annual log drive on the Gatineau. That night a serious log jam occurred at a point known as the Cascades, and Sam was called back to the river. He worked through the night and left for Ottawa at dawn, completely exhausted, in a buggy. He was last seen, asleep at the reins, as he passed through the village of Wakefield. A short time later his horse stepped into the river, and his carriage was swept away. Sam Bingham was drowned, and his body was not recovered until 23 June. Among his bequests were funds for a Roman Catholic school and a Protestant school to be built in the valley of the Gatineau.

Bingham Square, situated just east of the General Hospital (bounded by Bolton and Dalhousie streets), has given pleasure to generations of Lower Town residents. This playground—which for years bore the sign "Free to every living man and boy who behaves himself"—contains a wading pool and has recently been landscaped and refurbished. Anson Gard, author of *The Hub and Spokes*, a history of Ottawa published in 1904, noted the popularity of the little park, and wrote: "Such citizens as Ex-Mayor Bingham are the real bene-factors of a city. Long after he has gone will little Ottawans throw up their hats and shout: "Three cheers and a tiger for good Mister Bingham!"

In 1897, the same year that Sam Bingham was elected mayor, Wilfrid Laurier, Canada's Prime Minister, was knighted by Queen Victoria in London. Few Canadians were more deserving of this honour. Sir Wilfrid, in addition to being a statesman of international status, was also a well-loved resident of Ottawa who did much for the capital during his fourteen-year tenure (from 1896 to 1911) as Prime Minister.

Born in the hamlet of St. Lin, north of Montreal, Laurier came to Ottawa in 1874 as a backbencher for the Liberal Party. He spent his first years in the capital living the lonely life of a lodger—in the Russell House—and loathed the city. Ten years later his opinion of the community had softened to the extent that he was able to tell a Montreal audience: "I would not wish to say anything disparaging of the capital, but it is hard to say anything good of it. Ottawa is not a handsome city and does not appear destined to become one either."

In 1893, after Laurier had spent nearly two decades in the capital and risen through the ranks to be Leader of the Opposition, he said in an address to the Reform Association of Ottawa:

"I keep a green spot in my heart for the city of Ottawa, and when the day comes, as it will come by and by, it shall be my pleasure and that of my colleagues, I am sure, to make the city of Ottawa as attractive as possibly could be; to make it the centre of the intellectual development of this country and above all the Washington of the North."

More than any other Prime Minister—with the possible exception of Sir John A. Macdonald—Laurier considered the capital as his home. He was a familiar and courtly figure on the streets of the city, and was kept busy doffing his hat to numerous acquaintances. Sir Wilfrid was also a faithful patron of the Ottawa Electric Railway, whose trams he rode to and from the office.

In 1897, the year after Laurier became Prime Minister, several of his friends helped him to buy a substantial yellow brick residence at 335 Theodore Street in Sandy Hill. (Theodore Street, named for one of Louis Besserer's sons, was later renamed Laurier Avenue.) Sir Wilfrid lived in this house until his death in 1919. He is buried near the main gate in Notre Dame Cemetery, where his stone monument—a casket borne by nine female mourners—can be seen from the Montreal Road. When Lady Laurier died in 1921, she bequeathed the house to the leader of the Liberal Party, William Lyon Mackenzie King, who was elected Prime Minister the same year. King moved into the residence, which he renamed "Laurier House," in 1923. King occupied Laurier House until his death in 1950 and left it to the nation as a museum. Laurier House contains many interesting pieces of memorabilia from these two men who influenced Canada's destiny. It has been open to the public for conducted tours since 1951.

Laurier's stated intention to make Ottawa "the Washington of the North" was considered by some people as empty rhetoric. However, in 1899, he created the Ottawa Improvement Commission whose mandate was: " . . . to purchase, acquire and hold real estate in the City of Ottawa and vicinity thereof for the purpose of public parks or squares, streets, avenues, drives or thoroughfares, and for their maintenance."

Initially this federal agency was run by four commissioners, three of whom were appointed by the Crown, the fourth by the city of Ottawa. The first chairman of the Ottawa Improvement Commission was Sir Henry Bate, a respected wholesale grocer from the capital. Annual funding amounted to a paltry $100,000, but a great deal was accomplished with this sum in the early years. In 1927 the Ottawa Improvement Commission was succeeded by the Federal District Commission, which in turn became the National Capital Commission in 1959. Today the National Capital Commission, a federal government agency corporation, is run by a board of twenty commissioners who come from all parts of Canada—only two, the chairman and the vice-chairman, receive salaries. The NCC has broadened its mandate to include the acquisition and preservation of historic buildings, and now concerns itself with approximately 1,800 square miles of territory on both sides of the Ottawa River. The annual budget is in the region of $70 million.

The Ottawa Improvement Commission and its successors have always worked within the framework of a master plan. The first such plan was executed in 1903 by Frederick Todd, an internationally famous landscape architect from Montreal. Many of Todd's recommendations were incorporated in a more comprehensive report—involving Hull and the surrounding municipalities—completed in 1915, under the chairmanship of a Montreal industrial baron, Sir Herbert Holt. In 1937 Prime Minister King engaged Jacques Gréber, a world-renowned town planner from France, to redesign the central portion of the capital. Some of Gréber's recommendations were acted upon, but World War Two caused a long delay and brought about unforeseen changes in the city. Gréber returned to Canada in 1945 and drew up a revised master plan for the development of the national capital region. The Gréber Plan provides the basis for the present program of beautification in the Ottawa area.

One of the first priorities of the Ottawa Improvement Commission was to clean up the Rideau Canal, which was lined with ramshackle boathouses and shabby buildings. When this was completed, a scenic drive was constructed beside the Canal, and a causeway was built across Dow's Lake. Another early project was the conversion of King Edward Avenue into a broad, tree-lined boulevard. From the outset the city and the Commission have worked in concert to develop parks in Ottawa.

In 1893 the city purchased eighty acres of raw land from the MacKay beneficiaries which became Rockcliffe Park. Following the creation of the Ottawa Improvement Commission, this tract was leased to the federal agency for one dollar. The OIC not only maintained the park but acquired an additional 110 acres to the east which they christened the National Park. Among the improvements to the adjoining parks was a speedway, fifty feet in width and a mile long, which ran from the western end of the Rockeries to the eastern boundary of the Royal Canadian Mounted Police barracks. This speedway—or "drag strip"—now forms part of a scenic but sedate driveway along the Ottawa River.

In addition to co-operating with the Ottawa Improvement Commission, the city undertook to improve the capital on its own in the closing years of the century. One example of civic initiative was the paving of Sparks Street, between Elgin and Bank, in 1895. This refinement prompted R. J. Devlin, Ottawa's leading furrier, to publish the following announcement:

> Take a final look at Sparks St.
> That is Sparks St. as it is.
> This is your last chance to see a panorama of Alpine
> scenery, the ruins of Pompeii, a section of South
> Dakota after a cyclone and about two acres of the
> Slough of Despond, all under one canvas.
> You will spear no more frogs in the gutter.
> You will catch no more mud-pouts at the corners of
> the crossings.
> For behold, the asphalt cometh, and a drive along the
> thoroughfare will remind you no more of a trip on
> the backbone of an earthquake.
> Yes the asphalt cometh, but it cometh through great
> tribulation.
> It looks as though the city council were getting ready
> for the Last Trump and were behind hand as usual.

The paving of Sparks Street was marked by a dignified ceremony in front of the post office at the corner of Elgin Street that drew a crowd of more than 300 people. This civic occasion was chronicled in the *Ottawa Citizen* of 31 July 1895:

> ... Mayor Bothwick stood with shovel in hand while Mr. Stubbe, contractor of Montreal, addressed the crowd. He said: "In the name of the General Asphalt Co. of France, which has the honour to supply the city of Ottawa with the first asphalt laid down in the Capital of the Dominion of Canada, I congratulate you and all the members of the corporation for the initiative you have taken with regard to this desirable pavement." The Mayor made quite a lengthy speech and, with a silver shovel, threw the first instalment of asphalt, followed by several aldermen, who also contributed a shovelful. The party adjourned to the Russell House where refreshments were served. The small finished patch was subjected to tests from canes and umbrella points, while bicyclists gazed on the enticing surface and smiled in sweet contentment.

The Ottawa Improvement Commission and its successors have made an immense contribution to the beauty of the capital. From their inception they have never lacked for a challenge; this was particularly true in the early days. When the first Deputy Minister of the Department of Labour came to Ottawa in 1900, he was moved to write: "The business part of the town is small and like that of a provincial town, not interesting but tiresome. Ottawa is not a pretty place save about the Parliament Buildings."

The man who wrote these lines was only twenty-six years old at the time, and had been born in Kitchener, a community rarely noted for metropolitan elegance. His name was William Lyon Mackenzie King.

16

A Momentous Year

1900

OTTAWA MARKED THE dawn of the twentieth century with little fanfare, and for a city of nearly 60,000 souls, few misdemeanors.

When court opened on 2 Janaury 1900 there were only four prisoners in the dock. The magistrate, wishing everyone to have a chance to start the New Year on the right foot, was lenient with the offenders. The first case concerned Jean Giroux, who had had an altercation with Moses Bilsky over the payment of $4.00, the sum required to redeem a watch he had pawned. Giroux had become abusive and broken one of Bilsky's showcases. For this, he was fined $5.00 and ordered to pay $6.00 in damages. Another man, a grocer whose surname was also Giroux, was found guilty of having "internal communication" with the liquor store. This curious offence earned a fine of $20 plus $2.00 in costs. A young woman from Casselman admitted to stealing articles worth $2.00 from her employer, but because she was deeply repentant she was given a suspended sentence. The last case involved a man named Miles who had been apprehended while attempting to steal a ham (valued at $1.60) from Cluff's Grocery on Bank Street. The defendant explained that he was drunk at the time, and received a suspended sentence.

On New Year's Day Sir Wilfrid Laurier was the first gentleman to pay his respects to the Governor-General at the annual Levee. Having done so, Sir Wilfrid and many of the other dignitaries then cast their ballots in the civic election. Thomas Payment was re-elected as mayor, but the local newspapers gave much greater coverage to the situation in the South African War. The reason they focused on this distant conflict was that approximately two hundred men from the Ottawa area were fighting with the Empire forces against the Boers.

The first contingent of Ottawa soldiers had sailed for South Africa on the *Sardinia*, which left Quebec City on 31 October 1899. A second thousand-man contingent, including volunteers from Ottawa, was dispatched in November. Although the war against the Boers drew criticism from many parts of the world, Ottawa and the rest of English-speaking Canada responded to the call from Great Britain with intense patriotism. Canadians sincerely believed it was a question of defending the Queen's honour and of protecting the rights of British subjects in a hostile continent.

On 20 October 1899, while recruiting was still in progress, the *Ottawa Citizen* ran a front-page article entitled "Men who will fight for the Empire" which began: "When the stirring bugle call sounds the charge, and the trained troops of Imperial Britain sweep onward to the battle, in all the formidable array of the Empire's soldiers, there will be no braver, more capable and intelligent body of officers and men than the Canadian contingent."

The newspaper then went on to describe the throngs of men at the Drill Hall on Cartier Square waiting to enlist and the strict requirements for enrolment:

> To be accepted a man must be between the age of twenty-two and forty. His chest must measure thirty-four inches, and his height must be five feet nine inches. His teeth must be perfect, his toes straight as a string, his lungs sound as a bell. And in addition to this, he must be a trained soldier, and a deadly shot. And it is only if a man fulfils all these conditions, and has a clean military and civil record, that he stands a fighting chance.

Most of those chosen for the contingent were members of Ottawa's two militia infantry regiments, the 43rd Battalion (Carleton Blazers), and the Governor-General's Foot Guards. They would serve in Africa as soldiers of the Royal Canadian Regiment, a permanent force infantry unit. In 1893 the Queen had honoured

the Royal Canadian Regiment by permitting her personal cipher—
VRI—which stands for *Victoria Regina Imperatrix* (Victoria Queen
Empress), to be incorporated into the regimental insignia. The men
of the Royal Canadian Regiment wear her cipher to this day, and
have forged a reputation for gallantry, spit and polish, and unswerv-
ing loyalty to their sovereign.

When the first Ottawa contingent left on 24 October, half the
city turned out to bid them farewell. The troops marched in a
column from the Drill Hall to the Union Depot (opposite the Chateau
Laurier Hotel) where they boarded two special railway cars. People
crowded to see them all along the route; on the east bank of the
Canal, they were lined forty deep. The Ottawa *Free Press* of 25
October vividly described the event under the headline:

OTTAWA'S GOOD-BYE TO ITS VOLUNTEERS
... Lined up in front of the volunteers were the bands of the
Governor General's Foot Guards and Forty-third Battalion, and the
bugle band of the latter regiment.

At twenty minutes to six, amid an enthusiastic outburst of cheering
and to the enlivening music of *Soldiers of the Queen* by the Guards band,
the detachment moved out across Cartier Square. After the detachment came the officers of the Ottawa brigade in uniform and the
veterans of '66-70, while thousands followed behind....

The men marched to perfect time, and their soldierly bearing won
compliments from all quarters. All along the line of march thousands
of people were assembled and waving of hankerchiefs, displays of
fireworks and enthusiastic cheers indicated that the people of Ottawa
are proud of their contingent and confident that in the fullest manner
they will uphold the honour of the city. Many residences along the
line were decorated and this added to the spectacular effect....

A prominent society lady, who viewed the march from Wellington
Street, was literally forced into the ranks of the Forty-third band. She
was alive to the situation, however, and clinging to the big drum,
made her way along till a break in the crowd enabled her to make her
escape....

At the Union depot the scene was one of the utmost excitement
and enthusiasm. Every possible position in the neighbourhood was
occupied; the grass plot near Sappers bridge on the west side of the
Canal was crowded....

On the platform, within the roped enclosure, just at the turn
leading to the cars, was His Excellency the Earl of Minto, accompanied
by Capt. Graham, the aide-in-waiting, Mrs. Drummond, and some
few additional members of the government house party. When the
column reached this point, Capt. Rogers gave the command "eyes

left," and as the men marched past the Governor General, they were loudly cheered and applauded.

As soon as the company was safely ensconced in its cars, the crowd on every hand made a mad rush forward. The people clambered over the ropes or crawled under them. The police for a moment made an effort, but a vain one, to keep the crowd in check. But a considerable army of police could scarcely have done that. Recognizing the futility of their efforts, the guardians of the law assumed a passive attitude and allowed the people to have their way.

...Precisely at 6.35 the whistle of the engine blew, the bell rang, and the train moved out. Both regimental bands struck up *The Girl I Left Behind Me*, merging at length in *Auld Lang Syne*; fifteen thousand throats cheered themselves hoarse, and the rear end of the last car passed into darkness.

In addition to infantry, Canada sent other units to South Africa, including a 537-man troop of mounted rifles, the Lord Strathcona's Horse. This troop was raised and maintained at the personal expense of Lord Strathcona, the man who drove the last spike of the transcontinental railway, and who in 1900 was both Canadian High Commissioner to Great Britain and governor of the Hudson's Bay Company. The Canadian forces acquitted themselves with honour in a total of twenty-nine engagements. One of the first and most significant encounters with the enemy was the Battle of Paardeberg, which took place on 18 February 1900. This was a major victory for the Empire, and the Royal Canadian Regiment earned a battle honour for its part in the action. Because D Company of the regiment was comprised of Ottawa men, the Governor-General's Foot Guards were also awarded a battle honour for this engagement.

Since then the Royal Canadian Regiment has observed the anniversary of the Battle of Paardeberg each year. Members of the regiment stationed in Ottawa and retired members living in the area hold an annual dinner at the Army Headquarters Officers Mess on Somerset Street. For several decades local veterans of the South African War, regardless of their military affiliation, were also invited to this function.

The last surviving Boer War veteran from Ottawa to attend a Paardeberg Dinner was Sergeant William Hare, who died in 1972. Both he and his father, W. R. Hare, were with D Battery of the Royal Canadian Artillery when its guns were surrounded at Liliefontain. This section, commanded by Lieutenant E. W. B. Morrison, a former editor of the *Ottawa Citizen*, staved off repeated attacks from a huge force of Boers. Three Victoria Crosses were awarded to Canadians in the action. Sergeant E. W. Holland of Ottawa (son of Andrew Holland, for whom Holland Avenue is named) was one of those who won Britain's highest decoration for valour. Lieutenant Morrison received the Distinguished Service Order and subsequently rose to the rank of major-general. In World War One Morrison commanded the 1st Division artillery and was knighted for his service. Number 5 gun—one of the two twelve-pounders saved at Liliefontain—now stands in Confederation Park.

The Ottawa area enjoyed unseasonably warm weather in the spring of 1900. The 26th of April was particularly fine, with clear skies and a fresh breeze from the northwest. Around ten o'clock on that day a chimney fire ignited the roof of a small frame dwelling on St. Redempteur Street in the congested central section of Hull. This occurrence was so common—and of such minor significance—that the Hull Fire Department responded to the alarm in a leisurely fashion. By the time the pump arrived, the adjoining house was also ablaze, and burning shingles were being blown onto the roofs of adjacent dwellings. Within an hour Hull was in the throes of a catastrophe.

As the fire spread, the wind increased in velocity, fueling the flames like a blow torch. The conflagration consumed a wide swath of the central and southern part of the city as it worked toward the Eddy complex on the shore of the Ottawa River. Mr. Eddy described the approach of the fire in these words: "If one could imagine a snow storm of particles of fire instead of snow, it would give some idea of the intensity."

The fire gained further momentum when it licked into the piles of wood surrounding the Eddy plants. Aided by the wind, firebrands as well as clouds of dense smoke were carried across the river to the Ottawa shore. By one o'clock J. R. Booth and H. F. Bronson's lumber yards were in flames. All of Ottawa's firefighting equipment was rushed to the Chaudière district. Buglers went through the streets of the capital sounding a call-out to members of the militia regiments. Mayor Payment telegraphed Montreal, Toronto, Brockville, Smiths Falls, and Peterborough for aid. Montreal responded by sending two detachments. The first, consisting of eight men, five horses, a pump, and a reel of hose, arrived around five o'clock, after a rail journey of just under two hours.

As soon as the fire crossed the river, a mass evacuation took place from the Chaudière Flats. While the people were fleeing with their belongings, one man was seen struggling up Wellington Street with his obese wife in a handcart. Suddenly the tailgate of the cart broke under the woman's weight, and she rolled back down the incline. Her distraught husband yelled to those behind him, "Stop her! Stop her!" From the surging throng a voice yelled back: "Let her slide. There are plenty more, and you can get a lighter one next time!"

By five o'clock the Chaudière region including the lumber mills, the flour mills, the electric generating stations, and hundreds of dwellings were all ablaze. The fire fighters and the militia did their best, but their equipment was unequal to the task. At one point attempts were made to dynamite a fire break, but this only resulted in live embers being scattered at random, which set off more fires. Had it not been for the high escarpment to the east of the Chaudière, and the fact that the wind dropped at sundown, all of Ottawa might have been destroyed. A Parliamentary Press Gallery reporter, Frank Gadsby, described the scene as it appeared from Parliament Hill at seven-thirty that evening:

> The shades of night are falling, and a glorious sunset flames behind the purple Laurentians. But Nature's splendour is eclipsed by the red hell that flares and flickers in the valley of the Ottawa . . . I note one roof after another twinkle, glow and burst out in garish effulgence. The millions of feet of lumber all along the river banks are alight . . . There is nothing to divert the attention from the menacing grandeur of the conflagration. The River flows along black and sullen save where it is traversed by broad red shafts of light from burning deals or mill flumes.

The fire finally guttered out around midnight. It had destroyed a half-mile swath from the Ottawa River to Carling Avenue, a distance of approximately two and a half miles. When dawn came, the area resembled a bombed city. That afternoon the *Ottawa Citizen* wrote of the desolation:

> Oh, the sad spectacle that is now presented in the aforementioned picturesque gay Capital of the fair Dominion, and its adjoining city! The contents of thousands of comfortable houses scattered about everywhere, grey-haired tottering men and women wandering about the streets, younger women sobbing, and children crying bitterly for the comfort they were wont to experience. And saddest of all, the

deep heart-rending grief of the families whose loved ones had fallen prey to the flames—snatched before their eyes when their willing hearts and hands were powerless to render assistance. The sight will be indelibly engraven on the memory of thousands.

The Great Fire of Ottawa and Hull was responsible for seven deaths, 15,000 people were left homeless, more than 3,000 buildings were destroyed, and property damage exceeded $10 million.

The devastation in Ottawa covered 440 acres; 1,900 buildings were destroyed, and 8,370 people were left without a roof over their heads. J. R. Booth lost both his milling complex and his handsome residence in the Le Breton Flats (Ezra B. Eddy, who had practically no insurance, suffered the heaviest loss in Hull). Prior to the Great Fire, some of the capital's most influential citizens had lived in the Chaudière region. In addition to J. R. Booth, several members of the Pinhey family, Andrew Fleck, the owner of an iron foundry, John Rochester, a lumberman and former mayor (1870-71), and Dr. Hamnett Hill had homes there. After the fire these people moved to Sandy Hill or to Centre Town. Many businesses were re-established, but the only new dwellings were those of low-income workers. During the next half-century the area gradually deteriorated into an industrial slum.

Before the ashes had cooled, both local and foreign benefactors came to the aid of the stricken. A ladies' committee, headed by Her Excellency, the Countess of Minto, and Lady Laurier, distributed food and clothing at the Drill Hall on Cartier Square, and at other temporary depots. Food and clothing for Hull was sent across the river by boat because the Chaudière Bridge had been burned. Queen Victoria cabled a message of condolence as soon as she heard the news. On 27 April the *London Times* said in an editorial: "Great Britain must help Canada, who is lavishing her blood and treasure in South Africa by contributing funds for the victims of the Ottawa fire." In Ottawa that evening a General Relief Committee for Ottawa and Hull was formed. This committee was chaired by George H. Perley, a local lumber merchant, and included prominent citizens from both communities. (Perley was subsequently knighted and served as Canada's High Commissioner to Great Britain from 1917 to 1922.) The main task of the Committee was to administer a fund which eventually totalled just over $950,000. Donations to the fund came from the following sources:

Canada $500,781
Great Britain $363,248
British Colonies $53,605
United States $33,505
France $1,036

France's response was noteworthy in view of the fact that 30 percent of Ottawa's population, and 90 percent of Hull's population, were of French descent.

The Ottawa and Hull Relief Fund disbursed payments to 3,051 claimants before its books were closed on 31 December 1900. In 1912 the *Ottawa Journal* said in a retrospective article: "It was the only big fire fund that caused neither scandal nor reproach and whose administration was universally praised." The fund helped to finance the erection of 750 new buildings before year end, and was a major factor in getting the two cities back on their feet.

Another reason for Ottawa's phenomenal recovery was the resilient attitude of its population. While the ruins were still smoking, people picked through the debris to salvage heat-tempered nails for rebuilding. In a sense the city's mettle was also tempered by the holocaust—and the capital emerged stronger for the ordeal.

17

The End of an Era

1901 to 1914

DESPITE THE RAVAGES of the Great Fire in 1900, Ottawa was a prosperous and growing city in 1901. An article in the *Ottawa Journal* that year attributed Ottawa's progress to three causes. The first was the lumber industry—made possible by the Chaudière Falls power—which was producing more than 500 million board feet annually. The second was the trade generated by the railways; Ottawa had four systems with nine different rail lines. The third reason was the presence of the federal government. The *Journal* exulted over the financial harvest reaped in the capital:

Aside from the large amounts of money left by transient visitors on business with the government, the regular monthly payroll of the civil service put into circulation a vast and annually increasing amount of money, which could not but tend to help the material prosperity of all. The merchant and business men in all ranks have ever felt the exhilarating touch of the national gold bags, and the presence of so large an army of workers, with, for the most part, luxurious tastes and generous spending ability, gave the city an advantage to which it has splendidly responded.

The last statement was not entirely accurate. While it was true that the federal government was Ottawa's largest single employer, most of the 3,500 civil servants earned relatively low wages. Those with "luxurious tastes and generous spending ability" were either Cabinet ministers or senior government appointees. These people—Ottawa's newly arrived gentry—either lived in Sandy Hill or the Metcalfe Street neighbourhood of Upper Town.

Sandy Hill, bounded by Rideau Street to the north, Waller Street to the west, Theodore Street (later Laurier Avenue) to the south, and the Rideau River to the east, had been granted to Louis-Theodore Besserer in 1828. Prior to the influx of civil servants in 1865 the area remained sparsely settled, and the real estate market was so poor that Besserer was forced to sell several hundred lots to settle a debt of just over £2,000. Between Confederation and the turn of the century Sandy Hill was transformed into a luxurious residential area noted for its stately homes. By 1900 there were more people of rank and title in this enclave than any other comparable district in Canada.

The advantages of Sandy Hill made it the most pleasant place to live in Ottawa. It was within easy walking distance or a short tram ride of the business district and the Parliament buildings. It had local educational facilities, including the University of Ottawa, and several fine parks. Strathcona Park, formerly the Dominion Rifle Range, and later the Royal Ottawa golf course, was at that time connected by foot bridge to the Rideau Lawn Tennis Club on the opposite bank of the Rideau River. It was also well served by churches of all denominations.

The first church in Sandy Hill (excluding the Methodist Chapel on Rideau Street) was St. Paul's Presbyterian, built on Daly Avenue in 1845. At Church Union in 1925 St. Paul's absorbed the congregation of the Eastern Wesleyan Methodist Church on King Edward Avenue (erected in 1873) and changed its name to St. Paul's Eastern United Church. The old Eastern Wesleyan Church was subsequently purchased by the Ottawa Little Theatre company, which staged performances in the building until it was destroyed by fire in 1970. The modern Ottawa Little Theatre stands on the original site of the Methodist Church.

In 1856 the Oblate Order erected St. Joseph's Church at the corner of Cumberland and Wilbrod streets. St. Joseph's was designated an English-speaking church in 1889, when the Oblates built Sacre Coeur on Laurier Avenue for the French-speaking members of the parish. St. Joseph's was enlarged in 1892 and demolished by fire in 1930. The present church was built in 1932. Sacre Coeur, one block south of St. Joseph's, was completed in 1889, destroyed by fire in 1907, rebuilt in 1910, and in 1978 totally gutted in a spectacular fire. Sacre Coeur parishioners hope to build a smaller church on the same site.

In 1866 construction was started on the second Anglican church in Ottawa—St. Alban the Martyr—at the corner of Daly and King Edward avenues. Because of unstable clay formations, difficulties were encountered while digging the foundation, and Thomas Fuller's design for the church had to be abandoned. Fuller quit in disgust, handing the project over to his assistant, King Arnoldi (who six years later redesigned Christ Church Cathedral). During the next decade St. Alban's was plagued by financial woes and dissension among the congregation. Construction proceeded so slowly that in 1875 Canon Bedford-Jones protested by offering his resignation. This drastic move galvanized his parishioners into finishing the job. The congregation of St. Alban's has included many distinguished personages. Among the first to attend this church were the Governor General, Lord Monck, Prime Minister Sir John A. Macdonald, and six of Macdonald's Cabinet ministers. Ottawa's first woman mayor, the late Charlotte Whitton, who died in 1975, also attended the Church of St. Alban the Martyr.

In 1898 another Anglican church, All Saints, was established in Sandy Hill. This beautiful grey stone edifice, at the corner of Chapel Street and Laurier Avenue, was promoted and built at the personal expense of one man, Sir Henry Newell Bate. Because of Sir Henry's generosity (and his large family) it was jocularly called "All Bates Church." By 1900 All Saints had drawn nearly one hundred families from St. Alban's, and was the most fashionable house of worship in Sandy Hill. In 1910 All Saints had a congregation of more than 1,200. The most important figure in the history of All Saints was the late Archdeacon Channel Galbraith Hepburn, who was associated with the parish from 1920 to 1956. Archdeacon Hepburn served as a padre in World War One and won the Military Cross for rescuing wounded men under heavy fire. He also went overseas with the troops in World War Two, and was awarded the Order of the British Empire. Archdeacon Hepburn was an immensely popular and able minister. When he died in 1971, messages of condolence came from across the country. A letter from a veteran in British Columbia, published in the *Ottawa Journal*, summed up the sentiments of many Ottawans: "He exuded Christian love and understanding born of a life dedicated to Christ. Interspersed with witticisms he brought us startling gems of philosophy based on some biblical truth. He was not just another 'sky pilot'—he was our Padre, counsellor and friend."

As mentioned earlier, the Metcalfe Street area was also a preferred residential district at the turn of the century. Most of this property, including sections of Somerset, Cartier, O'Connor, Gilmour, Cooper, and James streets had belonged to Colonel By. In 1876 the land was purchased from Colonel By's estate by the Freehold Association of Ottawa, a development company owned by the lumber magnate, James Maclaren; Robert Blackburn, a prominent merchant; and Charles Magee, president of the Bank of Ottawa. During the 1880s and 1890s the land was subdivided and sold as lots. By 1900 a number of influential citizens had built large homes in the area.

Queen Victoria died in January 1901, having reigned for more than sixty years. She was succeeded by her son, Edward VII, whose connection with Ottawa went back to 1860, the year that he laid the cornerstone of the Parliament building.

On 22 April 1900 the Alexandra Bridge, linking Ottawa and Hull was opened to train traffic. This bridge, named for Edward's beautiful consort, Queen Alexandra, is now usually called the Interprovincial Bridge. It had a cantilever span of 556 feet, which at that time was the longest in the Dominion, and the fourth longest in the world. The over-all length of the bridge, including approaches, was 2,684 feet. Squeezed into its width of sixty-seven feet were two roads for wheeled vehicles, two sets of streetcar tracks, two foot paths, and one set of train tracks. Because of its size, and the difficulty of constructing piers in the river bottom, the Alexandra Bridge took nearly nine years to complete. The problem with the supports was greatly aggravated by the fact that the river bed was covered with a layer of sawdust and mill debris, which was sixty feet deep in places.

The railway on the Alexandra Bridge led to a central depot just south of Rideau Street which had been built by J. R. Booth in 1895. This depot, reached by a covered stairway from Sappers Bridge, was the hub of a network of lines, including the Canada Atlantic Railway. In 1879 Booth had bought control of that railway, which ran east from Ottawa to Montreal and then branched off to the Vermont border near the head of Lake Champlain. The CAR gave Booth access to the Quebec markets and to those of the Atlantic seaboard. In 1896 he built another railroad, the Ottawa, Arnprior and Parry Sound, which ran west to Georgian Bay, servicing his timber limits en route. A portion of this line now forms part of the roadbed of the Queensway through Ottawa. When Booth merged the two systems a few years later, the Canada Atlantic Railway became the largest privately owned railroad in the world. In 1905 J. R. sold the Canada Atlantic Railway to the Grand Trunk Line for $14 million. The sale included more than 400 miles of track, 67 steam locomotives, and approximately 3,000 units of rolling stock.

In July 1901, three months after the first train clattered across the Alexandra Bridge, a second bridge was opened in Ottawa. This 400-foot steel structure, built in a parabolic curve, was the only bridge in Canada without a level plane. It spanned the Rideau Canal and adjacent railway tracks a half-mile south of Sappers Bridge, connecting Theodore and Maria streets. Both these streets and the span that linked them were later named for Sir Wilfrid Laurier. A few weeks before Sir Wilfrid formally opened this bridge, the *Ottawa Citizen* printed a detailed description of the new facility with the cogent observation: "Should an elephant or any other heavy weight come back to Ottawa it need have no fears about walking over the new handsome steel structure which now joins Maria and Theodore Sts., in an enduring grip."

The Laurier Avenue Bridge has carried countless vehicles—many of them considerably heavier than an elephant—for more than three-quarters of a century. It also possesses a Victorian charm that is particularly noticeable after dark, when lights illuminate its graceful arch.

The year 1901 was a vintage one for bridges in Ottawa. In addition to the Alexandra and the Laurier, two narrow steel truss bridges spanning the Rideau River at Green Island were christened in honour of the Governor General, Lord Minto. These quaint structures are still in excellent condition, but their width forces drivers of large vehicles to proceed with caution.

In the autumn of 1901 the Duke and Duchess of Cornwall and York made an extended tour of Canada. The visit of the heir-apparent (later King George V, grandfather of Queen Elizabeth II) to Ottawa was marked by a variety of entertainments. In addition to formal ceremonies on Parliament Hill which included the unveiling of Queen Victoria's statue, the royal couple took a scenic drive through the capital in a richly appointed streetcar. Not only did the Duke and Duchess ride down a timber slide, but they also lunched on pork and beans in an authentic shanty erected for their benefit in Rockcliffe Park. One of the Duke's most pleasant duties was to watch the play-off game for the Minto Cup. This trophy, donated by Lord Minto, was emblematic of the world championship in lacrosse. The match was won by the Ottawa Shamrocks, and the Duke enjoyed the uninhibited play so much that he kept the ball as a souvenir.

Ice skating has always been a major winter pastime in the capital. Most Ottawa youngsters learn to skate soon after they learn to walk. At the turn of the century this sport took on added prestige when Lady Minto, foundress of Ottawa's Minto Skating Club, gave weekly skating parties at Government House.

In addition to manmade rinks, the city had huge expanses of natural ice in the form of the Canal, the Rideau River, and the Ottawa River, which were ideal for day-long excursions. One drawback of these waterways, however, was that in the early winter, and prior to the spring break-up, the ice became dangerously thin in places.

At dusk on 6 December 1901 two prominent young Ottawans drowned while skating on the Ottawa River. Miss Bessie Blair, daughter of the Minister of Railways and Canals, and her partner plunged through a weak spot in the ice near the mouth of the Gatineau River. Henry A. Harper, a senior official in the Department of Labour, who was some distance behind the pair, tried to rescue Miss Blair by lying spread-eagled on the ice and extending his walking stick. When this failed, Harper calmly shed his coat and gauntlets and dived into the icy water. Miss Blair's companion miraculously made it to safety, but Henry Harper and Bessie Blair perished.

This tragedy saddened many people in the capital, especially William Lyon Mackenzie King, Canada's future Prime Minister, who had been Henry Harper's colleague and close friend. To commemorate Harper's heroism, King arranged for a statue of Sir Galahad to be erected on Wellington Street opposite the Parliament buildings. It was a fitting memorial, because Henry Harper had owned a print of George Watt's painting of Sir Galahad (from which the statue was modelled), and would sometimes look at it and say: "There is my ideal knight!"

Ottawa's skating heritage has also produced some fine hockey teams. Between 1894, when Lord Stanley's trophy for the senior championship was first awarded, and 1934, the year Ottawa dropped out of the National Hockey League, the city captured the Stanley Cup nine times.

Before departing for England in 1894 Lord Stanley placed the Stanley Cup in the trusteeship of two Ottawa men; P. D. Ross, an outstanding athlete and publisher of the *Ottawa Journal*, and Dr. John Sweetland, who was also Sheriff of Carleton County. Until 1926, when it was restricted to teams in the National Hockey League, the Stanley Cup was a challenge trophy open to any team approved by the trustees.

Ottawa's team at the turn of the century, the Silver Seven (so named because there were seven to a side at that time), won the Stanley Cup in 1903 and repeated the feat in 1904. In 1905 the Silver Seven were challenged by a Klondike team from Dawson City. This plucky squad took nearly a month to reach Ottawa, travelling by dogsled, boat, and transcontinental train. After watching the Silver Seven at practice, one of the Klondikers told an interviewer that Ottawa's star forward, Frank McGee, "doesn't look like much." In the first match of the three-game series McGee contributed only one goal in Ottawa's 9-2 victory. In the second game McGee broke loose and scored fourteen goals—eight of them in eight minutes—to set an all-time record for Stanley Cup play.

A few weeks after Ottawa vanquished Dawson City, the Silver Seven were challenged by a team from Rat Portage (which has since been given the less evocative name of Kenora). This series was so rough that in the second game the referee wore a hard hat. Both he and his hat were knocked flying on a number of occasions, to the delight of the crowd. Ottawa won two out of three games and retained the Stanley Cup for the third consecutive year.

In 1909 the Ottawa team changed its name from the Silver Seven to the Senators. The Ottawa Senators won the Stanley Cup in 1909 and 1911 before a hiatus set in which lasted until after World War One. Between 1920 and 1927 the Senators captured the trophy four more times. In 1926 the *Ottawa Citizen* ran a full-page article on hockey in the capital which began:

WONDER MACHINE OF CANADA'S GREAT WINTER PASTIME
GIVES CITY PROMINENCE EVERYWHERE
For Forty Years Colors of the Ottawa Hockey Team Have Flashed Up
and Down the Ice, Bringing Kudos to the Capital, and Always Proving
the Best Drawing Card on Any Circuits on Which It Has Played.

In 1931 the Ottawa All Stars, a ten-man squad of "amateur" players, set off on a gruelling overseas exhibition tour. Billed as "Ottawa vs. Europe" the team played thirty matches in six weeks in half a dozen countries: England, France, Poland, Germany, Italy, and Switzerland. Some of the games were closely contested, but most were easy victories for the Canadians. Because it was a good-will tour, the All Stars played clean hockey, and whenever the score became too lopsided they refrained from adding unnecessary goals. As a result of their gentlemanly conduct the Ottawans were warmly received wherever they went. At the end of this sporting odyssey the All Stars had a record of twenty-eight wins and two ties. The tour was such a success that another Ottawa team, the Shamrocks, went to Europe the following year.

Ottawa has had many outstanding players over the years. In addition to Frank McGee, some of the more famous were: Fred "Cyclone" Taylor, who bet that he could score a goal skating backward, and did so; Alex Connell, who played goal for the Ottawa Senators and set a record with six consecutive shut-outs; Frank Boucher, who won the Lady Byng Trophy (for gentlemanly conduct) seven times; Harvey Pulford, a ferocious defenceman whose specialty was body-checking opponents over the boards into the second row of spectators; Frank Nighbor, who won the Lady Byng Trophy three times and the Hart Trophy (for the most valuable player) once; Bouse Hutton, who played on three championship teams in the same year, the Silver Seven, the Ottawa Rough Riders (football) and the Ottawa Capitals (lacrosse); Bill Cowley, an Ottawa native who won the Hart Trophy in 1941 while playing for the Boston Bruins; and Syd Howe, another Ottawan, who set a National League Record in 1944 when he scored six goals for the Detroit Red Wings in a game against the New York Rangers. One of the longest hockey careers was that of Francis Michael "King" Clancy, who played on two Stanley Cup teams for Ottawa in the 1920s, later coached both Montreal and Toronto, became an NHL referee, and finally retired in 1953 as assistant manager of the Toronto Maple Leafs.

Up until 1924 Ottawa's senior hockey was played in Dey's Arena

Horse-drawn tram crossing Sappers Bridge 1877. Building in centre background was the main post office. *(OMA #CA 0419)*

"D" Battery, Royal Canadian Artillery, departing for the Boer War, February 1900. The pedestrian entrance to J. R. Booth's Union Depot was the covered stairway at left. *(PAC #C 3950)*

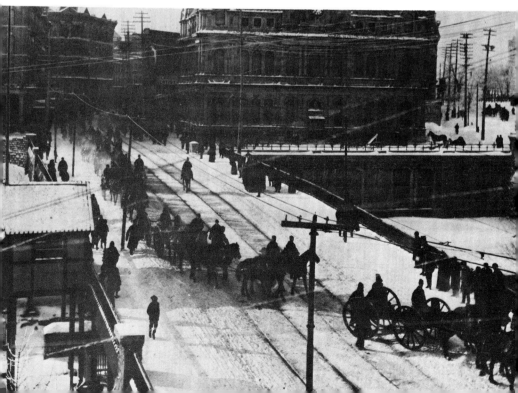

TOP: The Great Fire, 26 April 1900, crossing the Ottawa River at the Chaudière Falls. *(OMA #CA 0121)*
MIDDLE: The fire reaching the corner of Wellington Street and Pooley's Bridge Turn-Off (now Duke Street). *(Booth Family Collection)*
BOTTOM: Devastation of the Chaudière District the day after the fire. *(OMA #CA 0128)*

Royal visit 1901. Sir Wilfrid Laurier and Mayor W. D. Morris escort the Duchess of York. The Duke of York (later King George V) is in the centre of the procession. Langevin Building at left, Rideau Club at right. *(Queen Mary's collection)*

The Duke and Duchess of York riding a crib—complete with Royal Standard—down a timber slide at the Chaudière, September 1901. *(PAC—Topley Collection)*

LEFT: Sleighs lined up on Wellington Street, March 1914. Chateau Laurier Hotel looms in background. *(PAC #PA 60985)*
CENTRE: Regatta on the Ottawa River, September 1901. *(PAC #PA 11863)*

RIGHT: Facade of Rideau Hall in 1914. This view is essentially the same today. *(PAC #PA 43784)*
BELOW: Ottawa panorama from Nepean Point circa 1890. *(OMA #CA 0158)*

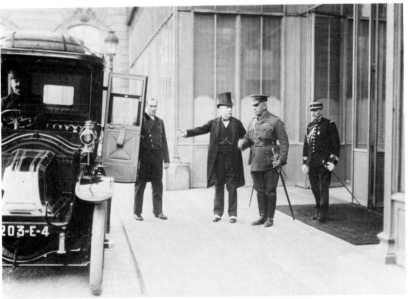

TOP: First Battalion, Princess Patricia's Canadian Light Infantry, leaving Lansdowne Park for France in August 1914. Of the 1098 officers and men in this battalion all but 44 were killed. (OMA #CA 0200)
BOTTOM: Major-General Sir Sam Hughes leaving the president's palace in Paris after interviewing the President of France. (PAC #PA 4706)

TOP: Clearing the ruins of the Houses of Parliament after the 1916 fire. Fire doors saved the Library of Parliament. *(PAC #C 38766)*
BOTTOM: Reconstruction of the Centre Block in the summer of 1916. *(PAC #C 38767)*

ABOVE: Colonel Charles
Lindbergh just after land-
ing in Ottawa on 2 July
1927. Moments later one of
his escort planes crashed.
(PAC #C 18070)
RIGHT: Parliament Hill
ceremonies marking the
1927 Diamond Jubilee of
Confederation. Wearing
Windsor uniforms are
Prime Minister King *(right)*
and The Honourable Hugh
Guthrie, Leader of His
Majesty's Loyal Opposi-
tion. *(PAC #C 24728)*

on Laurier Avenue, opposite the Drill Hall. In 1924 Tom Gorman, one of the city's leading sports promoters, opened the Auditorium, a barnlike brick arena at the corner of O'Connor Street and Argyle Avenue. The Auditorium, or "Aud" as it was familiarly known, served the capital well for more than forty years. During this period the Ottawa Senators switched to the Quebec Senior Hockey League. The Auditorium had a section behind the visitors' goal, called the Rush End, which catered to those hardy souls who, for a ticket costing 50 cents, were willing to stand and watch the play from a restricted angle. While the game was in progress the exuberant clientele of the Rush End were kept caged to prevent them from slipping into the higher priced seats.

In 1966 the Auditorium was sold to provide a site for the new YMCA—YWCA building. This move was influenced in part by the fact that the Civic Centre Arena at Lansdowne Park, which would comfortably seat nearly 10,000, was due to open the following year. This new arena has for some years been the home ice of the Ottawa 67s, the city's entry in the Ontario Junior Hockey Association. The 67s wear the same colours—red, white, and black—as the Silver Seven and the Senators. Like their predecessors, the Ottawa 67s play fast and exciting hockey.

Ottawa society was sharply stratified at the turn of the century. Membership in a gentleman's club was restricted to those who were well connected (by birth or by marriage) and those in certain favoured professions. So pronounced was the social pecking order that while medical doctors were usually welcomed, dentists were normally refused membership. Retail merchants and men engaged in trade—unless they were both educated and wealthy—were excluded from the more prestigious clubs.

In 1904 this situation prompted three well-known members of the Rideau Club to establish a new entity, the Laurentian Club. These men, Edward R. Bremner, R. Gordon Edwards, and Colonel (later Sir) Percy Sherwood, took this action because they wanted a club where they could mingle with friends from all walks of life. That same year the three founders signed a bank loan for $10,000, which was used to buy modest premises on Slater Street. Colonel Sherwood, who at that time was commissioner of the Dominion Police Force, which had jurisdiction over the Parliament buildings, was the first president of the Laurentian Club.

By 1913, when the membership was approaching 200, the club moved to a newly erected building at the corner of Albert and Elgin streets (where the National Gallery now stands). Twenty years later the club was hit by the Depression, and the situation eventually deteriorated to the extent that it was unable to pay its taxes. The club managed to survive this ordeal, but in 1941 the federal government expropriated its building and this forced a move to 233 Metcalfe Street. The next five years were difficult ones; at times it was feared that the club would go out of existence.

The turning point came in 1947, when the executors of the C. Jackson Booth Estate sold Jackson Booth's former residence at 252 Metcalfe Street to the Laurentian Club. The sale, made for a token price, was executed with the understanding that the club would try to keep the house in its original state. Booth's turreted red brick mansion, which has eight fireplaces, large rooms, and ornate wood panelling, makes a fine club. It is also a link with Ottawa's past because it was here that J. R. Booth lived his last years.

A resurgence in membership during recent decades has once again placed the Laurentian Club on a sound financial footing. Today the old Booth home provides a comfortable haven for nearly 400 members.

Parliament has had a fine library building since 1876, but the city of Ottawa did not get a public library until 1906. Even then it was a struggle. Nine years earlier, in 1897, a Public Library Board was formed, but their efforts to persuade Council to petition the rate payers for a library proved fruitless. Council's objection to a library was based on the fact that it would cost money, and such an expenditure would be frivolous. Finally, goaded by Wilson Southam (proprietor of the *Ottawa Citizen*), Mayor William Morris agreed in February 1901 to write Andrew Carnegie, the American Philanthropist, for a grant to build a library. Southam's directive was sound: during his lifetime, Andrew Carnegie endowed 2,500 libraries and gave more than $350 million to worthy causes. Carnegie's reply to the mayor's flowery request was brief and to the point:

Dear Sir,
Yours of 23rd received. If the City of Ottawa will furnish a site, and agree through Council to tax itself to the extent of $7500 a year for the maintenance of the library, I shall be glad to give $100,000 for a Free Library Building.

Very Truly Yours,
(Signed) Andrew Carnegie

Most people in Ottawa were delighted with Carnegie's proposal, but the City Fathers were less enthusiastic. Several councillors went so far as to vote against acceptance of Carnegie's offer because they believed the cost of the site and the annual maintenance was too great a liability. Mayor Morris then approached the federal authorities to see if they would *give* the city some Crown land for a site. When this ploy failed, the whole matter was shelved. Eventually however, public opinion forced Council to take action.

In 1905 the city bought a site at the corner of Metcalfe Street and Laurier Avenue and built an elegant stone library at a cost of approximately $200,000. The building was named for Andrew Carnegie, who formally opened it on 1 May 1906. (Years later, when the memory of Carnegie's generosity had faded, the building was rechristened the Ottawa Public Library.) From the outset the library was staffed by dedicated men and women who did their best to provide reading entertainment, knowledge, and culture to people of all ages.

The library added a children's section in 1907 and three years later opened its first branch, in New Edinburgh. Seven more branches were opened in various parts of the city between 1918 and 1963. The original branch, New Edinburgh, was closed in 1967 and the district is now served by bookmobile, but most of the other branches have expanded their facilities.

In 1971 the old Carnegie Library was demolished and a modern six-story structure was erected on the same site. This building, called the Central Library, also serves as headquarters for the Eastern Ontario Regional Library System, which was established in 1965. The EORLS is a resource-sharing arrangement that encompasses the Ottawa Public Library and those in ten neighbouring counties.

Today the Ottawa Public Library circulates more than 2 million books, periodicals, and records each year. There is a bookmobile service for those in distant parts of the city, and a Home Reader Service (with "talking books" on tape cassettes) for homebound readers. One of the busiest areas in the library is the Reference Section, which answers some 200,000 questions annually—questions ranging from the birth date of a Greek philosopher to the theoretical value of a used car. The auditorium and meeting rooms in the Central Library are booked heavily by the staff and community groups.

Andrew Carnegie's generosity in 1901 has undoubtedly created an ongoing liability for the city. The library's annual budget is now

$5 million, or fifty times the amount of Mr. Carnegie's initial donation, but the library is of immense benefit—and pleasure—to a broad cross-section of the community.

The Public Archives of Canada, custodian of the nation's heritage, was created somewhat casually by the Canadian Government in 1872. Douglas Brymner, an emigrant Scot, was given the use of three rooms with vague instructions to collect material relating to Canada's past. Brymner at that time was a second-class clerk in the Civil Service. Working with a small staff and a severely limited budget, Brymner accomplished a great deal during the next three decades. When he retired in 1901 he had laid a sound foundation for the future.

In 1902 an Order-in-Council decreed that public papers "be assembled in one place and put in the custody of one person." Two years later construction began on a Scottish baronial stone building on Sussex Drive (near the Basilica) to house the Archives. The same year, 1904, an Englishman named Arthur Doughty was appointed Dominion Archivist.

Doughty came with excellent credentials, for he was a qualified historian and he had served as Joint Librarian of the Quebec Assembly. Aided by the Order-in-Council of 1902, which gave him a clear mandate and the authority to carry it out, Doughty did a remarkable job during his thirty-one-year tenure. Not only did he enlarge the collection greatly but he also ensured that these documents were made available to the public. It was Doughty who instituted the practice of permitting accredited researchers access to the Archives twenty-four hours a day, seven days a week. This privilege is a boon to people whose regular employment restricts their free time during the day. In addition to being an able administrator, Arthur Doughty also published several scholarly works. Upon his retirement in 1935 he was knighted for his service to the country. Sir Arthur Doughty died in 1936, and in 1940 a bronze statue was erected to his memory outside the Archives.

While Doughty was Dominion Archivist, the archival collection increased so rapidly that a wing was added to the Sussex Drive Archives in 1926. Following World War Two, space again became a problem. After years of delay, work finally began in 1963 on a new National Library and Public Archives building situated on Wellington Street, opposite the Garden of the Provinces. The simple exterior of this structure is characterized by small windows whose purpose is to reduce the amount of light that would harm valuable papers and photographs. The interior has a spacious marble entrance hall and a broad marble staircase. Throughout the building there are many paintings and wall murals as well as a number of finely etched glass panels. Although the National Library and the Public Archives are separate entities, they share the thirteen acres of floor space in such a way that researchers can conveniently move from one source of information to the other.

The Public Archives has custody of approximately 20,000 sound recordings, 30,000 movie films, 100,000 historical volumes, 100,000 paintings and illustrations, 750,000 maps and atlases, and more than 6 million photographs. Many documents date back to the beginning of Canada's history. One example is a collection of Sir Humphrey Gilbert's papers pertaining to his final voyage in 1583, when he and his crew perished in their tiny ship, the *Squirrel*. Sir Humphrey was a famous navigator and sometime pirate who claimed Newfoundland for his sovereign, Queen Elizabeth I, in August 1583. Another example is a letter dated 18 August 1634 from Samuel de Champlain, "the Father of New France," to Cardinal Richelieu.

Because the role of the Archives is not only to collect and preserve material but also to make it available to the public, there are large reading and reference rooms where researchers may physically handle historic documents. There are, in addition, thirty-eight small rooms where individuals may work on lengthy projects in seclusion.

For the casual visitor there are three Exhibition Salons, and the National Library has a Newspaper Reading Room on the ground floor. This room is an intriguing place in which to browse (it is also invaluable for researchers), for here one may leaf through back issues of newspapers from across the country. These newspapers invariably yield a personal, and often amusing, insight into Canada's past.

When the Public Archives moved to Wellington Street in 1967, Sir Arthur Doughty's statue was relocated to a site behind the new building, facing the Ottawa River. The Archives' venerable quarters on Sussex Drive were subsequently taken over by the National War Museum. Now the old stone structure is surrounded by a Centurion tank, a naval gun battery, a Harvard Trainer airplane, and a German *Jagdpanzer* (tracked tank destroyer).

The National War Museum contains memorabilia from all the conflicts in which Canadians have participated, dating back to the French and Indian Wars. Some of the exhibits are highly evocative, particularly the reconstructed section of a World War One trench. You enter the trench through a heavy burlap curtain. It is night. As you walk along the wooden duckboards you hear the muffled voices of men and the sound of gunfire; above the parapet you glimpse the battlefield, which is illuminated briefly by the flash of exploding shells. All that is lacking are the stench and the mud. Weapons, equipment, war art, and photographs are included in the other displays, which are arranged by sections to represent the various periods in history. The National War Museum, despite the grim nature of its contents, is a popular attraction for people of all ages. In addition to its fascinating artifacts, this institution fairly reflects Canada's role in history and also serves to remind one of the realities of war.

The War Museum is flanked by the Royal Canadian Mint, another stone structure of the same vintage, which stands on a bluff over-looking the Ottawa River. This site is historically significant because it was occupied by an isolation hospital during the cholera epidemics of 1832 and 1834. In an effort to prevent the disease from spreading through Bytown, all vessels coming up the Ottawa were compelled to stop at a wharf below the hospital for a medical inspection. Those found to be suffering from cholera were obliged to disembark at this point and report to the hospital for treatment. Unfortunately, the inspection procedure at Cholera Wharf was only partially successful in controlling the epidemic. The same may be said for treatment at the ramshackle hospital shed. In 1832, the worst year, nearly 50 percent of the poor souls who were hospitalized, died.

The Mint, completed in 1907, has a feudal appearance, which is heightened by its soot-stained turrets, its steel spike fence, and the presence of armed guards. Security is of paramount importance, for this building contains millions of dollars' worth of gold bullion (refined gold) and currency. The first coin was struck in the capital on 2 January 1908 by Lord Grey, the Governor General. The coin, a gold sovereign, had a value before World War One of around seven dollars. Today it is more than one hundred times that amount.

Under Canadian law all gold mined in Canada is purchased by the Canadian Government. This gold is sent from the mines to the Royal Canadian Mint, where it is assayed, refined to .999 purity, and then made into bars and wafers. Some of the gold bullion is retained by the Mint to make coins and medals, some is marketed to the public through the Bank of Nova Scotia, and the balance is stored in the vaults of the Bank of Canada as part of the nation's gold reserves.

Canada adopted the American system of decimal currency in 1858. From that time until a branch of the Royal Mint was established in Ottawa in 1908, all of Canada's coins were made by the Royal Mint in England. In 1931, by Act of Parliament, the Mint at Ottawa ceased to be a branch of the Royal Mint, and was renamed the Royal Canadian Mint. In 1969 another Act of Parliament changed the status of the Mint from an agency of the Department of Finance to a Crown Corporation.

The Royal Canadian Mint makes all of Canada's coins as well as currency for foreign countries such as Israel, Iceland, Venezuela, and Bangladesh. Canadian medals and decorations, including the Order of Canada, are struck at the Mint. In recent years the average annual production of the Ottawa plant (there are now branches in Hull and Winnipeg) has exceeded 700 million pieces. Because of its intrinsic value, the 1980 issue of the $50 Maple Leaf coin has attracted international attention. This piece contains exactly one ounce of pure gold, which makes it convenient to trade and worthwhile to hold.

The public is permitted to visit the Royal Canadian Mint in small groups by appointment. Tours begin with a short movie on the history and manufacture of currency; then the group is conducted through a portion of the plant where high-speed machines spew coins at an astonishing rate. It is an interesting and educational experience, but there are no free samples.

In 1908, the year that Lord Grey struck the first coin at the Mint, an exclusive club came into existence on the Quebec shore of the Ottawa River. It was called quite simply The Country Club. The petition for incorporation was signed by the Right Honourable Sir H. E. Taschereau, the Honourable Sir Charles Fitzpatrick, the Honourable Sir Adolphe Caron, the Honourable N. A. Belcourt, the Honourable W. C. Edwards, and ten other prominent Ottawans, who prayed for permission "to carry on among other things, a club for the encouragement of riding, driving, motoring, boating, fishing, tennis, bowling and like sports and for social purposes, and for purposes of amusement."

The Country Club, consisting of ninety-three proprietory members from Ottawa society, had ample funds to develop its forty-acre property which included shoreline above the Remic rapids and a small island near the Champlain Bridge. A large clubhouse complete with ballroom was built. The grounds were transformed into a stately park with flower beds, a trellised walk, and vast stretches of lawn. Two grass tennis courts and a bowling green were placed at a discreet distance from the clubhouse, and a dock for small craft was built at the river's edge. In the Thirties, despite the strenuous objections from some members, an Olympic-size pool was installed within sight, but out of earshot, of the clubhouse. The pool proved to be an instant success.

Through the years The Country Club evolved into a social rather than a sporting institution. One could still swim, bowl, or play tennis, but it was mainly a place to relax in an atmosphere of old-fashioned elegance. Indeed, the setting was so idyllic and the service so excellent that many government functions, especially important dinners, were held on the premises. During the summer of 1967 (Centennial Year) twenty-seven heads of state were entertained by the Canadian Government at The Country Club.

Because the club had a tiny membership in relation to its facilities, government business paid for a significant amount of the overhead. When the Lester B. Pearson Building opened in 1973, with a state dining room for functions that would normally have been held at the Country Club, it was a severe blow. Within a few years the financial position of the club became untenable due to the combination of reduced revenues and inflation.

In 1977 a real estate company headed by several club members purchased the shares of The Country Club for a token price. The company intends to sell lots on the property while at the same time maintaining a social club with the old name. The "new" Country Club differs from the original entity in many respects, but still observes some of its pleasant traditions.

The Roxborough, Ottawa's first luxury apartment, was opened in 1910 when the population of the capital numbered approximately 86,000. Located at the corner of Laurier Avenue and Elgin Street, this eight-story structure contained eighty-two suites, many of which were furnished. The Roxborough may not have been an architectural gem, but it was solidly built, the rooms were well proportioned—most living rooms had fireplaces—and the service was excellent. With its marble steps, panelled foyer, and wrought-iron grillwork, the building had an air of Edwardian elegance. Between 1910 and 1965 the Roxborough was home to more senior Parliamentarians, Senators, Supreme Court justices, and diplomats than any other residence in the city.

The central location of the Roxborough was one reason for its popularity. Many distinguished tenants, including William Lyon

Mackenzie King and Louis-Stephen St. Laurent, enjoyed walking to work. This democratic practice was not without hazard. One day in 1950 St. Laurent (whose dignity and benign manner earned him the nickname of Uncle Louis) was nearly run over by a truck while crossing Confederation Square. To add insult to injury, when the driver slammed on his brakes, he put his head out of the cab and yelled at the Prime Minister: "Look where you're going, you silly old bastard!"

A first-class restaurant, the *La Touraine* (named for the chateaux district in France) was opened on the ground floor of the Roxborough in 1948. The *La Touraine* included a cocktail bar, the *Cockatoo Lounge*, which had as its mascot an irascible old parrot named Cocky, who in an earlier career had starred in several movies. Cocky was intolerant of patrons who tried to feed him hors d'oeuvres and would respond by biting their fingers. In consequence, the bartender at the *Cockatoo Lounge* routinely dispensed medical aid as well as liquid refreshments.

In 1965 the National Capital Commission expropriated the Roxborough Apartments to provide a site for the proposed National Museum complex. The tenants were so upset that they petitioned Parliament to postpone this action, but their plea was ignored. Following a farewell dinner on the night of 30 September 1965 which culminated with a piper playing a lament, the Roxborough came under the wrecker's hammer. Among the dispossessed were two senior Cabinet ministers, several Senators, a Supreme Court justice, and six ambassadors. Fifteen years after the event nothing has been built on the site which today forms part of Confederation Park.

The Roxborough was built by Lieutenant-Colonel James W. Woods, who was described by the *Dictionary of Canadian Biography 1875 - 1933* as a "capitalist and philanthropist." Colonel Woods had many business interests, his main enterprise being a factory that made canvas goods and supplies for the lumber industry. In 1900 Colonel Woods developed a light, non-absorbent cotton duck tent for the Imperial Forces in the Boer War. Modified versions of this tent were used extensively by Canadian troops in World Wars One and Two. Woods also manufactured down-filled sleeping robes, which quickly became standard bedding throughout the North. His second son, the late Shirley E. Woods, was the inventor of the down-filled vest, which he designed for Canadian troops during World War Two. Colonel Woods's products were used on the arctic expeditions of such famous explorers as Byrd, Peary, and Amundsen. In Ernest Hemingway's novel *For Whom the Bell Tolls* (where much of the action takes place after dark), the hero of the story frequently extolls the virtues of a Woods sleeping bag. The Woods plant on the Hull shore of the Ottawa River was a landmark from the turn of the century until the 1950s, when it was expropriated to make a park. A smaller factory, located on Queen Street in Ottawa, is still standing.

Colonel Woods was well known for his generosity. During his term as president of the Protestant General Hospital (a forerunner of the Ottawa Civic Hospital) he presented this institution with the first dental clinic in Canada. Three years later, in 1910, when he was commanding officer of the Governor General's Foot Guards, he outfitted the entire regiment in new dress uniforms. Being patron of this unit also had its advantages. Of a summer evening the regimental band would sometimes give a concert in front of his residence, Kildare House, on Chapel Street, while he and his neighbour, Sir Wilfrid Laurier, listened in easy chairs on the verandah.

In September of 1911 the Central Canada Exhibition Committee tried to engage John A. D. McCurdy to give a flying demonstration in his aircraft, the *Silver Dart*. McCurdy had made aviation history two years earlier with a successful flight—the first in the British Empire—at Baddeck, Nova Scotia. McCurdy was too busy to accept their invitation, but he arranged for an American colleague, Captain Thomas Baldwin, to put on a performance.

Captain Baldwin, one of the early barnstormers, owned several aircraft and had as his protégé a young pilot named Lee Hammond. Baldwin arrived in Ottawa with the *Red Devil*, a skeletal biplane, on 10 September, the day before the opening of the fair. Because of the congestion at the Exhibition Grounds, Baldwin chose to assemble his machine at Slattery's Field, just east of the Rideau Canal. His base for this operation was a tent pitched beside the aircraft. As no one in Ottawa had ever seen an airplane in flight, these preparations provoked intense interest as well as questions about Baldwin's pilot, who was nowhere to be seen. Baldwin told the reporters that Lee Hammond was a "real comer" who had shown his courage numerous times during his three-month career. He also explained that his protégée had been late catching the train from New York because he had crashed at Coney Island the previous day and had been thrown into the sea.

The *Ottawa Citizen* gave this account of the performance on Opening Day at the Exhibition:

Mr. Hammond only arrived in Ottawa shortly after noon from New York and proceeded directly to the grounds. On his arrival there he found that the machine was in shape for an ascent and as the weather conditions were all that could be desired he immediately got ready for a start.

Capt. Baldwin explained to the crowd the necessity of keeping clear of the machine once it started. The people were quick to realize that an accident might easily happen should any of them get in or near the path of the machine, as Capt. Baldwin stated that before it left the ground it attained a high rate of speed. Chief Ross had four bluecoats on hand to see that the crowd in the field did not encroach on the aviator. Their services were not necessary as the crowd was orderly.

Shortly after one o'clock the biplane was wheeled out for its first attempt. It was taken to the easterly end of the field, and after a preliminary whirl of the propellor to see that it was working in good order, Mr. Hammond mounted the seat and gave the word. Skimming over the ground the moment it was released, the plane went about one hundred and fifty yards. When it had gathered sufficient momentum Hammond lunged forward elevating the front planes, and with a bird like motion the machine shot onto the air well above the tree tops.

Going at a high speed Hammond guided his aeroplane well over the exhibition grounds, going as far as Dow's Lake on the trip west. Turning towards the north he shot back again over the grounds like a bolt from the blue, the people at the fair being warned of his presence in the air above them by megaphones and by the purring of the engine. Skirting to the south of the grounds over the canal, he again turned its nose northward, completing a figure eight and then sailing off westward once more. Turning above Dow's Lake again, he drove the machine back to his starting point in the field, making the landing in fine style. Capt. Baldwin waved a hankerchief in the centre of the field and Hammond came down almost at his feet. The flight lasted a little over five minutes.

The second flight was ... practically a repetition of the first with the exception that the aviator drove the machine down almost in front of the grand stand, where the people had a splendid opportunity of seeing it whirling through the air. On the second landing Hammond tore off two of the tires on the wheels under the planes. These were easily repaired.

Hammond's flights attracted a record crowd to the opening of the Exhibition. On that day, 11 September 1911, more than 20,000 people attended the fair. Because many of them were children (who got in free) there are still a surprising number of Ottawans who remember seeing the *Red Devil*—the first air machine to fly above the capital.

Ottawa's first central rail depot, built by J. R. Booth in 1895, was a limited success. One reason was that Booth acted as though the depot had been built for his personal benefit as owner of the Canada Atlantic Railway. This distressed his competitors, who understood it to be a public facility. It also upset City Council, who had paid Booth a $50,000 bonus for completing the station on time. In 1901 City Council sent a Resolution to the Prime Minister and the Minister of Railways which began:

> That this Council learns with deep concern that difficulties arise in connection with the use by all railways on equal and convenient terms of the Central Railway Station site and its approaches.
>
> That the Council particularly regrets the appearance of obstacles placed by officials of the Canada Atlantic Railway in the way of access to and from the Central Station via the Interprovincial bridge.

The Central Station also had aesthetic shortcomings. In 1904 a tongue-in-cheek advertisement appeared in the Ottawa newspapers. It was in the form of a letter to Santa Claus, and said in part:

> ...I would like first of all a nice new Central Station, built from the ground up, not laid in sections, a plank, or a coat of whitewash at a time. The present so-called depot wouldn't be acceptable as a lobster packing warehouse and it was a blot on the landscape when you filled the home-made hosiery of the By family."

In 1910 a settlement was reached between the government and the heirs of the Nicholas Sparks Estate regarding the Rideau Canal Reserve. This cleared the way for the government to cede a portion of the property (including the Central Railway Station) to the Grand Trunk Railway as the site for a new depot and a luxury hotel. The Union Station and the Chateau Laurier Hotel—both of which were grander than anything Ottawa had known—took two years to build, and were opened with little fanfare on 2 June 1912.

The Union Station, unlike its predecessor, was a great source of pride to the city. Built of granite in the Classic Revival style, it has a magnificent domed ceiling in the main concourse which is supported by graceful stone pillars. In 1919 the Grand Trunk Railway was nationalized to prevent its collapse and the Union Station became an asset of the Crown. The station served as the rail hub of the capital until 1966. In that year it was closed as part of the Gréber Plan to reroute railways to the outskirts of the city, and a new station was opened in the Walkley Road area. The Union Station was originally slated to be torn down, but there was such a public outcry in defence of the landmark, that this action has been postponed. The building was renovated in 1967, and is now the Canadian Government Conference Centre.

When the station and hotel were being built the city replaced the Sappers and Dufferin bridges with a single wide bridge, which had in its centre a triangular plot of grass. This area, now part of Confederation Square, was named Connaught Place in honour of Prince Arthur, Duke of Connaught, who was Governor General at that time. The hotel itself is surrounded by history, for it overlooks the Entrance Locks of the Rideau Canal, to the east are the Parliament buildings, to the west is Lower Town, and behind it is Major's Hill Park.

The Chateau Laurier, named for Sir Wilfrid Laurier, was built to resemble a stately French chateau. It has a granite and buff sandstone exterior, with a copper roof that has oxidized to a pastel shade of green. When the Grand Trunk was nationalized following World War One, the Chateau Laurier became part of the government-owned Canadian National Railway chain of hotels. Originally the Chateau had 306 rooms, but a new wing was added in 1929 which increased the total to 546 rooms. The hotel underwent extensive renovations in 1963, including the installation of air-conditioning. Now, the Chateau combines the best features of the old and the new; it has spacious rooms with high ceilings (and thick walls) as well as such modern amenities as an indoor swimming pool, which was added in the 1929 building program.

From the day it opened its doors the Chateau Laurier became Ottawa's prestige hotel. Because of its proximity to the Hill, and the excellent service, it has always had a good number of Senators and members of the House of Commons during Parliamentary sessions. While R. B. Bennett was Prime Minister from 1930 to 1935, he lived in a special suite in the hotel. Despite the establishment of several first-class hotels in the capital in recent years, the Chateau still enjoys steady patronage from businessmen and tourists.

This hotel is such an integral part of Ottawa's skyline that it has been designated an historic building by the National Capital Commission. By day it is a handsome structure that harmonizes pleasantly with the Parliament buildings. It is also attractive at night, even though coloured floodlights on its spires and towers transform the style of architecture from French Gothic to Modern Disneyland.

In 1912, the same year the Chateau Laurier and the Union Station were completed, the Victoria Memorial Museum, another important Ottawa institution, was officially opened. This building, located at the south end of Metcalfe Street, was designed for the exhibition and custody of Canada's national treasures. From 1880 until 1910 the museum collection had been an adjunct of the Geological Survey Department, housed in a four-story stone building at 541 Sussex Street. This historic structure, built in 1853, had once been a barracks and is now occupied by the National Capital Commission.

The eight-acre site of the new museum, bounded by Argyle Avenue, Elgin, McLeod, and O'Connor streets, was purchased by the Canadian Government in 1902 for $73,000. This property had previously been the home of Catherine Stewart, who had lived in Appin Place, a large Gothic house surrounded by magnificent grounds, until her death in 1900. Catherine was the widow of William Stewart, who had come to Bytown in 1827, opened a store on Rideau Street, and later became the member of the Legislative Assembly for Bytown. The museum site was part of a seventy-acre parcel of land that Stewart had bought for £300 in 1834. William Stewart died in 1856 and his acreage, named Stewarton, was subdivided into lots in 1871. Many of the streets in the vicinity of the museum, such as Flora, William, Isabella, McLeod, and Catherine, were named for the Stewarts' nine children.

The Appin Place property was chosen by the government because they envisaged the museum as the terminus of a stately avenue— Metcalfe Street—leading directly to the Parliament buildings. However, as a building site, it had one serious drawback: beneath the overburden of topsoil there was a 140-foot-thick layer of Leda clay. The government's architects were made aware of this problem but insisted over the contractor's protests that construction proceed. It was a long and exceedingly difficult task, which started in 1905 and was not completed until 1912. Three hundred stone masons were imported from Scotland to deal with the intricate stonework of the turreted design. Soon after the massive outer walls were erected, the building began to sink in the clay, and many of the labourers refused to work in the basement because of alarming shifts in the floor. Three years after the museum was completed, the tall central tower (which resembled a Victorian wedding cake) started to shear away from the main structure. Most of the tower was dismantled in 1916, and with it went the symmetry of the whole building.

During the construction period the staff of the museum on Sussex Drive learned to their dismay that several other government agencies planned to join them in their new quarters. To claim as much space as possible, the curators and their assistants moved into the Victoria Memorial Museum in 1910, while the walls were still ringing with the sound of hammers and Gaelic cries of the artisans. By the time the building was officially opened in 1912 the National Gallery and some departments of the Geological Survey were also tenants.

The museum separated from the Geological Survey in 1925 when an Order-in-Council created the National Museum of Canada. Through the years the National Museum of Canada has suffered some serious reverses and has also had to cope with a chronic shortage of funds. In 1913 a research expedition to the Canadian Arctic resulted in the death of five staff members on Wrangel Island and the icefloes of the Chuckchi Sea. When the Parliament buildings burned in 1916, most of the museum exhibits were removed so that the House of Commons and the Senate could use the building to conduct the nation's business. This hasty evacuation resulted in the damage and loss of some valuable artifacts. During the Depression the operation of the museum almost came to a halt; in World War Two most of the building was taken over by wartime agencies. By the 1950s the Victoria Memorial Museum was in a state of disrepair, and far too small for its occupants.

In 1959 the Geological Survey moved to a newly opened twenty-one-story building for the Department of Mines and Technical Surveys at 580 Booth Street. The following year the National Gallery also left the premises and took over the Lorne Building on Elgin Street. After half a century the Victoria Memorial Museum was now available for the purpose for which it had originally been designed. However, the building needed such extensive repairs that the government agreed to build a modern facility for the museum on the site of the Roxborough Apartments. This decision was subsequently reversed in favour of building the National Arts Centre.

In 1968 the National Museums of Canada—which included the National Museum of Natural Sciences, the National Museum of Man, the National Museum of Science and Technology, and the National Gallery—became a Crown Corporation with a secretary-general and a board of trustees who were responsible to Parliament through the Secretary of State. This changed the status of the agencies but did little to improve the condition of the Victoria Memorial Museum, which housed both the Museum of Man and the Museum of Natural Sciences. In 1969 the director of the Museum of Man became so exasperated that he told the press that the Victoria Memorial Museum was a "squalid disaster." The following year the old stone building underwent a $6 million renovation and facelift that included the installation of a new basement floor. Since then, no further sinking has taken place, and experts agree that the problem has finally been overcome.

Today the National Museums are engaged in a vigorous program to reach the public by means of publications and touring exhibits such as the half-mile-long "Discovery Train." In Ottawa there are creative displays at four permanent locations, each of which is different from the other. On St. Laurent Boulevard a huge warehouse-type building—distinguished from its neighbours by a seventy-foot Atlas missile mounted on the front lawn—is the home of the National Museum of Science and Technology. This museum contains everything from music boxes to steam locomotives, as well as exhibits that provide "fun and learning through involvement." One example is the "Crazy Kitchen," which appears normal even though the floor is tilted at a sharp angle. People who try this test of the senses end up staggering through the room hanging on to the guard rail. Another demonstration literally makes one's hair stand on end through static electricity. The aeronautical collection of the Science and Technology Museum, consisting of nearly one hundred aircraft, from bush planes to supersonic fighters, is housed in three hangars at Rockcliffe Airport. A number of these aircraft came from the National War Museum (a division of the Museum of Man), located in the former Archives building on Sussex Street.

A visit to the Victoria Memorial Museum is a rewarding experience. As soon as you enter the eighty-foot-high rotunda, which has as its centrepiece an ancient Haida totem pole, you are surrounded by history. The National Museum of Man occupies the west wing of the building, where it uses nine halls to display items of Canada's heritage, including artifacts from the Canadian Indian and Inuit cultures. The National Museum of Natural Science occupies the east wing and has a similar amount of space devoted to exhibits that range from gem stones to dinosaurs.

The Victoria Memorial Museum has survived two world wars, a world depression, and years of political indifference. Like its namesake, Queen Victoria, it becomes more popular with the passage of time.

Le Droit, Ottawa's French-language daily newspaper, published its first issue on 27 March 1913. The name of the paper, *Le Droit* (meaning equity or justice), symbolized its purpose, which was to defend the rights and to preserve the culture of French-speaking Roman Catholics in the national capital region. One specific reason *Le Droit* was founded was to rally support for a change in a provincial law that restricted the amount of French taught in Roman Catholic separate schools. Due in part to the influence of *Le Droit's* editorials, the Ontario Government eliminated this restriction in 1927.

Although the newspaper is run by laymen, it is owned by Les Pères Oblats d'Ottawa, the French community of the Oblate Order in the capital. Because of this sponsorship, *Le Droit* is noted for responsible journalism and editorial comment directed at cultural rather than political matters. The paper and its two affiliated companies employ approximately 440 people, most of whom live on the Quebec side of the Ottawa River. The average daily circulation, which is distributed throughout the Ottawa Valley as well as to communities such as Cornwall and Mont Laurier, amounts to 50,000 copies. The newspaper is associated with a large and competent commercial press that prints a wide range of publications and also executes a substantial number of custom orders. In 1973 Les Pères Oblats d'Ottawa formed a third company, Novalis, which has its own staff of specialists who publish liturgical and educational texts in both languages.

It has always been *Le Droit's* editorial policy to devote most of its attention to parochial matters and relatively little space to national or world events. For this reason the paper continues to fill a community need in the Ottawa area and also helps to preserve the French culture.

18

The Great War

1914 to 1918

"HELL'S LET LOOSE" was the headline of the *Ottawa Free Press* on 4 August 1914, the day Britain declared war against Germany. Most Ottawans were dismayed at the prospect of war, but at least one resident—Colonel Sam Hughes, the flamboyant and eccentric Minister of Militia—was delighted. The day before, Hughes had become so angry at Britain's attempts at appeasement that he had exclaimed to a colleague, "England is going to skunk it!" He then ordered the Union Jack hauled down from Militia Headquarters (which was in the Woods Building on Slater Street) but was dissuaded from this gesture. As soon as war was declared, Hughes issued a nation-wide call for volunteers for a Canadian contingent. Within three weeks he was able to report to the House that more than 100,000 young men had offered their services and that trains bound for the capital were being besieged by volunteers: "They are climbing on so persistently that we can't keep them off."

Among the first to respond to the call were men from Ottawa and the nearby Valley towns. Long line-ups formed at the Drill Hall and Lansdowne Park to join units such as the Governor-General's Foot Guards, the Princess Louise Dragoon Guards, the 43rd Ottawa and Carleton Battalion, the 8th Brigade Field Artillery, the

Service Corps, and the Medical Corps. Phenomenal recruiting was experienced by a new regiment, the Princess Patricia's Canadian Light Infantry, which had only come into existence on 8 August.

The Princess Patricia's Canadian Light Infantry was raised at the personal expense of A. Hamilton Gault, a Montreal millionaire who had served as a subaltern in the Boer War. The regiment (now based in western Canada) was named for the Governor-General's daughter, HRH Princess Patricia of Connaught, who was one of the outstanding beauties of her day. The first commanding officer of the regiment was Lieutenant-Colonel Francis Farquhar, Coldstream Guards, who until the outbreak of war had been Military Secretary to the Governor-General. Between 8 and 19 August, Colonel Farquhar and his second-in-command, Major Hamilton Gault, personally screened three thousand applicants for the PPCLI. Of these, they chose 1,098, including an entire pipe band that had come by train from Edmonton. Most of the men selected had seen service before, and 85 percent were first-generation immigrants from the British Isles.

Following a church parade at Lansdowne Park on 23 August, Princess Patricia presented her regiment with its Colour. She had made the crimson silk flag herself, which had her cipher VP (Victoria Patricia) woven in gold upon a blue centre. The staff for the Colour was made from a tree in the Government House grounds. This Colour had such significance that prior to embarkation it was guarded day and night by a sentry whose orders read that he was responsible for its safety "dead or alive." It has since won a place in military history because it was the only Colour to be carried into action by an Allied regiment in World War One. To achieve this distinction the Patricias ignored a War Office directive which stated that Colours could not be taken into battle. By the end of the war the Colour was bullet-torn and the staff had been broken in an artillery barrage. These scars help to make it one of the regiment's most cherished possessions today.

At the end of August 1914 the PPCLI joined the Canadian Expeditionary Force (which included the 2nd Provisional Battalion, made up of men from the GGFG and the 43rd) at Camp Valcartier, on the shore of the St. Lawrence River. In October the Canadian Expeditionary Force—numbering 31,000 men and 8,500 horses—sailed in convoy for England.

The first Canadian soldiers to see action were the Princess Patricia's Canadian Light Infantry. Their introduction to trench warfare was a grim one. When they moved into the line at St. Eloi on 4 January 1915 they found the trench a shambles. Not only was it vulnerable to attack, but human limbs protruded from its broken walls and they had to watch their footing as they waded to their positions lest they trip over corpses buried in the mud.

Three months later the balance of the Canadian Expeditionary Force fought as a division at the Ypres Salient in Belgium. This was the first time the Germans used gas, which had been forbidden by the Geneva Convention of 1906. On the first day of the battle, clouds of deadly chlorine forced the French Algerian force on the left flank of the Canadians to retreat, leaving a huge gap in the line. The Canadians helped to close the gap that night and then withstood three days of heavy assaults from the enemy. Each German attack was preceded by an artillery barrage and the release of gas. This battle won world renown for the Canadian Expeditionary Force—at a cost of more than six thousand casualties—and earned the 2nd Provisional Battalion its nickname, "The Iron Second." In a dispatch to the Secretary of State for War, Field-Marshal Sir John French said of the Canadians" . . . the bearing and conduct of these splendid troops averted a disaster which might have been attended with the most serious consequences."

The 38th Battalion, recruited in Ottawa by Lieutenant-Colonel Cameron Edwards, was among the units comprising the Second Contingent which arrived in France in September 1915. This contingent formed the nucleus of the 2nd Canadian Division, commanded by Brigadier-General (later Sir) Richard Turner, who had won the Victoria Cross in the Boer War. Both Canadian divisions were involved in a succession of bloody engagements in the ensuing year, the most notable being the Battle of Mont Sorrel, in June 1916, which cost 8,400 Canadian casualties, and the lengthy Battle of the Somme.

For the first two years of the war Canada's most prominent military personage was Colonel Sam Hughes, the Minister of Militia. Prior to his election in 1891 as a Conservative member of the House of Commons, Hughes had owned a newspaper in Lindsay, Ontario. During the Boer War he served in a supernumerary capacity with the British forces and also managed, while careening about the veldt in search of the enemy, to act as a correspondent for his hometown paper. Most of his dispatches (told in the third person) contained glowing accounts of his personal valour. For many years after the war Hughes was galled by the fact that these exploits did not win him a Victoria Cross, and he waged a vigorous but unsuccessful campaign to right this perceived injustice.

When Robert Borden was elected Prime Minister in 1911, he appointed Sam Hughes as his Minister of Militia and Defence. Seventeen years later Sir Robert Borden wrote in his memoir an assessment of "Colonel Sam's" performance:

> ...his mood might be divided into three categories; during about half of the time he was an able, reasoned and useful colleague working with excellent judgement and indefatigable energy; for a certain other portion he was extremely excitable, impatient of control, and almost impossible to work with; and during the remainder his conduct and speech were so eccentric as to justify the conclusion that his mind was unbalanced.

Despite his obvious flaws Sam Hughes contributed to Canada's war effort in a number of ways. Convinced that war was inevitable with Germany, as soon as he was appointed to the Cabinet he took steps to revitalize the militia, which included the establishment of cadet corps, and the construction of armouries. The swiftness with which he dispatched the Canadian Expeditionary Force was a remarkable feat (even though most of the men were ill equipped and half trained). Hughes was a genuine patriot who had the courage to insist, over the objections of Field-Marshal Lord Kitchener, that Canadians must fight with their own units rather than being dispersed as reinforcements to the British Army. This confrontation with the British Secretary of War could have damaged Commonwealth relations, but the following year Hughes was knighted, and in 1916 he was elevated to the rank of honorary Lieutenant-General in the British Army.

As a result of his conflicts with the Cabinet, and a munitions scandal that involved a contract he had given to a friend, Lieutenant-General Sir Samuel Hughes was forced to resign his portfolio in October 1916. He continued as a Conservative backbencher until he became terminally ill in 1920. In recognition of his service a special train was provided by the government to take him from Ottawa to his home in Lindsay. Asked by the engineer if he would like the train to proceed slowly, Sam Hughes replied, "No, go like blazes!"

By the beginning of 1916 Ottawa residents were feeling the effects of the war, which they now knew would be a long one. Inflation made goods increasingly expensive, and shortages were an everyday occurrence. The entire country was also suffering from a manpower shortage—by this time approximately 300,000 Canadians were in the armed forces—and the continuing demand for recruits was certain to aggravate this situation. There was relatively little social activity, and most functions were designed to raise money for relief funds or other war-related causes. Many Ottawa women devoted a great deal of their time to making woollens and bandages for the troops; the Duchess of Connaught (with the aid of a knitting machine) made more than one thousand pairs of socks for the men overseas. Although the news from the front was presented in the most optimistic light, casualty lists of local men in the same newspapers told a different story. To make matters worse, on the night of 3 February 1916, fire destroyed the Centre Block of the Parliament Buildings.

The original Centre Block was an ornate three-story building with a frontage of 472 feet and a depth of 247 feet. Because it was constructed of stone and concrete, with large water tanks in some of its towers, this structure was believed to be fire-proof. For this reason, even though the building housed both the Senate and the House of Commons, it contained inadequate firefighting equipment, and there were no fire escapes. The fire not only gutted the entire building but also took the lives of seven people.

The conflagration started in the Commons Reading Room at about nine o'clock on that icy winter night. Two Dominion constables tried to extinguish the blaze, but it licked fiercely across the matting on the floor and "fairly chased them" out of the room. Mederic Martin, the mayor of Montreal, saw the black smoke billowing into the corridor and rushed into the Commons chamber where a member was addressing a small audience on the subject of fishing rights. Martin shouted, "Fire, and a big one!" Within three minutes the Commons chamber and the connecting corridors were also filled with dense smoke. The fire spread so quickly from the Reading Room that the people in the Chamber and the Gallery barely had time to leave. The last man out, Dr. Clarke, the Member for Red Deer, was knocked down by a stream from a fire hose and had to crawl on his hand and knees to the main entrance.

Having warned his colleagues, Mederic Martin hurried out of the burning building and went to his room in the nearby Chateau Laurier where he telephoned the Chief of the Montreal Fire Brigade, and told him to send as many men to Ottawa as possible. However, the mayor's order was not acted upon, because a short time later the Superintendent of the Ottawa Fire Department telephoned Montreal and said the fire was under control.

Fed by the richly varnished wood panelling, the fire roared through the draughty corridors, trapping people in their rooms and cutting off avenues of escape. The next morning, the *Citizen* recounted the experiences of some of Canada's Parliamentarians:

Sir Robert Borden stated that he was in his office when his undersecretary hurried in and informed him that the building was afire. He turned back for his hat and coat, but was persuaded that it would be dangerous to wait for them. Sir Robert said that he was glad that he had accepted the advice as he experienced considerable difficulty in making his way out of the building as it was.

Mr. John Stanfield, chief Conservative whip, was trapped in his room, and had to escape down a ladder which was extended to him by some firemen with the assistance of some newspapermen. . . .

Mr. Thomas McNutt, M.P. for Saltcoats, Sask., and Dr. Cash, M.P. for Yorkton, Sask., had a thrilling escape. Both men were in the lavatory when the fire assumed big proportions, but were unaware of the fact.

"I went in the wash room," said Mr. McNutt in telling his story, "and I had not been in there three minutes when I opened the door and I could see a mass of flames at the other end of the corridor. Dr. Cash, M.P., came out at the same time. We could not go through the smoke and flame, so we looked around for a means of escape. We went to the nearest window. Never considering what was below, we seized the towels and made a rope of towels. This rope of towels we tied to a stick which is used to open the windows. Dr. Cash went first through the window and down the rope. He must have fallen twenty feet. By now one of the caretakers, a French-Canadian, joined me. He came running along with a ladder. This we lowered and placed on the floor of the well outside. I went first and reached the ladder with my feet. Then after making sure it was safe I called for the caretaker. He came through the window and I placed his feet on the rungs of the ladder. That is how we got out.

After the fire consumed the west wing, it changed direction and swept toward the east wing, which contained the Senate Chamber. In the few minutes before the flames reached the Chamber, the Senate staff managed, at great personal risk, to remove the Throne and several valuable paintings. One of the paintings saved was the portrait of Queen Victoria by the English artist John Partridge. This painting had been rescued by four men in 1849, when a mob burned the Parliament building in Montreal. Alpheus Todd, Assistant Librarian to the Legislative Assembly, was one of the four men. Sixty-seven years later, on 3 February 1916, the person responsible for saving the same portrait was Alpheus Todd's nephew, A. Hamlyn Todd, Chief Clerk of the Parliamentary Library. This portrait, which now hangs in the Senate foyer, is also of interest because it shows the young Queen with a foreshortened left arm; a disability some tour guides delight in pointing out to their charges. In fact, Victoria's arms were perfectly normal; the deformity is the fault of the artist's brushwork.

When the fire doubled back to the east, M. Connolly MacCormac, a clerk on the library staff, bolted the steel fire-door that annexed the Library of Parliament from the Centre Block. This action—combined with a strong north wind and the work of the firemen, who hosed its stone walls and domed roof all night—saved the Library.

The inferno on the Hill attracted a tremendous crowd, including the Duke and Duchess of Connaught, who had been at the Russell Theatre. Dominion Police and troops of the 77th Battalion maintained order while sliding about the grounds, which had turned into a gigantic skating rink. The most dramatic spectacle of the night began when the flames reached the base of the 160-foot-high central tower. The clock in the tower ran until half-past twelve, but its bell crashed to the ground in a fiery shower of sparks at the last stroke of midnight. The fall of the tower itself, recorded by the *Citizen*, occurred at twenty-one minutes past one:

> For a long time the giant tower remained silhouetted against the dark background of the Gatineau Hills. Gallantly Chief Graham and his men poured thousands of tons of water into the enfilading flames, but their fight proved a losing one and spectators sighed with regret as it capitulated to the fury of the flames, shuddered on its massive foundations and came down with a tragic crash that shook the place for blocks around.

At eleven o'clock that night Sir Robert Borden met with his Cabinet Council in the Honourable Robert Rogers' room at the Chateau Laurier. The following afternoon the House of Commons convened in the auditorium of the Victoria Memorial Museum.

Both the Senate and the Commons remained at the Museum until they returned to the enlarged Centre Block in 1920.

Many people believed the fire was caused by "Hun treachery." Two suspected spies were arrested the next day but subsequently released for lack of evidence. The results of a Parliamentary Investigation were also inconclusive, although they indicated that the fire may well have been the work of an arsonist.

During 1917 Canadian troops played a major role in a number of engagements; the most outstanding being the Battle of Vimy Ridge in April of that year. Because of the valour of the Canadians, who lost 11,000 men in the space of five days, Vimy Ridge was later chosen as the site for an impressive memorial to Canadian dead. In June 1917 the number of volunteers had dwindled so drastically that conscription was enacted to enlist the remaining men eligible for service. Canadians were also subjected to a "temporary" income tax, and Prohibition came into effect throughout the country, except for the province of Quebec. This latter measure irritated some residents of the capital, even though it was still possible (but not legal) to cross the Ottawa River and purchase liquor in Hull.

In the spring of 1918 the news from the front took a sinister turn when the Kaiser launched a massive counteroffensive. After alarming initial successes the Germans were stopped at the Battle of Amiens on 8 August. This decisive encounter—the turning point of the war—produced more than nine thousand Canadian casualties.

September 1918 should have been a happy month in Ottawa, for the war news was genuinely optimistic. However, like the rest of the world, the capital was hit by a virulent epidemic of influenza. At the height of the epidemic more than 10,000 Ottawans were stricken; during the last week of September and the first two weeks of October 520 residents died of influenza and pneumonia.

In an attempt to reduce the contagion, Mayor Harold Fisher closed the city's schools, churches, laundries, theatres, and pool halls. Stores and offices were compelled to close at four o'clock in the afternoon, and all public gatherings were banned. The mayor also wrote Tom Ahearn asking him that passengers not be allowed to stand in the street cars (to avoid crowding) and that the trams be better ventilated if possible. Several schools were turned into temporary hospitals, and a barracks for orphaned children was established in the Manufacturers Building at Lansdowne Park.

The people of the city, particularly women of the May Court Club, the Ottawa Day Nursery, and other service organizations, responded to the crisis, but by 10 October the mayor had to appeal for additional volunteers. A *Citizen* report of that date read in part:

> If anyone doubts the urgent need for volunteers who will work in the homes of the sick of Ottawa, and help out in any way that conditions demand, then a visit to the city hall, where the organization committee is working night and day endeavouring to meet the call for nursing service, for hot broths and soups, for fuel, bedding and clothes, would quickly dispel this illusion.
>
> Five telephones are busy throughout the day and night, and all calls especially among the destitute are responded to with some form of help at once. But the committee is finding it dreadfully hard to get workers. Mayor Fisher, again emphasizes the need for women to go into the homes and help nurse the sick. Bedding is also much needed, and anyone who has blankets, quilts or any warm bed coverings to spare is requested to telephone the city hall.
>
> MEN ARE HELPING
>
> Constables Gleeson, Downey and Coombes of the city police force acted as nurses last night in homes where there are several patients, and their good work is highly recommended by the committee. Chief Ross is also taking other men off their beats and sending them wherever their services will be needed in any way, either for chopping wood, bringing in fuel, or to see that those families where there is illness have a supply of necessary fuel.

On the same page of the *Citizen* the mayor addressed another subject that concerned him deeply. The article, captioned "Mayor Says That Lives Are Saved By Prohibition," was based on an interview with His Worship that began:

> Records in the past have shown that when attacked by sickness the men addicted to excessive use of liquors were among the first to go under. Just now, he says, the privilege of getting a bottle of liquor on the order of a physician is being much abused. He ventured the opinion that half the orders issued are for liquor not needed for medicinal purposes. He would be strongly opposed to any move which would make it easier to secure liquor, he said, referring to the feeler being put out in certain circles to have the ban on liquor loosened to the extent of having a doctor's certificate made unnecessary at present....

The influenza epidemic passed through the capital with the speed and violence of a tornado. After peaking in October the number of cases proceeded to drop rapidly. Early the next month Mayor Fisher announced that his interdiction on public gatherings and other emergency restrictions would be lifted the following Monday, November 11.

The days preceding that Monday were exciting ones. On Saturday Kaiser Wilhelm abdicated his throne. This news was relayed to the residents of Ottawa by a prearranged signal; the power companies turned the street lights on and off twice and reduced the current to commercial and residential customers so that lights in houses and businesses flickered at the same time. The signal, given at 3:28 in the afternoon, caused pandemonium in the capital. People poured into the streets carrying flags and noise-makers and then converged upon Connaught Square, where an effigy of the Kaiser was to be burnt. They were joined by the Veterans' Band, which marched up Sparks Street playing "We'll Hang Kaiser Wilhelm to a Sour Apple Tree." As the band approached Connaught Square, the crowd fell in behind them while male spectators joyfully threw their hats in the air.

In its report of the festivities, the *Citizen* remarked on the phenomenon of adults tossing their hats, and their dignity, to the wind:

> Under ordinary circumstances, any man who saw his new dollar headgear lying on the ground and being reduced to a pulp by a frantic dance performed by a total stranger, would have wept tears of rage. But when the "Vet's" band was passing more than one man viewed the utter destruction of his hat unmoved. Indeed, he was probably doing exactly the same thing to some one else's hat. The boys were cheered to the echo.

While the Kaiser's abdication was an important milestone that signalled the end of the Hohenzollern dynasty, it did not stop the war. This would only come when an armistice was signed. On Saturday and Sunday, news dispatches indicated that the Armistice could be expected at any hour. It was signed shortly after midnight on Monday, 11 November.

Ottawa was the first city in Canada to receive the momentous news. This happened because all the telegraphers of the Canadian Press, except for the man in Ottawa, were on a coffee break when the dispatch came over the wire from Europe. The *Journal* of 11 November proudly recounted its part in spreading the tidings:

> Within two minutes of the receipt of the news in Ottawa that the armistice had been signed, scores of whistles at industrial plants conveyed, as per arrangements made by the Journal Newspapers, the great news that the world war had come to a successful conclusion in favour of the Allies. Even at the early hour of 3.01 scores of citizens arose from their beds and made their way down town. In front of *The Journal* building there was quite a demonstration.
>
> The fire department, church bells, and citizens with guns and revolvers created a din that could be heard in the four corners of the city. Ottawa was awakened.

The crowds milled and surged in every direction. At around four o'clock, several thousand gathered on Parliament Hill where they sang patriotic songs for half an hour. The next attraction was a huge bonfire, at the corner of Sparks and O'Connor streets, which not only stopped traffic but also scorched the overhead telephone and trolley wires. Most of the celebrants, thoroughly exhausted, went home around eight o'clock. The *Ottawa Journal's* Armistice Day issue contained many vignettes of the festivities, among them:

> Within the confines of Castle Dawson [the Nicholas Street Gaol] the gloom was penetrated by the joyous news and the prisoners forgot their unfortunate plight and celebrated. Aroused from their bunks by the shrill whistles, although locked behind iron bar doors, they joined in the cry of gladness. The dark and gloomy cell corridor resounded with lusty cheers.
>
> . . . An old gentleman seated in a carriage proudly held aloft a large white rooster. "We're cock o' the walk," he cried. The bird would not crow however.
>
> . . . One of the Capital's most prominent and otherwise dignified barristers was seen at the break of day tramping along Bank street trailing a couple of wash boilers at the end of a rope and joyfully banging together two sauce-pan lids.
>
> . . . "Pack Up Your Troubles in Your Old Kit-Bag, and Smile, Smile, Smile," played the Veterans' Band, and the hundreds who followed lustily sang. The advice was unnecessary for there were no grouches in the Capital."

The *Citizen* of November 11 also gave comprehensive coverage to the day's events. However, its one-word headline, in three-inch letters, told the most important news "PEACE."

Throughout the months of January, February, and March 1919, practically every train that pulled into the Union Station had some Ottawa servicemen aboard. The 38th Battalion returned to the city under the command of the man who had originally raised the regiment, Lieutenant-Colonel Cameron Edwards. In the interim the 38th had fought in many of the great battles, Colonel Edwards had been wounded once and he had been awarded the Distinguished Service Order three times. Shortly after the 38th was disbanded, it was reactivated as a Highland militia regiment, the Cameron Highlanders of Ottawa. Colonel Edwards, who had several Cameron ancestors, was responsible for the choice of the 38th's new name.

The Princess Patricia's Canadian Light Infantry returned to the Capital on 19 March 1919. They were addressed by a civic welcoming committee in Connaught Square and then marched through cheering crowds to Lansdowne Park, where they were demobilized. The regiment was led by Lieutenant-Colonel A. Hamilton Gault, DSO, who had been wounded three times and had lost a leg in the conflict. Colonel Gault was one of the forty-four who survived out of the 1,098 who enlisted in the Patricias in 1914. Such was the price of the Great War.

19

The Buoyant Years
1919 to 1929

THE GREAT WAR swept Canada from the horse-and-buggy era into the age of mechanization. The postwar period was characterized by its emphasis on speed, efficiency, and social change. Between 1914 and 1918 membership in Canadian trade unions more than doubled and the number of automobiles in the country tripled. Under the pressure of war Canada's industrial output surged dramatically. Following the Armistice, many engineering developments relating to the production of tanks and warplanes were applied to the manufacture of automobiles and civilian aircraft. The first airmail delivery was made on 17 August 1918, when a biplane flew from Toronto to Ottawa—a distance of approximately 220 miles—in three hours and forty minutes. The Great War also resulted in an expansion of the Civil Service and changed the fortunes of a number of Ottawa's leading business concerns.

One such firm was the Ottawa Car Manufacturing Company. Founded in 1893 by Thomas Ahearn and Warren Soper in partnership with William Wylie, a local carriage builder, this company had a large plant at the corner of Kent and Albert streets. Initially the firm produced tram cars for the Ottawa Electric Railway (owned by Ahearn and Soper) and horse-drawn vehicles for the public. During the Great War the company changed its production to the manufacture of gun carriages for 4.5 howitzer and 18-pounder guns.

In 1920, when the last of the defence contracts was completed, the Ottawa Car Manufacturing Company obtained the patent to make Brill gas/mechanical and gas/electric railway cars. These self-propelled coaches, similar to the modern dayliner used by urban commuters, were sold throughout Canada. In 1933 the company discontinued the manufacture of rolling stock, and focussed their efforts on the production of bus bodies and related equipment.

The Ottawa Car Manufacturing Company entered the aviation business in 1938 when it was awarded a contract from the British government to make engine mountings, retractable landing gear, and gas tanks for bombers. Shortly after the outbreak of World War Two, the firm changed its name to the Ottawa Car and Aircraft Limited and turned its entire capacity—which encompassed 250,000 square feet of floor space—to the production of aircraft parts. This business ceased at the conclusion of the war. The company made four buses for the Ottawa Electric Railway in 1947 and then wound up its affairs. The plant was sold the same year, and most of it was subsequently torn down. The remaining brick building on Albert Street is now used as an indoor parking garage.

R. L. Crain Limited, Canada's second-largest manufacturer of business forms, was another company affected by the Great War. It was founded in 1888 in Merrickville (a town thirty miles from Ottawa) by Rolla Law Crain, a bricklayer whose hobby was printing. Because bricklaying was a seasonal occupation and Crain hated to be idle, he opened a printing shop in his basement. The first thing he printed on the hand press was his business card, which read

The Merrickville Cheap Job Printing Office.

Being a hamlet, Merrickville offered a limited market, so Crain moved to Winchester, a somewhat larger town, and then in 1894 established a printing shop at 402 Wellington Street in Ottawa. He differed from most printers in that he was an innovator who would study the needs of his clients and then print special forms to suit them. This approach won him many customers and his business grew steadily. In 1896 he moved to larger quarters on Sparks Street, then in 1900 back to another building on Wellington Street, and eventually, in 1912, to the corner of Bank Street and Fifth Avenue.

The Great War produced an avalanche of paper, a problem compounded by the chronic shortage of personnel. Crain studied the situation and subsequently devised a method of printing forms on a continuous roll rather than on separate sheets of paper. This process proved so successful with the government that Crain was sure it would have a broad application in industry after the war. Anticipating the demand, he moved to much larger premises on Spruce Street in 1918.

In the two decades following the Great War Crain business forms came into general use throughout Canada. Rolla Crain's success was due in part to his own ingenuity and hard work, but also to the support he received from his employees. Crain was fond of saying, "People don't work for me, they work with me." (To this day, Crain employees are not unionized; all their dealings with management are through their own Council.)

Rolla Crain died in 1947, the year his firm moved to a 10.6-acre site on the Richmond Road. He was succeeded by his son Rolla Crain, Jr., who like his father hated to waste time. During his tenure as president it was unusual for the Annual General Shareholders' meeting to last longer than nineteen minutes, from start to finish. Rolla Crain, Jr.died in 1967, and was succeeded by his brother, Harold F. Crain, who is now chairman of the board.

R. L. Crain Limited is still controlled by the Crain family, although it has been a public company since 1946. Today the firm has more than one thousand employees and there are branch plants in Hull, Toronto, Moncton, and Medicine Hat. The company's new trademark, a triangle with a dot in the centre, has an interesting story behind it. This logotype is a magnified version of the "printer's bug" (a tiny mark used by printers to identify their own products), which was employed by Rolla Law Crain at the turn of the century.

The Great War was also a turning point for the Ottawa Hunt Club. This club owned a sandy 186-acre tract at the junction of the Bowesville and Rideau roads which had been purchased in 1908 by its first president, Colonel James Woods. The following year a clubhouse, stables, and kennels for the hounds were erected on the property. Because of the open nature of the terrain the grounds were ideal for polo, flat racing, and fox hunting. During the war the club was forced to suspend these sports and subsequently renamed itself the Ottawa Hunt and Motor Club.

After the Armistice the Hunt Club resumed its original name but dropped many of its former activities—including horseback riding, cricket, and lawn bowling—in favour of golf. In 1919 most of their

ABOVE: Boys hauling pig on sleigh in the By Ward market, December 1926. *(PAC #PA 87683)*
RIGHT: Chicken peddler in the market, December 1926. *(PAC #PA 87686)*
BELOW: York Street section of the By Ward market in 1911. *(OMA #CA 0222)*

TOP: Olympic gold medalist Anne Heggtveit in competition. *(OMA—Sports Hall of Fame Collection)*
LEFT: Francis Michael "King" Clancy circa 1925. *(OMA #CA-0211)*
RIGHT: Olympic skating champion Barbara Ann Scott circa 1948. *(OMA— Andrews-Newton Collection)*

King George VI and Queen Elizabeth after unveiling ceremony of National War Memorial in Confederation Square, May 1939. *(PAC #C 2179)*

TOP LEFT: King George VI and Queen Elizabeth at Royal Assent ceremony in Senate Chamber, May 1939. Prime Minister King at left, robed justices of Supreme Court in foreground *(PAC #C 33278)*

TOP CENTRE: Lord Tweedsmuir's funeral, 14 February 1940. Cortege is about to depart from St. Andrew's Church for the Union Station. *(Queen's University Collection)*

TOP RIGHT: Charlotte Whitton (1896-1976), Ottawa's first woman mayor, in full regalia. *(OMA—Andrews-Newton Collection)*

LOWER LEFT: Lieutenant Commander Thomas Fuller, "The Pirate of the Adriatic," Malta, October 1944. *(Fuller Family albums)*

LOWER RIGHT: Queen Elizabeth II and Prince Philip with Governor-General Vincent Massey at Rideau Hall in 1957. Mr. Massey's golden retriever, Duff, is the Royal Purse Bearer. *(PAC #NFB 84295)*

TOP LEFT: St. Andrew's Presbyterian Church, Wellington Street. Original structure erected by Thomas Mac-Kay's masons in 1828, enlarged 1854, completely rebuilt 1873. Bank of Canada at left, Holiday Inn in background. (OMA #80-20-23)

TOP RIGHT: Notre Dame Roman Catholic Cathedral, Sussex Street. Cornerstone laid in 1841, completed in 1853. Elevated to status of basilica in 1879. (OMA #80-20-1)

LOWER LEFT: Christ Church Cathedral. Built on land donated by Nicholas Sparks in 1833, enlarged in 1841, rebuilt in 1873. Elevated to status of cathedral in 1896. (OMA #80-20-33)

Honours ceremony in ballroom of Rideau Hall, October 1979. Governor-
General Edward Schreyer invests hockey star Bobby Orr with the insignia of
the Order of Canada. *(John Evans)*

The Deep Cut of the Rideau Canal as a winter playground today. Parliament Buildings at left, Chateau Laurier at right. *(Malak, Ottawa)*

acreage was turned into an eighteen-hole course, and a mammoth landscaping project that involved the planting of 60,000 coniferous trees was undertaken. Golf proved so popular with the members that a special clubhouse was built in 1922, and another nine-hole course was added in 1956.

In 1959 a six-sheet artificial-ice curling rink was built as an annex to the main clubhouse. Fortunately the curling rink was joined to the rambling old structure by a forty-foot fire-proof tunnel. This saved the rink when the clubhouse was demolished by fire on 23 February 1962. The members set about rebuilding immediately and moved into fine new quarters on the same site in November of the same year.

Today the Ottawa Hunt is a family club with approximately 1,500 members of all ages. Its main activities are golf and curling, and it has hosted national and international tournaments in both sports. The evolution of the Ottawa Hunt, which started with the Great War, is now complete. The only hunting on the premises is for lost golf balls.

On 20 May 1920 a memorable demonstration took place before five hundred people at the Chateau Laurier Hotel. For the first time in history a radio broadcast was received from a distance of more than one hundred miles. Later the same evening Ottawa's pioneer radio station—call letters OA—sent a transmission from its studio in the hotel back to Montreal.

Station OA, owned by the government, was operated by the Department of Marine and Fisheries. During the next four years the facilities of Station OA were also used by a group of local enthusiasts, the Ottawa Amateur Radio Association. In February 1924 the government placed Station OA under the control of the Canadian National Railways and changed its call letters to CNRO. In March of the same year the Ottawa Amateur Radio Association commenced broadcasting on its own station, which had the call letters CKCO.

The licence for CKCO—the first issued to an individual in Canada—was made out in the name of Dr. George Geldert, the president of the Ottawa Amateur Radio Association. Dr. Geldert, a man with many talents and exceptional energy, was at that time one of only two anaesthetists in the city. In the early days CKCO was a joint venture of the Ottawa Amateur Radio Association, but later became the property of Dr. Geldert. From the beginning CKCO was literally part of the doctor's home: his living room doubled as the control room and his dining room served as the broadcasting studio. This arrangement caused some inconvenience to the Geldert family, who were obliged to eat their evening meal at five o'clock in the afternoon so that the studio would be free when the station went on the air a few hours later.

Most local programs were performed by enthusiastic amateurs who donated their services; thus the week's entertainment was in some respects like a continuous amateur talent show. Church services were a regular feature, as were speeches made at public functions. There was no advertising. Among the star performers at CKCO was a canary, which lived in the Gelderts' living room, and a cuckoo clock, which stood on their mantelpiece.

Because CNRO and CKCO used the same wave length, the stations broadcast on different days. Initially, few Ottawans actually listened to the radio; to do so one had to buy an expensive neutrodyne tube set, which had a speaker, or one had to endure the inconvenience of sitting with a pair of earphones at a short-range crystal set. With both receivers, reception was often poor, and when an Ottawa station was on the air, it blocked the transmission of popular American stations. For this reason, CNRO and CKCO were criticized as much for interfering with outside reception as they were for their program content. A few months after the local stations went on the air there was a flurry of letters to the Ottawa papers. The following are excerpts from the *Citizen* and the *Journal* in the spring of 1925:

> I wish to add my protest to the very numerous others which have been made recently, to the way in which the local stations are allowed to control the air. Surely the time has come for the Government to exercise a little more judgement in their licencing. Why not limit private broadcasting to one night a month, and others to one night a week with hours 8 to 10? ...

> In the past CKCO has constituted itself a nuisance in some quarters. It has come on the air during weekdays far behind its newspaper advertised time, has had painful, time-wasting pauses of even up to a half an hour's silence between its program divisions, often ten minute gaps on its immediate program, and has at every point possible, uttered tiresome long winded reiterations of its status as a radio station. ...

My chief complaint against CNRO is the constant repetition by the announcer of the station broadcasting. The iteration and reiteration of the advertisement for the Canadian National Railways has so got on my nerves that positively I dread to turn on the machine....

At this time when a little friction is evident in respect to local broadcasting, I as an owner of an inexpensive crystal set would like to voice my appreciation for the various concerts etc., I listened to last week....

...Mr. Donald Heins and company entertained us to a royal treat. On another night we listened to a splendid concert by well-known French artistes. Friday night we were entertained in a most pleasing manner through the courtesy of Mr. J. R. Booth Jr., and Saturday we were carried away by the delightful voice of Mr. Jack Grace as he warbled in that touching way of his, "All Alone," and "Bringing Home the Bacon." The jazz if not elevating certainly reflected a radiance on the musicians.

As there have been so many kicks at the concerts given by the CNRO lately, I would just like to say a word in praise of Saturday evening's program.

The singing of Miss C. Baxter and Mr. W. Roach was of the highest order, and the programs selected by these two singers left nothing to be desired.

The number that pleased me most was the "Londonderry Air," my favourite Irish classic. Mr. Roach's rendering of this song was indeed very artistic, and he should be congratulated for this difficult song. I think it is the first time I ever heard it over the radio....

By the close of the Twenties, radio broadcasting in the capital had matured to a professional standard. In 1930 Dr. Geldert moved CKCO and his residence to a nearby mansion at 272 Somerset Street. As a concession to his wife the doctor installed the broadcasting equipment and the studio in the attic, which had a separate entrance. Three years later Geldert bought the old organ from the Imperial Theatre, which necessitated an addition to his house to enclose its tall pipes and accessories.

In 1936 Station CNRO was transferred to the newly formed Canadian Broadcasting Corporation and redesignated with the letters CBO. The original station OA studio in the Chateau Laurier was retained, and is still in use today.

For more than two decades, from 1924 until 1947, CKCO was the only privately owned radio station in Ottawa. During this period it served the community well and built up a large listening audience. In the same period Dr. Geldert entered civic affairs, serving as an alderman and a controller on City Council. In 1949, Dr. Geldert sold CKCO (and his house) to a group of local investors. There were several reasons for this action, including his crushing workload and competiton from television as well as CFRA, another private radio station.

The new owners of CKCO changed its call sign to CKOY and engaged a communications firm to manage the station. For many years CKOY beamed its signal at the twelve-to-seventeen age group, known in the trade as the "bubble gum" audience. In 1969 the owners of CKOY added a Frequency Modulated (FM) station, CKBY, which was aimed at the Country and Western audience. CKBY may not enhance the culture of the capital, but it is enjoyed by a broad cross-section of city and rural listeners. Some of the songs—such as "Love Don't Grow on Trees"—contain a nugget of wisdom, or in the case of "Take This Job and Shove It" an insight into personal relationships. Both CKOY and CKBY have continued Dr. Geldert's tradition of community service and regularly air public announcements, including a daily bulletin on behalf of the Ottawa Humane Society. In 1979 CKOY and its affiliate were purchased by the Toronto-based publishing firm of Maclean-Hunter Limited.

The Ottawa Civic Hospital was created by a Provincial Act in 1919 that merged the Protestant General Hospital, St. Luke's Hospital, and the Ottawa Maternity Hospital. This municipal hospital was sorely needed because the population had reached 100,000 some years earlier, but it was not until the 1918 flu epidemic revealed a critical shortage of beds that any action was taken. The new hospital was located on twenty-three acres bordering Carling Avenue, opposite the Experimental Farm. Because of its remote location, the Civic was dubbed by the press "Fisher's Folly" after Mayor Harold Fisher, who had promoted the concept and chosen the site. The Ottawa Civic Hospital opened its doors in December 1924 with five hundred beds; since then additions have increased its capacity to nearly one thousand beds.

For years the standard of medicine in the capital was adequate but undistinguished. Indeed, many residents of the city preferred to go to Montreal or Toronto for diagnosis and surgery rather than be treated locally. However, in the past two decades both the Civic Hospital and Ottawa University have won recognition at the international level. Today the Civic has an outstanding reputation for cardio-vascular medicine and surgery, having performed more than seven hundred open-heart operations. It is also one of the leading hospitals in the country for kidney transplants, micro-vascular surgery (the reattachment of severed limbs), and orthopaedic surgery. The Civic has been a pioneer in the practice of surgical day care, which permits patients to come in, undergo minor surgery, and return home the same day. In addition to all the normal services the Civic is a teaching hospital with the second largest school of nursing in Canada.

At this writing the Ottawa Civic is undergoing a $44 million modernization program that will also expand the facilities of the Cardiac Unit. Although the Civic is now the fourth-largest hospital in Canada, it has managed to retain much of the warmth and friendliness of a small-town hospital. This is due to the cheerful care of the staff and the location of "Fisher's Folly," which, though now in the midst of the city, still overlooks hundreds of acres of quiet farmland.

Ottawa was shaken by an earthquake for the first time in its history on the night of 28 February 1925. The epicentre of the disturbance —the most severe ever recorded in eastern Canada—was more than three hundred miles from the capital, at the mouth of the Saguenay River. The first tremors occurred at 9:20 P.M., and continued intermittently for approximately two hours. Relatively little damage was suffered by the city, but many residents got a bad fright. One young woman in a Rideau Street drugstore was so terrified by the vibrations that she ran out in the street shrieking, "The end of the world is here!"

Another young lady, Miss Roxie Carrier, was in the midst of a song at the annual Lisgar Collegiate concert when the first tremors shook the hall, causing the gallery to sway dangerously. Some of the audience bolted for the exits, but Miss Carrier continued with her performance. Her courageous example calmed the crowd and averted a general panic.

The largest gathering in the city that night was at the Auditorium, where a crowd of more than eight thousand was watching an exciting game between the Ottawa Senators and the Montreal Canadiens. The *Ottawa Citizen* of 2 March described the scene:

... It was in the middle of the second period, after a fight had occurred between Ed Gorman and Billy Boucher, and the crowd had just settled back in their seats, when there was a sudden commotion in the eastern section of the big amphitheatre. Hundreds of those sitting in the upper tiers of seats were alarmed when, to the accompaniment of a deep rumbling sound, the whole structure commenced a series of sharp sways, and there were ominous creaking sounds. At first, no one realized what was happening until someone yelled earthquake, and then there was panic in the making, until a number of ushers, with considerable presence of mind, advised all and sundry that there was no danger, and everyone, with the exception of a few timid persons, resumed their seats....

Because of the clay and sand that underlies central Ottawa and Sandy Hill, these districts felt the most violent tremors. However, only one building, the Victoria Memorial Museum, suffered any damage of consequence. On all four floors of the museum, all the arches cracked at their apexes and plaster fell from the ceilings in some of the rooms. One of the few people to benefit from the upheaval that Saturday night was the Reverend Ernest Sayles, pastor of the First Baptist Church on Laurier Avenue. In his sermon the following morning Reverend Sayles used the earthquake as an example of the "all powerful nature of things Divine."

Since 1925 there has only been one significant earthquake in Ottawa. This disturbance occurred on 5 September 1944, and because its epicentre was just fifty miles away, near the town of Cornwall, it was slightly more intense than the first one. The capital is within the boundaries of the West Quebec Seismic Zone, which is classified as an intermediate seismic-risk area.

Rugby football has been a major sport in Ottawa for more than one hundred years. In the early days the capital had two senior teams, Ottawa University and the Ottawa Football Club, which competed with each other for the Dominion Championship. Both teams won the national title in the 1890s, but since 1902 the Ottawa Football Club has been the capital's sole representative in the senior league. In 1909 the Governor General, Lord Grey, donated a cup to be awarded annually to the best rugby football team in Canada. For many years the contest for this trophy—the Grey Cup—has been the most important sporting event in the country.

The Ottawa Football Club won the Grey Cup for the first time in 1925, when they beat the Winnipeg Tammany Tigers by a score of 24 to 1. This game, played at Lansdowne Park on 5 December, was marred by huge puddles on the field and near-freezing temperatures. The Westerners were completely outclassed, but their conduct won them many friends among the spectators and the press. The following excerpts on the game are from the *Ottawa Journal* of 7 December 1925:

> The invaders might not be of Dominion Championship calibre, yet they revealed themselves as gentlemen athletes both on and off the field. They accepted defeat like well-bred sportsmen. Their lusty cheer for the Ottawas at the close of the game was a gesture of true sportsmanship. Come back again Winnipeg!
>
> After the game, the losers tripped into the Ottawa dressing room and insisted on shaking hands all round with the winners. The Winnipeg boys lost no time in peeling off their sweaters and asking the Ottawas to exchange the famous red, white and black shirts for them. An exchange was made all-round.

The Ottawa Football Club's team acquired its name "Rough Riders" in 1898, the same year that Theodore Roosevelt's Rough Rider cavalry unit won a decisive victory at Santiago de Cuba in the Spanish-American War. The term "Rough Riders" was used in a derogatory sense by a Hamilton sports writer to describe the conduct of the Ottawa team when it defeated the Hamilton Tigers 9 to 1 in a match at Ottawa on 15 October 1898. Harry S. Southam, treasurer of the *Ottawa Citizen*, starred for the Ottawa side in the victory. After the game one of Southam's reporters interviewed Jack Counsell, captain of the Hamilton fifteen. The interview concluded with the question "Did you consider there was any undue roughness?"

"I consider that Ottawa has," said the Tiger captain warmly, "three of the dirtiest players that ever played on a Canadian gridiron. That is about all I care to say about the game."

The following Monday the Hamilton papers had a great deal more to say about the brutality of the Ottawa team. The Hamilton *Evening Times* noted, among other things:

> When Secretary Barker saw the battered and bloody faces of some of the Tigers, he was strongly inclined to refuse to play the Ottawas again.
>
> Rayside (an Ottawa forward) is a manly fighter at least. He punches in the face, and does not kick from behind.

Two weeks later, on 29 October, a return match was played at the Hamilton Cricket Grounds before a crowd of five thousand. Everyone agreed it was an excellent contest, even though the Tigers lost by a score of 8 to 0, and the Hamilton club only collected a fraction of the receipts because they made the mistake of employing beer wagon drivers as gate-keepers. On Monday the Hamilton *Evening Times* wrote: "The Ottawa players by their fairness and gentlemanly play, as well as their dash and vim, won the respect of all who saw the game."

As a result of the Hamilton series in 1898, the Ottawa Football Club adopted the Rough Rider name and have used it ever since, except for three years (1925 to 1927) when they called themselves the Senators. In total, Ottawa has won the Grey Cup nine times. One reason for its success in recent years is that the team has been able to recruit talented Canadian players who are of special value because of the league restrictions on "imported" players.

In the late Thirties and immediately after World War Two, Ottawa's outstanding fullback, Tony Golab, was known as the "Golden Boy" of Canadian football. In the Fifties, Bobby Simpson, an end for the Riders, was both a sure-handed receiver and a savage downfield tackler. In 1956 Simpson caught passes for a total of 1,030 yards. The Sixties was a vintage decade for the Riders, who won the Grey Cup three times in this period. Ottawa had half a dozen exceptional Canadians including Russ Jackson, Ron Stewart, and Whit Tucker.

Jackson was a husky quarterback who could run the ball with authority (one of his favourite tricks was to hide the ball on his hip and then set off down the field), he could throw the ball with precision, and he had the academic approach of a schoolmaster, which was his career in the off season.

Stewart, a dimunitive backfielder, used to delight the fans by going through the opposition like a cannonball, leaving a trail of defenders in his wake. In a game against Montreal on 10 October 1960, Stewart established a league rushing record of 287 yards. After his fourth touchdown the crowd in Molson Stadium paid him the unheard-of compliment of a standing ovation.

Tucker, who played flanker with the speed of a deer, was famous for catching long passes from Jackson. Tucker's career average of 22.4 yards is a league record.

Tony Gabriel, a tight end, has been Ottawa's and one of Canada's best players in the Seventies. Gabriel won both Schenley Awards (for most valuable player and most valuable Canadian) in 1978 and has been on many All-Star teams. He has caught passes in more than one hundred consecutive games. One of these receptions—

with twenty seconds left on the clock—won the Grey Cup for the Riders in 1976.

The Rough Riders have a tremendous following—football is the only "big league" sport in the capital—and it is not unusual for 30,000 to attend their games at Lansdowne Park. Although the team is now owned by a Toronto company, the senior management consists in the main of local people. Frank Clair, the vice-president in charge of player personnel, came to Ottawa in 1956. Since then he has served the club in a variety of capacities, and coached the Riders to three Grey Cups. The general manager is John "Jake" Dunlap, Q.C., a former all-star lineman who started as a player with the team in 1945. Dunlap is a big jovial Valley Irishman who is much in demand as an after-dinner speaker.

The Ottawa Football Club was for many years an amateur, nonprofit association. Professionalism came to the game in the 1930s. Because the Ottawa club was chronically short of funds, jobs—in lieu of salaries—were found for imported players in the Civil Service and the Ottawa Fire Department and Police Force. Until 1954 the directors, who were frequently obliged to sign bank loans for the club, received no remuneration other than free tickets and the occasional trip with the team. This situation changed in 1955 when the directors bought the club, for $1.00 each, and deftly turned it into a limited company. In 1967 the number of director/shareholders was increased from six to twelve. The following year David Loeb (one of the new directors) purchased 85 percent of the shares for just over $700,000. In 1977 Loeb sold the Ottawa Football Club to CFRA Limited, a local radio station, which is a wholly owned subsidiary of CHUM Limited of Toronto.

Ottawa's most prestigious residential district—Rockcliffe Park—was incorporated as a village in 1926. Most of its 460 acres originally belonged to Thomas MacKay, the Canal contractor whose widow lived in a stone mansion on the northern boundary of the village. This house, Rockcliff Manor, was named for the limestone cliffs that border the Ottawa River. The village took its name (spelt with an "e") for the same reason. MacKay's son-in-law and chief executor, Thomas Coltrin Keefer, planned the community and laid out its streets between 1870 and the end of the century.

Rockcliffe Park was incorporated as a municipality to preserve its pastoral nature, which was threatened by the building boom of the Twenties. At that time the village only had a score of permanent homes, some summer cottages, and two private schools—Ashbury College for boys, built in 1910, and Elmwood School for girls, established in 1915. Today there are approximately 650 residences (the cottages have all been converted to permanent use), and the village has an excellent public school in addition to the two private schools. The total population is approximately 2,400.

Rockcliffe is an unusual community for a number of reasons. Because of a bylaw that states "no person shall erect or use any building for any purpose other than as a single detached family dwelling" there are no apartments or businesses of any kind—not even a doctor's office. Another bylaw further ensures a low population density by stipulating a minimum lot size of eighty feet by one hundred feet. Many of the old houses are so large that they require a domestic staff to maintain them. Rockcliffe has been fortunate in this regard because foreign nations have bought these mansions for ambassadorial residences. At the end of 1979 representatives of forty-eight countries—ranging from the Russian Ambassador to the Papal Nuncio—live in the village.

In addition to a host of diplomats, Rockcliffe is the home of many old Ottawa families, successful professional people, a variety of judges, Senators, and other Crown appointees, as well as some senior civil servants. The great appeal of the village is its rural ambience, combined with its convenience to the city—downtown Ottawa is less than a ten-minute drive away. In 1954 *Maclean's* Magazine published a five-page article on Rockcliffe entitled "The Haughtiest Suburb of Them All." The author said of the village:

> Rockcliffe stands out from the surrounding city like a rose among a patch of thorns. Where Ottawa is crowded, Rockcliffe is spacious. Where Ottawa children often have to dodge cars to play on the hot streets, Rockcliffe children seem to frolic in a village set aside as a safe playground. Privacy, an almost forgotten luxury in Ottawa, is a Rockcliffe stand-by, doubly assured by the wide lawns and shrubs and by the thousands of great old trees which make the village's busiest thoroughfares seem like winding country lanes.
>
> Even the privacy of bird and animal life is respected, since Rockcliffe is a Crown game preserve. Dogs breathe a kindlier air, for a special bylaw permits them to run without leashes in the village.

Real estate values are high in Rockcliffe; the average value of a house being approximately $200,000. In a recent transaction the Republic of Korea purchased a large stone house on Acacia Avenue from a retired admiral for $880,000. The vendor then bought a smaller and more manageable home a few streets away for $450,000. Because the village has no commercial rate-payers and a very small population, taxes are also high. Much of the tax revenue is spent on education and the preservation of the environment, especially the trees. Roads receive minimum attention and there are few sidewalks. To protect the hedges and lawns the roads are sprinkled in the winter with gravel rather than with salt.

The village of Rockcliffe has no police force or fire department of its own. These services are provided under contract by the Ontario Provincial Police and the Ottawa Fire Department. Local government consists of a elected reeve and four councillors. Those who seek office—or have it thrust upon them—are motivated by a sense of civic responsibility rather than political gain. For this reason the affairs of the community have always been well managed. The present reeve is Beryl Plumptre, former chairman of the Food Prices Review Board. The council consists of two prominent barristers, a leading opthalmic surgeon, and an internationally known architect.

Walter P. Stewart, author of *The Village of Rockcliffe Park*, published in Ottawa in 1976, wrote in the foreword to his book:

> For those who think of the Village as populated by snobs, I suggest that this, too, is untrue. A little insulated from the less well-endowed world, perhaps, but most are hard-working, community oriented people much aware of the needs of humanity.... how excellent it would be if all men, women and children could enjoy similar living circumstances.

The cornerstone for the new Centre Block of the Parliament buildings was laid on 1 September 1916 by the Governor General, HRH the Duke of Connaught. At the ceremony the Duke noted that it was exactly fifty-six years since his late brother, Edward VII (then Prince of Wales) had laid the same stone for the original structure. Although the new Parliament building was not completed until 1922, both the Senate and the Commons were able to move into their quarters in February 1920. The new block resembled the original except that it had six rather than five stories. By adding another story and modifying the interior, the architect, John Pearson of Toronto, had managed to increase the floor space in the new building by 50 percent.

Pearson was also the architect for the Peace Tower, a symbol familiar to all Canadians. The cornerstone of this three-hundred-foot Gothic spire—originally called the Victory Memorial Tower—was laid on 1 September 1919 by the Prince of Wales (who later renounced his throne as Edward VIII and became the Duke of Windsor). The base of the Peace Tower forms the front entrance to the Centre Block. One floor above the main rotunda is a memorial chamber. The next level of the tower contains a ninety-one-foot belfry with a carillon of fifty-three bells. The top level of the spire has a four-faced clock and an observation balcony. Rising from the peak of the sharply sloping roof is a thirty-five-foot bronze flag mast topped by a cluster of lights. These lights are only turned on during nights when the House is in session.

The Peace Tower was finished by stages, the last being the Memorial Chamber, which was dedicated by Prime Minister King on 11 November 1928. This small room has three stained-glass windows, pillared walls decorated with engraved tablets and carved insignia, a mosaic floor made of stone taken from European battle-fields, and a high vaulted ceiling. In the centre of the room is a raised altar containing a beautifully illuminated Book of Remembrance. The parchment pages of this book list the names of the 66,651 Canadians who fell in the Great War. Four smaller caskets—which are destined for another site—contain Books of Remembrance for the South African War and Nile Expedition, World War Two, the Korean War, and the province of Newfoundland. Each morning at eleven o'clock the pages of the books are turned to display a different set of names.

One enters the Memorial Chamber through an archway that bears the inscription "The Tunnellers' Friends, the Humble Beasts that Served and Died." Above these words are carved the likenesses of a caribou, a mule, some carrier pigeons, a horse, and a dog with a first-aid cannister attached to his collar. In the midst of these carvings is a cage of canaries surrounded by mice.

The sound of the Carillon, whose bells hang directly above the chamber, does not disturb the aura of peace within the chapel, described by the late Charlotte Whitton as "the holiest place on Canadian soil."

The Carillon was opened by the Governor-General, Viscount Willingdon, on 1 July 1927. This was the first major event in a three-day celebration of Canada's sixtieth anniversary. The bells of the Carillon, which harmonize with each other, were especially cast by a foundry in England. Their total weight is more than sixty tons, and individual bells range in weight from ten pounds to over ten tons. Played by a wooden keyboard which the carilloner strikes with his hands and feet, the tonal range of the Carillon is four and one half octaves, from the key of A to the key of E. Since the Carillon was installed in 1927 visitors and residents of the capital have been treated to hundreds of open-air concerts. In his speech at the inaguration ceremonies Prime Minister King said that the Carillon was "... The voice of the nation in thanksgiving and praise which will sound over the land and sea to the uttermost parts of the earth, and which, in the course of time, from the place where we are now assembled, may yet be borne down the centuries to come."

The highlight of the second day of Canada's Diamond Jubilee was a good-will visit by Colonel Charles Lindbergh. Six weeks earlier, on 21 May 1927, Lindbergh had made history when he piloted his Ryan monoplane, *The Spirit of St. Louis*, on a nonstop solo flight across the Atlantic from New York to Paris. Lindbergh, nicknamed "the Lone Eagle," arrived over Ottawa in *The Spirit of St. Louis* accompanied by a squadron of twelve United States Air Force planes. After circling the Peace Tower he flew south for approximately seven miles to a makeshift landing field near the Ottawa Hunt Club. Lindbergh, the first to land, received a tremendous ovation from the spectators, who were then "... thrilled by the awe-inspiring sight of the twelve American pursuit planes hurtling around the circle in close formation, dropping out one by one at the landing place." The sixth plane, piloted by Lieutenant J. Thad Johnson, peeled out of formation to land but then changed its direction and climbed sharply. This sudden manoeuvre resulted in a mid-air collision with one of the other aircraft. Johnson bailed out of his crippled machine, but his parachute did not have time to open and he was killed when he struck the ground.

Although Lindbergh was stunned by this tragedy, he consented to being driven in an open car through the city for an official welcome on Parliament Hill. En route, thousands of Ottawans who turned out to see him—unaware of the death of Lindbergh's comrade —were surprised that the Lone Eagle did not flash his famous smile. The Ottawa *Evening Citizen* of 4 July reported Lindbergh's reception on the Hill:

> ... when Lindbergh finally arrived shortly before three o'clock he was the darling of the hour. Crowds shouted, children roared, frock-

coated dignitaries forgot themselves and jumped about excitedly, while ladies clambered to chairs and points of vantage in and about the canopy on Parliament Hill to catch sight of the fair-haired young lad who had won the hearts of two continents. And he won the hearts of many young ladies, too, if the enthusiasm they displayed be any criterion of female approbation.

This was the only joyous occasion of the good-will visit because Prime Minister King, overcome by Lieutenant Johnson's death, ordered that a state funeral be held for the airman the next day. King's extraordinary decision forced the cancellation of the Jubilee celebrations and plunged the capital into mourning.

Lieutenant Johnson's funeral took place outside the Prime Minister's office in the East Block. The service was attended by the Governor General, representatives of the diplomatic corps, the Senate, the Commons, the mayor of Ottawa, and other dignitaries. Fifty thousand people watched the cortège wend its way from Parliament Hill to the Union Station. The band of the Governor General's Foot Guards marched with muffled drums ahead of the gun carriage, which was flanked by scarlet-coated Mounties. As the procession moved off, the Carillon pealed forth Chopin's Funeral March. On the way to the station the band played "God Be With You Till We Meet Again." When the cortège reached the black- and purple-draped station, the band played "The Star Spangled Banner" and the guard of honour fired a three-volley salute. Buglers then sounded The Last Post and Reveille. Viscount Willingdon, Mr. King, William Phillips (the American Ambassador), and Vincent Massey (Canadian Ambassador to the United States), were on the platform when the casket was transferred to the black-draped mortuary car.

The American escort squadron—with a gap in their formation for their missing comrade—followed the train for the first few miles of its journey to Johnson's home in Michigan. Colonel Lindbergh in *The Spirit of St. Louis* made successive low-level passes over the funeral car, dropping flowers of remembrance. This gesture was so moving that Ottawans who witnessed it remember the scene clearly after more than half a century.

At the time of Lindbergh's visit there were relatively few aircraft in Canada. Most of those in the Ottawa area belonged to the newly formed Royal Canadian Air Force, which was based at the former Rockcliffe Rifle Range. The airstrip near the Hunt Club used by

Colonel Lindbergh was part of a large parcel of arid wasteland owned by the Uplands Realty Limited. This private company was controlled by Colonel James Woods and several friends who had bought the land with the hope that it would be chosen as the site for the new Connaught Rifle Range. This speculation proved unsuccessful when, in 1913, Colonel Sam Hughes (the Minister of Militia) decided upon an equally convenient and desolate tract for the range near Shirley's Bay, on the Ottawa River.

Except for Lindbergh's visit, the Uplands property lay fallow until the Ottawa Flying Club was founded in 1928. That year, the club—a nonprofit organization dedicated to the promotion of pleasure flying—rented Lindbergh's Field from the Uplands Realty for the price of the annual taxes on the property. The club was fortunate because the flat terrain eliminated the need to build runways, and their only expenditure was a small shed to house their two De Havilland Moth biplanes.

In 1936, when the club was unable to pay its rent, one of its members, A. Barnet Maclaren, bought the property from the Uplands Realty. Maclaren took this action for two reasons; to ensure that his newly formed company, Laurentian Air Services, would have an airport, and to aid the financially stricken Ottawa Flying Club. In 1938 Maclaren sold his holding of approximately three hundred acres to the federal government so that the Crown could convert it into a public airport. The result of this transaction, which was typical of the way Canada's first airports were established, was that both Laurentian and the flying club became tenants of the government.

Soon after the airport changed hands it was renamed Ottawa Airport, and the Department of Transport built two permanent runways, a large concrete hangar, and a wooden terminal building. By the end of 1938 Trans-Canada Airlines (the forerunner of Air Canada) instituted a scheduled passenger service from Lindbergh's Field to other parts of the country.

During World War Two, Ottawa Airport was one of the largest training centres for pilots from the Commonwealth countries. The airport underwent a major expansion program in 1950 to accommodate jet aircraft. By means of expropriation the total area was increased to 5,285 acres, permitting the installation of much longer runways. After years of grumbling from Parliamentarians and residents, a large modern terminal was opened in 1960. Several walls in this gleaming structure were made of glass. Just before the official opening of the terminal a United States Air Force fighter broke the sound barrier over Uplands, and the sonic boom caused $250,000 damage to the building. Today Ottawa International Airport serves civilian, commercial, and military traffic; two runways ten thousand and eight thousand feet long are for jet airliners, while two smaller runways four thousand and three thousand feet in length, are for smaller craft. Canadian Forces Base Uplands has its own administrative buildings and hangars just west of the main terminal.

Laurentian Air Services (now owned by Maclaren's nephew, John M. Bogie) has its headquarters at the airport and a base at Schefferville, Quebec. The company's fleet of bush planes consists of nine De Havilland Otters and Beavers. Laurentian has established a solid reputation in the charter-flight business, catering in the main to the tourist and mining industries. Its planes, usually equipped with pontoons, fly to the remotest areas of northeastern Canada.

The Ottawa Flying Club came very close to folding during the Depression. Jack Charleson (an instructor at that time) recalled that his greatest risk was not from flying but from starvation. During World War Two the club was transferred to an airfield near Hawkesbury, some sixty miles east of Ottawa, where its members formed the nucleus of the staff for the 13th Elementary Training School. Since its formation in 1928 the club has had an enviable safety record, which is a tribute to the standard of its own instructors. Today the OFC has a modern clubhouse for its four hundred members at the Ottawa International Airport, and a fleet of nine Cessna aircraft. For the past fifteen years the club has held a "Crippled Childrens' Fly Day." On this day the members give the public sightseeing flights around the capital. The net proceeds from the sale of flight tickets is donated to the Ontario Society for Crippled Children.

Shortly before noon on 29 May 1929 a violent gas explosion rocked the main sewer line between the Ottawa River and Centre Town. During the next nine hours a series of explosions ran the entire three-and-one-quarter-mile length of the main line, terrifying residents in New Edinburgh, Sandy Hill, and the suburb of Eastview.

In its report on this bizarre occurrence the Ottawa *Evening Citizen* said:

> As explosion followed explosion along the line of the sewer travelling east and branching into cross streets, the iron covers of the sewer

manholes were thrown in some instances high in the air. J. A. Taylor, 335 Somerset Street east, was in front of his home when he noticed the explosions and saw three manhole covers, one after the other, being lifted into the air.

The heavy iron covers were carried higher than the wires on the streets, and in one case the electric light globe was smashed.

Mr. Taylor states that the lifting of the covers was followed by bursts of flame about the size of a barrel, which immediately died down, to be followed by black smoke.

Miraculously, only one person was killed although the blasts destroyed a number of buildings, including St. Martin's Reform Episcopal Church in New Edinburgh. Two inquiries were held following the explosions but the results were inconclusive because all parties—the city, the Ottawa Gas Company, and the service station owners—denied any blame. To prevent a recurrence of this phenomenon, ventilators were installed in the sewer lines and a bylaw was passed to prohibit the dumping of volatile liquids in Ottawa sewers. (These measures were not entirely successful because another series of explosions took place two years later.)

The seething conditions beneath the streets of the capital in May 1929 were similar in some respects to the speculative inferno of North America's stock markets. The stock markets exploded on 24 October, and then on 29 October, "Black Tuesday," disintegrated. The collapse of the markets ushered in a new era—the Depression.

20

A Dreary Decade

1929 to 1939

A PAIR OF ELDERLY bachelors, W. L. M. King and R. B. Bennett, dominated the political stage during the Depression. Both men were clever and both had few friends. King, the leader of the Liberals, was a stout little grey man noted for his political cunning, his fondness for empty rhetoric, and his ability to compromise. Bennett, the leader of the Conservatives, was a tall and imposing millionaire whose haughty manner made him a caricature of a Tory. In his speeches Bennett was fond of using the words "my government," a phrase normally employed in formal addresses by the sovereign.

King, who was Prime Minister at the onset of the Depression, failed to grasp the seriousness of the situation, dismissing it as a minor downturn in the economic cycle. After consulting a fortune-teller (who predicted a Liberal victory) King called a general election in the summer of 1930 and was soundly defeated. During the next five years Bennett and his Conservatives initiated a number of measures to help the economy—including a 10 percent cut in the wages of civil servants—but the business slump continued. Western Canada was particularly hard hit because of low grain prices and drought. In the 1935 election both the Conservatives and the socialist

Co-operative Commonwealth Federation (predecessor of the New Democratic Party) ran on platforms that called for massive government intervention in the economy. King, who had no discernible platform, won by a landslide. Bennett stayed on as Leader of the Opposition until 1938 and then moved to England, where he was subsequently elevated to the peerage.

Ottawa, as the seat of government, was insulated from the worst effects of the Depression. Indeed, during 1929 business in the capital continued as usual, and it was not until 1932, when the National Research Council building on Sussex Drive was completed, that the federal building program slowed to a halt. Because the government, the city's largest employer, laid off relatively few people and the Civil Service pay cuts were more than offset by a decrease in the cost of living, the demand for goods and services in Ottawa stayed at a reasonable level. In the worst years, 1932 to 1935, many of the destitute people in the city were not local residents but transients who had come to Ottawa in search for work. The capital was also fortunate to emerge from the slump sooner than other Canadian communities because of a federally sponsored program of public works and government buildings that began in 1935. Since the Thirties, Ottawa has been regarded by the rest of Canada as a "depression-proof" city.

History was made on 15 February 1930 when Cairine Wilson became the first woman in Canada to be appointed to the Senate. Until 1928, when England's Privy Council reversed a decision of the Supreme Court of Canada, a woman was not considered to be a person within the terms of the British North America Act, and hence was not permitted to sit in the Senate.

Mrs. Wilson, the mother of eight children and chatelaine of Rockcliff Manor, was chosen for her political credentials rather than her participation in the struggle for women's rights. Both her husband and her father were prominent Liberals: Norman Wilson was a former Member of Parliament for Russell, and her father, the Honourable Robert Mackay, had been a Liberal Senator. Mrs. Wilson's most significant contribution to the party took place in 1928 when she organized and founded the National Federation of Liberal Women of Canada.

Notwithstanding these political considerations, Prime Minister King could hardly have selected a more deserving woman for the Senate. Cairine Wilson worked throughout her life for social reforms, particularly those concerning the rights of women and the treatment of children. During World War Two she arranged for the care of hundreds of refugees and also lobbied for better treatment of interned Japanese on the West Coast. She was a pillar of the Kirk (St. Andrew's Church on Wellington Street) and contributed to numerous charities. One local legacy is the Ottawa Neighbourhood Services, which she founded in 1930. This philanthropic organization provides employment for the handicapped and the needy.

Senator Wilson, who died in 1962, received many awards during her lifetime. In 1950, for example, she was chosen Canadian Mother of the Year and was also created a Knight of the Legion of Honour for her work with French refugee children. A bronze bust of the Honourable Cairine Wilson stands at the entrance to the Senate.

The depth of the Depression was reached in Ottawa during the last half of 1933 and the first half of 1934. To compound everyone's misery, it was also the coldest winter on record. The snow came in October and stayed until April. On 29 December 1933 the temperature dropped to -38°F; for the whole month of February 1934 the mean temperature was a bone-chilling -2.7°F. During that winter approximately 22,000 people or 16 percent of the population were on relief, in addition to several thousand destitute transients. Most of the transients lived in crowded wooden barracks at Rockcliffe Airport or in shack settlements at Brewer Park and the Lees Avenue dump.

In those grim days even the A. J. Freiman department store suffered from a dearth of business. When Archibald Freiman went out of town on a buying trip, his son Lawrence—then in his twenties and just out of Harvard Business School— hit upon a novel sales promotion scheme. Lawrence engaged Sally Rand (an American stripper who had created a sensation at the 1933 Chicago World's Fair) to put on a fashion show in the store, using her chorus girls as models. Young Freiman's idea succeeded beyond his wildest expectations. People literally fought to get into the store, the crowd was so unruly that the police had to be called, and several women were shoved through the plate-glass windows. The show was watched with intense interest but when Miss Rand and her troupe departed, the customers, left also. Although the event failed to stimulate business, it did attract the attention of the Canadian Press, who ran the story across the country. Archibald Freiman read the news in Montreal. He was not amused.

The Bank of Canada was created by a special Act of Parliament in 1934. The purpose of this institution was to regulate credit and currency in the national interest, to control the external value of Canadian money, and to take fiscal measures to stabilize the economy of the country. The bank is the sole issuer of Canadian currency and the custodian of the nation's gold reserves. The first governor of the bank was the late Graham F. Towers, who held this position for three consecutive terms until his retirement in 1954.

Prior to the formation of the Bank of Canada, both the chartered banks and the Dominion Government issued paper currency. Most of the notes issued by the chartered banks were for $5.00 or more, while the government was responsible for the smaller denominations. Until 1938 the nation's gold reserves and securities were lodged in the vaults of the East Block on Parliament Hill. Adjacent to these vaults is an incinerator that was used to destroy worn bills and redeemed securities. The vaults were (and still are) secure, but the incinerator was prone to malfunction. On at least one occasion a faulty draught in the furnace blew half-burnt $2.00 bills over the East Block lawn like confetti.

The Bank of Canada began operation in March 1935 from temporary quarters in the Victoria Building at 140 Wellington Street. Three years later the staff of the central bank moved into their own newly completed building at 234 Wellington Street. Beneath the rock foundation of this austere five-story structure were two floors of steel vaults. Over the Victoria Day weekend in 1938 various government securities and approximately 180 tons of gold—some 5,400,000 troy ounces—were transferred from the East Block vaults to the basement of the Bank of Canada building. The East Block vaults still contain some securities, as well as narcotics and drugs seized by the RCMP, but worn currency is now destroyed in the efficient Bank of Canada furnaces.

By coincidence, the Bank of Canada building was located on Wellington Street between its two main suppliers, the British American Bank Note Company Limited and the Canadian Bank Note Company Limited. Since the early days of Confederation these two companies had been printing banknotes, bond certificates, and postage stamps for the Dominion Government. Competition, which the government has always encouraged, has been a constant factor in the business relationship of the banknote companies. When the Bank of Canada came into existence, it became their largest single customer. In their dealings with the central bank, the two firms are akin to a pair of porcupines feeding on the same succulent tree: they attend to their own affairs and stay well away from each other.

Security is of paramount importance to the banknote companies. In addition to the latest electronic devices to protect their plants, the entire security program for each firm is regularly checked by the RCMP. At the end of the day every single sheet of paper used in the manufacture of currency or securities must be accounted for. The documents they print are also designed to outwit counterfeiters. Notes and certificates are printed on special paper with special inks, and most include an engraved illustration of a human form. Quite often the figure is a voluptuous female in a clinging robe. The reason for this choice of subject is that it is almost impossible to reproduce subtle flesh tones and cloth texture in a steel engraving. The banknote companies do a substantial business with private industry in addition to their dealings with the three levels of government in Canada.

The British American Bank Note Company came to Ottawa in 1866 and moved back to Montreal in 1871. The firm planned to return permanently to the capital in 1888, but had to wait a year because its building on Wellington Street collapsed. British American Bank Note prospered in Ottawa during the next six decades except for some lean years in the Depression. The company moved to a modern single-story building at 975 Gladstone Avenue in 1948. Today this Canadian-owned firm has branches across Canada and also deals with customers in foreign countries.

The Canadian Bank Note Company was originally a subsidiary of the giant American Bank Note Company. In 1897 the American Bank Note was awarded a contract by the Dominion Government to supply postage stamps, paper currency, and revenue stamps on the condition that the company build a printing plant in Ottawa by the end of the same year. The American firm fulfilled its obligation by erecting a fireproof four-story building on Wellington Street in the astonishingly short time of thirteen weeks. In 1922 the American Bank Note reorganized their subsidiary as the Canadian Bank Note Company. The plant on Wellington Street underwent successive expansions through the years, until finally in 1950 the company built modern premises at a thirteen-acre site on the Richmond Road.

Charles B. Worthen, who had previously been with a textile firm in Brockville, joined the Canadian Bank Note as a labour relations officer in 1955. At the end of his first day in this position he went home to his wife and told her that coming to Ottawa was the worst mistake he had made in his life. Ten years later Worthen was elected president of the company. In 1973 Worthen bought 60 percent of the shares of the Canadian Bank Note from the parent firm. In 1976 he sold his holding to two Toronto investors, who have since acquired the balance of the shares from the American Bank Note Company. The Canadian Bank Note, like its competitor, has an international clientele and branches from coast to coast.

The growth of the banknote companies has been matched by that of the Bank of Canada. In 1972 the central bank began a massive building project that encompassed the entire block bounded by Bank and Kent streets. Completed in August 1979, this complex consists of twin twelve-story towers with the original structure in the centre. All three buildings are connected by a garden court as well as covered walkways on the upper levels. The shining glass exterior of the Bank of Canada complex makes it the brightest landmark in the capital, in contrast to the old building, which, with its severe façade and granite urns, reminded one of a mausoleum.

Ottawa's employment situation brightened in 1935 when construction started on the Justice Building on Wellington Street and Postal Terminal A on Besserer Street. When Postal Terminal A was completed in 1937, the old post office on Connaught Square was demolished and a new Central Post Office (now called Postal Terminal B) was built at the corner of Elgin and Sparks streets. This was not a make-work exercise but part of an over-all plan to prepare Connaught Square, renamed Confederation Square, for the National War Memorial.

Prior to 1937 the square had been enlarged by the removal of Bate's warehouse, the ruins of City Hall (burnt in 1931), the ruins of the Russell Hotel (burnt in 1928), and Knox Presbyterian Church. The French town-planner Jacques Gréber was invited to Ottawa by Prime Minister King in 1937 to act as a consultant on the project. Gréber was opposed to having the memorial in the core of the capital because it would impede traffic, but he was overruled by King, who wanted as many people as possible to see it. Both men were right; the traffic is so heavy and congested in this area that it has since been nicknamed Confusion Square.

The War Memorial, executed by the British sculptor Vernon March, is a soaring granite arch seventy feet in height. Atop the arch stand two bronze figures representing Peace and Freedom.

Passing through the arch are twenty-two human figures and a horse pulling a field gun. The human figures, whose uniforms and equipment are correct to the last detail, represent Canada's forces who served in the Great War, including the Medical Corps and the Canadian Nursing Association. It is a compelling and poignant scene. Carved on the north and south faces of the granite pedestal are the dates 1914—1918.

While Confederation Square was being terraced and landscaped, the monument (which had been shipped in thirty-five crates from England) was being assembled on the site. At the same time Elgin Street was being widened from Sparks Street to Laurier Avenue to create a boulevard leading to the memorial. These works took on a sense of urgency when it was learned in the autumn of 1938 that His Majesty King George VI and Queen Elizabeth would make a Royal Tour of Canada the following spring.

The King's visit to Canada in May 1939 was the first by a ruling British sovereign. The royal couple arrived in Ottawa on the morning of 19 May aboard the Governor-General's train, which had been freshly painted blue and silver. They were greeted by Lord Tweedsmuir, the Governor-General, W. L. M. King, the Prime Minister, Mayor Stanley Lewis of Ottawa, and a flock of other dignitaries at a station that had been erected for the occasion near Island Park Drive. After receiving a Royal Salute from the Cameron Highlander Guard of Honour, Their Majesties were driven in an open carriage to Rideau Hall, escorted by a troop of the Princess Louise Dragoon Guards (one of whom was thrown from his mount). Their seven-mile journey included a circuit of Lansdowne Park, where they were given a rousing ovation by 15,000 subjects. The *Ottawa Journal* summarized the first hours of the three-day visit:

> At 11.09 the Queen was assisted into the open landau, so busily waving at the shouting crowd who could now see her clearly that she nearly tripped upon the step. The King then took his place beside her at the left side of the rear seat.
> At 11.10 the four horses with their six-man equipage drew away their Royal charges to show them to the people and the city of Ottawa.
> The sun shone momentarily as the procession moved off. It was a glittering blood-tingling spectacle, a thing of shining brass and helmets, well groomed steeds, dancing pennants on rigid lances, bobbing white plumes.
> It was God's will that permitted the use of the open landau—and it

was a favour that made all the difference between an automobile ride and a Royal Progress....

Waving and smiling as they went, noticing little children and nodding at old men the King and Queen appeared more as two happy people than as Monarch and Consort entering a Capital City. They needed no "protecting" and there was nothing of organized propaganda inspired adulation. The welcome was bade to a King, not from fear but from affection and esteem.

Ottawa's Driveway system was a chain of humanity, yet the carriage moved through this veritable Cinderella-land right to schedule. The King and Queen reached Government House at 12.20, thus fulfilling their appointment to the minute.

That afternoon, the Royal Standard flew from the Peace Tower when the King gave Royal Assent to certain bills in the Senate chamber. In the evening there was a large state dinner at Government House. The next day the Governor-General's Foot Guards trooped the Colour before the King on Parliament Hill, and the Queen laid the cornerstone of the new Supreme Court building on Wellington Street. In the afternoon there was a formal garden party for 5,000 guests at Government House; that same evening, the Prime Minister gave a dinner for seven hundred at the Chateau Laurier.

The highlight of the royal visit came on the last morning when the King unveiled the War Memorial. At the close of the ceremony the royal couple waived protocol to mingle with the Veterans Guard in front of the monument. The veterans then broke ranks, and the King and Queen disappeared in a sea of blue and brown berets. This unexpected development caused the security officers some anxious moments, but did much to endear the monarch to his Canadian subjects.

After the King and Queen left for Toronto that afternoon, the *Ottawa Journal* estimated that at least 500,000 people had seen them in Ottawa during "the three most historic days in the Capital's annals."

On 10 September 1939—less than four months after King George VI unveiled the War Memorial—Canada was once again at war with Germany.

21

World War Two

1939 to 1945

THE WAR ABRUPTLY ended the Depression. Because it was both the seat of government and the headquarters for Canada's war effort, Ottawa's population—approximately 145,000 in 1939—was swelled by an influx of military and civilian personnel. More than a dozen huge wooden temporary buildings were erected on vacant Crown land, several existing office buildings were purchased, and contracts were let for a complex of National Research Council laboratories on the Montreal Road. The laboratory complex was the first group of government buildings to be linked by underground tunnels in the capital. Because practically no new residential construction had taken place in the previous decade, housing was in very short supply. Business, especially war-related industries, boomed. Between 1940 and 1943 the Ottawa Car Company increased its staff from fifty to 1,800 people.

Many prominent Canadians took up residence in Ottawa during the war. Some of these were Dollar-a-Year-Men talented business and professional people who donated their services to the country for a token salary of $1.00 a year. Among them were E. P. Taylor, who was appointed chairman of the Department of Munitions and Supply (Taylor was born and educated in Ottawa); E. V. Scully, later president of the Steel Company of Canada, who became president of Victory Aircraft Limited, a Crown Corporation; and H. R. Mac-Millan, the West Coast lumber magnate, who was appointed timber controller for Canada. J. A. D. McCurdy, the pioneer pilot who was unable to give a demonstration in his *Silver dart* at the 1911 Central Canada Exhibition, finally came to Ottawa in 1939 and remained in the capital for the next eight years as assistant director of Aircraft Production.

In addition to being the headquarters for all three armed services, Ottawa was an important recruiting depot and the largest air-training centre in the country. From 1939 to 1945 both Rockcliffe and Uplands operated at maximum capacity and the air was filled with the constant drone of aircraft. The city's militia regiments were brought to full strength within a matter of weeks and given new fighting roles. The Governor-General's Foot Guards, which had always been an infantry unit, was reorganized as the 21st Armoured Regiment. The Princess Louise Dragoon Guards was also mechanized, and became the 4th Reconnaissance Squadron. The Cameron Highlanders, formerly an infantry battalion, was re-equipped as a machine gun battalion.

People throughout Canada were saddened by the death on 11 February 1940 of the Governor-General. John Buchan, first Baron Tweedsmuir, was not only an extremely popular figure, but also the author of numerous books including *The Thirty-nine Steps*, a classic spy novel. More than 14,000 Ottawans filed past the Governor-General's bier in the Senate chamber, and memorial services were held for him in many parts of the country. His state funeral in Ottawa on 14 February was attended by three thousand servicemen as well as many dignitaries. Thousands of residents braved the bitter cold to pay their last respects to his flag-draped coffin when it was borne from St. Andrew's Church to the Union Station on the traditional gun carriage, pulled by sixty naval ratings. The *Ottawa Citizen* described the last touching moments of the ceremony, which brought together Lieutenant Alastair Buchan, the Governor-General's youngest son, and Prime Minister King:

As the casket was carried up the steps of the platform at the end of the Governor-General's private car, heads were bared and officers snapped to the salute. Lieut. Buchan, along with his fellow-officers, stood silently at the salute while the casket was placed in the end compartment of the car which was lit dimly by five soft electric candles.

Just before Lieut. Buchan entered the train, Prime Minister King went to his side and shook hands with him. Mr. King was visibly moved and there were tears glistening in his eyes as he stood with head bared as the train moved slowly out of the station. It was exactly 4.25 when the train left.

Quite a few refugees—particularly children from the United Kingdom—stayed with Ottawa families during World War Two. The largest single contingent of refugees consisted of approximately one hundred boys from Abinger Hill, an English public school, who boarded at Ashbury College in Rockcliffe Park.

Crown Princess Juliana, daughter of Queen Wilhelmina of the Netherlands, was undoubtedly Ottawa's most distinguished wartime guest. Princess Juliana, forced to flee from Holland when the Nazis invaded her country, arrived in Ottawa with her two daughters, Beatrix and Irene, in June 1940. She was accompanied by the children's nurse and Mrs. Martine Roell, the wife of the Treasurer of the Royal Household. Queen Wilhelmina stayed in London, as did Prince Bernhard, Princess Juliana's husband. Queen Wilhelmina visited Ottawa only once during the war, but Prince Bernhard—who commanded the Dutch Military Mission in England—managed to visit his family in Canada a number of times.

Princess Juliana arrived in Canada with little more than a few suitcases. Her first weeks in Ottawa were spent at Government House as a guest of the Earl of Athlone and Princess Alice (to whom she was related). In July 1940, Princess Juliana and her small retinue moved into 120 Lansdowne Road, a secluded house on the shore of MacKay's Lake in Rockcliffe Park. This stone house was built for the late Shirley E. Woods in 1938, and was rented to the royal exile fully furnished. Soon after she had moved in, Princess Juliana named her residence *Noot Gedach* ("Never Thought") because it was inconceivable, a few months earlier, that she would find herself more than three thousand miles from her true home.

Although she was a royal personage, the princess lived a simple life in the capital. Much of her time was devoted to looking after her children, to helping with the housework—she even shovelled snow on occasion—and to working for war effort causes. She became a familiar figure in the city, and while her privacy was always respected, she never asked for any special treatment. To the surprise of many people she enrolled her two daughters at Rockcliffe Park

Public School rather than at a private school. Beatrix, her eldest, who at that time was a rather chubby child, delighted the audience at a Rockcliffe school concert one year with her rendition of the nursery song "I'm a Little Teapot, Short and Stout."

On 19 January 1943, Princess Juliana gave birth to a daughter, Princess Margriet, at the Ottawa Civic Hospital. To ensure that the royal infant would only have Dutch citizenship, the Canadian Government declared the delivery room to be Netherlands territory for that day. For the first time in history a foreign flag—the Royal Standard of the House of Orange—was flown from the Peace Tower. Queen Wilhelmina came from England for Princess Margriet's baptism at St. Andrew's Church, which was held on 29 January 1943.

Soon after the birth of her third daughter, Princess Juliana moved her family to a larger house, Stornoway, at 541 Acacia Avenue in Rockcliffe Park. This house, which is now the official residence of the Leader of the Opposition, was at that time owned by the late Mrs. I. K. Perley-Robertson, daughter of Sir George Perley.

Princess Juliana returned with her family to the Netherlands in June 1945 and ascended to the throne in September 1948. Shortly after returning to her native soil she sent 15,000 tulip bulbs to Ottawa as a gesture of thanks for the city's hospitality. Ever since the end of the war Queen Juliana has repeated this gift so that now the National Capital Commission plant 2 million Dutch tulip bulbs annually. The huge display of tulips in the capital each spring is a glowing reminder of the affection that exists between the people of Ottawa and a Queen of the Netherlands.

In July 1940 "Operation Fish" took place. Operation Fish was the code name for a scheme to move most of Britain's currency reserves, as well as bullion and securities belonging to Norway, France, and Belgium, from the United Kingdom to Canada for safekeeping. Six ships, *The Monarch of Bermuda*, the *SS Sobieski* and the *SS Batory* (former luxury liners), *HMS Bonaventure* and *HMS Emerald* (cruisers), and *HMS Revenge* (a battleship) were used to carry the cargo across the Atlantic. After being unloaded at Halifax the treasure was then sent by rail under great secrecy to Montreal. It was a massive operation involving scores of trains, all of which had to be heavily guarded yet sufficiently unobtrusive to avoid public suspicion. When the trains arrived in Montreal, the cars bearing gold were separated from those carrying securities. The securities were then lodged in the vaults of the Sun Life Assurance Company in Montreal, while the gold was dispatched by train to Ottawa for storage in the vaults of the Bank of Canada.

The delivery from the Union Station in Ottawa to the Bank of Canada was made at night in Canadian National Express trucks, each of which was guarded by two armed men disguised in overalls. For security reasons the Ottawa Police were not told what was taking place. The amount of the gold and coins—in excess of 60 million ounces—made storage a staggering task. Two thirty-man crews worked around the clock in twelve-hour shifts for several weeks. Although the gold bars were quickly stacked to the ceiling (a height of nearly twenty feet) the men sweating in the vaults were unable to keep pace with the deliveries from the station. At one stage the backlog was so great that Royal Canadian Mounted Police officers literally sat on 1,500 unopened crates piled in the basement corridors of the bank. Eventually everything, including the crown jewels of Norway, was catalogued and safely packed away.

During the course of the war a substantial portion of Britain's gold was transferred to Fort Knox in payment for American aid. At the end of the war the balance of the hoard in Canada was returned to Europe and Great Britain. One of the most amazing features of Operation Fish was that although hundreds of Canadians were involved in the transaction, the secret was never revealed. Not one Ottawa pedestrian in a thousand who walked past the Bank of Canada on Wellington Street was aware of the foreign treasure stored beneath his feet.

Many Allied leaders, among them Winston Churchill, Franklin Roosevelt, and Charles de Gaulle visited Ottawa during the war years. The first world figure to come to the capital was Britain's Prime Minister, Winston Churchill, who on 30 December 1941 addressed a joint gathering of Parliament.

Churchill was given a tumultuous ovation when he entered the House of Commons accompanied by the Canadian Prime Minister. After a brief introduction by his host, Churchill launched into a rousing thirty-two-minute speech that covered a wide range of subjects. The most memorable part of this speech (the first to be broadcast from the Commons by radio) concerned the Vichy French generals who had told their countrymen that within three weeks of France's surrender "Britain's neck would be wrung like a chicken." Churchill savoured their prophecy—France having fallen some eighteen months earlier—and then, with superb timing and great emphasis, said, "Some chicken! Some neck!"

At the conclusion of his address the British statesman was escorted by Prime Minister King to the Senate chamber for an official photograph. Churchill stood impatiently in the glare of the floodlights while the photographer, thirty-three-year-old Yousuf Karsh, made last-minute adjustments to his camera. Just before he squeezed the bulb, Karsh darted forward and, with a murmured apology, plucked the cigar from the Prime Minister's mouth. Churchill glared at the camera and Karsh snapped his picture. The resulting photograph was so powerful that it made history. It also marked the turning point in the fortunes of Yousuf Karsh.

Karsh, an Armenian immigrant, came to Canada in 1925 as the ward of his uncle, George Nakash, a photographer in Sherbrooke, Quebec. After serving an apprenticeship under his uncle and George H. Garo, a well-known American photographer, Karsh moved to Ottawa in 1932 as a photographer's assistant. The following year he borrowed $150 and set up his own studio at 130 Sparks Street. It was a difficult time to start a business and Karsh was forced to provide such modest services as passport pictures for one dollar. His first recognition came in 1934, when he executed a portrait of Lord and Lady Bessborough, which was published in England as well as in Canada. By the time Churchill came to Ottawa, Karsh was well established in the capital, and numbered among his admirers Prime Minister King.

Yousuf Karsh is a short, gentle person who speaks with almost Oriental courtesy. At work, he darts about the studio like a bird, pausing from time to time to study his subject intently. Because of the incredible number of famous people he has met, he has an inexhaustible fund of amusing anecdotes. One can mention the name of almost any world figure and he can respond with a story from his personal experience. His own fame is such that the term "Karshed" (to be photographed by Karsh) has been in common usage for years. Karsh loves to photograph musicians but his favourite subject of all was Winston Churchill.

In the autumn of 1943 Karsh spent from September to November in England. During this short period he took forty-two major portraits, which ranged from King Haakon of Norway to George Bernard Shaw. After the war he opened a permanent studio in New York; since then he has travelled extensively, photographing notables in all parts of the globe. Because of his towering reputation he could live and work anywhere he wished. However, he has kept both his main studio and his home in Ottawa. Today his Ottawa studio is located in a suite in the Chateau Laurier Hotel. His home, situated on four acres at a bend in the Rideau River, is a personal retreat that he has enjoyed since 1940. Because his property is also a miniature bird sanctuary, his house is called White Wings.

There are actually two talented Karsh photographers in Ottawa. Malak Karsh, Yousuf's younger brother, emigrated to Canada in 1937. After working with his brother Yousuf for a number of years, Malak opened his own studio in the capital. Malak Karsh specializes in commercial photography rather than portrait work, and to further avoid confusion uses his Christian name, Malak, rather than the family surname.

Canadians in general, and Ottawans in particular, are proud of Yousuf Karsh. For his part, Karsh has never forgotten the country and the city that fostered his legendary success in the world. One tangible and typically gracious indication of Karsh's gratitude is that he has always maintained a special fee scale for Ottawa residents.

Carleton College, Ottawa's first nonsectarian school of higher learning, was established in 1942. The driving force behind this institution was Dr. Henry Marshall Tory, the founding president of the University of Alberta and a past president of the National Research Council. Dr. Tory, who was seventy-eight at the time, began a series of night classes at the High School of Commerce in the autumn of 1942. He and his staff of two assistants expected one hundred students to enroll for the Grade 13 and first-year university courses, but more than seven hundred registered for the first semester. The following year a charter was granted to "The Ottawa Association for the Advancement of Learning" (the sponsoring body of the infant college).

Carleton College continued to operate out of church basements and high school rooms until 1946, when it bought the former Ottawa Ladies College building at 268 First Avenue from the Canadian Government. This building permitted Carleton to expand the scope of its courses and to offer full-time day classes. In April 1952 a provincial act elevated Carleton to the status of a university, with authority to grant diplomas and degrees. At the same time the school, which had previously been financed by public donations and student fees, became eligible for government grants. In 1957 Carleton College changed its name to Carleton University.

In 1959 the university moved from First Avenue to a 129-acre site on Bronson Avenue between the Rideau River and the Rideau Canal. Three prominent Ottawans; Harry S. Southam, Wilson M. Southam, and Colonel Cameron Edwards donated thirty-seven acres of this land. Both the purchase of the property and the four original buildings were paid for by a combination of government grants and private subscriptions, including a $500,000 gift from Senator Norman M. Paterson. (The Loeb family also donated $500,000 toward the construction of the Loeb Building for Social Sciences, which was completed in 1967.) In the intervening years Carleton acquired more property and erected other buildings; there are now twenty-four, including the MacOdrum Library. This library houses a collection of nearly 1 million volumes, as well as several hundred thousand microfilms, maps, and archival documents. Five residence buildings on the 152-acre campus can accommodate more than 1,300 students.

Carleton University has a renowned School of International Affairs, which is enhanced by the fact that Ottawa is the seat of government and the home of many foreign diplomats. The presence of the federal government has also increased the stature of the university's School of Public Administration. Carleton has long been famous for its School of Journalism. Harking back to its original role—to provide advanced night classes—the university has a substantial program of night classes. Of the total enrolment of approximately 14,000, some 6,000 attend Carleton on a part-time basis.

Germany surrendered to the Allies on 7 May 1945. This news, in the words of the *Evening Citizen*, resulted in

> ...the greatest mass demonstration of relief and joy ever to be witnessed in Canada's Capital.
> A great silence fell over Victory Loan ceremony crowds on Confederation Square as the sun streamed down, and the blue coated massed bands of the RCAF broke out into the strains of "O Canada." As soon as the last note had died away there was an incomparable outburst of cheering from an enthusiastic crowd that just would not be silenced.
> The news picked up and spread like wildfire throughout the city. And as it did, Ottawa citizens turned out to celebrate.
> Tons of paper poured out of office windows on the heads of the crowds below. Torn up tax papers appeared to be the most popular

form of ammunition, with confetti, bathroom tissue, letterheads and great long ribbons of adding machine paper added.

Led by thousands of youngsters on bicycles, citizens joined in a giant impromptu parade that snaked its way through the center of the city tying traffic in knots.

The *Evening Citizen* of 7 May 1945 also took a backward look at Ottawa's contribution to the war over the preceding six years. During this period some 40,000 Ottawans had volunteered for the armed services and a similar number had joined the fighting forces from surrounding towns in the Ottawa Valley. By mid-1945 the National Research Council had developed a significant number of weapons and techniques for the Allied cause and the Civil Service had grown to more than 37,000 people.

Ottawa was one of the first cities in Canada to set up Red Cross blood donor clinics. This facet of the war effort, in which more than 100,000 local donors participated, was luridly described by the *Evening Citizen*: "Gallons of rich red blood flowed from the veins of her people through the blood donor service in a crimson stream of mercy to gallant men and women struck down by the ruthless enemy action."

In addition to their contributions through military service, war work, and blood donations, residents of the capital bought more than $350 million of the seven Victory Loan bond issues. They also reached into their pockets for a number of other good causes including the Mayor of Ottawa's Relief Fund (organized by Mayor Stanley Lewis), which raised approximately $30,000 to aid children orphaned by the bombing of London.

It is impossible to recount the achievemnts of the many Ottawans who served their country in World War Two, but the stories of three outstanding people—a public servant, an airwoman, and a naval captain—may serve as examples.

In 1939 Mrs. Phyllis Turner was the chief research economist for the Dominion Tariff Board. This handsome, highly educated widow lived with her two young children, Brenda and John, in a house on Daly Avenue near Charlotte Street. At the outbreak of the war Mrs. Turner was seconded to the newly formed Wartime Prices and Trade Board. In 1941 she became the highest-ranking woman in the Canadian Government when she was appointed Oils and Fats Administrator. This position gave Mrs. Turner jurisdiction over the allocation and consumption of all processed and unprocessed animal, vegetable, and fish oils. Among the familiar products within these categories were starches, lard, shortening, soaps (95 percent of the glycerine used in the manufacture of explosives was a soap by-product), paints, varnishes, adhesives, printing inks, and waxes. For four years, from 1941 to 1945, Mrs. Turner's decisions determined the production and availability of these goods for the entire country.

At the end of the war Phyllis Turner resigned from the Civil Service and married the Honourable Frank M. Ross, who later became Lieutenant-Governor of British Columbia. Her son John, who attended Ashbury College and St. Patrick's College in Ottawa, now practises law in Toronto. From 1968 to 1976 John Turner was a Liberal member of the House of Commons for the riding of Ottawa Carleton. During this period he served as both Minister of Justice and Minister of Finance. In 1961 Mrs. Ross became the first woman to head a Canadian university when she was appointed chancellor of the University of British Columbia.

War was declared three days after Willa Walker returned to Ottawa from her honeymoon in Scotland. Her husband, Captain David Walker, one of Lord Tweedsmuir's aides, immediately rejoined his regiment, the Black Watch, in Scotland. The next two years were bleak for the young couple: their first baby died in February 1941 and her husband—listed as missing for three months—was captured with the remnants of his battalion at St. Valerie in France.

In the summer of 1941 Willa Walker returned to her parents' home in Montreal and organized the Canadian Prisoners of War Association. In October of that year she enlisted in the Royal Canadian Air Force Women's Division and was later commissioned as an assistant section officer. Being one of the few women in Canada to hold a commission (the RCAF was the first service to establish a women's division), she had to contend with an element of male chauvinism, such as being barred from the Officers' Mess at a large Canadian air base. However, her obvious competence and tact soon removed any bias on the part of her male colleagues. In June 1942 Walker was made squadron officer of the Women's Division at Rockcliffe Air Base, which trained more than one thousand air women each month. In March 1943 she was appointed senior staff officer at RCAF Headquarters in Ottawa, and two months later promoted to wing officer (equivalent to wing commander). She was the first woman in the RCAF to attain this rank. Wing Officer Walker was made a member of the Order of the British Empire by

King George VI in the New Year's Honours List of January 1944. She was the first Canadian servicewoman to receive this award. When Wing Officer Walker retired from the service in the autumn of 1944, she was responsible for the entire division of 17,000 air-women.

Willa Walker was reunited with her husband, Major David Walker, in Scotland in 1945. David Walker, who also received the MBE for several daring prison camp escapes, has since become a well-known Canadian novelist. Two of his books, *Digby* and *The Pillar*, won the Governor General's award for fiction. Willa and David Walker have lived at Strathcroix, their seaside home in St. Andrews, New Brunswick, since 1947.

Thomas G. Fuller—whose grandfather designed the Parliament buildings, and whose father was also chief architect for the Dominion Government—earned a swashbuckling reputation in the Royal Canadian Naval Volunteer Reserve. During the period 1939 to 1945 Fuller had thirteen ships shot out from under him and won the Distinguished Service Cross three times.

A few months after joining the RCNVR in 1939 Fuller was seconded to the Royal Navy. For the next two years he served on motor gun boats and motor torpedo boats (seventy to one hundred-foot craft with a top speed of forty knots) patrolling the English Channel. This type of warfare, which included attacking enemy ships off the coast of France, placed a premium on speed and daring. One stormy night in 1942 Fuller was forced to shoot his way out of an engagement with twenty-two enemy gunboats in the Channel. For this feat he was awarded his first Distinguished Service Cross. He won the second one in 1943 when German paratroops captured the naval base on the Greek island of Léros. Fuller assumed command of the outnumbered garrison and was subsequently captured. Two days later he led a group that escaped to Turkey by commandeering the German admiral's launch. Fuller was then promoted to lieutenant commander and appointed senior British naval officer for the Aegean theatre. In this posting he headed a combined flotilla of motor gun boats and motor torpedo boats based at Vis, an island off the coast of Yugoslavia controlled by Tito's guerrillas.

His tactics during this phase of the war earned him the nickname of "The Pirate of the Adriatic." Each night Fuller's boats would stealthily follow the indentations of the coastline—a technique known as "periwinkling"—in search of enemy shipping. When Fuller sighted a single vessel, he would pounce upon it and send a boarding party over the rail. The captured vessel would then be towed back to Vis. When a convoy was encountered he would approach it silently and then tear through the centre of it with guns blazing. This daring ploy created such havoc and confusion in the darkness that the enemy ships would often engage in a fierce gun battle *with each other* after Fuller had run the gauntlet.

Fuller won his third Distinguished Service Cross in 1944, when during a ten-day period he seized nine armed enemy vessels and sank five others. On one of those nights he boarded a 400-ton frigate and then towed it fifty-two miles—under the muzzles of the German coastal batteries—to Vis, where he was greeted at dawn by a brass band. The captured frigate contained a valuable cargo, including ten tons of Dutch butter. Fuller's booty was so appreciated by the Yugoslav Resistance that Marshall Tito presented him with a cask of vintage wine and made him an honorary commandant of the National Army of Liberation.

In 1945, after being discharged with the rank of captain, Thomas Fuller reactivated his small construction company. Since then, he has been as successful in business as he was in the navy, and is regarded by those in the trade as an exceedingly tough competitor. In addition to many major projects for others, Fuller has built and owns nine substantial office buildings in Ottawa. His handsome house overlooks the Britannia Yacht Club, of which he is a past commodore, and his brigantine *Blackjack*, is the pride of the club's fleet.

World War Two ended with the surrender of Japan on 14 August 1945. Less than three weeks later the start of the Cold War—the political and ideological struggle between the Soviet Union and the United States and her allies—was heralded by the defection of a Russian cipher clerk in Ottawa.

On the night of 5 September 1945 Igor Gouzenko left the Soviet Embassy on Charlotte Street with a sheaf of telegrams and other secret documents stuffed inside his shirt. Gouzenko tried to see the editor of the *Ottawa Journal* who had left for the day, and was advised by two *Journal* employees to give his information to the Royal Canadian Mounted Police. Instead, Gouzenko went to the Justice building on Wellington Street, where he tried to see the Minister of Justice. The Minister had also gone home, and Gouzenko was told to come back again the next morning. He did so, bringing with him his wife Anna and his son Andrei, but after waiting all morning he was informed that he could not see the Minister.

After two more fruitless visits to the office of the *Journal* and an unsatisfactory interview at the Crown Attorney's office, Gouzenko returned, frightened and exhausted, to his apartment at 511 Somerset Street. That evening he noticed some men watching his apartment from across the street, and in desperation went to Sergeant Harold Main, his next-door neighbour. Sergeant Main took Gouzenko and his family in for the night, and then arranged for two Ottawa Police constables to watch the building. During the night four Soviet Embassy staff broke into Gouzenko's empty apartment. The next morning, 7 September, Gouzenko was driven by the Ottawa Police to the Justice Building, where he was interviewed by the RCMP and granted asylum.

On the strength of Gouzenko's information, twenty Canadians were arrested on 15 February 1946, and charged with breaches of the Official Secrets Act. Ten people, the most prominent being Fred Rose, the Member of Parliament for the Montreal riding of Cartier, were subsequently convicted and sentenced to prison terms.

During the prosecution of these cases a technicality arose concerning the verification of the Russian military attaché's signature. Colonel Nikolai Zabotin, a personable former Czarist officer, was believed to be the master spy of the network, but it was impossible to verify his signature on the incriminating documents because he had always had one of his staff sign diplomatic correspondence and guest books on his behalf. This problem was solved when the late Shirley E. Woods produced the logbook of the Black Bay Duck Club which contained Colonel Zabotin's signature. Woods had been entertained a number of times at the Soviet Embassy by Colonel Zabotin; in return, he had invited Zabotin down to his duck-shooting camp on the Ottawa River near Thurso.

The Gouzenko case created such an international sensation that Hollywood made a movie of it titled *The Iron Curtain*. The movie, much of it filmed on location in Ottawa, starred Dana Andrews in the role of Igor Gouzenko, and Gene Tierney as Anna, his wife. There were other, more sinister ramifications from the incident. Gouzenko's information from the Soviet Embassy in Canada also led to the discovery of Russian espionage networks in the United States and Great Britain.

22

Growth and Change

1946 to 1979

OTTAWA HAS UNDERGONE an astonishing change since World War Two. Indeed, a person returning to the capital today for the first time since the war would find much of the city unrecognizable. The transformation began in August 1945, less than two weeks after the surrender of Japan, when Prime Minister King invited the French town-planner Jacques Gréber back to Canada. The Prime Minister took this action because he believed that the capital of the country should be a city of which all Canadians could be proud.

At that time Ottawa, far from being "the Washington of the North," was a shabby place. Aside from a few beauty spots, such as Parliament Hill and stretches of the Canal, rail lines crisscrossed the slums and the drab streets in the core of the community. The rail problem was particularly serious. More than one hundred trains, noisily belching smoke and cinders, entered Ottawa each day, and the residents also had to put up with the danger and inconvenience of one hundred and fifty level crossings within the city limits.

Following a visit to Ottawa in October 1945, Gréber agreed to act as a consultant to the National Capital Planning Committee. This body, established in 1946, was authorized to draw up an over-all plan for the development of the National Capital Region, which initially encompassed 900 square miles of territory on both sides of the Ottawa River. Three years later, in 1949, the committee submitted a comprehensive plan, known as The Gréber Report, to Prime Minister St. Laurent. The report, approved by Parliament in 1951, included in its main recommendations the establishment of a "green belt" around the capital, the removal of slums, the creation of parks and parkways, the acquisition of land on the outskirts for government buildings, the purchase of property in Quebec for the Gatineau Park, and the removal or relocation of railways in the area. These changes and innovations were to be funded by the federal government, and executed by the Federal District Commission. In 1959 the national capital region was enlarged from 900 square miles to 1,800 square miles, and the Federal District Commission was replaced by the National Capital Commission. Two provisions of the Gréber Report—those dealing with the Green Belt and the rail lines— deserve special mention.

The Green Belt, a two-and-one-half-mile-wide swath of low-density land that encompasses sixty-five square miles of metropolitan Ottawa, was described by Gréber as "a necklace for the National Capital." Its purpose is to prevent urban sprawl and to enhance the environment of the city by the presence of open parkland. Although it has served these functions admirably, the acquisition of land for the Green Belt was a difficult process until 1958, when the government increased the authority of the Federal District Commission. Farmers and land speculators blamed "Mr. Grabber" for the expropriation of their property, and the adjoining townships of Gloucester and Nepean also objected strenuously to the Green Belt because it slowed the pace of urban development in their areas. Today most Ottawans are extremely grateful to be surrounded by the Green Belt.

The rail lines that gripped the heart of the city like tentacles also posed an immense problem. The situation reached a stalemate in 1957, by which time the Federal District Commission had lifted thirty-five miles of track and removed half of the level crossings. Prime Minister Diefenbaker resolved the impasse in 1959 by giving the National Capital Commission sweeping authority to deal with the railways. Today there are few level crossings in the city, the Union Station has been moved from Confederation Square to the Alta Vista area, and the old Canada Atlantic Railway bed is a limited-access freeway. This freeway, the Queensway, started in

1957 and completed in 1965, spans the capital from east to west, a distance of seventeen miles.

Most of the public works executed by the National Capital Commission are maintained by that body, and come under federal jurisdiction. For this reason many parks and driveways in the National Capital Region are protected by the Royal Canadian Mounted Police. Thus a motorist on Wellington Street is subject to the laws of the municipality (enforced by the Ottawa Police), but when he turns off Wellington onto the Ottawa River Parkway he is on NCC or federal property and, if caught speeding, will be apprehended by the RCMP. This situation becomes even more complex when a motorist enters Rockcliffe Park: the park itself is patrolled by the RCMP, but the village comes under the jurisdiction of the Ontario Provincial Police. There are many such examples of intermingled federal, provincial, and municipal jurisdiction in Canada's capital.

This is not to suggest that the efforts of the National Capital Commission have led to confusion. The reverse is true. Because of the National Capital Plan, both the city and the federal authorities have been able to co-ordinate their projects to improve Ottawa. The importance of Gréber's master plan can not be overstated. It has profoundly influenced development in the Ottawa region for more than three decades, and it has also changed many unsightly features of the capital.

Ottawa had an influx of diplomatic missions during World War Two. In 1939 the diplomatic community in Canada's capital consisted of two high commissions, five legations, and five consulates. In 1945 Ottawa had ten embassies, five high commissions, eight legations, and two consulates. These figures are particularly significant when one considers that in the diplomatic "pecking order" the most senior representation of a country is an embassy, or in the case of a fellow Commonwealth member, a high commission. A legation ranks below an embassy (or a high commission); a consulate, which is primarily concerned with personal travel and commercial affairs rather than diplomacy and is usually located outside the capital, ranks below a legation.

Italy, which opened a consulate in Ottawa in 1924, was the first foreign country to be accredited to Canada. China opened a consulate the following year, upgraded the consulate to the status of a legation in 1942, and elevated the legation to an embassy in 1944. Canada's two founding nations, Great Britain and France, and the

United States (with whom Canada shares more than two thousand miles of undefended border), did not become accredited until 1928. That year Great Britain opened a high commission in Ottawa, while France and the United States opened legations.

The diplomatic community continued to mushroom in Ottawa after World War Two and now occupies an important niche in the social life of the city. At the close of 1979 ninety-five countries had accredited missions in the capital, the most recent arrival being the High Commission of St. Vincent.

CFRA, Ottawa's second private radio station, was launched on 3 May 1947 with a gala performance at the Auditorium. More than eight thousand people attended the show, which featured such luminaries as Mayor Stanley Lewis, conductor Percy Faith, former hockey star King Clancy, reporter Gordon Sinclair, and the Glebe Collegiate Lyres Club. The Canadian Broadcasting Corporation extended a gracious welcome to their new competitor by broadcasting CFRA's birthday party over the CBC national network.

The owner and driving force behind Station CFRA was Frank S. Ryan, who was born in Arnprior, Ontario. Ryan completed his education at Queen's University, where he majored in economics and psychology,two subjects that stood him well in the future. He married Kathleen Whitton of Renfrew (Mayor Charlotte Whitton's younger sister), who was also a graduate of Queen's. When Frank Ryan settled at Kilreen Farm on the outskirts of Ottawa in 1946, he had many successful years behind him in advertising, publishing, and broadcasting.

CFRA's first studio was beneath the "Rush End" stands of the Auditorium, and the initial output was a modest 1000 watts. Some years later CFRA moved to its own building on Isabella Street which was replaced with a larger structure in the late 1960s. During this period CFRA's broadcast signal was increased to an impressive 50,000 watts.

Almost from the day it went on the air, CFRA captured the largest listening audience in the national capital region. This was no accident but the result of shrewd programming by Frank Ryan, who each day at quarter-past twelve beamed his own program, "The Farmer's Notebook," at listeners in the Ottawa Valley. After a few introductory bars of "The Surrey with the Fringe on Top" Ryan would discuss rural topics in his rich Valley accent. For eighteen years this program was a favourite of both city and urban dwellers.

His commitment to the Ottawa Valley was reinforced by frequent appearances in the surrounding towns by the station's country band, "The Happy Wanderers," and its baseball team, "The Happy Blunderers." Frank and Kathleen Ryan were also supporters of numerous community projects in the Valley and made an outstanding personal contribution to the town of Lanark after it was destroyed by fire in 1959.

Ryan spoke with considerable knowledge on agricultural matters because he and his wife raised prize-winning livestock and Hackney horses at their farm on the Baseline Road. When this farm was sold, and they moved to another Kilreen farm farther out in the country, the Ryans donated eight acres of their former property to Algonquin College. After Frank Ryan died in March 1965 while on vacation in Florida, his wife Kathleen, a highly competent manager in her own right, took over as chief executive officer of CFRA and its subsidiary CFMO for the next two years. During this period the programming emphasis shifted gradually to the urban listening audience.

In 1967 Mrs. Ryan sold CFRA and CFMO to radio station CHUM Limited of Toronto. The following year Mrs. Ryan opened the Ryan Tower, a 750-foot communications mast set atop Skyline Ridge in the Gatineau Hills. This tower, which has greatly improved radio and television reception in the Ottawa area, is unique because of the multiple radio and television frequencies it carries.

Today CFRA is still the most popular radio station in the region. During the morning and afternoon it gears its programming to the adult audience; in the evening it caters to younger tastes. CFMO, which came on the air in 1959, is by far the most popular FM station in the area. CFMO features music and commentary for adult listeners.

J. Terrence Kielty, who is now vice-president and general manager of CFRA, is the only employee with the station who was present when it opened in 1947. Kielty, a protégé of the late Frank Ryan, is a well-known radio personality. In his early days as a broadcaster Terrence Kielty originated the now-familiar introduction: "This is CFRA, the voice of the nation's capital."

Barbara Ann Scott—a pretty Ottawa eighteen-year-old with a dazzling smile—was given a huge welcome when she returned to the capital on 7 March 1947, after winning both the European and the World figure-skating championships. At a reception held for her at the Chateau Laurier, Mayor Lewis, on behalf of the city of Ottawa, presented Miss Scott with a cream-coloured 1947 Buick convertible. In the House of Commons that afternoon a resolution (written by Prime Minister King) was passed congratulating Miss Scott on "her great achievement, bringing distinction to herself and honour to Canada."

Three days later Avery Brundage, president of the International Olympic Committee, advised Miss Scott that if she accepted the gift of an automobile she would lose her amateur status and thus be disqualified from the 1948 Winter Olympics. Barbara Ann returned the car, and the city held it for her and had it repainted powder blue, her favourite colour. During the next twelve months, while the car remained on display in a Sparks Street show window, she systematically won the Canadian, North American, European, World, and Olympic ladies championships.

Her homecoming after winning the Olympic gold medal was unmatched in the history of the capital. Both papers headlined the event, which dominated the news. The *Ottawa Evening Citizen* described her arrival in these words:

> At 12.40 exactly on schedule, Barbara Ann's special railway car rolled to a stop. Prime Minister King was the first to spot the beautiful skating star and like any schoolboy, he doffed his beaver hat and waved it enthusiastically.
>
> Barbara Ann, wearing a black suit under her beaver coat, with its Red Cross arm-band, and a jaunty, new white straw hat with a black and orange ribbon topped by a perky orange poppy—was the first to step down from the train.
>
> She rushed right into Mayor Lewis' open arms and planted a hearty kiss on the Chief Magistrate's cheek. She then turned as if for a more decorous handshake for the Prime Minister, but then, smiling happily, put her arms around Mr. King and gave him a kiss.
>
> "Welcome home, Barbara Ann," the Prime Minister smiled.
>
> "Oh, I'm so happy to be back," Barbara Ann responded. "It's wonderful to be home again."

The *Citizen* summed up the young skater's welcome:

> Barbara Ann Scott, Champion of Champions, returned in triumph to her home town today.
>
> In the biggest spontaneous demonstration this 122-year-old city has ever seen, Ottawa's own Barbara Ann returned like a queen. No Roman conqueror, returning from his greatest hour, ever got more

vociferous acclaim than did the Olympic, European, and World skating champion. But here were no victims chained to chariot wheels. Here instead were loyal Ottawans tied to Barbara's heartstrings.

At the conclusion of a parade in a flower-bedecked automobile, Miss Scott was presented with a gilt key bearing the colours of the city. When Mayor Lewis handed her this symbolic key before a huge crowd on Confederation Square, he said: "It is a visible reminder that Ottawa's door is open to you always. Its traditional meaning is that you, Barbara Ann Scott, are hereby made a Freewoman of the City of Ottawa."

Some time later Miss Scott was also given the keys to the blue Buick convertible that had been held in escrow for her by the city. She skated professionally for a few years and then retired to marry a Chicago business executive. Today there are two constant reminders in the capital of "the queen of the blades": the Barbara Ann Scott Arena on Torquay Avenue and the extraordinary number of Ottawa women—born between 1947 and 1950—whose Christian names are Barbara Ann.

Barbara Ann Scott was trained at Ottawa's renowned Minto Skating Club. This institution was founded in 1903 at Rideau Hall by the Earl and Countess of Minto. The initial membership consisted of fifteen gentlemen, one of whom was William Lyon Mackenzie King. In 1904—the year that Lady Minto broke her leg on the open-air rink at Government House—ladies were admitted to the club.When the Earl and Countess left for India in 1905, the Minto Skating Club had already arranged for skating privileges at the Rideau Rink on Laurier Avenue.

Membership in the club increased greatly with the admission of children in 1910. Although members had to have a certain social standing, the main objective of the club was to promote skill at figure-skating. To this end, a professional instructor was hired in 1911, and classes were given to junior members two years later. Between 1903 and 1928 the Minto won sixty-seven of the ninety-seven major Canadian and North American skating awards. Led by the late Melville Rogers, the Minto Club continued to dominate the North American competitions during the Thirties. Between 1923 and 1938 Rogers personally won eighteen gold medals for Canadian and North American singles, pairs, fours, and ten-step events. Rogers, an Ottawa barrister, was a member of the Minto for more than half a century and served on the club executive for forty-two years. His contribution covered every facet of the sport, including judging at the Olympics.

In 1922 the Minto acquired its own rink on Waller Street. This ramshackle tin building burned down in 1949, and the club built a new rink three years later on Henderson Avenue which was subsequently sold to the University of Ottawa in 1959. Since then the Minto has operated from rented premises. The club has staged a gala ice show for the public, "The Minto Follies," since 1926, except for the years 1968 to 1973. The Minto Follies is a popular winter institution that employs the talents of every member of the club, regardless of age or proficiency. (The tiny ones, lurching around the ice on their ankles, are often uproariously funny show-stealers.)

Although the Minto no longer has its own permanent quarters, it still produces champions, one of the most recent being Lynn Nightingale, who from 1974 to 1977 was Senior Canadian Ladies Champion. With four hundred members and eight dedicated instructors, the Minto Club continues to play a major role in Canadian figure-skating.

The Loon's Necklace, an eleven-minute movie on the Indian legend of how the loon acquired its striated white collar, was chosen Canadian Film of the Year for 1949. This 16-mm colour picture was a notable success for the young Ottawa firm of Crawley Films Limited. In a sense the formation of Crawley Films Limited was an example of serendipity.

The founder, Frank "Budge" Crawley, had married Judith Sparks, a descendant of Nicholas Sparks, in 1938. On their honeymoon Budge Crawley, who at that time was a practising chartered accountant, took several reels of 16-mm colour film of l'île d'Orleans (opposite Quebec City). When he returned to Ottawa he edited his footage of the historic island and entered it in a New York contest. His film won the 1939 Hiram Percy Maxim Award for the world's best amateur moving picture.

During the first years of the war Crawley became increasingly involved in film-making, but it was not until 1943, when he purchased a church hall on Fairmont Avenue for a studio, that he decided to make his hobby his vocation. Since then, his firm has produced more than three thousand documentary, industrial, sports, animated, and feature films, and won more than 250 national and international awards. *The Loon's Necklace*, for instance, has won fifteen awards, and the demand for the picture is still so brisk that two hundred copies are sold each year.

Because he would rather lose money on a good picture than make money on a poor one, Budge Crawley has not become immensely rich from his firm. However, his dedication to excellence is rewarded by the loyalty of his staff, many of whom have been with him for more than twenty years, and the high percentage of repeat business that the company enjoys (sixty clients have reordered from four to forty times). International recognition, such as the 1977 Academy Award for his feature-length film, *The Man Who Skied Down Everest*, is also gratifying.

In addition to producing films for clients, Crawley offers a selection of "stock items," in French and English, for sale to schools and libraries. These films range from *Merchants in a Changing Land*, the story of the Hudson's Bay Company, to *Anik*, which traces the development of Canada's first communication satellite. One of the most popular is *Ottawa—Canada's Capital*, a sparkling fourteen-minute documentary on the city that has been seen by more than 125 million television viewers.

On 1 January 1950 the city of Ottawa annexed 14,605 acres from the township of Gloucester and 7,420 acres from the township of Nepean. This move, sanctioned by the Ontario Government, increased the size of the city five-fold, from 6,109 acres to 30,482 acres. The reason for acquiring this vast amount of property, which extended to the Ottawa River and surrounded the capital like a giant horseshoe, was to provide room for the postwar housing boom. Because most of the land was undeveloped, the annexation only increased the population by some 30,000 (to 193,000) and the increase in taxable assessment was a mere 2.5 percent. Over the short term the annexation saddled the city with a huge liability to provide services for the burgeoning suburbs. Over the long term it insured that their development would be an orderly part of the over-all plan.

As a result of the annexation Ottawa's electoral boundaries were redrawn and six alderman from three new wards were added to City Council. Following these changes, the slate of municipal representatives consisted of the mayor and four controllers (who were elected from the city at large) and twenty-eight aldermen (two of whom were elected from each of fourteen wards). The aldermen, in addition to representing the interests of their own particular wards also served on various city-wide committees. The mayor, as chief executive officer, was assisted by the controllers—known collectively as Board of Control—whose function was similar to that of a cabinet. In the event of the mayor's absence, the controller with the largest majority in the last election acted in the mayor's place. All bylaws or proposals involving the collection or expenditure of money had to be approved by City Council, which consisted of the mayor, the four controllers, and the twenty-eight aldermen.

History was made in the 1950 municipal election when a fifty-four-year-old spinster, Charlotte Elizabeth Whitton, was elected to Board of Control. Not only was she the first woman to be elected as a controller, but her majority was the largest ever accorded a candidate in the capital.

Miss Whitton was a remarkable person. Born in Renfrew, she graduated from Queen's University with a master's degree and a number of prizes, including the Governor-General's Award. Although she was barely five feet tall and weighed 130 pounds (built, in her words, "on good Shetland pony lines"), she played on the girls' basketball and hockey teams. By the time she was elected to Board of Control, Whitton was an accomplished author and had had a distinguished career as a social worker, being both the founder and first director of the Canadian Council on Child Welfare. Along the way she had received several honorary degrees and had been appointed a Commander of the Order of the British Empire. Her entry into politics came as a result of a dare made by The *Ottawa Citizen*, following a speech in which she had urged women to take a more active role in government.

When Mayor Grenville Goodwin died in office in August 1951 Charlotte Whitton, as senior controller, was chosen by Council to finish the balance of his term. Whitton thus became the first woman to be mayor of a Canadian municipality. Not only did she serve for Goodwin's term, but she was re-elected mayor for two more terms in 1952 and 1954. She retired from municipal politics in 1956 and was subsequenly defeated as a Progressive Conservative candidate for Ottawa West in the 1958 general election. Whitton returned to civic politics and served as mayor from 1960 until 1964. She was defeated in her attempt for a third consecutive term in December 1964 but later represented Capital Ward as an alderman from 1967 to 1972.

Charlotte Whitton dominated City Hall during her years in office.

She had a flair for attracting headlines, and was undoubtedly the capital's most colourful mayor. Because of her quick temper and sharp tongue, she was described by the press at various times as "a pint-sized pepper pot," "a stormy petrel," "a bantam-weight fighter," and "able but impossible." She was all of these things, but underlying her fractious behaviour was a core of exceptional competence.

One of the first things she did when she became mayor was to reinstate pomp and ceremony at City Hall. She loved to wear her gold chain of office, her scarlet fur-trimmed robe, and her tricorne hat, and she also saw that the members of Council wore their robes. She ran Council meetings like a schoolmarm. When a councillor wished to speak, he first had to stand and address her formally as "Your Worship" or "Madam Mayor" before he could address his colleagues. On many occasions Whitton clashed with Council, but she was a gifted orator and usually managed to have the last word. For years she engaged in a highly publicized feud with Paul Tardif, a senior member of Board of Control. This feud was in fact largely for the benefit of Whitton's and Tardif's respective supporters. When a serious matter came up at City Hall, the two combatants would settle the problem privately and amicably behind closed doors.

She was a knowledgeable historian, and the author of *A Hundred Years A-Fellin'*, the saga of Gillies Brothers, Limited, a Valley lumbering concern. Her pride in her local ancestry was tempered by a sense of humour; she once observed that Bytown in the early days was populated by 10,000 lumbermen—8,000 of them drunks. Although she had an army of women volunteers (known as Lottie's Girls) her political support extended far beyond the feminist vote. Her political appeal was based on the fact that she was better qualified than her opponents, and she was absolutely honest.

Her notable achievements during her nine years as mayor include the selection of Green Island as the site for City Hall, the conversion of Porter's Island from a derelict smallpox hospital to the site of a modern senior citizens' home, a greatly improved city welfare program, the construction of eight hundred low-rental housing units, and a 300 percent increase in federal grants.

Charlotte Whitton died on 25 January 1975. Two years before her death, Council passed a bylaw that changed the name of the Council Chamber to Whitton Hall. It was a fitting tribute to one of Ottawa's finest mayors.

Shortly after midnight on 4 August 1952 fire broke out in the domed roof of the Library of Parliament. The fire, started by a failure in the wiring, smoldered between the copper sheathing of the roof and the plaster ceiling of the interior. Because the source of the fire was hidden and the dome was more than one hundred feet above the ground, it presented a difficult and dangerous problem for the Ottawa Fire Department. After covering some of the bookshelves with tarpaulins, firemen hacked holes in the roof and sprayed the inside of the dome with their hoses. This tactic eventually quenched the stubborn blaze.

Although the flames never touched the interior of the building the library was filled with greasy black smoke that triggered the automatic sprinkler system. By the time the sprinkler system was shut off, six hours later, some 200,000 gallons of water had drenched the contents of the library and more than two inches of water covered its beautiful parquet floor. Approximately 150,000 of the library's 400,000 volumes suffered water and smoke damage.

The task of restoration was enormous. Every single item in the library had to be removed and refurbished. All the pine panelling and other woodwork, including the warped parquet floor, was sent out to be cleaned, refinished, and painted on the back with fire-retardant material. Hundreds of volunteers—from the Boy Scouts to the Keeper of the Collections of the Library of Congress—as well as professional people worked at restoring the damaged volumes of which 500 were destroyed and 45,000 had to be rebound. While this was taking place, the building underwent structural improvements to make it more fire-resistant. The restoration took nearly three years to complete and cost approximately $2,400,000.

Today the library looks much like it did before the fire, but it is now a more efficient and safer home for Canada's Parliamentary collection. When you step through the sliding doors from the Centre Block it is like stepping into a vanished era, for you are surrounded by the most enchanting Victorian woodwork. It is hard to believe, when you gaze at the gold leaf dome high above the rotunda, that you are looking at the site of a near-catastrophe.

Mayor Whitton extended "the freedom of the city" to the 1st Battalion of the Royal Canadian Regiment when it returned from Korea on 27 April 1953. In her welcoming address at the Union Station, the mayor noted that Ottawa's connection with the RCR dated back to the South African War. The men of the battalion, clad in khaki uniforms and maroon berets, then paraded to Parliament

Hill where they were congratulated by Prime Minister St. Laurent and given their Colours (which had been laid up while the unit was overseas) by the Minister of Labour, Brigadier Milton F. Gregg. The Minister was also the honorary colonel of the regiment, having served with it in World War One when he won the Victoria Cross as well as the Military Cross and Bar. Following this ceremony, the battalion exercised its right "to march through the streets of the city with bayonets fixed, Colours flying, and drums beating."

Five weeks later, on 2 June 1953, Ottawa celebrated the coronation of Canada's sovereign, Queen Elizabeth II. The main event on that historic day was the Trooping of the Colour by the Governor General's Foot Guards on Parliament Hill. A huge crowd watched the Guards, resplendent in their scarlet dress uniforms and tall bearskins, perform the ancient ritual. The Right Honourable Vincent Massey, the nation's first Canadian Governor General, took the salute on the reviewing stand in front of the Peace Tower.

That evening thousands of Ottawans clustered around television sets to watch a black and white movie of the coronation ceremony which had taken place in London earlier in the day. Because there were no global satellite transmitters, the showing was made possible by a Vampire jet, which had taken advantage of the five-hour time difference between the two countries to fly the Kinescope film across the Atlantic. This television program—the first to originate in Ottawa—was transmitted from the Canadian Broadcasting Corporation's newly completed facility on Lanark Avenue.

Initially, space was so limited in the forty-by-fifty-foot structure that the staff of twenty were forced to use a wooden outhouse behind the building. Regular television programming for CBOT (the English station) and CBOFT (its French counterpart) began in the autumn of 1953. Colour broadcasting commenced on 1 September 1966. The original transmitting plant, because of successive additions during the past three decades, now occupies most of the block. Today this rambling brick structure contains spacious offices, well-equipped studios, and adequate plumbing facilities for its four hundred and fifty employees.

The Soviet Embassy on Charlotte Street caught fire on New Year's Day, 1956. People noticed smoke pouring from the top floor windows at four-fifteen on that frigid afternoon, but the Ottawa Fire Department was not notified until a neighbour, Esmond Butler, telephoned the alarm forty minutes later. Within three minutes Fire

Chief John Foote was on his way to the blaze, as were one hundred of his men. Although the fire was burning brightly, they were refused access to the embassy by the Russians who were frantically removing secret documents from the building. Chief Foote, concerned that the conflagration would spread to the nearby residence of Senator Norman Paterson, then telephoned Mayor Whitton for advice. The mayor, who was suffering from a heavy cold and had just emerged from a mustard bath, said she would come down and read the Riot Act.

Miss Whitton was dissuaded from this course by the Honourable Paul Martin, Acting Secretary of State for External Affairs, who reminded the mayor that the Soviet Embassy was technically on foreign soil, and if the Soviet Ambassador wished, he could allow his embassy to burn to the ground—providing it did not endanger other properties. The mayor and Mr. Martin then met with the Soviet Ambassador, Dmitri S. Chuvanin on Charlotte Street, and after intense negotiations the Russian gave permission for the firemen to enter the embassy. However, by that time it was too late and the building could not be saved. A minor incident occurred when a Russian tried to prevent Chief Foote from entering the second-floor west wing, which was sectioned off by a heavy iron door and contained eight wireless and decoding rooms. The chief later told reporters that when his way was blocked, "I gave him my shoulder, because I had a job to do, and the Russian took a swing at me. I ducked." By eleven o'clock that night the fire was out and the building was an ice-covered ruin.

The old mansion, built for J. R. Booth's son, J. Frederick Booth, had been the scene of happier times. It was here on 11 February 1924 that a magnificent reception was held for Frederick Booth's daughter Lois when she married Prince Erik of Denmark. One of the two silk-clad pages at the wedding was John Bassett, Jr., the now-famous broadcasting magnate. (Master Bassett left the reception early in the grip of his German nanny after he had the misfortune to sit in a plate of lemon sherbet.) The Soviets also gave a memorable reception in October 1943 to celebrate Red Army Day. More than 1,200 guests, including Prime Minister King and most of his Cabinet, attended this party. The guests realized they were no longer welcome when their host closed the six bars, and then switched off the lights briefly, a signal normally employed by taverns to indicate closing time.

The Soviets occupied temporary quarters at 24 Blackburn Avenue, the office of their commercial counsellor, until a new embassy was erected on their vacant property at 285 Charlotte Street. There have been few gala parties in this maximum-security granite building.

At the Governor General's Levee on 3 January 1956 no fewer than six ambassadors made a point of assuring Mayor Whitton that if their premises caught fire, they would not impede the entry of the Ottawa Fire Department.

The city was decorated with bunting, and seventeen Union Jack flags flew from the Carleton County Gaol on Nicholas Street, when Her Majesty, Queen Elizabeth, visited Ottawa for the first time as monarch on 12 October 1957.

The Queen and her husband Prince Philip, Duke of Edinburgh, arrived at Uplands from England at four twenty-two on that sunny Saturday afternoon. An estimated 200,000 people lined the route from the airport to Rideau Hall, and the crowds were so dense that twice the royal limousine was forced to stop. The following day the royal couple attended a Thanksgiving service at Christ Church Cathedral on Wellington Street and then paid tribute to Canada's war dead in a ceremony at the National War Monument. That evening the Queen, sitting at a desk in the Governor General's study made the first live television broadcast of her career. Her address was not only transmitted across Canada, but was also viewed by some 50 million people in the United States. After dinner the late Wing Commander Joseph G. Stephenson (conducting officer of the tour) drove Prince Philip from Rideau Hall to the Black Bay Duck Club, situated on the Quebec shore of the Ottawa River twenty miles from Ottawa.

The Prince enjoyed an early-morning duck shoot at the club and then set off for Ottawa with Wing Commander Stephenson. When they turned on to Highway 8 from the private road, Philip asked if he might drive the powerful maroon convertible, which had been lent for the royal tour by the Chrysler Corporation. Possibly because of his unfamiliarity with the vehicle, the Prince rocketed down the highway leaving his RCMP escort far behind. A few minutes later a Quebec Provincial Police cruiser stopped the convertible for speeding and gruffly asked the Prince for his driver's licence and ownership papers. Stephenson quickly explained the identity of the driver, but the policeman thought he was being facetious and became quite angry. At this juncture the RCMP arrived on the scene and the matter was soon resolved. Stephenson drove the car for the rest of the journey to Rideau Hall.

That afternoon Her Majesty, accompanied by Prince Philip, rode in the state carriage to the Hill where she opened Parliament. The highlight of this brilliant full-dress ceremony came when the Queen read the Throne Speech.

By coincidence, on the same day it was announced that the Honourable Lester B. "Mike" Pearson had been awarded the Nobel Peace Prize. Had it not been for the royal visit, Pearson's historic achievement would have received much greater press coverage. When Pearson was telephoned at his residence by a local paper and told of the award, he was astonished at the news. Pearson, the former Secretary of State for the recently defeated Liberal government, was chosen to lead his party the following year and subsequently served as Prime Minister of Canada from 22 April 1963 to 20 April 1968. This distinguished statesman and popular resident of the capital died at his Rockcliffe home on 27 December 1972.

The Queen's visit in 1957 only lasted four days, but she returned two years later, in June 1959, for an extended forty-five-day tour of Canada. She used Rideau Hall as her main residence from which she and Prince Philip made numerous trips to other parts of the country. During this visit the regiment of Canadian Guards (a permanent force infantry unit stationed at Camp Petawawa) mounted a household guard at Rideau Hall similar to the ones at Buckingham Palace and Windsor Castle. Each morning at precisely ten o'clock the Guard was changed in an impressive ceremony on Parliament Hill. This daily pageant proved so popular with the public that the Canadian Guards continued to mount a Guard each summer at Rideau Hall until 1970, when the regiment was disbanded. For the next eight years the household duties were assumed by two affiliated militia regiments, the Canadian Grenadier Guards and the Governor General's Foot Guards.

In 1979 the militia units were withdrawn from the role and replaced by a new entity, the Ceremonial Guard. The Ceremonial Guard was established by the Department of National Defence to accommodate women who wished to be employed as soldiers on Parliament Hill. During the summer of 1979 approximately one dozen women served with the Guard. Stuffed into scarlet tunics, with regulation trousers and army boots, these determined women —their bearskins pulled over their eyes and chin straps hiding their faces—blended inconspicuously with the men in the ranks. In its first season the Ceremonial Guard received favourable comment from many tourists in the capital.

The National Gallery of Canada moved into the newly completed Lorne Building on Elgin Street in February 1960. This eight-story structure, named for the Marquess of Lorne—was designed so that it could be converted to office use, and was intended to be a temporary home for the gallery. Twenty years later, with the gallery still in residence, it stands as a classic example of the term "temporary," which in Ottawa can mean a time lapse of from one month to half a century.

The Marquess of Lorne founded the National Gallery in 1880 on the prompting of his wife, Princess Louise, who was a talented painter and the youngest daughter of Queen Victoria. The Gallery came into existence as a result of the inaugural exhibition of the Royal Canadian Academy which was opened by the Governor-General on 6 March of that year. The diploma paintings of the Academy's members—now the country's most important collection of early Canadian art—were hung in the Clarendon Hotel at 541 Sussex Street. For the next two years this stone building (now occupied by the National Capital Commission) served as the National Gallery of Canada. In 1882 the collection was transferred to two converted workshops on Parliament Hill, and John J. Watts, Assistant Chief Government Architect, was appointed its first curator. From 1888 until 1912 the gallery occupied rooms in the Fisheries Exhibit building on O'Connor Street. This location was a surprising boon for attendance because many of the people who came to see the popular marine exhibits also took time to look at the paintings.

In 1910 an Englishman named Eric Brown was appointed the first full-time curator of the Gallery. Brown was a forceful proponent of the Canadian school of art, personified by the work of the Group of Seven. During his twenty-nine years as curator, Brown made an immense contribution to the gallery by broadening the scope of its collection and, despite limited funds, pursuing an aggressive policy of acquisition.

In 1912 the gallery moved into relatively grand quarters on three floors in the east wing of the Victoria Memorial Museum. The following year Parliament passed the National Gallery Act, which defined the gallery's role and arranged for its management to come under a board of trustees. When the Centre Block burned in 1916 and Parliament convened at the museum, the gallery was forced to vacate its space and place most of its collection in storage. However, this reverse prompted the gallery in 1917 to mount its first touring exhibition, which was sent to a number of cities across Canada. The gallery moved back to the Museum in 1921, and remained there for the next thirty-nine years. From 1929 to 1948 Harry S. Southam, the publisher of the *Ottawa Citizen* and a noted art collector, was chairman of the board of trustees. In December 1968 Parliament passed the National Museum Act, which placed the National Gallery under the same board of trustees as the national museums.

Today the National Gallery has a collection of more than 20,000 paintings, sculptures, prints, and drawings. Nearly 80 percent of these works are by Canadian artists. It also has a public reference library containing some 44,000 volumes and a collection of approximately 8,000 fine art photographs. In addition to lectures, films, and regular publications, the gallery sends at least ten exhibitions to sixty communities across Canada each year.

The National Gallery of Canada is recognized throughout the world, and Ottawans are particularly fortunate to have its collection in their city. Because space restricts the number of works that may be shown at one time, the exhibitions are changed frequently. For this reason a visit to the Lorne Building can be an enriching experience at any time of the year.

Anne Heggtveit, a slim, fair-haired twenty-one-year-old, was given a tumultuous welcome when she returned to Ottawa on 10 March 1960. She had just won the Ladies' Olympic Slalom, the World Slalom, and the Combined Alpine ski events at Squaw Valley, Idaho. Forty fellow members of the Ottawa Ski Club formed a ski-pole arch for her when she stepped from her airplane at Uplands Airport. After an official greeting from the mayor and the Minister of Citizenship, Miss Heggtveit was enthroned on an open float (which had been Ottawa's entry in the Grey Cup parade) and driven to the Chateau Laurier. At MacLaren Street the fifty-car motorcade was joined by six bands and a troupe of majorettes.

That evening five hundred guests attended a civic banquet where the young athlete was presented with a silver tea service by the city of Ottawa. Mayor George Nelms read a telegram of warm congratulations from the Queen and also praised Miss Heggtveit in a personal speech. Prime Minister John Diefenbaker said that the Ottawa skier was an inspiration to all young Canadians, and borrowed Kipling's phrase to christen her "Our Lady of the Snows."

Anne Heggtveit's triumph at Squaw Valley was the culmination of an arduous skiing career, which started on the lawn of her New Edinburgh home when she was two years old. For the next few years she skied at Rockcliffe Park under the watchful eyes of her father, Halvor Heggtveit, and her uncle, Bruce Heggtveit, both of whom were former Canadian cross-country champions. She then graduated to competitive skiing at Camp Fortune and went to Europe to gain experience at the age of fourteen. She won her first world-class race, the Holmenkollen Giant Slalom at Oppdal, Norway, in 1954 when she was fifteen. During the next five years she was plagued by bad luck, and eventually decided that the 1960 Olympics would be her last competition. On a practice run at Grindelwald, Switzerland, in January 1960 she was struck on the leg by a man who was shovelling snow on the trail. The shovel cut her shin to the bone, and she was forced to stop training and return to Canada. Despite this injury and a three week lay-off, she entered the United States Nationals at Alta, Utah, and won both the Ladies' Slalom and the Ladies' Giant Slalom. She then went to Aspen, Colorado, and won the Ladies' Giant Slalom in the prestigious Roche Cup competitions. By the time she reached Squaw Valley, Anne Heggtveit was the top-ranked woman skier in the world. This rating was well deserved: not only was she awarded three gold medals, but her winning margin in the slalom was so great that it still stands as a record.

Anne Heggtveit's formative years were spent on the hills of the Ottawa Ski Club. This club, the largest in the world, was started in 1910 by a group of ski-jumping enthusiasts at Rockcliffe Park. Every weekend during the winter Ottawans would gather to watch these dare-devils soar from a jump near Governor's Bay onto the frozen river. The site of this spectacle was appropriately called Suicide Hill. During the Twenties the members of the club shifted their attention to downhill and cross-country skiing, at Camp Fortune in the Gatineau. The Rockcliffe jump was dismantled in 1937; by this time the club had sixty miles of groomed trails and several lodges at Camp Fortune. Jumping is still a facet of the club's activities (a sixty-metre jump was built at Lockeberg Hill in 1967) but the majority of the members prefer downhill and cross-country skiing.

Today the club owns or leases some seven hundred acres in the heart of Gatineau Park, which is only a twelve-minute drive from the capital. Management of the club is in the capable hands of a syndicate of businessmen/skiers headed by John Graham, Jr., who is a sixth-generation Ottawan. The facilities at Camp Fortune are impressive. For the cross-country skiers there are 140 miles of packed and patrolled trails; for the downhill enthusiasts there are sixteen runs, which range from the gentle Pee Wee slope to Vanier and Expo, which are more than a mile in length. These hills are serviced by eight tows, the most modern being a triple chairlift, the oldest being a simple rope tow. Thirteen lodges of various sizes are scattered about the property.

Formal ski lessons started in 1923. Since then the club's expert instructors have produced countless first-class skiers, many of whom have won Canadian and international titles. However, most of the Ottawa Ski Club's six thousand members are pleasure skiers. For them Camp Fortune is an ideal place for the whole family to enjoy a winter day.

The Sparks Street Mall—Ottawa's celebrated pedestrian thorough-fare—was first opened on a trial basis on 20 May 1960. That summer the three-block stretch between Elgin and Bank streets was transformed by 10,000 tulips planted in concrete beds, fifty-three potted trees, some park benches, a fountain, and a wading pool. At the opening a local resident expressed his opinion to the *Ottawa Journal*: "What amazes me are the trees, which are the most attractive feature. The benches will be a good thing unless they are monopolized by certain types who find them restful before the taverns open. The Mall is something new, and that's what we need in Ottawa."

First suggested by Jacques Gréber in 1958, the mall was a move by the Sparks Street merchants to recapture the trade they had lost to suburban shopping centres. In September of 1959, the Ottawa Board of Trade flew some of their members as well as civic and federal officials to Toledo, Ohio, to view the shopping mall in that city. Following their visit the Sparks Street Development Association was formed by Emerson R. Fisher, the proprietor of a Sparks Street men's store. Ottawa architect Watson Balharrie then drew up a plan for a temporary mall which was submitted to City Council for approval. Council was lukewarm to the idea, but passed the necessary bylaws and also agreed to contribute $15,000 toward the cost of the three month trial.

The mall was such a success in the summer of 1960 that the merchants financed it themselves for the following two summers. In the autumn of 1963 a Citizens Committee recommended to

Council in a comprehensive report that the city of Ottawa create a permanent Sparks Street Mall. Despite protests from some businessmen who feared that a permanent mall would turn Sparks Street into "a carnival," "encourage loafers," and "kill the carriage trade," Council approved this proposal. Construction began soon after the Ontario Legislature ratified the project in June 1966 and Mayor Don B. Reid officially opened the permanent mall on 27 June 1967, just in time for Canada's centennial birthday celebrations.

The mall, which has since been extended two blocks west to Lyon Street, has revitalized Ottawa's central business district. All the buildings on the mall have been cleaned or redecorated, and now the thoroughfare is one of the city's proudest tourist attractions. The street attracts the lion's share of the carriage trade, and the jingle of cash registers confirms that its original aim—to stimulate business —has been achieved. Fears concerning the mall have largely proved groundless, although in the summer it does host a few impecunious loafers. Because of its tranquil atmosphere, the mall is appreciated by both shoppers and office workers in the vicinity. Although it has now been in operation for two decades, the Sparks Street Mall is still considered a model for other communities in North America.

In June 1961 Madame Georges Vanier, wife of Canada's popular Governor-General, opened the May Court Convalescent Home at 114 Cameron Avenue. This forty-one-bed institution was the largest project undertaken by the May Court Club, which had been engaged in charitable work in Ottawa for more than three quarters of a century.

The May Court Club had a most unlikely beginning. On 1 May 1898 the Countess of Aberdeen gave a fête at Rideau Hall where one hundred Ottawa maidens, dressed in flowing robes and garlanded with flowers, revived the ancient custom of dancing around the May Pole. One of the dancers, Ethel Hamilton, was crowned with a wreath as May Queen by Lady Aberdeen. When the young ladies gathered again at Government House that October, Miss Hamilton suggested to her court that they form a club whose objectives would be to "accord girls of leisure opportunities of improving their own talents and characters, and of helping girls with less time at their disposal."

The May Court Club was formally established by the end of 1898, and immediately began charitable work through various committees. One of the first committees gave assistance to the Victorian

Order of Nurses, which had also been sponsored by the Countess of Aberdeen. In 1905 the club furnished a children's ward at the Protestant General Hospital, and in 1912 also donated a children's ward to the Ottawa General Hospital. Funds for the club's activities were raised by public entertainments such as concerts, teas, and theatricals. The first May Court Ball (which raised $675) took place on New Year's Eve, 1907, under the patronage of Their Excellencies, Lord and Lady Grey.

In 1916 the club rented a building on O'Connor Street for a twelve-bed convalescent home, which was subsequently turned into an emergency hospital during the influenza epidemic of 1918. Sir George Perley (father of the late Mrs. I. K. Perley-Robertson, a former May Queen) donated a large house at 270 Cooper Street to the club in 1920. This house was turned into the May Court Convalescent Home, and the patients were transferred from the rented premises on O'Connor Street.

In 1959 the May Court Club sold the house given by Sir George Perley to help pay for the new convalescent home on Cameron Avenue. Because this home receives no government grants, it continually operates at a deficit. In 1971 the May Court Club opened The Bargain Box, a store staffed by its members that sells donated clothing. During the past decade The Bargain Box has raised more than $50,000 to assist the Convalescent Home.

Despite the social nature of the club (in the early days the first duty of an Ottawa debutante was to register for junior membership) the May Court has long been known for solid achievement. Today the primary aim of its 450 members is to meet the changing needs of the community. One of the club's current projects is the sponsorship of a Palliative Care Unit at the Riverside Hospital. Palliative care— ministering to the terminally ill—is quite different from skipping around the May Pole at Rideau Hall.

In May 1966 Paul Joseph Chartier—a forty-five-year-old unemployed security guard living in Toronto—wrote the Clerk of the Commons requesting permission to make a speech to the House. Chartier, who had been undergoing treatment for a severe emotional disorder, was convinced that Parliament was collectively responsible for most of Canada's social ills, including divorce, separation, and suicide. When he was advised by the Clerk of the Commons that only Members of the House could speak in the Commons, he came to Ottawa. Papers found in Chartier's Toronto lodgings indicate that he intended to kill as many Members of Parliament as possible.

Chartier arrived in Ottawa on 17 May. The following afternoon he went to the Public Gallery at the south end of the Commons chamber with a home-made bomb concealed beneath his coat. Shortly before three o'clock he asked a Commons guard for directions to the nearest washroom and asked the policeman to save his seat.

Chartier then made his way to a third-floor lavatory, where he activated the fuse of his bomb. As he left the washroom the bomb exploded with an ear-splitting crash that shattered the marble walls of the room and blew out the windows. Chartier was killed instantly.

This tragedy—the first such violence in the history of Parliament—could have had even more frightful consequences, had the bomb detonated in the Public Gallery, which was filled with school children, or on the floor of the House of Commons. Security precautions were immediately tightened on Parliament Hill following this terrifying incident.

By the close of 1966 Ottawa's two leading real estate developers, Robert Campeau and William Teron, were engaged in projects that would have long-term effects on the capital. Campeau had nearly completed the first phase of Place de Ville, a massive office tower and hotel complex, which would extend the city's business district west to the area of Kent and Lyon streets. Teron, for his part, had finished planning Kanata, a model community west of the Green Belt, and had built the first houses in the three-thousand-acre development.

Robert Campeau, a native of Sudbury, came to Ottawa in 1947 to work as a machinist at the Canadian International Paper Company plant in Gatineau. In 1949 he built a house for his bride at Alfred, a town some forty miles east of Ottawa. While this house was being built, he sold it for a handsome price. With the profit he built another bungalow and bought some land on which he later erected twelve houses. In 1950 Campeau left his job as a machinist and became a home builder. His first major development, the seven-hundred-acre subdivision of Elmvale Acres, in Ottawa south, proved to be a springboard for much greater expansion. By the time he embarked on the Place de Ville project in 1966, he had built and sold more than 12,000 housing units in the Ottawa area.

In 1969 Campeau Corporation Limited became a public company.

The following year 51 percent of its shares were purchased by Power Corporation Limited of Montreal, which paid for the shares by transferring to Campeau Corporation a major interest in Canadian Interurban Properties Limited (which owned more than fifty income-producing properties, including twenty-two shopping centres and undeveloped land in Kanata) and Blue Bonnets Raceway, outside of Montreal. Two other small real estate companies were included in the payment. In March 1972 Campeau Corporation borrowed $28 million, and with this money bought back its shares from Power Corporation. Later, through public tender offers, Campeau Corporation purchased the balance of shares in Canadian Interurban Properties and Blue Bonnets Raceway. In 1977 the company bought approximately four million of its own shares from the public for cancellation. As a result of these transactions Robert Campeau and his family now own 72 percent of the shares in Campeau Corporation. At the end of 1979 this multinational company had more than two thousand employees and assets valued at nearly $1 billion.

William Teron, who was born in the Manitoba hamlet of Gardenton, came to Ottawa in 1949 at the age of seventeen. After working as a draughtsman in the Civil Service for six weeks, Teron joined an Ottawa house builder as his designer. Five years later, with the aid of his savings (which totalled $412) and a bank loan, he established his own contracting firm, William Teron Limited. In the first three years his sales jumped from $116,000 to more than $5 million, and by the age of twenty-five he was a millionaire. In 1965, when he started to build Kanata—his dream community—he had built more than three thousand houses in the capital, including Lynwood Village, on the outskirts of the city.

Kanata (an Iroquois word for an encampment) was Teron's most ambitious project. Because he wanted the houses to blend with the environment, he personally sited each house so that it would take advantage of the natural contours, and left as many trees standing as possible. The exteriors of the houses were built of materials that would blend rather than clash with their surroundings. Those who bought homes in Kanata were obliged to comply with his standards, and he cheerfully admitted to being a "dictator" in this regard.

To obtain the capital to finish developing Kanata, Teron sold his interest in the community in 1967 to Power Corporation. However, when Power Corporation bought control of his rival, Campeau Corporation, in 1970 and he learned that the Campeau operation would be the dominant entity, Teron sold his shares in Canadian Interurban Properties and withdrew from Kanata. Two years later, through the purchase of Canadian Interurban Properties, Campeau became the owner of the undeveloped acreage in Kanata. Since then Teron has publicly criticized Campeau for sacrificing low-density housing in Kanata for maximum profits.

During the past decade Teron has built approximately two thousand housing units in Ottawa as well as the Carleton Towers (now the Four Seasons) Hotel, the prestigious Park Square condominium apartments, and the Inn of the Provinces hotel and office complex. When he was appointed president of Central Mortgage and Housing Corporation (a Crown company) in 1973, he placed his assets in a blind trust to prevent any conflict of interest. In August 1979 Teron resigned his position at Central Mortgage and Housing to return to private business.

Robert Campeau and William Teron are similar in some respects and quite different in others. Both are developers on a grand scale. Teron is noted for the imagination of his work, while Campeau is renowned for the size of his projects. Each has been immensely successful. Between them they have changed the face of the capital.

The summer of 1967, Canada's Centennial year, was marked by pomp and ceremony. Between April and October fifty-four heads of state or their representatives paid good-will visits to the capital. Never in Ottawa's history had so many foreign dignitaries come to the city in one year. These envoys ranged from the Shah of Iran to the President of Iceland. For each visit the route between Rideau Hall and Parliament Hill was lined with the flags of the guest nation. By the end of the summer Ottawans were quite used to the sight of long black limousines being shepherded down Sussex Street by a motorcycle escort.

Haile Selassie, Lion of Judah and Emperor of Ethiopia, was the first personage to come to Canada. The Emperor's stay at Rideau Hall was complicated by the presence of Lulu, his Mexican Hairless dog. Lulu had not been house-trained, and consequently left her signature on many of the carpets at Government House. Lulu also set a diplomatic precedent by urinating on the foot of one of the guests at the state dinner given for her master.

Queen Elizabeth and Prince Philip were in Ottawa for the highlight of the year, Canada's birthday celebration on 1 July. The festivities started the night before when 30,000 people gathered on

Parliament Hill to witness the close of Canada's first century of Confederation. As the clock on the Peace Tower tolled midnight, it was joined by church bells throughout the city. The crowd standing below responded with a thunderous cheer.

On the morning of 1 July, Her Majesty attended an ecumenical service of Thanksgiving in front of the Centre Block. That afternoon the Canadian musician Bobby Gimby, wearing a green cape and blowing a gaily decorated horn, led a throng of children to a mammoth birthday party on Parliament Hill. The song "CA-NA-DA," which this modern-day Pied Piper had written for the Centennial, was on every child's lips. Shortly after two o'clock the royal couple arrived and the Queen ceremoniously cut a slice from a twenty-four-foot-high cake. Following this formality ice cream, soft drinks, and sticky cupcakes were served to the 50,000 children and adults assembled on the lawn. During the rest of the day there were also festivities in other parts of the capital.

That evening the *son et lumière pageant* (which combines special lighting and sound effects) was presented on Nepean Point, a bluff overlooking the Ottawa River. Canada's birthday celebrations ended with a dazzling fireworks display on Parliament Hill. This show came to a spectacular climax a few moments before midnight. Then a hush fell over the darkened Hill, and at the stroke of twelve the Carillon sounded the first notes of "O Canada." Seventy thousand voices joined in singing the national anthem.

On 1 January 1969 Ottawa became the first city in Ontario to be subject to regional government. The Regional Municipality of Ottawa-Carleton is a federation of local municipalities and townships which encompasses an area of 1,100 square miles with a total population of more than 500,000 people. The purpose of regional government is "to provide a political and administrative framework to govern and plan more effectively for the future."

To this end, regional government allows townships and municipalities to co-ordinate their efforts on common problems, but leaves them free to meet the specific needs of their own residents. Regional government assumes responsibility for such things as water supply, sewage treatment, pollution control, public transportation, traffic control, social services, emergency measures, and debt financing.

The Regional Municipality of Ottawa-Carleton is governed by a Council of thirty representatives, who are elected officials from the eleven townships and municipalities. The Council, which is appointed, elects a chairman every two years. Because the city of Ottawa has approximately two-thirds of the assessment and more than 60 percent of the population in the region, Ottawa has sixteen of the thirty seats on the Council. Ottawa is represented at the regional level by its mayor and its fifteen-member City Council.

Regional government has created controversy. It has been praised for planning measures that have inhibited urban sprawl, and it has been damned for causing jurisdictional confusion. On balance, it has achieved general acceptance.

The National Arts Centre, Ottawa's cultural showplace, opened on 4 June 1969 with the world première of Roland Petit's ballet *Kraanerg*. Twenty-three hundred people in full evening dress attended the gala performance.

Until 1969 facilities in the capital for the performing arts had been dreadfully inadequate. During the past half-century there had been a number of attempts to rectify this situation, but all were unsuccessful. In 1919, for example, Wilson M. Southam, the publisher of The *Ottawa Citizen* had written to J. R. Booth proposing that they sponsor an opera house as a memorial to the men who fell in the Great War. His brother, Harry S. Southam (who was also publisher of The *Citizen*), tried to enlist civic support after World War Two for a combined theatre and concert hall on the site of the National Arts Centre.

In 1963 fifty-five cultural groups in the Ottawa area banded together under the leadership of G. Hamilton Southam to form the National Capital Arts Alliance. This body commissioned a firm of consultants to make a feasibility study on a national centre for the performing arts. The report, known as the Brown Book, recommended that a concert hall and theatre complex be built on Nepean Point at an estimated cost of $9 million. The Alliance was enthusiastic but could not raise the funds from its members, so it turned to the federal government.

The timing could not have been better because Prime Minister Pearson was looking for a Centennial project for the capital. The Alliance submitted its Brown Book proposal to the Prime Minister in November 1963 and received his approval in principle less than six weeks later. When Mayor Whitton learned that the government was going to sponsor a centre on Nepean Point, she offered a parcel of land that had been donated by the Nicholas Sparks family to Bytown in 1848. This property, together with the Crown-owned former Russell Theatre site, totalled approximately six and one half acres on the west bank of the Canal, just south of Confederation Square.

The government accepted Mayor Whitton's offer and set about modifying the original plans for the centre. One of its first actions was to appoint four advisory committees comprised of knowlegeable people from across Canada. Prime Minister Pearson referred to this important step when the Queen visited the construction site in 1967: "In planning this centre, the federal government sought the most expert advice available in the country. We did more. We took it!"

When the government created the advisory committees, it seconded G. Hamilton Southam from his post at External Affairs to act as co-ordinator of the committees. In July 1966 Parliament passed the National Arts Centre Act, which stated that the centre would be responsible to a board of trustees; the first chairman of this board was Lawrence J. Freiman. In April 1967 G. Hamilton Southam was appointed director general of the National Arts Centre for a five-year term. The appointment of this patrician Ottawa native (son of Wilson M. Southam) was a logical one because of his long and knowledgeable connection with the performing arts.

Construction started in January 1965. From the outset it was obvious that the original estimate of $9 million was far too low. The change of location from Nepean Point introduced three costly changes: the provision for underground parking, the shoring of the Canal bank, and special precautions against seepage from groundwater. Before construction on the buildings could begin, more than 100,000 truckloads of stone and fill had to be excavated and removed from the site. There were other unforeseen expenses brought about by changes during the course of construction, which took nearly four years. Criticism mounted as the price doubled, tripled, and then quadrupled. The final cost was in excess of $46 million. One can more easily understand the escalation in price when one considers that it took six hundred men six months to finish the interior.

From the outside, the National Arts Centre appears to be three separate hexagonal buildings, but all three towers have the same base. It is built on a slope, with the top story at the level of Elgin Street and the two lower ones graduating down to the level of the Canal. Because of its rectangular lines and the scarcity of windows, the exterior of the Centre is plain. However, the interior of the complex is spacious and richly finished with lasting materials. The Centre contains an opera hall, a theatre, a studio, and a salon.

The Opera, which has a seating capacity of 2,372, has a large orchestra section and three tiers of balcony seats. Extending from the balconies along the side of the hall are three tiers of boxes, including a royal box. Every seat in the Opera is comfortable, and each gives a fair view of the stage. The stage is the largest in Canada, and when it was built it was the second-largest in North America (Lincoln Centre in New York being the largest). A major portion of the stage can be lowered to a basement room for loading heavy scenery or properties. Two orchestra pits in front of the stage are also hydraulically operated. One of the pits can be altered to increase the size of the stage; both can be converted to provide additional seating capacity. The Opera has two ceilings; the lower one is a decorative design of lighted panels, while the upper ceiling (which is hidden from view) is a cleverly engineered sound dome. One of the most arresting features of the Opera is its stage curtain, which is made of shimmering loops of nylon and weighs nearly two tons. The play of light on the brilliant colours in the curtain create the effect of a moving tapestry.

The Theatre, which seats 813, was deliberately restricted in size to preserve the intimacy between the artists and the audience. Like the Opera, it has comfortable seats arranged in such a way that everyone is as close as possible to the stage. The Studio seats 350, and is designed for experimental productions. The salon is a multi-purpose room that can be used for receptions, art exhibitions, auditions, and rehearsals.

In addition to the performance halls, the National Arts Centre has a gourmet restaurant and a more moderately priced restaurant. There are twelve bars in the complex, most of which are only open during the intermissions of performances. In the summer there is an outdoor terrace bar that overlooks the Canal, and a beer garden. The entire complex is air-conditioned and great care has been taken to eliminate extraneous noise from the performing areas. The nine-hundred-car parking garage is so well designed that a capacity crowd at the Opera can leave the building within fifteen minutes.

The National Arts Centre is also the home of Canada's national orchestra and two (one English and one French) theatre companies. The internationally recognized orchestra has been conducted by

Canadian-born Mario Bernardi since 1968. In the intervening years Maestro Bernardi and his forty-six musicians have toured the United States and Europe as well as many Canadian cities.

The National Arts Centre has clearly achieved its fundamental purpose, which was stated in the Brown Book: "... to provide facilities which will nurture and encourage growth and excellence in the performing arts and among artists, both in the National Capital and throughout Canada, and which will provide a showcase wherein Canadians can enjoy and take pride in our dual cultural attainments..."

Sunny days, crisp nights, and brilliant autumn foliage combine to make Thanksgiving one of Ottawa's favourite holiday weekends. However, in 1970 it was a time of tension, when most residents stayed close to their radios and television sets to learn of the latest developments in the FLQ Crisis.

The FLQ (Front de la Libération du Québec) was an extremist organization dedicated to the overthrow of the government of Quebec. On 5 October 1970 FLQ terrorists kidnapped the senior British Trade Commissioner, James R. Cross, from his home in Montreal. Five days later an FLQ cell kidnapped the second most important man in the Quebec Cabinet, Pierre Laporte, Minister of Labour and Immigration. The FLQ then demanded the release of twenty-three "political prisoners" in exchange for their two hostages. These prisoners included three convicted murderers, five people awaiting trial on manslaughter charges, a man serving a life sentence for bombings, and a man who had been convicted of seventeen armed robberies.

On Thanksgiving Day, 12 October, the federal government ordered the Canadian Armed Forces to assist the Royal Canadian Mounted Police on protective and security duties in the Ottawa area. At dusk that evening the vanguard of the Second Combat Group were whisked by helicopter from Camp Petawawa to the capital. More troops and a 121-truck convoy of supplies, came by road. By midnight approximately 2,500 soldiers were deployed in the city. The headquarters of this military operation (code-named "Ginger") was the Drill Hall on Cartier Square. Taking twelve-hour shifts, detachments of from two to six men stood guard at public buildings and at the homes of Cabinet Ministers, Parliamentary leaders, diplomats, and others who might be in peril. The soldiers, who were armed and dressed for combat, tried to be as unobtrusive as possible and said little except to challenge visitors for their identification.

Ottawa residents were stunned by the appearance of the troops. Charles King, associate editor of The *Ottawa Citizen* summed up the reaction of many Ottawans in his column on 14 October: "... I share the chagrin of most Canadians that such a display of force is necessary ... I hope they don't have to stay ... but I'm damned glad to see them after the events of the past week, and I wonder whether we haven't been living dangerously without them in the past."

The situation remained tense in Ottawa after the arrival of the soldiers, and there were increasing signs of anarchy in the province of Quebec. On the night of 15 October, more than three thousand FLQ sympathizers held a rally at the Paul Sauvé Arena in Montreal where they chanted "FLQ! FLQ! FLQ!" Earlier that day the Attorney General for the province had formally requested military aid from the government of Canada. Within two hours of this request the first elements of the Fifth Combat Group (which included the famous Royal 22nd Regiment) were deploying in Montreal. During the next twenty-four hours they were joined by combat units from other Canadian bases. The military operation in Quebec, codenamed "Essay," was quite separate from Operation Ginger in Ottawa. On the morning of 16 October, Prime Minister Trudeau invoked the War Measures Act, which gave the military and civil authorities sweeping powers of search and arrest. Two days later, on 18 October, Pierre Laporte's body was found in the trunk of a car on the outskirts of Montreal. He had been strangled by his abductors. The following day the War Measures Act was ratified by an overwhelming majority in the House of Commons.

The murder of Pierre Laporte was the last outrage perpetrated by the Front de la Libération du Québec. There were no incidents in Ottawa. Despite the presence of so many soldiers Ottawans led perfectly normal lives, and the children were able to enjoy "trick or treating" at most of the guarded residences. On 21 November Operation Ginger was terminated, and the soldiers left the capital as quietly as they had come. On 3 December James Cross was released in exchange for safe passage of his abductors to Cuba. The troops engaged in Operation Essay were withdrawn from the province of Quebec on 4 January 1971.

The FLQ Crisis was a grim experience for the nation. Although there was no violence in Ottawa, it cast a pall over the city. The most notable effect on the village of Rockcliffe, which had the heaviest concentration of troops (because of its embassies and prominent citizens), was that the crime rate dropped to nil.

Douglas H. Fullerton, an able man with strong convictions, was appointed chairman of the National Capital Commission on 4 September 1969. Prior to his appointment the National Capital Commission had attracted little attention from the press and was generally regarded as a remote planning body. During Fullerton's tenure, from 1969 to 1973, the NCC became directly involved in the lives of area residents and generated a great deal of publicity.

Fullerton's frankness and his love of controversy soon earned him the adjective "abrasive" in press reports. This impression was heightened by his use of four-letter words and a speech impediment which made him sound blunt and aggressive. In fact, his overriding ambition was to make the National Capital Region a "shining symbol" for the rest of the nation. To this end he was convinced that Hull should receive a much greater share of federal spending. For Ottawa, one of his priorities was to revitalize the old residential districts in the core of the city. He was implacably opposed to the automobile, which he considered a serious enemy of the urban environment.

As soon as he took office, he stopped the NCC road-building program, except for the airport parkway. This action immediately brought him into conflict with several municipal bodies. He then pressed for the construction of the Portage Bridge, from Wellington Street in Ottawa to Maisonneuve Boulevard in Hull, causing further disagreement with the Ontario municipalities, which felt they were being neglected. By May 1970 there was open speculation that Fullerton would be forced to resign, but he weathered the storm and the Portage Bridge was built. This modern bridge has obliterated a significant portion of one of Ottawa's heritage sites, the Richmond Landing.

During the next two years Fullerton implemented many of his ideas to improve the quality of life in the National Capital Region. To encourage walking and cycling, he built a network of paths in and around the capital. He banned snowmobiles from the Gatineau Park and redesignated it a wilderness area so that people could hike or cross-country ski in a tranquil environment. In his war against the automobile he tried unsuccessfully to have civil servants charged for their parking privileges. This measure, designed to encourage the use of public transit, has since been partially adopted. To give dwellers in the core of the city a chance to have their own gardens, he made NCC land available for this purpose in several locations. In 1979 more than five thousand people rented twenty-five-by-fifty foot plots from the NCC for a nominal fee of ten dollars.

Fullerton's most popular move was the exploitation of the Rideau Canal as a summer and winter recreation area. In the summer he made boats available for rent, and in the winter the ice surface was maintained by the NCC as a skating rink. The five-mile stretch of the Canal, from the National Arts Centre to Dow's Lake, is frequently referred to as the longest rink in the world. On a fine winter day as many as twenty thousand Ottawans take advantage of this unique facility.

In February 1972 Fullerton concluded the purchase of the E. B. Eddy sulphite mill located opposite the Parliament buildings on the Hull shore of the Ottawa River. This mill was an eyesore, and had for years been a major source of air and water pollution. When the Eddy Company sold the mill and forty-four acres of waterfront property to the NCC, it also agreed to remove its gigantic white swan sign. This neon-lit advertisement for Eddy's best-selling line of toilet paper had long marred the view from Parliament Hill.

Douglas Fullerton resigned as chairman of the National Capital Commission at the end of May 1973. As a result of his imagination, Ottawa came a little closer to being a shining symbol—and a much more pleasant place in which to live.

The year 1979 was a trying one for members of the Rideau Club. On 22 November 1978, a special general meeting had been called to consider the admission of ladies to full and equal membership. This meeting attracted the largest turnout in the club's history; it also provoked much heated discussion. Early in the proceedings an eminent barrister pointed out to the chairman that the question could not be put to a vote because the motion contained several errors in its wording. This news meant that another meeting would have to be held, but it did not stop the flow of rhetoric.

The lightest moment of the evening occurred when a well-known journalist, who was an ardent advocate of the motion, reminded his fellow members that the Liberal government would not entertain at the Rideau Club because of its "discrimination." Shaking with emotion, he begged his audience to reflect on this sad state of affairs, and harking back to the club's founder (Sir John A. Macdonald), he finished with the question, "What would Sir John say?"

There was a brief silence and then a voice answered, "Vote Tory!"

At a more tranquil special general meeting on 28 March 1979 an amended motion was passed admitting ladies to full membership in the Rideau Club. Five months later Mrs. Jean Pigott became the first female member to be elected in the club's 114-year history. It is likely that Sir John would have heartily approved, for in addition to being a charming and accomplished person, Mrs. Pigott was a senior advisor to Prime Minister Clark and a former Conservative Member of Parliament for Ottawa-Carleton.

The club suffered a catastrophe in the autumn of 1979. On the afternoon of 23 October fire broke out in the basement of its ancient premises. The only member in the club at the time was the Right Honourable Roland Michener, who was having a cup of tea in the reading room on the second floor. When he was told of the fire, Canada's former Governor-General made a leisurely departure, thinking that the blaze was of little consequence. However, soon after he left, the fire worked its way between the walls and then burst out on the upper floors. The Ottawa Fire Department appeared on the scene within minutes, but shortly after their arrival the structure turned into a gigantic torch. There was an ironic touch to this spectacle, which many watched from the windows of the Centre Block: sixty-three years earlier, members of the Rideau Club had stood at their windows watching the Centre Block burn.

At the height of the blaze it was feared that the Langevin Block, across the street, and the United States Embassy immediately west of the club would also be engulfed. A west wind saved the embassy, but the roof of the Langevin Block caught fire, sending sheets of flame ten feet in the air. This fire was brought under control, but while the threat lasted, a fleet of vans stood ready to remove documents from the Prime Minister's Office and the offices of the Privy Council. By eleven o'clock all that was left of the club was a burned-out shell.

The loss of this old landmark was felt by more than the members of the Rideau Club. The day after the fire columnist Christopher Young wrote in The *Ottawa Citizen*: ". . . Many other Ottawans who cared not at all for the Rideau Club as a club cared a lot about the building. It presented an elegant, finely proportioned but unobtrusive facade that stared steadily across Wellington Street, decade after decade, towards the Parliament of Canada . . ."

A few weeks after the fire the club moved into former Prime Minister Bennett's luxurious suite at the Chateau Laurier. At the end of November the Rideau Club held its annual black-tie dinner in these new quarters. The guest of honour that evening was His Excellency Edward Schreyer. There was room for only one hundred and thirty members, but all agreed that it was an excellent dinner and unquestionably the most pleasant event of a tempestuous year.

23

The Capital in 1979

WHEN THE ENGLISH poet Rupert Brooke visited Canada in 1913, he wrote: "... what Ottawa leaves in the mind is a certain graciousness ..." This is also true in 1979, for the pace of life in the capital is less frantic than in most cities of comparable size. Those who live in Ottawa like it because it has both the amenities of a big city and the charm of a small town. Ottawa is especially noted for its water and its parks, and its proximity to unspoiled country. After more than a century the grey stone buildings on Parliament Hill are still the focal point of the community and its most famous symbol to the rest of the world.

The city of Ottawa encompasses approximately 30,000 acres. Its main geographical features are the Rideau and Ottawa rivers, and the Rideau Canal. The Green Belt, mentioned in the previous chapter, is unique to Canada's capital; no other North American city is encircled by a band of parkland. Ottawa is renowned for its trees, although in recent years many of its stately elms have been killed by Dutch elm disease.

In 1979 the population of the city of Ottawa was just over 300,000. The mother tongue of its population was approximately 70 percent English, 20 percent French, and 10 percent other ethnic origins. The ratio of English-to-French-speaking residents is interesting because it has remained relatively unchanged since Bytown was founded in 1826.

Because nearly half of Ottawa's population is Roman Catholic, there are two school systems: the Ottawa Board of Education, and the Ottawa Roman Catholic Separate School Board. These two boards administer a total of 151 elementary, secondary, and junior high schools. In thirty-one of the elementary schools French is the language of instruction. There are eleven nondenominational hospitals in the capital.

Since Colonel By laid out Upper Town and Lower Town in 1826, residential districts have sprung up to the east, west, and south of the Canal. Twenty new housing developments have been built on the perimeter of the city in the last decade. During the same period a vigorous program of redevelopment has taken place in the shabby central residential areas. Slum clearance has been going on for the past twenty years. Today there are still some poor neighbourhoods, but none could be classed as slums.

Ottawa's main business district lies within a two-mile radius of Parliament Hill. There are, however, major concentrations of government office buildings at more distant locations, such as Tunney's Pasture to the west, Confederation Heights to the south, and the National Research Council area to the east. There are six industrial parks (two owned by the municipality) and a dozen large shopping centres, most of which are located on the outskirts of the city.

The Canadian Government is the mainstay of Ottawa's economy. Indeed, the federal payroll is so important to the capital that local calendars carefully note Civil Service paydays. By and large, Ottawa is a prosperous city. In 1979 the average income for a family was more than $18,000, and the level of unemployment was less than 6 percent. Both figures are considerably better than the national average.

Because it is the capital of Canada, Ottawa is the headquarters for several hundred national organizations. Most of these organizations maintain a close liaison with the federal government. Some are listening posts, while others are active lobbyists on behalf of their members. Among those with headquarters in the city are such diverse groups as the Academy of Medicine, the Association of Canadian Distillers, the Boy Scouts of Canada, the Canadian Pork Council, the Canadian Water Polo Association, and the Canadian Labour Congress.

Ottawa's economic base is slowly shifting toward the private sector. In the last half of the seventies, the government's program of decentralization (which transfers federal offices to other parts of Canada) has virtually stopped the growth of federal employment in the capital. The most dramatic example of decentralization in the Ottawa area has been the massive building program in the city of Hull, across the river. As a result of the government offices in Hull, which literally change the skyline, more than 10,000 Ottawans commute to the Province of Quebec each day. This huge office complex has had a salutary effect on the economy of Hull, which for years was a low-income community.

To offset the government decentralization program, Ottawa is encouraging high-technology companies to locate in the city. The capital is an excellent site for this type of industry because of the research facilities of the two universities and the National Research Council. Two other important factors are the number of skilled people in the area and the presence of the Canadian government, the industry's largest customer. At the end of 1979 there were forty high-technology companies in the Ottawa region, manufacturing such sophisticated devices as mini-computers, lasers, telephone equipment, avionics, and electronic systems.

Ottawa's beauty, its historic buildings, and its colourful ceremonies attract an increasing number of tourists every year. Hosting tourists and conventions is a substantial local industry; in 1979 more than 300 conventions were held in the capital, and there were more than 2 million tourists. It has been estimated that these visitors spent in excess of $150 million in the city.

Although some elected officials have displayed limited competence, Ottawa has historically been well administered. There has never been a financial scandal at City Hall. The relationship of the municipal government to the federal government and its agency, the National Capital Commission, has for the most part been a happy one. Both the federal government and the NCC have contributed in a significant way to the planning and the beauty of the city. Neither the NCC nor the federal government pay taxes to the city, but grants are paid to the municipality by the Crown in lieu of taxes.

The Ottawa Fire Department has a long-standing and well-deserved reputation for excellence. It has also won a number of significant merit awards.

Ottawa takes justifiable pride in its Police Force, which has approximately six hundred sworn officers and a perpetual waiting list of more than one hundred who wish to join. Ottawa policemen are noted for their size—most are burly six-footers—their smart appearance, and their courtesy to the public. Ottawa has few serious crimes in comparison to other large cities. In 1979 there were only three murders in the capital. There is also little evidence of organized crime in Ottawa. Aside from the city force, Ottawa is the site of the Canadian Police College and the headquarters of the Royal Canadian Mounted Police. There are approximately 1,500 RCMP officers stationed in the capital. Possibly the best evidence of the fine reputation of the Ottawa Police Force is the fact that each year it receives more than 200 letters of praise from tourists and local residents.

Despite the growth and modernization that has taken place in Ottawa, the city has retained its beauty and its warmth. Daily life in the capital contains many reminders of the past. The By Ward Market, which is more than one hundred years old, is a good example. Today the main market building and many surrounding structures have been refurbished, but there are still open stalls where people from the country sell their fresh produce. Ottawa residents from all walks of life—housewives, diplomats, professional people—trek to Lower Town to shop at the By Ward Market. The market's great appeal over modern supermarkets is that each transaction is, in part, a pleasant social encounter.

Much of Sussex Drive, on the western boundary of the By Ward Market, has been restored by the National Capital Commission. Many of the buildings have been completely renovated so that their interiors are suitable for apartments and offices, while their façades appear as they did in Confederation days. One block of Sussex Drive, between York and Clarence streets, still houses the Jeanne d'Arc residence for single girls, started by Sister Marie de St. Thomas d'Aquinas in 1917. This nondenominational hostel is actually three adjoining buildings, which were acquired piecemeal over a four-year period. In 1919 Sister St. Thomas founded the Jeanne d'Arc Congregation, which has had an excellent elementary school in the west end of the city for more than half a century.

Rideau Hall, at the east end of Sussex Drive, has not changed a great deal over the years. Cricket is still played on the broad lawns during the summer, and during the winter guests engage in curling matches on the outdoor rink. The ceremonial duties of the Governor-General date back to Confederation. When a new ambassador comes to Canada he goes through the formality of presenting his credentials to the Governor-General as "ambassador extraordinary and plenipotentiary" of his country. The ambassador is driven to this ceremony in the state carriage. It is a splendid and nostalgic sight to see the coach bowling down Sussex Drive, escorted by six scarlet-coated RCMP outriders whose lances are topped with fluttering guidons.

Despite such modern conveniences as digital clocks (which are on several buildings in the city) the Noon Gun continues to boom from Major's Hill Park at midday. This three-ton cannon, cast in 1807, was purchased by the Canadian Government in 1860 from the British garrison of Upper Canada. Nine years later Sir John A. Macdonald passed an Order-in-Council stating that the cannon be fired in the capital each day at noon. The cannon belches a six-inch flame and makes an impressive roar when it is fired. Even with the noise of traffic the sound of the Noon Gun can be heard for a great distance. The other classic time-keeper in Ottawa is the clock on the Peace Tower.

At midnight on 31 December 1979 the Bourdon bell in the Peace Tower tolled the end of one decade and the beginning of another. Skaters glided to a sudden stop on the Canal when they heard its deep tone in the frosty air. Turning to the Parliament buildings, they could see the hands of the clock pointed to the heavens. Their skating rink—the ice-covered Canal—had fostered the birth of Bytown more than a century and a half ago. In the intervening years an immense amount of history had taken place in Canada's capital.

Appendix A

Mayors of Bytown

1847 John Scott
1848 John Bower Lewis
1849 Robert Hervey
1850 John Scott
1851 Charles Sparrow
1852 Richard W. Scott
1853 J. B. Turgeon
1854 Henry J. Friel

N.B. Bytown mayoralty term, one year

Mayors of Ottawa

1855—1857 John Bower Lewis
1858—1859 Edward McGillivray
1860—1862 Alexander Workman
1863   Henry J. Friel
1864—1866 M. K. Dickinson
1867   Robert Lyon
1868—1869 Henry J. Friel

1870—1871	John Rochester
1872—1873	E. Martineau
1874—1875	J. P. Featherston
1876	G. B. L. Fellows
1877	W. H. Waller
1878	C. W. Bangs
1879—1881	Charles H. Mackintosh
1882—1883	Pierre St. Jean MD
1884	C. T. Bate
1885—1886	Francis McDougal
1887—1888	McLeod Stewart
1889—1890	Jacob Erratt
1891	Thomas Birkett
1892—1893	Olivier Durocher
1894	George Cox
1895—1896	William Borthwick
1897—1898	Samuel Bingham
1899—1900	Thomas Payment
1901	W. D. Morris
1901	James Davidson
1902—1903	Fred Cook
1904—1906	James A. Ellis
1906	Robert Hastey
1907—1908	D'Arcy Scott
1908	Napoleon Champagne
1909—1912	Charles Hopewell
1912	Edward H. Hinchey
1913	James A. Ellis
1914	Taylor McVeity
1915—1916	Nelson D. Porter
1917—1920	Harold Fisher
1921—1923	Frank H. Plant
1924	Henry Watters
1924	Napoleon Champagne
1925—1927	John P. Balharrie
1928—1929	Arthur Ellis
1930	Frank H. Plant
1931—1933	John J. Allen
1934—1935	Patrick Nolan
1936—1948	J. E. S. Lewis
1949—1950	E. A. Bourque

1951	Grenville Goodwin
1951—1956	Charlotte Whitton
1957—1960	George H. Nelms
1961—1964	Charlotte Whitton
1965—1969	Don B. Reid
1970—1971	Kenneth H. Fogarty
1972—1974	Pierre Benoit
1975—1978	Lawrence Greenberg
1979—	Marion Dewar

N.B. Ottawa mayoralty terms were one year 1855 to 1940; two years from 1941 to 1966; three years from 1967 to 1972. Since 1973 the term has been two years.

Appendix B

Chairmen of the National Capital Commission (and its predecessors*)

1899—1917	Sir Henry N. Bate
1917—1920	Sir Henry K. Egan
1920—1926	J. B. Fraser
1927—1932	The Honourable Thomas Ahearn
1932—1936	W. E. Matthews
1936—1951	Frederick E. Bronson
1951—1952	The Honourable Duncan K. MacTavish
1952—1960	Major General Howard Kennedy
1960—1961	Alan K. Hay
1961—1967	Lieutenant General S. F. Clark
1967—1969	A. John Frost
1969—1973	Douglas H. Fullerton
1973	Jean-Claude LaHaye (Acting Chairman)
1973—1976	Edgar Gallant
1976—1978	Pierre Juneau
1979	Brigadier the Honourable Charles M. Drury

*Ottawa Improvement Commission 1899 to 1927, Federal District Commission 1927 to 1959.

Appendix C

Governors-General of Canada

1867—1868	Viscount Monck
1868—1872	Baron Lisgar
1872—1878	The Earl of Dufferin
1878—1883	The Marquess of Lorne
1883—1888	The Marquess of Lansdowne
1888—1893	Lord Stanley of Preston
1893—1898	The Earl of Aberdeen
1898—1904	The Earl of Minto
1904—1911	Earl Grey
1911—1916	Prince Arthur, Duke of Connaught
1916—1921	The Duke of Devonshire
1921—1926	Lord Byng of Vimy
1926—1931	Viscount Willingdon
1931—1935	The Earl of Bessborough
1935—1940	Baron Tweedsmuir
1940—1946	The Earl of Athlone
1946—1952	Viscount Alexander of Tunis
1952—1959	The Right Honourable Vincent Massey
1959—1967	Major General Georges-Philias Vanier
1967—1974	The Right Honourable D. Roland Michener
1974—1979	The Right Honourable Jules Léger
1979—	The Right Honourable Edward R. Schreyer

Appendix D

Prime Ministers of Canada

1867—1873	Sir John A. Macdonald
1873—1878	The Right Honourable Alexander Mackenzie
1878—1891	Sir John A. Macdonald
1891—1892	Sir John J. C. Abbott
1892—1894	Sir John S. D. Thompson
1894—1896	Sir Mackenzie Bowell
1896	Sir Charles Tupper
1896—1911	Sir Wilfrid Laurier
1911—1920	Sir Robert L. Borden
1920—1921	The Right Honourable Arthur Meighen
1921—1926	The Right Honourable William L. M. King
1926	The Right Honourable Arthur Meighen
1926—1930	The Right Honourable William L. M. King
1930—1935	The Right Honourable Richard B. Bennett
1935—1948	The Right Honourable William L. M. King
1948—1957	The Right Honourable Louis-S. St. Laurent
1957—1963	The Right Honourable John G. Diefenbaker
1963—1968	The Right Honourable Lester B. Pearson
1968—1979	The Right Honourable Pierre E. Trudeau
1979—1980	The Right Honourable C. Joseph Clark
1980—	The Right Honourable Pierre E. Trudeau

Bibliography

AUDET, FRANCIS JOSEPH. *Thomas McKay, Rideau Hall and Earnscliffe.* Ottawa: King's Printer, 1936.

Belden, H. and Co., Publishers. *Historical Sketch of the County of Carleton.* Introduction by C. C. J. Bond, Belleville, Ontario: reprinted by Mika Silk Screening, 1971.

_____ . *Illustrated Atlas of the Dominion of Canada.* Toronto: H. Belden and Co., Publishers, 1878.

BILLINGS, CHARLOTTE. "The Great Fires of 1870," Women's Canadian Historical Society of Ottawa *Transactions,* vol. III, 1910.

_____ . "The Rideau Canal," Women's Canadian Historical Society of Ottawa *Transactions,* vol. II, 1909.

BOND, C. C. J. "Alexander Christie, Bytown Pioneer, His Life and Times, 1787-1843," *Ontario Historical Society,* 1964.

_____ . *City on the Ottawa.* Ottawa: Queen's Printer, 1961.

_____ . *Hurling Down the Pine.* Old Chelsea, Quebec: Historical Society of the Gatineau, 1964.

_____ . *The Ottawa Country.* Ottawa: Queen's Printer, 1968.

BOUCHETTE, JOSEPH. *General Report of an official tour through the new settlements of the Province of Lower Canada, performed in the summer of 1824, in obedience of the commands and instructions of His Excellancy, George, Earl of Dalhousie.* Quebec: Thomas Carey and Co., 1825.

327

————— . *The Topographical Dictionary of the Province of Lower Canada.* London: Longman, Rees, Orme, Brown, Green and Longman, 1832.

BRAULT, LUCIEN. *Ottawa: Old and New.* Ottawa: Ottawa Historical Information Institute, 1946.

BUSH, EDWARD F. "Thomas Coltrin Keefer," *Ontario History,* vol. 66 no. 4, 1974.

CAMPBELL, WILFRED. "The Old Bytown Canal," *The Canadian Magazine,* vol. XLII no. 5, March, 1914.

Canadian Legion. *The Legionary,* vol. 38 no. 1, June 1963.

Central Canada Exhibition Association. *The Central Canada Exhibition Association Through 65 Years, 1888-1953.* Ottawa: Runge Press, 1954.

Commonwealth Relations Office. *Earnscliffe.* Downing Street, London: Commonwealth Relations Office, 1955.

COOK, FREDERICK. "Appreciations: Hon. Thomas Ahearn, P.C.," Printed for private circulation, c. 1935.

CREIGHTON, DONALD. *Canada's First Century 1867-1967.* Toronto: MacMillan Company Ltd., 1970.

————— . *John A. MacDonald: The Old Chieftain.* Toronto: MacMillan Company Ltd., 1955.

————— . *John A. MacDonald the Young Politician.* Toronto: MacMillan Company Ltd., 1952.

CROSS, MICHAEL. "Stoney Monday, 1849: the Rebellion Losses Riots in Bytown," *Ontario History,* vol. LXIII no. 3, 1971.

————— . "The Age of Gentility: The Formation of an Aristocracy in the Ottawa Valley," Canadian Historical Association, *Report of the Annual Meeting,* 1967.

————— . "The Dark and Druidical Groves: The Lumber Community and the Commercial Frontier in British North America," PhD. thesis, University of Toronto, 1968.

————— . "The Lumber Community of Upper Canada 1815-1867," *Ontario History,* vol. LIII no. 4, 1960.

DAVIES, BLODWEN. *Ottawa: Portrait of a Capital.* Toronto: McGraw-Hill, 1954.

DEVLIN, R. J. *The Devlin Old-Time Advertisements.* Ottawa: James Hope and Sons, Ltd., 1954.

DONALDSON, GORDON. *Fifteen Men: Canada's Prime Ministers from Macdonald to Trudeau.* Toronto: Doubleday Canada Ltd., 1969.

DOUGLAS, H. TOWNLEY. "John Burrows Honey," Women's Canadian Historical Society of Ottawa *Transactions*, vol. XI, 1954.

DUFFERIN AND AVA, THE MARCHIONESS OF. *My Canadian Journal, 1872-1878.* London: 1891.

EDGAR, SIR JAMES D. *Canada and Its Capital; with Sketches of Political and Social Life at Ottawa.* Toronto: G. N. Monang, 1898.

EGGLESTON, WILFRID. *The Queen's Choice: A Story of Canada's Capital.* Ottawa: Queen's Printer, 1961.

EVANS, PATRICK M. O. *The Wrights: a geneological study of the first settlers in Canada's National Capital Region.* Ottawa: National Capital Commission, 1975.

EWART, JOHN S. *The Ottawa Branch of the Royal Mint.* Ottawa: Queen's Printer, 1930.

FEE, NORMAN. *The Knox Presbyterian Church Centenary: A History of the Congregation.* Ottawa: Mortimer Ltd., 1944.

FRASER, JOSHUA. *Shanty, Forest and River Life in the Backwoods of Canada.* Montreal: J. Lovell and Sons, 1883.

FREIMAN, LAWRENCE. *Don't Fall Off the Rocking Horse.* Toronto: McClelland and Stewart, 1978.

FRENCH, DORIS. "The Booths of Ottawa," *Chatelaine*, Dec., 1963 and Jan. 1964.

Fuller and Jones, Architects Departmental block, Ottawa, front view 2nd prize, (Architectural drawing by Messrs. Fuller and Jones, Toronto, 1859). Mounted photograph of drawing.

FULLERTON, DOUGLAS H. *The Capital of Canada: How Should it Be Governed?* Ottawa: Information Canada, 1974. 2 vol.

GARD, ANSON A. *Pioneers of the Upper Ottawa and the Humours of the Valley.* (South Hull and Aylmer edition). Ottawa: Emerson Press, 1906.

_____. *The Hub and the Spokes, or, The Capital and Its Environs.* Ottawa and New York: Emerson Press, 1904.

GOURLAY, J. L. *History of the Ottawa Valley.* Ottawa: Department of Agriculture, 1896.

GOUZENKO, IGOR. *This Was My Choice.* Toronto: Dent Publishing, 1948.

GUILLET, EDWIN C. *Pioneer Inns and Taverns.* Toronto: Ontario Publishing, 1954.

HAIG, ROBERT B. *Ottawa: City of the Big Ears.* Ottawa: Haig and Haig, 1970.

HAMILTON, ROBERT M. "The Library of Parliament Fire," Canadian Library Association *Bulletin,* vol. 9, 1952.

HAYDON, ANDREW. *Pioneer Sketches in the District of Bathurst.* Toronto: The Ryerson Press, 1925.

Heritage Ottawa. "Walking in New Edinburgh." Ottawa: 1974.

————. "Walking in Sandy Hill." Ottawa: 1974.

HILL, HAMNETT PINHEY. *History of Christ Church Cathedral, Ottawa, 1832-1932.* Ottawa: Runge Press, 1932.

————. *Robert Randall and the LeBreton Flats.* Ottawa: James Hope and Sons, 1919.

————. "The Construction of the Rideau Canal, 1826-1832," Ontario Historical Society, *Papers and Records,* vol. 22, 1925.

HUBBARD, ROBERT H. *Cathedral in the Capital: A Short History of Christ Church Cathedral.* Ottawa: Cathedral Committee, Mutual Press, 1972.

————. *Rideau Hall: An Illustrated History of Government House.* Montreal and London: McGill-Queen's University Press, 1977.

HUNTER, WILLIAM S. "Hunter's Ottawa Scenery in the Vicinity of Ottawa," Ottawa City: W. S. Hunter, 1855.

JAMIESON, M. "Schools and Schoolmasters of Bytown and Early Ottawa," Women's Canadian Historical Society of Ottawa *Transactions,* vol. III, 1910

JEFFERSON, RIGHT REVEREND ROBERT and JOHNSON, L. *Faith of Our Fathers.* Ottawa: The Anglican Book Society, 1950.

KARSH, YOUSUF. *In Search of Greatness.* New York: Alfred A. Knopf, 1962.

KEEFER, THOMAS C. *Philosophy of Railroads.* Toronto: University of Toronto Press, 1972 (new edition).

KEITH, JANET. *The Collegiate Institute Board of Ottawa: A Short History 1843-1969.* Ottawa: 1969.

KETCHUM, C. J. *Federal Capital District, Ottawa.* Ottawa: 1939.

KING, W. L. M. *The Secret of Heroism: A Memoir of Henry Albert Harper.* New York: Revell Ltd., 1906.

KIRBY, DONALD S. *A Historical Sketch of the Brittania Yacht Club 1891-1967.* Ottawa: 1967.

KNIGHT, DAVID B. *Choosing Canada's Capital: Jealousy and Friction in the 19th Century.* Toronto: McClelland and Stewart, 1977.

Laurentian Club. *The Laurentian Club Ottawa, Ontario 1904-1979.* Ottawa: Dollco Press, 1979.

LEGGET, ROBERT F. "Early Ottawa and Engineering," *The Engineering Journal,* vol. 44 no. 2, 1961.

————. *Ottawa Waterway: Gateway to a Continent.* Toronto: University of Toronto Press, 1975.

————. *Rideau Waterway.* Toronto: University of Toronto Press, 1961.

LELIEVRE, S. "Settlement in Hull," Women's Canadian Historical Society of Ottawa *Transactions,* vol. III, 1910.

LETT, WILLIAM PITMAN. "Bytown to Ottawa, 1827-1872," Women's Canadian Historical Society of Ottawa *Transactions,* vol. VIII, 1922.

————. *Recollections of Bytown and Its Old Inhabitants.* Ottawa: Ottawa Citizen Publishing Co., 1874.

Lisgar Collegiate. *Lisgar Collegiate Centenary 1843-1943.* n.d., n.p.

LITTLE, C. H. *All Saints' Church Sandy Hill, Ottawa: A Short History 1898-1975.* n.p., n.d.

————. *The Rideau Club; a short history, the first 100 years 1865-1965.* Ottawa: The Rideau Club, 1965.

LYON, J. BOWER. "Westboro: Ottawa's Westmount," Ottawa: 1913.

MacBETH, MADGE. *Inside Government House.* Toronto: Ryerson Press, 1954.

————. *Over My Shoulder.* Toronto: Ryerson Press, 1953.

MacTAGGART, JOHN. *Recollections of Early Bytown.* n.p., n.d.

————. *Three Years in Canada: An Account of the Actual State of the Country in 1826-7-8.* London: Henry Colburn, 1829.

Maple Leaf Ottawa Number (special edition). *Maple Leaf,* 1923.

MARSHALL, HERBERT. *History of the Ottawa Ski Club.* Ottawa: Ottawa Ski Club, 1973.

MacDONALD, MALCOLM. "The Birds of Brewery Creek," London: Oxford University Press, 1947.

MacDONALD, W. E. *The Waterworks System of the City of Ottawa.* n.d., n.p.

McPHAIL, J. G. *St. Andrews Church, Ottawa: The First Hundred Years 1828-1928*. Ottawa: Dadson Merrill Press Ltd., 1932.

MINTON, ERIC. *Ottawa: Reflections of the Past*. Toronto: Nelson, Foster and Scott, 1974.

MOFFATT, MARGARET E. *Dr. Edward Van Cortlandt*. n.p., 1973.

MORRISON, E. W. B. *With the Guns in South Africa*. Hamilton: Spectator Printing Co., 1901.

NAGY, THOMAS L. *Ottawa in Maps: a brief cartographical history of Ottawa 1825-1973*. Ottawa: Public Archives of Canada, 1974.

National Capital Commission. "Early Days in the Ottawa Country: History of Ottawa, Hull and the National Capital Region," Ottawa: National Capital Commission, 1967.

_____ . *Guide to Canada's Capital; Le Guide de la capitale du Canada*. Ottawa: National Capital Commission, 1974.

_____ . *Statues/Monuments*. Ottawa: National Capital Commission, 1974.

_____ . *The Capital of Canada; a full description of Ottawa and its Metropolitan area in the year 1965*. Ottawa: National Capital Commission, 1966.

NEWTON, MICHAEL. *Lower Town Ottawa Volume I 1826-1854*. Ottawa: National Capital Commission, 1979.

OGILVY, C. *Ottawa: Canada's Capital*. Ottawa: 1940.

Ottawa and Hull Fire Relief Fund. *Report of the Ottawa and Hull Fire Relief Fund, 1900*. Ottawa: R. L. Crain, 1900.

Ottawa Citizen. *Bytown-Ottawa 1826-1976 Sesquicentennial, Special Edition*. Ottawa, Sept. 24, 1976.

Ottawa, City of. *Ottawa 79/80*. Ottawa: Information and Public Relations Division, 1979.

Ottawa Collegiate Institute Board. *A History of the Ottawa Collegiate Institute, 1843-1903*. Ottawa: Mortimer and Co., 1904.

Ottawa Field Naturalists Club. "Trail and Landscape," Ottawa: Field and Naturalists Club, Ottawa, n.d.

Ottawa Hydro Electric Commission. *History of Electric Power in Ottawa*. Ottawa: Hydro Electric Commission, n.d.

Ottawa Improvement Commission. *Ottawa Improvement Commission 1904 Reports*. Ottawa: 1905.

PAUL-EMILE, SISTER, S.C.O. *A Pioneer of Bilingual Education: Mother Elisabeth Bruyère*. Ottawa: Sisters of Charity, n.d.

_____ . *Mother Elisabeth Bruyère*. Ottawa: Sisters of Charity, n.d.

_____ . *Typhus of 1847 in Bytown*. Ottawa: Sisters of Charity, n.d.

PERLEY-ROBERTSON, ALEX, editor. *One Hundred Years: 1864-1964 Protestant Children's Village*. Ottawa: Protestant Children's Village, 1964.

PIGEON, L. B. "Notes on Some of the Prominent Citizens of the Early Days of Bytown," Women's Canadian Historical Society of Ottawa *Transactions*, vol. VIII, 1922.

RITCHIE, T. "Samuel and Thomas Keefer: Pioneers of Canadian Engineering," *Engineering Journal*, vol. 51 no. 9, 1968.

ROSS, ALEXANDER H. D. *Ottawa Past and Present*. Ottawa: Thorburn and Abbott, 1927.

Saint Joseph's Parish. *St. Joseph's Parish History 1856-1956*. Ottawa: St. Joseph's Parish, 1956.

SCOTT, R. W. "Recollections of Bytown: some incidents in the history of Ottawa." Ottawa: Mortimer Press, 1911.

_____ . "The Choice of the Capital: Reminiscences. . . ." Ottawa: Mortimer Co., 1907.

SHIRREFF, CHARLES. "Memorial to Lord Dalhousie re Timber Trade of the Ottawa," Nov. 10, 1828. n.p.

SHORTER, G. W. "Ottawa-Hull Fire of 1900," National Research Council *Publications*, 1962.

SMALL, HENRY BEAUMONT. *Medical Memoirs of Bytown*. Ottawa: R. L. Crain and Co., 1903.

Sparks Street Development Association. *The Sparks Street Mall*. Ottawa, n.d.

STEWART, McLEOD. *The First Half Century of Ottawa*. Ottawa: The Esdale Press Ltd., n.d.

STORY, NORAH. *The Oxford Companion to Canadian History and Literature*. Toronto, London, New York: Oxford University Press, 1967.

THORBURN, C. H. "Ottawa 1867-1927," Women's Canadian Historical Society of Ottawa *Transactions*, vol. X, 1928.

THORBURN, MARIA J. *Orphan's Home of the City of Ottawa: a Sketch of the First Forty Years 1864-1904*. Toronto: Briggs Ltd., 1904.

VAN COURTLANDT, GERTRUDE. "Records of the Rise and Progress of Ottawa . . . from the Foundation of the Rideau Canal to the Present Time." Ottawa: Citizen Publishing Co., 1858.

WALKER, HARRY J. *The Ottawa Story Through 150 Years.* Ottawa: Ottawa Journal, 1953.

WELCH, EDWIN, editor. *Bytown Council Minutes 1847-1848.* Ottawa: City of Ottawa Archives, 1978.

————. *Sights and Surveys: Two Diarists on the Rideau.* Ottawa: Historical Society of Ottawa, Bytown Museum, 1979.

WHITTON, CHARLOTTE. *A Hundred Years A-Fellin' 1842-1942.* Ottawa: printed for Gillies Bros. Ltd., by Runge Press, 1943.

WILSON, ANDREW. *A History of Old Bytown and Vicinity, Now the City of Ottawa.* Ottawa: printed at the *News* office, 1876.

WRIGHT, LILY CUNNINGHAM. *Philemon Wright—A Sketch of the Pioneer of the Ottawa Valley.* Ottawa: Order of Daughters of the Empire leaflet, 1918.

WRIGHT, PHILEMON. "An Account of the First Settlement of the Township of Hull, on the Ottawa River, Lower Canada," Appendice R; Journaux de l'assemblée legislative 1823-1824, reproduit dans *Asticou,* Cahier no. 5, 03/70.

YOUNG, A. H. "Ottawa, a Hundred Years Ago," Ontario Historical Society *Papers and Records,* vol. XXVII, 1932.

Private Collections

JUDITH BURNS. *William Stewart,* M.P., merchant, founder of Stewarton; *McLeod Stewart,* Vankleek Hill resident; personal correspondence.

MRS. G. W. SHORTER. *G. M. Geldert Collection,* Medical Doctor, City of Ottawa Controller 1931-1948, President and Founder of CKO Radio Station; personal papers and newspaper clippings.

MOIYA WRIGHT. *Philemon Wright Collection,* Ottawa Valley pioneer, Founder of Hull, lumber merchant; personal correspondence and family papers.

Acknowledgements

I could not have written this book without the help of many people.

Before putting pen to paper I read with profit the earlier works on the capital by Bond, Brault, Davies, Edgar, Eggleston, Gard, Haig, Haydon, Lett, Ross, Van Courtlandt, and Walker. These books set a standard for me to emulate and provided much worthwhile information.

Ottawa's two venerable English-language daily papers, the *Ottawa Citizen* and the *Ottawa Journal,* have yielded first-hand accounts of past events and numerous quotations. Both have a history of responsible journalism.

I wish to thank Dr. Claude Aubry for extending special privileges to me at the Ottawa Public Library. For those interested in the history of the capital and surrounding region, the Ottawa Room is a treasure trove of information. All the library staff have been most kind, but I would particularly like to thank Lynn Legate and Gordon Adshead for their contribution to this book.

Dr. Edwin Welch of the Ottawa Historical Society has given me many interesting documents and excellent background material on the Bytown period. The staff of the Bytown Museum have also shown many courtesies.

Louise Roy of the City of Ottawa Archives was most helpful in numerous instances, particularly with regard to municipal government records.

Rolf Latté, Chief of the Heritage Section, National Capital Commission, took an active and valuable interest in the assembly of research material for the manuscript.

The National Library, the Parliamentary Library, the National Archives, and the War Museum were all valuable sources of reference documents. I should like to thank the staffs of these institutions for their assistance and unfailing courtesy.

I was aided in gathering research information by Barbara Emmett and Leslie Scanlon; to them I extend my sincere appreciation.

Among those who lent me valuable family papers, or provided assistance of a special nature, were:

George F. Ault, John A. Aylen, Edwin R. Beddoe, Mrs. Marjorie Blyberg, John M. Bogie, Courtney C. J. Bond, Lucien Brault, Mrs. Margaret A. O. Brown, Mrs. Judith Burns, Esmond Butler, Mrs. Nini Cape, Père Gaston Carrière OMI, John F. Charleson, Harold F. Crain, Major General Michael Dare, Mrs. Margaret F. H. Doran, Kerry J. Dunphy, Thomas G. Fuller, Graeme Fraser, Lawrence Freiman, Audrey Gill, John W. Grace, John Graham, Jr., N. Gregor Guthrie, Major E. J. Hare, Bruce Heggtveit, H. L Heggtveit, R. H. Hubbard, J. Wyburn Lawson, Commander C. H. Little, Sister Madeleine (Sisters of Charity of Ottawa), Charles J. Mackenzie, Hugh MacLennan, Mrs. Lynn McGuffin, Mervin Mirsky, J. Barry O'Brien, A. James Phillips, E. N. Rhodes Jr., Major General Roger Rowley, Doctor J. N. Rushforth, Colonel Cuthbert Scott, Frederick H. Sherwood, Mrs. Shirley Shorter, Mrs. Harold W. Soper, G. Hamilton Southam, Miss Dilys Thomas, Mrs. Willa Walker, George S. Watts, Richard P. White, Richard D. Whitmore, Miss Cairine Wilson, John R. Woods, Henry P. Wright, and Mrs. Moiya A. Wright.

Erik Spicer has contributed to the book in several important ways. Not only did he recommend my name to Doubleday, but after I was commissioned to write this work he gave me access to all the research material he had collected on the capital. In addition, he kindly consented to write the Foreward and also proofread the entire manuscript before it was sent to the publisher. His suggestions and encouragement have been an immense help.

Mrs. Betty Jane Corson, Managing Editor of Doubleday, has

shown both interest and patience in the completion of the manuscript. Her editing skill has greatly enhanced the book.

From the outset Robert Legget has been both my technical and literary advisor. He has also fed me with some exquisite morsels of unpublished research material. Despite the heavy demands of his own publishers, he has taken the time to read the complete manuscript, and his corrections have done much to improve my credibility—and save me future embarrassment.

Sandrea, my wife, has acted as my preliminary editor, proofreader, and counsellor for two years. During this period she has shown admirable judgement, exceptional tolerance, and a sorely tried sense of humour. Not only am I grateful for her contribution to the book, but also for the fact that despite my preoccupation with my typewriter and irritating behaviour, she has not sued for divorce.

S.E.W., Jr.

Index